T0305178

Credit Risk Modeling

Credit Risk Modeling: Theory and Applications
IS A PART OF THE
PRINCETON SERIES IN FINANCE

SERIES EDITORS

Darrell Duffie   Stephen Schaefer
Stanford University   London Business School

Finance as a discipline has been growing rapidly. The numbers of researchers in academy and industry, of students, of methods and models have all proliferated in the past decade or so. This growth and diversity manifests itself in the emerging cross-disciplinary as well as cross-national mix of scholarship now driving the field of finance forward. The intellectual roots of modern finance, as well as the branches, will be represented in the Princeton Series in Finance.

Titles in this series will be scholarly and professional books, intended to be read by a mixed audience of economists, mathematicians, operations research scientists, financial engineers, and other investment professionals. The goal is to provide the finest cross-disciplinary work in all areas of finance by widely recognized researchers in the prime of their creative careers.

OTHER BOOKS IN THIS SERIES

Financial Econometrics: Problems, Models, and Methods by Christian Gourieroux and Joann Jasiak

Credit Risk: Pricing, Measurement, and Management by Darrell Duffie and Kenneth J. Singleton

Microfoundations of Financial Economics: An Introduction to General Equilibrium Asset Pricing by Yvan Lengwiler

Credit Risk Modeling

Theory and Applications

David Lando

Princeton University Press

Princeton and Oxford

Copyright © 2004 by Princeton University Press

Published by Princeton University Press,
41 William Street, Princeton, New Jersey 08540

In the United Kingdom: Princeton University Press,
3 Market Place, Woodstock, Oxfordshire OX20 1SY

Library of Congress Cataloguing-in-Publication Data

Lando, David, 1964–
    Credit risk modeling: theory and applications / David Lando.
        p.cm.—(Princeton series in finance)
    Includes bibliographical references and index.
    ISBN 0-691-08929-9 (cl : alk. paper)
        1. Credit—Management. 2. Risk management. 3. Financial management. I. Title. II. Series.

HG3751.L36 2004
332.7'01'1—dc22   2003068990

British Library Cataloguing-in-Publication Data

A catalogue record for this book is available from the British Library

This book has been composed in Times and typeset by T&T Productions Ltd, London
Printed on acid-free paper ⊚
www.pup.princeton.edu

Printed in the United States of America

10 9 8 7 6 5 4 3 2 1

For Frederik

Contents

Preface

In September 2002 I was fortunate to be on the scientific committee of a conference in Venice devoted to the analysis of corporate default and credit risk modeling in general. The conference put out a call for papers and received close to 100 submissions—an impressive amount for what is only a subfield of financial economics. The homepage www.defaultrisk.com, maintained by Greg Gupton, has close to 500 downloadable working papers related to credit risk. In addition to these papers, there are of course a very large number of published papers in this area.

These observations serve two purposes. First, they are the basis of a disclaimer: this book is not an encyclopedic treatment of all contributions to credit risk. I am nervously aware that I must have overlooked important contributions. I hope that the overwhelming amount of material provides some excuse for this. But I have of course also chosen what to emphasize. The most important purpose of the book is to deliver what I think are the central themes of the literature, emphasizing "the basic idea," or the mathematical structure, one must know to appreciate it. After this, I hope the reader will be better at tackling the literature on his or her own. The second purpose of my introductory statistics is of course to emphasize the increasing popularity of the research area.

The most important reasons for this increase, I think, are found in the financial industry. First, the Basel Committee is in the process of formulating Basel II, the revision of the Basel Capital Accord, which among other things reforms the way in which the solvency requirements for financial institutions are defined and what good risk-management practices are. During this process there has been tremendous focus on what models are really able to do in the credit risk area at this time. Although it is unclear at this point precisely what Basel II will bring, there is little doubt that it will leave more room for financial institutions to develop "internal models" of the risk of their credit exposures. The hope that these models will better account for portfolio effects and direct hedges and therefore in turn lower the capital requirements has led banks to devote a significant proportion of their resources to credit risk modeling efforts. A second factor is the booming market for credit-related asset-backed securities and credit derivatives which present a new "land of opportunity" for structural finance. The development of these markets is also largely driven by the desire of financial institutions to hedge credit exposures. Finally, with (at least until recently) lower issuance rates for treasury securities and low yields, corporate bond issues have gained increased focus from fund managers.

This drive from the practical side to develop models has attracted many academics; a large number due to the fact that so many professions can (and do) contribute to the development of the field.

The strong interaction between industry and academics is the real advantage of the area: it provides an important reality check and, contrary to what one might expect, not just for the academic side. While it is true that our models improve by being confronted with questions of implementability and estimability and observability, it is certainly also true that generally accepted, but wrong or inconsistent, ways of reasoning in the financial sector can be replaced by coherent ways of thinking. This interaction defines a guiding principle for my choice of which models to present. Some models are included because they can be implemented in practice, i.e. the parameters can be estimated from real data and the parameters have clear interpretations. Other models are included mainly because they are useful for thinking consistently about markets and prices.

How can a book filled with mathematical symbols and equations be an attempt to strengthen the interaction between the academic and practitioner sides? The answer is simply that a good discussion of the issues must have a firm basis in the models. The importance of understanding models (including their limitations, of course) and having a model-based foundation cannot be overemphasized. It is impossible, for example, to discuss what we would expect the shape of the credit-spread curve to be as a function of varying credit quality without an arsenal of models.

Of course, we need to worry about which are good models and which are bad models. This depends to some extent on the purpose of the model. In a perfect world, we obtain models which

- have economic content, from which nontrivial consequences can be deduced;
- are mathematically tractable, i.e. one can compute prices and other expressions analytically and derive sensitivities to changes in different parameters;
- have inputs and parameters of the models which can be observed and estimated—the parameters are interpretable and reveal properties of the data which we can understand.

Of course, it is rare that we achieve everything in one model. Some models are primarily useful for clarifying our conceptual thinking. These models are intended to define and understand phenomena more clearly without worrying too much about the exact quantitative predictions. By isolating a few critical phenomena in stylized models, we structure our thinking and pose sharper questions.

The more practically oriented models serve mainly to assist us in quantitative analysis, which we need for pricing contracts and measuring risk. These models often make heroic assumptions on distributions of quantities, which are taken as exogenous in the models. But even heroic assumptions provide insights as long as we vary them and analyze their consequences rigorously.

The need for conceptual clarity and the need for practicality place different demands on models. An example from my own research, the model we will meet in Chapter 7, views an intensity model as a structural model with incomplete information, and clarifies the sense in which an intensity model can arise from a structural model with incomplete information. Its practicality is limited at this stage. On the other hand, some of the rating-based models that we will encounter are of practical use but they do not change our way of thinking about corporate debt or derivatives. The fact is that in real markets there are rating triggers and other rating-related covenants in debt contracts and other financial contracts which necessitate an explicit modeling of default risk from a rating perspective. In these models, we make assumptions about ratings which are to a large extent motivated by the desire to be able to handle calculations.

The ability to quickly set up a model which allows one to experiment with different assumptions calls for a good collection of workhorses. I have included a collection of tools here which I view as indispensable workhorses. This includes option-based techniques including the time-independent solutions to perpetual claims, techniques for Markov chains, Cox processes, and affine specifications. Mastering these techniques will provide a nice toolbox.

When we write academic papers, we try to fit our contribution into a perceived void in the literature. The significance of the contribution is closely correlated with the amount of squeezing needed to achieve the fit. A book is of course a different game. Some monographs use the opportunity to show in detail all the stuff that editors would not allow (for reasons of space) to be published. These can be extremely valuable in teaching the reader all the details of proofs, thereby making sure that the subtleties of proof techniques are mastered. This monograph does almost the opposite: it takes the liberty of not proving very much and worrying mainly about model structure. Someone interested in mathematical rigor will either get upset with the format, which is about as far from theorem–proof as you can get, or, I am hoping, find here an application-driven motivation for studying the mathematical structure.

In short, this book is my way of introducing the area to my intended audience. There are several other books in the area—such as Ammann (2002), Arvanitis and Gregory (2001), Bielecki and Rutkowski (2002), Bluhm et al. (2002), Cossin and Pirotte (2001), Duffie and Singleton (2003), and Schönbucher (2003)—and overlaps of material are inevitable, but I would not have written the book if I did not think it added another perspective on the topic. I hope of course that my readers will agree. The original papers on which the book are based are listed in the bibliography. I have attempted to relegate as many references as possible to the notes since the long quotes of who did what easily break the rhythm.

So who is my intended audience? In short, the book targets a level suitable for a follow-up course on fixed-income modeling dedicated to credit risk. Hence, the "core" reader is a person familiar with the Black–Scholes–Merton model of option-pricing, term-structure models such as those of Vasicek and Cox–Ingersoll–Ross, who has seen stochastic calculus for diffusion processes and for whom the notion of an equivalent martingale measure is familiar. Advanced Master's level students in the many financial engineering and financial mathematics programs which have arisen over the last decade, PhD students with a quantitative focus, and "quants" working in the finance industry I hope fit this description. Stochastic calculus involving jump processes, including state price densities for processes with jumps, is not assumed to be familiar. It is my experience from teaching that there are many advanced students who are comfortable with Black–Scholes-type modeling but are much less comfortable with the mathematics of jump processes and their use in credit risk modeling. For this reader I have tried to include some stochastic calculus for jump processes as well as a small amount of general semimartingale theory, which I think is useful for studying the area further. For years I have been bothered by the fact that there are some extremely general results available for semimartingales which could be useful to people working with models, but whenever a concrete model is at work, it is extremely hard to see whether it is covered by the general theory. The powerful results are simply not that accessible. I have included a few rather wimpy results, compared with what can be done, but I hope they require much less time to grasp. I also hope that they help the reader identify some questions addressed by the general theory.

I am also hoping that the book gives a useful survey to risk managers and regulators who need to know which methods are in use but who are not as deeply involved in implementation of the models. There are many sections which require less technical background and which should be self-contained. Large parts of the section on rating estimation, and on dependent defaults, make no use of stochastic calculus. I have tried to boil down the technical sections to the key concepts and results. Often the reader will have to consult additional sources to appreciate the details. I find it useful in my own research to learn what a strand of work "essentially does" since this gives a good indication of whether one wants to dive in further. The book tries in many cases to give an overview of the essentials. This runs the risk of superficiality but at least readers who find the material technically demanding will see which core techniques they need to master. This can then guide the effort in learning the necessary techniques, or provide help in hiring assistants with the right qualifications.

There are many people to whom I owe thanks for helping me learn about credit risk. The topic caught my interest when I was a PhD student at Cornell and heard talks by Bob Jarrow, Dilip Madan, and Robert Littermann at the Derivatives Symposium in Kingston, Ontario, in 1993. In the work which became my thesis I received a lot of encouragement from my thesis advisor, Bob Jarrow, who knew that credit risk would become an important area and kept saying so. The support from my committee members, Rick Durrett, Sid Resnick, and Marty Wells, was also highly appreciated. Since then, several co-authors and co-workers in addition to Bob have helped me understand the topic, including useful technical tools, better. They are Jens Christensen, Peter Ove Christensen, Darrell Duffie, Peter Fledelius, Peter Feldhütter, Jacob Gyntelberg, Christian Riis Flor, Ernst Hansen, Brian Huge, Søren Kyhl, Kristian Miltersen, Allan Mortensen, Jens Perch Nielsen, Torben Skødeberg, Stuart Turnbull, and Fan Yu.

In the process of writing this book, I have received exceptional assistance from Jens Christensen. He produced the vast majority of graphs in this book; his explicit solution for the affine jump-diffusion model forms the core of the last appendix; and his assistance in reading, computing, checking, and criticizing earlier proofs has been phenomenal. I have also been allowed to use graphs produced by Peter Feldhütter, Peter Fledelius, and Rolf Poulsen.

My friends associated with the CCEFM in Vienna—Stefan Pichler, Wolfgang Ausenegg, Stefan Kossmeier, and Joseph Zechner—have given me the opportunity to teach a week-long course in credit risk every year for the last four years. Both the teaching and the Heurigen visits have been a source of inspiration. The courses given for SimCorp Financial Training (now Financial Training Partner) have also helped me develop material.

There are many other colleagues and friends who have contributed to my understanding of the area over the years, by helping me understand what the important problems are and teaching me some of the useful techniques. This list of people includes Michael Ahm, Jesper Andreasen, Mark Carey, Mark Davis, Michael Gordy, Lane Hughston, Martin Jacobsen, Søren Johansen, David Jones, Søren Kyhl, Joe Langsam, Henrik O. Larsen, Jesper Lund, Lars Tyge Nielsen, Ludger Overbeck, Lasse Pedersen, Rolf Poulsen, Anders Rahbek, Philipp Schönbucher, Michael Sørensen, Gerhard Stahl, and all the members of the Danish Mathematical Finance Network.

A special word of thanks to Richard Cantor, Roger Stein, and John Rutherford at Moody's Investor's Service for setting up and including me in Moody's Academic Advisory and Research Committee. This continues to be a great source of inspiration. I would also like to thank my past and present co-members, Pierre Collin-Dufresne, Darrell Duffie, Steven Figlewski, Gary Gorton, David Heath, John Hull, William Perraudin, Jeremy Stein, and Alan White, for many stimulating discussions in this forum. Also, at Moody's I have learned from Jeff Bohn, Greg Gupton, and David Hamilton, among many others.

I thank the many students who have supplied corrections over the years. I owe a special word of thanks to my current PhD students Jens Christensen, Peter Feldhütter and Allan Mortensen who have all supplied long lists of corrections and suggestions for improvement. Stephan Kossmeier, Jesper Lund, Philipp Schönbucher, Roger Stein, and an anonymous referee have also given very useful feedback on parts of the manuscript and for that I am very grateful.

I have received help in typing parts of the manuscript from Dita Andersen, Jens Christensen, and Vibeke Hutchings. I gratefully acknowledge support from The Danish Social Science Research Foundation, which provided a much needed period of reduced teaching.

Richard Baggaley at Princeton University Press has been extremely supportive and remarkably patient throughout the process. The Series Editors Darrell Duffie and Stephen Schaefer have also provided lots of encouragement.

I owe a lot to Sam Clark, whose careful typesetting and meticulous proofreading have improved the finished product tremendously.

I owe more to my wife Lise and my children Frederik and Christine than I can express. At some point, my son Frederik asked me if I was writing the book because I wanted to or because I had to. I fumbled my reply and I am still not sure what the precise answer should have been. This book is for him.

Credit Risk Modeling

1

An Overview

The natural place to start the exposition is with the Black and Scholes (1973) and Merton (1974) milestones. The development of option-pricing techniques and the application to the study of corporate liabilities is where the modeling of credit risk has its foundations. While there was of course research out before this, the option-pricing literature, which views the bonds and stocks issued by a firm as contingent claims on the assets of the firm, is the first to give us a strong link between a statistical model describing default and an economic-pricing model. Obtaining such a link is a key problem of credit risk modeling. We make models describing the distribution of the default events and we try to deduce prices from these models. With pricing models in place we can then reverse the question and ask, given the market prices, what is the market's perception of the default probabilities. To answer this we must understand the full description of the variables governing default and we must understand risk premiums. All of this is possible, at least theoretically, in the option-pricing framework.

Chapter 2 starts by introducing the Merton model and discusses its implications for the *risk structure* of interest rates—an object which is not to be mistaken for a term structure of interest rates in the sense of the word known from modeling government bonds. We present an immediate application of the Merton model to bonds with different seniority. There are several natural ways of generalizing this, and to begin with we focus on extensions which allow for closed-form solutions. One direction is to work with different asset dynamics, and we present both a case with stochastic interest rates and one with jumps in asset value. A second direction is to introduce a default boundary which exists at all time points, representing some sort of safety covenant or perhaps liquidity shortfall. The Black–Cox model is the classic model in this respect. As we will see, its derivation has been greatly facilitated by the development of option-pricing techniques. Moreover, for a clever choice of default boundary, the model can be generalized to a case with stochastic interest rates. A third direction is to include coupons, and we discuss the extension both to discrete-time, lumpy dividends and to continuous flows of dividends and continuous coupon payments. Explicit solutions are only available if the time horizon is made infinite.

Having the closed-form expressions in place, we look at a numerical scheme which works for any hitting time of a continuous boundary provided that we know the transition densities of the asset-value process. With a sense of what can be done with closed-form models, we take a look at some more practical issues.

Coupon payments really distinguish corporate bond pricing from ordinary option pricing in the sense that the asset-sale assumptions play a critical role. The liquidity of assets would have no direct link to the value of options issued by third parties on the firm's assets, but for corporate debt it is critical. We illustrate this by looking at the term-structure implications of different asset-sale assumptions.

Another practical limitation of the models mentioned above is that they are all static, in the sense that no new debt issues are allowed. In practice, firms roll over debt and our models should try to capture that. A simple model is presented which takes a stationary leverage target as given and the consequences are felt at the long end of the term structure. This anticipates the models of Chapter 3, in which the choice of leverage is endogenized.

One of the most practical uses of the option-based machinery is to derive implied asset values and implied asset volatilities from equity market data given knowledge of the debt structure. We discuss the maximum-likelihood approach to finding these implied values in the simple Merton model. We also discuss the philosophy behind the application of implied asset value and implied asset volatility as variables for quantifying the probability of default, as done, for example (in a more complicated and proprietary model), by Moody's KMV.

The models in Chapter 2 are all incapable of answering questions related to the optimal capital structure of firms. They all take the asset-value process and its division between different claims as given, and the challenge is to price the different claims given the setup. In essence we are pricing a given securitization of the firm's assets.

Chapter 3 looks at the standard approach to obtaining an optimal capital structure within an option-based model. This involves looking at a trade-off between having a tax shield advantage from issuing debt and having the disadvantage of bankruptcy costs, which are more likely to be incurred as debt is increased. We go through a model of Leland, which despite (perhaps because of) its simple setup gives a rich playing field for economic interpretation. It does have some conceptual problems and these are also dealt with in this chapter. Turning to models in which the underlying state variable process is the EBIT (earnings before interest and taxes) of a firm instead of firm value can overcome these difficulties. These models can also capture the important phenomenon that equity holders can use the threat of bankruptcy to renegotiate, in times of low cash flow, the terms of the debt, forcing the debt holders to agree to a lower coupon payment. This so-called strategic debt service is more easily explained in a binomial setting and this is how we conclude this chapter.

At this point we leave the option-pricing literature. Chapter 4 briefly reviews different statistical techniques for analyzing defaults. First, classical discriminant analysis is reviewed. While this model had great computational advantages before statistical computing became so powerful, it does not seem to be a natural statistical model for default prediction. Both logistic regression and hazard regressions have a more natural structure. They give parameters with natural interpretations and handle issues of censoring that we meet in practical data analysis all the time. Hazard regressions also provide natural nonparametric tools which are useful for exploring the data and for selecting parametric models. And very importantly, they give an extremely natural connection to pricing models. We start by reviewing the discrete-time hazard regression, since this gives a very easy way of understanding the occurrence/exposure ratios, which are the critical objects in estimation—both parametrically and nonparametrically.

While on the topic of default probability estimation it is natural to discuss some techniques for analyzing rating transitions, using the so-called generator of a Markov chain, which are useful in practical risk management. Thinking about rating migration in continuous time offers conceptual and in some respects computational improvements over the discrete-time story. For example, we obtain better estimates of probabilities of rare events. We illustrate this using rating transition data from Moody's. We also discuss the role of the Markov assumption when estimating transition matrices from generator matrices.

The natural link to pricing models brought by the continuous-time survival analysis techniques is explained in Chapter 5, which introduces the intensity setting in what is the most natural way to look at it, namely as a Cox process or doubly stochastic Poisson process. This captures the idea that certain background variables influence the rate of default for individual firms but with no feedback effects. The actual default of a firm does not influence the state variables. While there are important extensions of this framework, some of which we will review briefly, it is by far the most practical framework for credit risk modeling using intensities. The fact that it allows us to use many of the tools from default-free term-structure modeling, especially with the affine and quadratic term-structure models, is an enormous bonus. Particularly elegant is the notion of recovery of market value, which we spend some time considering. We also outline how intensity models are estimated through the extended Kalman filter—a very useful technique for obtaining estimates of these heavily parametrized models.

For the intensity model framework to be completely satisfactory, we should understand the link between estimated default intensities and credit spreads. Is there a way in which, at least in theory, estimated default intensities can be used for pricing? There is, and it is related to diversifiability but not to risk neutrality, as one might have expected. This requires a thorough understanding of the risk premiums, and an important part of this chapter is the description of what the sources of excess expected return are in an intensity model. An important moral of this chapter is that even if intensity models look like ordinary term-structure models, the structure of risk premiums is richer.

How do default intensities arise? If one is a firm believer in the Merton setting, then the only way to get something resembling default intensities is to introduce jumps in asset value. However, this is not a very tractable approach from the point of view of either estimation or pricing credit derivatives. If we do not simply want to assume that intensities exist, can we still justify their existence? It turns out that we can by introducing incomplete information. It is shown that in a diffusion-based model, imperfect observation of a firm's assets can lead to the existence of a default intensity for outsiders to the firm.

Chapter 6 is about rating-based pricing models. This is a natural place to look at those, as we have the Markov formalism in place. The simplest illustration of intensity models with a nondeterministic intensity is a model in which the intensity is "modulated" by a finite-state-space Markov chain. We interpret this Markov chain as a rating, but the machinery we develop could be put to use for processes needing a more-fine-grained assessment of credit quality than that provided by the rating system.

An important practical reason for looking at ratings is that there are a number of financial instruments that contain provisions linked to the issuer rating. Typical examples are the step-up clauses of bond issues used, for example, to a large extent in the telecommunication sector in Europe. But step-up provisions also figure prominently in many types of loans offered by banks to companies.

Furthermore, rating is a natural first candidate for grouping bond issues from different firms into a common category. When modeling the spreads for a given rating, it is desirable to model the joint evolution of the different term structures, recognizing that members of each category will have a probability of migrating to a different class. In this chapter we will see how such a joint modeling can be done. We consider a calibration technique which modifies empirical transition matrices in such a way that the transition matrix used for pricing obtains a fit of the observed term structures for different credit classes. We also present a model with stochastically varying spreads for different rating classes, which will become useful later in the chapter on interest-rate swaps. The problem with implementing these models in practice are not trivial. We look briefly at an alternative method using thresholds and affine process technology which has become possible (but is still problematic) due to recent progress using transform methods. The last three chapters contain applications of our machinery to some important areas in which credit risk analysis plays a role

The analysis of interest-rate swap spreads has matured greatly due to the advances in credit risk modeling. The goal of this chapter is to get to the point at which the literature currently stands: counterparty credit risk on the swap contract is not a key factor in explaining interest-rate swap spreads. The key focus for understanding the joint evolution of swap curves, corporate curves, and treasury curves is the fact that the floating leg of the swap contract is tied to LIBOR rates.

But before we can get there, we review the foundations for reaching that point. A starting point has been to analyze the apparent arbitrage which one can set up using swap markets to exchange fixed-rate payments for floating-rate payments. While there may very well be institutional features (such as differences in tax treatments) which permit such advantages to exist, we focus in Chapter 7 on the fact that the comparative-advantage story can be set up as a sort of puzzle even in an arbitrage-free model. This puzzle is completely resolved. But the interest in understanding the role of two-sided default risk in swaps remains. We look at this with a strong focus on the intensity-based models. The theory ends up pretty much confirming the intuitive result: that swap counterparties with symmetric credit risk have very little reason to worry about counterparty default risk. The asymmetries that exist between their payments—since one is floating and therefore not bounded in principle, whereas the other is fixed—only cause very small effects in the pricing. With netting agreements in place, the effect is negligible. This finally clears the way for analyzing swap spreads and their relationship to corporate bonds, focusing on the important problem mentioned above, namely that the floating payment in a swap is linked to a LIBOR rate, which is bigger than that of a short treasury rate. Viewing the LIBOR spread as coming from credit risk (something which is probably not completely true) we set up a model which determines the fixed leg of the swap assuming that LIBOR and AA are the same rate. The difference between the swap rate and the corporate AA curve is highlighted in this case. The difference is further illustrated by showing that theoretically there is no problem in having the AAA rate be above the swap rate—at least for long maturities.

The result that counterparty risk is not an important factor in determining credit risk also means that swap curves do not contain much information on the credit quality of its counterparties. Hence swaps between risky counterparties do not really help us with additional information for building term structures for corporate debt. To get such important information we need to look at default swaps and asset swaps. In idealized settings we explain in Chapter 8 the interpretation of both the asset-swap spread and the default swap spread. We also look at more complicated structures involving baskets of issuers in the so-called first-to-default swaps and first-m-of-n-to-default swaps. These derivatives are intimately connected with so-called collateralized debt obligations (CDOs), which we also define in this chapter.

Pricing of CDOs and analysis of portfolios of loans and credit-risky securities lead to the question of modeling dependence of defaults, which is the topic of the whole of Chapter 9. This chapter contains many very simplified models which are developed for easy computation but which are less successful in preserving a realistic model structure. The curse is that techniques which offer elegant computation of default losses assume a lot of homogeneity among issuers. Factor structures can mitigate but not solve this problem. We discuss correlation of rating movements derived from asset-value correlations and look at correlation in intensity models. For intensity models we discuss the problem of obtaining correlation in affine specifications of the CIR type, the drastic covariation of intensities needed to generate strong default correlation and show with a stylized example how the updating of a latent variable can lead to default correlation.

Recently, a lot of attention has been given to the notion of copulas, which are really just a way of generating multivariate distributions with a set of given marginals. We do not devote a lot of time to the topic here since it is, in the author's view, a technique which still relies on parametrizations in which the parameters are hard to interpret. Instead, we choose to spend some time on default dependence in financial networks. Here we have a framework for understanding at a more fundamental level how the financial ties between firms cause dependence of default events. The interesting part is the clearing algorithm for defining settlement payments after a default of some members of a financial network in which firms have claims on each other.

After this the rest is technical appendices. A small appendix reviews arbitrage-free pricing in a discrete-time setting and hints at how a discrete-time implementation of an intensity model can be carried out. Two appendices collect material on Brownian motion and Markov chains that is convenient to have readily accessible. They also contains a section on processes with jumps, including Itô's formula and, just as important, finding the martingale part and the drift part of the contribution coming from the jumps. Finally, they look at some abstract results about (special) semi-martingales which I have found very useful. The main goal is to explain the structure of risk premiums in a structure general enough to include all models included in this book. Part of this involves looking at excess returns of assets specified as special semimartingales. Another part involves getting a better grip on the quadratic variation processes.

Finally, there is an appendix containing a workhorse for term-structure modeling. I am sure that many readers have had use of the explicit forms of the Vasicek and the Cox–Ingersoll–Ross (CIR) bond-price models. The appendix provides closed-form solutions for different functionals and the characteristic function of a one-dimensional affine jump-diffusion with exponentially distributed jumps. These closed-form solutions cover all the pricing formulas that we need for the affine models considered in this book.

2

Corporate Liabilities as Contingent Claims

2.1 Introduction

This chapter reviews the valuation of corporate debt in a perfect market setting where the machinery of option pricing can be brought to use. The starting point of the models is to take as given the evolution of the market value of a firm's assets and to view all corporate securities as contingent claims on these assets. This approach dates back to Black and Scholes (1973) and Merton (1974) and it remains the key reference point for the theory of defaultable bond pricing.

Since these works appeared, the option-pricing machinery has expanded significantly. We now have a rich collection of models with more complicated asset price dynamics, with interest-rate-sensitive underlying assets, and with highly path-dependent option payoff profiles. Some of this progress will be used below to build a basic arsenal of models. However, the main focus is not to give a complete catalogue of the option-pricing models and explore their implications for pricing corporate bonds. Rather, the goal is to consider some special problems and questions which arise when using the machinery to price corporate debt.

First of all, the extent to which owners of firms may use asset sales to finance coupon payments on debt is essential to the pricing of corporate bonds. This is closely related to specifying what triggers default in models where default is assumed to be a possibility at all times. While ordinary barrier options have barriers which are stipulated in the contract, the barrier at which a company defaults is typically a modeling problem when looking at corporate bonds.

Second, while we know the current liability structure of a firm, it is not clear that it will remain constant in the remaining life of the corporate debt that we are trying to model. In classical option pricing, the issuing of other options on the same underlying security is usually ignored, since these are not liabilities issued by the same firm that issued the stock. Of course, the future capital-structure choice of a firm also influences the future path of the firm's equity price and therefore has an effect on equity options as well. Typically, however, the future capital-structure changes are subsumed as part of the dynamics of the stock. Here, when considering corporate bonds, we will see models that take future capital-structure changes more explicitly into account.

Finally, the fact that we do not observe the underlying asset value of the firm complicates the determination of implied volatility. In standard option pricing, where we observe the value of the underlying asset, implied volatility is determined by inverting an option-pricing formula. Here, we have to jointly estimate the underlying asset value and the asset volatility from the price of a derivative security with the asset value as underlying security. We will explain how this can be done in a Merton setting using maximum-likelihood estimation. A natural question in this context is to consider how this filtering can in principle be used for default prediction.

This chapter sets up the basic Merton model and looks at price and yield impli-cations for corporate bonds in this framework. We then generalize asset dynamics (including those of default-free bonds) while retaining the zero-coupon bond struc-ture. Next, we look at the introduction of default barriers which can represent safety covenants or indicate decisions to change leverage in response to future movements in asset value. We also increase the realism by considering coupon payments. Finally, we look at estimation of asset value in a Merton model and discuss an application of the framework to default prediction.

2.2 The Merton Model

Assume that we are in the setting of the standard Black–Scholes model, i.e. we analyze a market with continuous trading which is frictionless and competitive in the sense that

- agents are price takers, i.e. trading in assets has no effect on prices,
- there are no transactions costs,
- there is unlimited access to short selling and no indivisibilities of assets, and
- borrowing and lending through a money-market account can be done at the same riskless, continuously compounded rate r.

Assume that the time horizon is $\bar{T}$. To be reasonably precise about asset dynamics, we fix a probability space $(\Omega, \mathcal{F}, P)$ on which there is a standard Brownian motion W. The information set (or σ-algebra) generated by this Brownian motion up to time t is denoted $\mathcal{F}_t$.

We want to price bonds issued by a firm whose assets are assumed to follow a geometric Brownian motion:

$$dV_t = \mu V_t \, dt + \sigma V_t \, dW_t.$$

Here, W is a standard Brownian motion under the probability measure P. Let the starting value of assets equal V_0. Then this is the same as saying

$$V_t = V_0 \exp((\mu - \tfrac{1}{2}\sigma^2)t + \sigma W_t).$$

We also assume that there exists a money-market account with a constant riskless rate r whose price evolves deterministically as

$$\beta_t = \exp(rt).$$

We take it to be well known that in an economy consisting of these two assets, the price C_0 at time 0 of a contingent claim paying $C(V_T)$ at time T is equal to

$$C_0 = E^Q[\exp(-rt)C_T],$$

where Q is the equivalent martingale measure[1] under which the dynamics of V are given as

$$V_t = V_0 \exp((r - \tfrac{1}{2}\sigma^2)t + \sigma W_t^Q).$$

Here, W^Q is a Brownian motion and we see that the drift μ has been replaced by r.

To better understand this model of a firm, it is useful initially to think of assets which are very liquid and tangible. For example, the firm could be a holding company whose only asset is a ton of gold. The price of this asset is clearly the price of a liquidly traded security. In general, the market value of a firm's assets is the present market value of the future cash flows which the firm will deliver—a quantity which is far from observable in most cases. A critical assumption is that this asset-value process is given and will not be changed by any financing decisions made by the firm's owners.

Now assume that the firm at time 0 has issued two types of claims: debt and equity. In the simple model, debt is a zero-coupon bond with a face value of D and maturity date $T \leqslant \bar{T}$. With this assumption, the payoffs to debt, B_T, and equity, S_T, at date T are given as

$$B_T = \min(D, V_T) = D - \max(D - V_T, 0), \tag{2.1}$$
$$S_T = \max(V_T - D, 0). \tag{2.2}$$

We think of the firm as being run by the equity owners. At maturity of the bond, equity holders pay the face value of the debt precisely when the asset value is higher than the face value of the bond. To be consistent with our assumption that equity owners cannot alter the given process for the firm's assets, it is useful to think of equity owners as paying D out of their own pockets to retain ownership of assets worth more than D. If assets are worth less than D, equity owners do not want to pay D, and since they have limited liability they do not have to either. Bond holders then take over the remaining asset and receive a "recovery" of V_T instead of the promised payment D.

---

[1] We assume familiarity with the notion of an equivalent martingale measure, or risk-neutral measure, and its relation to the notion of arbitrage-free markets. Appendix D contains further references.

The question is then how the debt and equity are valued prior to the maturity date T. As we see from the structure of the payoffs, debt can be viewed as the difference between a riskless bond and a put option, and equity can be viewed as a call option on the firm's assets. Note that no other parties receive any payments from V. In particular, there are no bankruptcy costs going to third parties in the case where equity owners do not pay their debt and there are no corporate taxes or tax advantages to issuing debt. A consequence of this is that $V_T = B_T + S_T$, i.e. the firm's assets are equal to the value of debt plus equity. Hence, the choice of D by assumption does not change V_T, so in essence the Modigliani–Miller irrelevance of capital structure is hard-coded into the model.

Given the current level V and volatility σ of assets, and the riskless rate r, we let $C^{BS}(V, D, \sigma, r, T)$ denote the Black–Scholes price of a European call option with strike price D and time to maturity T, i.e.

$$C^{BS}(V, D, T, \sigma, r) = VN(d_1) - D\exp(-rT)N(d_2), \qquad (2.3)$$

where N is the standard normal distribution function and

$$d_1 = \frac{\log(V/D) + rT + \frac{1}{2}\sigma^2 T}{\sigma\sqrt{T}},$$

$$d_2 = d_1 - \sigma\sqrt{T}.$$

We will sometimes suppress some of the parameters in C if it is obvious from the context what they are.

Applying the Black–Scholes formula to price these options, we obtain the Merton model for risky debt. The values of debt and equity at time t are

$$S_t = C^{BS}(V_t, D, \sigma, r, T - t),$$

$$B_t = D\exp(-r(T - t)) - P^{BS}(V_t, D, \sigma, r, T - t),$$

where P^{BS} is the Black–Scholes European put option formula, which is easily found from the put–call parity for European options on non-dividend paying stocks (which is a model-free relationship and therefore holds for call and put prices C and P in general):

$$C(V_t) - P(V_t) = V_t - D\exp(-r(T - t)).$$

An important consequence of this parity relation is that with $D, r, T - t$, and V_t fixed, changing any other feature of the model will influence calls and puts in the same direction. Note, also, that since the sum of debt and equity values is the asset value, we have $B_t = V_t - C^{BS}(V_t)$, and this relationship is sometimes easier to work with when doing comparative statics. Some consequences of the option representation are that the bond price B_t has the following characteristics.

- It is increasing in V. This is clear given the fact that the face value of debt remains unchanged. It is also seen from the fact that the put option decreases as V goes up.

- It is increasing in D. Again not too surprising. Increasing the face value will produce a larger state-by-state payoff. It is also seen from the fact that the call option decreases in value, which implies that equity is less valuable.

- It is decreasing in r. This is most easily seen by looking at equity. The call option increases, and hence debt must decrease since the sum of the two remains unchanged.

- It is decreasing in time-to-maturity. The higher discounting of the riskless bond is the dominating effect here.

- It is decreasing in volatility σ.

The fact that volatility simultaneously increases the value of the call and the put options on the firm's assets is the key to understanding the notion of "asset substitution." Increasing the riskiness of a firm at time 0 (i.e. changing the volatility of V) without changing V_0 moves wealth from bond holders to shareholders. This could be achieved, for example, by selling the firm's assets and investing the amount in higher-volatility assets. By definition, this will not change the total value of the firm. It will, however, shift wealth from bond holders to shareholders, since both the long call option held by the equity owners and the short put option held by the bond holders will increase in value.

This possibility of wealth transfer is an important reason for covenants in bonds: bond holders need to exercise some control over the investment decisions. In the Merton model, this control is assumed, in the sense that nothing can be done to change the volatility of the firm's assets.

2.2.1 The Risk Structure of Interest Rates

Since corporate bonds typically have promised cash flows which mimic those of treasury bonds, it is natural to consider yields instead of prices when trying to compare the effects of different modeling assumptions. In this chapter we always look at the continuously compounded yield of bonds. The yield at date t of a bond with maturity T is defined as

$$y(t, T) = \frac{1}{T - t} \log \frac{D}{B_t},$$

i.e. it is the quantity satisfying

$$B_t \exp(y(t, T)(T - t)) = D.$$

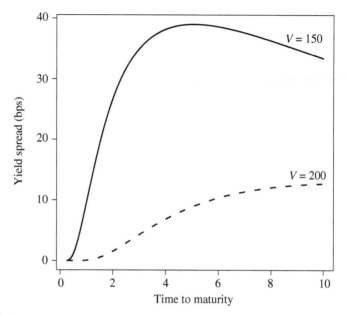

Figure 2.1. Yield spreads as a function of time to maturity in a Merton model for two different levels of the firm's asset value. The face value of debt is 100. Asset volatility is fixed at 0.2 and the riskless interest rate is equal to 5%.

Note that a more accurate term is really *promised yield*, since this yield is only realized when there is no default (and the bond is held to maturity). Hence the promised yield should not be confused with expected return of the bond. To see this, note that in a risk-neutral world where all assets must have an expected return of r, the promised yield on a defaultable bond is still larger than r. In this book, the difference between the yield of a defaultable bond and a corresponding treasury bond will always be referred to as the *credit spread* or *yield spread*, i.e.

$$s(t, T) = y(t, T) - r.$$

We reserve the term *risk premium* for the case where the taking of risk is rewarded so that the *expected return* of the bond is larger than r.

Now let $t = 0$, and write $s(T)$ for $s(0, T)$. The *risk structure* of interest rates is obtained by viewing $s(T)$ as a function of T. In Figures 2.1 and 2.2 some examples of risk structures in the Merton model are shown. One should think of the risk structure as a transparent way of comparing prices of potential zero-coupon bond issues with different maturities assuming that the firm chooses only one maturity. It is also a natural way of comparing zero-coupon debt issues from different firms possibly with different maturities. The risk structure cannot be used as a term structure of interest rates for one issuer, however. We cannot price a coupon bond issued by a firm by

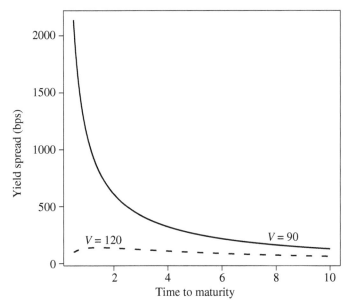

Figure 2.2. Yield spreads in a Merton model for two different (low) levels of the firm's asset value. The face value of debt is 100. Asset volatility is fixed at 0.2 and the riskless interest rate is equal to 5%. When the asset value is lower than the face value of debt, the yield spread goes to infinity.

valuing the individual coupons separately using the simple model and then adding the prices. It is easy to check that doing this quickly results in us having the values of the individual coupon bonds sum up to more than the firm's asset value. Only in the limit with very high firm value does this method work as an approximation—and that is because we are then back to riskless bonds in which the repayment of one coupon does not change the dynamics needed to value the second coupon. We will return to this discussion in greater detail later. For now, consider the risk structure as a way of looking, as a function of time to maturity, at the yield that a particular issuer has to promise on a debt issue if the issue is the only debt issue and the debt is issued as zero-coupon bonds.

Yields, and hence yield spreads, have comparative statics, which follow easily from those known from option prices, with one very important exception: the dependence on time to maturity is not monotone for the typical cases, as revealed in Figures 2.1 and 2.2. The Merton model allows both a monotonically decreasing spread curve (in cases where the firm's value is smaller than the face value of debt) and a humped shape. The maximum point of the spread curve can be at very short maturities and at very large maturities, so we can obtain both monotonically decreasing and monotonically increasing risk structures within the range of maturities typically observed.

Note also that while yields on corporate bonds increase when the riskless interest rate increases, the yield *spreads* actually decrease. Representing the bond price as $B(r) = V - C^{BS}(r)$, where we suppress all parameters other than r in the notation, it is straightforward to check that

$$y'(r) = \frac{-B'(r)}{TB(r)} \in (0, 1)$$

and therefore $s'(r) = y'(r) - 1 \in (-1, 0)$.

2.2.2 On Short Spreads in the Merton Model

The behavior of yield spreads at the short end of the spectrum in Merton-style models plays an important role in motivating works which include jump risk. We therefore now consider the behavior of the risk structure in the short end, i.e. as the time to maturity goes to 0. The result we show is that when the value of assets is larger than the face value of debt, the yield spreads go to zero as time to maturity goes to 0 in the Merton model, i.e.

$$s(T) \to 0 \quad \text{for } T \to 0.$$

It is important to note that this is a consequence of the (fast) rate at which the probability of ending below D goes to 0. Hence, merely noting that the default probability itself goes to 0 is not enough.

More precisely, a diffusion process X has the property that for any $\varepsilon > 0$,

$$\frac{P(|X_{t+h} - X_t| \geqslant \varepsilon)}{h} \xrightarrow[h \to 0]{} 0.$$

We will take this for granted here, but see Bhattacharya and Waymire (1990), for example, for more on this. The result is easy to check for a Brownian motion and hence also easy to believe for diffusions, which locally look like a Brownian motion.

We now show why this fact implies 0 spreads in the short end. Note that a zero-recovery bond paying 1 at maturity h if $V_h > D$ and 0 otherwise must have a lower price and hence a higher yield than the bond with face value D in the Merton model. Therefore, it is certainly enough to show that this bond's spread goes to 0 as $h \to 0$.

The price B^0 of the zero-recovery bond is (suppressing the starting value V_0)

$$B^0 = E^Q[D \exp(-rh) 1_{\{V_h \geqslant D\}}]$$
$$= D \exp(-rh) Q(V_h \geqslant D),$$

and therefore the yield spread $s(h)$ is

$$s(h) = -\frac{1}{h}\log\left(\frac{B^0}{D}\right) - r$$

$$= -\frac{1}{h}\log Q(V_h \geqslant D)$$

$$\approx -\frac{1}{h}(Q(V_h \geqslant D) - 1)$$

$$= \frac{1}{h}Q(V_h \leqslant D),$$

and hence, for $V_0 > D$,

$$s(h) \to 0 \quad \text{for } h \to 0,$$

and this is what we wanted to show. In the case where the firm is close to bankruptcy, i.e. $V_0 < D$, and the maturity is close to 0, yields are extremely large since the price at which the bond trades will be close to the current value of assets, and since the yield is a promised yield derived from current price and promised payment. A bond with a current price, say, of 80 whose face value is 100 will have an enormous annualized yield if it only has (say) a week to maturity. As a consequence, traders do not pay much attention to yields of bonds whose prices essentially reflect their expected recovery in an imminent default.

2.2.3 On Debt Return Distributions

Debt instruments have a certain drama due to the presence of default risk, which raises the possibility that the issuer may not pay the promised principal (or coupons). Equity makes no promises, but it is worth remembering that the equity is, of course, far riskier than debt. We have illustrated this point in part to try and dispense with the notion that losses on bonds are "heavy tailed." In Figure 2.3 we show the return distribution of a bond in a Merton model with one year to maturity and the listed parameters. This is to be compared with the much riskier return distribution of the stock shown in Figure 2.4. As can be seen, the bond has a large chance of seeing a return around 10% and almost no chance of seeing a return under -25%. The stock, in contrast, has a significant chance (almost 10%) of losing everything.

2.2.4 Subordinated Debt

Before turning to generalizations of Merton's model, note that the option framework easily handles subordination, i.e. the situation in which certain "senior" bonds have priority over "junior" bonds. To see this, note Table 2.1, which expresses payments to senior and junior debt and to equity in terms of call options. Senior debt can be priced as if it were the only debt issue and equity can be priced by viewing the entire debt as one class, so the most important change is really the valuation of junior debt.

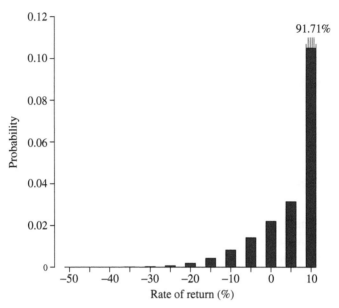

Figure 2.3. A discretized distribution of corporate bond returns over 1 year in a model with very high leverage. The asset value is 120 and the face value is 100. The asset volatility is assumed to be 0.2, the riskless rate is 5%, and the return of the assets is 10%.

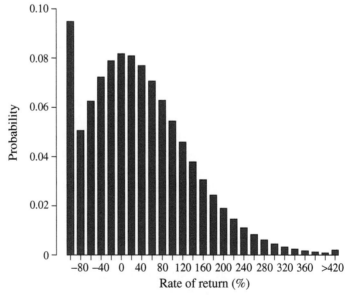

Figure 2.4. A discretized distribution of corporate stock returns over 1 year with the same parameter values as in Figure 2.3.

Table 2.1. Payoffs to senior and junior debt and equity at maturity when the face values of senior and junior debt are D_S and D_J, respectively.

	$V_T < D_S$	$D_S \leqslant V_T < D_S + D_J$	$D_S + D_J < V_T$
Senior	V_T	D_S	D_S
Junior	0	$V_T - D_S$	D_J
Equity	0	0	$V_T - (D_S + D_J)$

Table 2.2. Option representations of senior and junior debt. $C(V, D)$ is the payoff at expiration of a call-option with value of underlying equal to V and strike price D.

Type of debt	Option payoff
Senior	$V - C(V, D_S)$
Junior	$C(V, D_S) - C(V, D_S + D_J)$
Equity	$C(V, D_S + D_J)$

2.3 The Merton Model with Stochastic Interest Rates

We now turn to a modification of the Merton setup which retains the assumption of a single zero-coupon debt issue but introduces stochastic default-free interest rates. First of all, interest rates on treasury bonds *are* stochastic, and secondly, there is evidence that they are correlated with credit spreads (see, for example, Duffee 1999). When we use a standard Vasicek model for the riskless rate, the pricing problem in a Merton model with zero-coupon debt is a (now) standard application of the numeraire-change technique. This technique will appear again later, so we describe the structure of the argument in some detail.

Assume that under a martingale measure Q the dynamics of the asset value of the firm and the short rate are given by

$$dV_t = r_t V_t \, dt + \sigma_V V_t (\rho \, dW_t^1 + \sqrt{1 - \rho^2} \, dW_t^2),$$
$$dr_t = \kappa(\theta - r) \, dt + \sigma_r \, dW_t^1,$$

where W_t^1 and W_t^2 are independent standard Brownian motions. From standard term-structure theory, we know that the price at time t of a default-free zero-coupon bond with maturity T is given as

$$p(t, T) = \exp(a(T - t) - b(T - t)r_t),$$

where

$$b(T - t) = \frac{1}{\kappa}(1 - \exp(-\kappa(T - t))),$$
$$a(T - t) = \frac{(b(T - t) - (T - t))(\kappa^2\theta - \frac{1}{2}\sigma^2)}{\kappa^2} - \frac{\sigma^2 b^2(T - t)}{4\kappa}.$$

To derive the price of (say) equity in this model, whose only difference from the Merton model is due to the stochastic interest rate, we need to compute

$$S_t = E_t^Q \left(\exp \left(- \int_t^T r_s \, ds \right) (V_T - D)^+ \right),$$

and this task is complicated by the fact that the stochastic variable we use for discounting and the option payoff are dependent random variables, both from the correlation in their driving Brownian motions and because of the drift in asset values being equal to the stochastic interest rate under Q. Fortunately, the (return) volatility $\sigma_T(t)$ of maturity T bonds is deterministic. An application of Itô's formula will show that

$$\sigma_T(t) = -\sigma_r b(T - t).$$

This means that if we define

$$Z_{V,T}(t) = \frac{V(t)}{p(t, T)},$$

then the volatility of Z is deterministic and through another application of Itô's formula can be expressed as

$$\sigma_{V,T}(t) = \sqrt{(\rho \sigma_V + \sigma_r b(T - t))^2 + \sigma_V^2(1 - \rho^2)}.$$

Now define

$$\Sigma_{V,T}^2(T) = \int_0^T \| \sigma_{V,T}(t) \|^2 \, dt$$

$$= \int_0^T (\rho \sigma_V + \sigma_r b(T - t))^2 + \sigma_V^2(1 - \rho^2) \, dt$$

$$= \int_0^T (2\rho \sigma_V \sigma_r b(T - t) + \sigma_r^2 b^2(T - t) + \sigma_V^2) \, dt.$$

From Proposition 19.14 in Björk (1998), we therefore know that the price of the equity, which is a call option on the asset value, is given at time 0 by

$$S(V, 0) = V N(d_1) - D p(0, T) N(d_2),$$

where

$$d_1 = \frac{\log(V / Dp(0, T)) + \frac{1}{2} \Sigma_{V,T}^2(T)}{\sqrt{\Sigma_{V,T}^2(T)}},$$

$$d_2 = d_1 + \sqrt{\Sigma_{V,T}^2(T)}.$$

This option price is all we need, since equity is then directly priced using this formula, and the value of debt then follows directly by subtracting the equity value

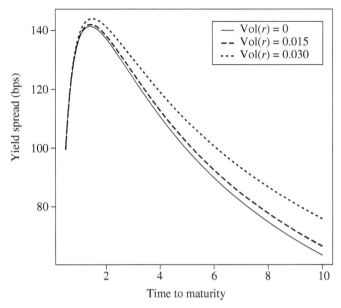

Figure 2.5. The effect of interest-rate volatility in a Merton model with stochastic interest rates. The current level of assets is $V_0 = 120$ and the starting level of interest rates is 5%. The face value is 100 and the parameters relevant for interest-rate dynamics are $\kappa = 0.4$ and $\theta = 0.05$. The asset volatility is 0.2 and we assume $\rho = 0$ here.

from current asset value. We are then ready to analyze credit spreads in this model as a function of the parameters. We focus on two aspects: the effect of stochastic interest rates when there is no correlation; and the effect of correlation for given levels of volatility.

As seen in Figure 2.5, interest rates have to be very volatile to have a significant effect on credit spreads. Letting the volatility be 0 brings us back to the standard Merton model, whereas a volatility of 0.015 is comparable with that found in empirical studies. Increasing volatility to 0.03 is not compatible with the values that are typically found in empirical studies. A movement of one standard deviation in the driving Brownian motion would then lead (ignoring mean reversion) to a 3% fall in interest rates—a very large movement. The insensitivity of spreads to volatility is often viewed as a justification for ignoring effects of stochastic interest rates when modeling credit spreads.

Correlation, as studied in Figure 2.6, seems to be a more significant factor, although the chosen level of 0.5 in absolute value is somewhat high. Note that higher correlation produces higher spreads. An intuitive explanation is that when asset value falls, interest rates have a tendency to fall as well, thereby decreasing the drift of assets, which strengthens the drift towards bankruptcy.

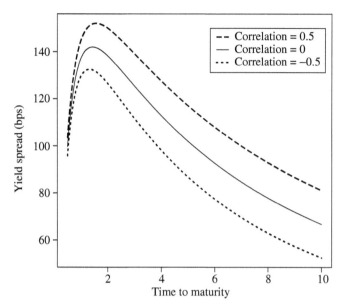

Figure 2.6. The effect of correlation between interest rates and asset value in a Merton model with stochastic interest rates. The current level of assets is $V_0 = 120$ and the starting level of interest rates is 5%. The face value is 100 and the parameters relevant for interest-rate dynamics are $\kappa = 0.4$ and $\theta = 0.05$. The asset volatility is 0.2 and the interest-rate volatility is $\sigma_r = 0.015$.

2.4   The Merton Model with Jumps in Asset Value

We now take a look at a second extension of the simple Merton model in which the dynamics of the asset-value process contains jumps.[2] The aim of this section is to derive an explicit pricing formula, again under the assumption that the only debt issue is a single zero-coupon bond. We will then use the pricing relationship to discuss the implications for the spreads in the short end and we will show how one compares the effect of volatility induced by jumps with that induced by diffusion volatility.

We start by considering a setup in which there are only finitely many possible jump sizes. Let $N^1, \ldots, N^K$ be K independent Poisson processes with intensities $\lambda^1, \ldots, \lambda^K$. Define the dynamics of the return process R under a martingale measure[3] Q as a jump-diffusion

$$\mathrm{d}R_t = r\,\mathrm{d}t + \sigma\,\mathrm{d}W_t + \sum_{i=1}^{K} h^i\,\mathrm{d}(N_t^i - \lambda^i t),$$

---

[2]The stochastic calculus you need for this section is recorded in Appendix D. This section can be skipped without loss of continuity.

[3]Unless otherwise stated, all expectations in this section are taken with respect to this measure Q.

and let this be the dynamics of the cumulative return for the underlying asset-value process. As explained in Appendix D, we define the price as the semimartingale exponential of the return and this gives us

$$V_t = V_0 \exp\left(\left(r - \tfrac{1}{2}\sigma^2 - \sum h^i \lambda^i\right)t + \sigma W_t\right) \prod_{0 \leqslant s \leqslant t} \left(1 + \sum_{i=1}^{K} h^i \Delta N_s^i\right).$$

Note that independent Poisson processes never jump simultaneously, so at a time s, at most one of the ΔN_s^i is different from 0.

Recall that we can get the Black–Scholes partial differential equation (PDE) by performing the following steps (in the classical setup).

- Write the stochastic differential equation (SDE) of the price process V of the underlying security under Q.

- Let f be a function of asset value and time representing the value of a contingent claim.

- Use Itô to derive an SDE for $f(V_t, t)$. Identify the drift term and the martingale part.

- Set the drift equal to $rf(V_t, t)\, dt$.

We now perform the equivalent of these steps in our simple jump-diffusion case. Define $\lambda = \lambda_1 + \cdots + \lambda_K$ and let

$$\bar{h} = \frac{1}{\lambda} \sum_{i=1}^{K} h^i \lambda^i.$$

Then (under Q)

$$dV_t = V_t\{(r + \bar{h}\lambda)\, dt + \sigma\, dW_t\} + \sum_{i=1}^{K} h^i V_{t-}\, dN_t^i.$$

We now apply Itô by using it separately on the diffusion component and the individual jump components to get

$$f(V_t, t) - f(V_0, 0)$$
$$= \int_0^t [f_V(V_s, s)r V_s + f_t(V_s, s) - f_V(V_s, s)\bar{h}\lambda V_s + \tfrac{1}{2}\sigma^2 V_s^2 f_{VV}(V_s, s)]\, ds$$
$$+ \int_0^t f_V(V_s, s)\sigma V_s\, dW_s + \sum_{0 \leqslant s \leqslant t} \{f(V_s) - f(V_{s-})\}.$$

Now write

$$\sum_{0\leqslant s\leqslant t} \{f(V_s) - f(V_{s-})\} = \sum_{i=1}^{K} \int_0^t \{f(V_s) - f(V_{s-})\}\,\mathrm{d}N_s^i$$

$$= \sum_{i=1}^{K} \int_0^t [f(V_{s-}(1 + h^i)) - f(V_{s-})]\lambda^i\,\mathrm{d}s$$

$$+ \sum_{i=1}^{K} \int_0^t [f(V_{s-}(1 + h^i)) - f(V_{s-})]\,\mathrm{d}[N_s^i - \lambda^i s]$$

and note that we can write s instead of $s-$ in the time index in the first integral because we are integrating with respect to the Lebesgue measure. In total, we now get the following drift term for $f(V_t, t)$:[4]

$$(r - \bar{h}\lambda)V_t f_V + f_t + \tfrac{1}{2}\sigma^2 V_t^2 f_{VV} + \sum_{i=1}^{K}\{f(V_t(1 + h^i)) - f(V_t)\}\lambda^i.$$

Letting

$$p^i := \lambda^i/\lambda$$

allows us to write

$$\sum_{i=1}^{K}\{f(V_t(1 + h^i)) - f(V_t)\}\lambda^i = \sum_{i=1}^{K}\{p^i[f(V_t(1 + h^i)) - f(V_t)]\}\lambda$$

$$\equiv \lambda E\Delta f(V_t),$$

and our final expression for the term in front of $\mathrm{d}t$ is now

$$(r - \bar{h}\lambda)V_t f_V + f_t + \tfrac{1}{2}\sigma^2 V_t^2 f_{VV} + \lambda E\Delta f(V_t).$$

This is the term we have to set equal to $rf(V_t, t)$ and solve (with boundary conditions) to get what is called an integro-differential equation. It is *not* a PDE since, unlike a PDE, the expressions involve not only f's behavior at a point V (including the behavior of its derivatives), it also takes into account values of f at points V "far away" (at $V(1+h^i)$ for $i = 1, \ldots, K$). Such equations can only be solved explicitly in very special cases.

We have considered the evolution of V as having only finitely many jumps and we have derived the integro-differential equation for the price of a contingent claim in this case. It is straightforward to generalize to a case where jumps (still) arrive as a Poisson process N with the rate λ but where the jump-size distribution has a continuous distribution on the interval $[-1, \infty)$ with mean k. If we let $\epsilon_1, \epsilon_2, \ldots$

---

[4]We omit V_t and t in f.

denote a sequence of independent jump sizes with such a distribution, then we may consider the dynamics

$$V_t = V_0 \exp((r - \tfrac{1}{2}\sigma^2 + \lambda k)t + \sigma W_t) \prod_{i=1}^{N_t}(1 + \varepsilon_i).$$

Between jumps in N, we thus have a geometric Brownian motion, but at jumps the price changes to $1 + \varepsilon_i$ times the pre-jump value. Hence $1 + \varepsilon_i < 1$ corresponds to a downward jump in price.

In the example below with lognormally distributed jumps, use the following notation for the distribution of the jumps: the basic lognormal distribution is specified as

$$E \log(1 + \epsilon_i) = \gamma - \tfrac{1}{2}\delta^2, \qquad V \log(1 + \epsilon_i) = \delta^2,$$

and hence

$$E\epsilon_i = k = \exp(\gamma) - 1,$$
$$E\epsilon_i^2 = \exp(2\gamma + \delta^2) - 2\exp(\gamma) + 1.$$

One could try to solve the integro-differential equation for contingent-claims prices. It turns out that in the case where $1 + \epsilon_i$ is lognormal, there is an easier way: by conditioning on N_t and then using BS-type expressions. The result is an infinite sum of BS-type expressions. For the call option with price C^{JD} we find (after some calculations)

$$C^{\mathrm{JD}}(V_t, D, T, \sigma^2, r, \delta^2, \lambda, k) = \sum_{n=0}^{\infty} \frac{(\lambda'T)^n}{n!} \exp(-\lambda'T) C^{\mathrm{BS}}(V_t, D, T, \sigma_n^2, r_n),$$

where C^{BS} as usual is the standard Black–Scholes formula for a call and

$$\lambda' = \lambda(1 + k),$$
$$r_n = r + \frac{n\gamma}{T} - \lambda k,$$
$$\sigma_n^2 = \sigma^2 + \frac{n\delta^2}{2T},$$
$$\gamma = \log(1 + k).$$

To understand some of the important changes that are caused by introducing jumps in a Merton model, we focus on two aspects: the effect on credit spreads in the short end, and the role of the source of volatility, i.e. whether volatility comes from jumps or from the diffusion part.

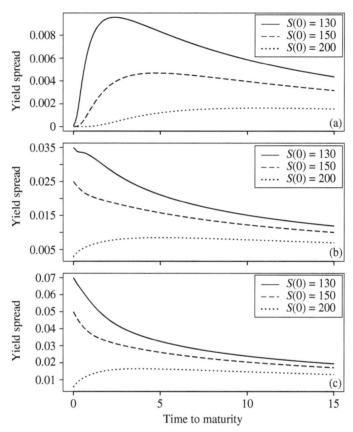

Figure 2.7. The effect of changing the mean jump size and the intensity in a Merton model with jumps in asset value. From (a) to (b) we are changing the parameter determining the mean jump size, γ, from $\log(0.9)$ to $\log(0.5)$. This makes recovery at an immediate default lower and hence increases the spread in the short end. From (b) to (c) the intensity is doubled, and we notice the exact doubling of spreads in the short end, since expected recovery is held constant but the default probability over the next short time interval is doubled.

We focus first on the short end of the risk structure of interest rates. The price of the risky bond with face value D maturing at time h (soon to be chosen small) is

$$
\begin{aligned}
B(0, h) &= \exp(-rh) E[D 1_{\{V_h \geqslant D\}} + V_h 1_{\{V_h < D\}}] \\
&= \exp(-rh) [D Q(V_h \geqslant D) + E[V_h \mid V_h < D] Q(V_h < D)] \\
&= D \exp(-rh) \left[1 - Q(V_h < D) + \frac{1}{D} E[V_h \mid V_h < D] Q(V_h < D) \right] \\
&= D \exp(-rh) \left[1 - Q(V_h < D) \left(1 - \frac{E[V_h \mid V_h < D]}{D} \right) \right].
\end{aligned}
$$

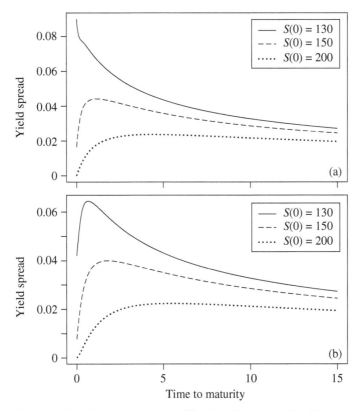

Figure 2.8. The effect of the source of volatility in a Merton model with jumps in asset value. (a) The diffusion part has volatility $\sigma = 0.1$, and the total quadratic variation is 0.4. (b) The diffusion part has volatility $\sigma = 0.3$, but the total quadratic variation is kept at 0.4 by decreasing λ. In both cases, three different current asset values are considered. Changing the source of volatility causes significant changes of the yield spreads in the short end for the high-yield cases. The difference between the spread curves in the case of low leverage is very small. Effects are also limited in the long end in all cases.

Now computing the yield spread limit as $h \to 0$ and using $\log(1 - x) \approx -x$ for x close to 0, we find that for $s(h) = y(0, h) - r$,

$$\lim_{h\downarrow 0} s(h) = \lim_{h\downarrow 0} \left[\frac{Q(V_h < D)}{h} \left(1 - \frac{E[V_h \mid V_h < D]}{D} \right) \right].$$

Now as $h \downarrow 0$ there is only at most one jump that can occur. The total jump intensity is λ, but the probability of a jump being large enough to send V_h below D happens with a smaller intensity $\lambda^* = \lambda Q[(1 + \varepsilon)V_0 < D]$. We recognize the second term in the expression as the expected fractional loss given default. Altogether we obtain

$$\lim_{h\downarrow 0} s(h) = \lambda^* E[\ell(V_0)],$$

where

$$\ell(V_0) = 1 - \frac{E[V_0(1 + \varepsilon) \mid V_0(1 + \varepsilon) < D]}{D}.$$

An immediate consequence is that doubling the overall jump intensity should double the instantaneous spread. Another consequence is, as is intuitively obvious, that lowering the mean jump size should typically lead to higher spreads. Both facts are illustrated in Figure 2.7.

When comparing the jump-diffusion model with the standard Merton model, it is common to "level the playing field" by holding constant the "volatility" in a sense that we now explain.

The optional quadratic variation of a semimartingale X can be obtained as a limit

$$[X]_t = \lim_{n \to \infty} \sum_{i \in \mathbb{N}} [X(t_{i+1}^n \wedge t) - X(t_i^n \wedge t)]^2,$$

where the grid size in the subdivision goes to 0 as $n \to \infty$.[5]

From the definition of *predictable* quadratic variation, $\langle X \rangle$ found in Appendix D, we know that when X has finite variance, $E[X_t] = E\langle X \rangle_t$, and since the jump-diffusion process R studied here is a process with independent increments, $\langle R \rangle_t$ is deterministic and we have that

$$E[R_t] = \langle R \rangle_t = \sigma^2 t + \lambda t E \varepsilon_i^2.$$

Holding $\langle R \rangle_t$ constant for a given t by offsetting changes in σ by changes in λ and/or $E \varepsilon_i^2$ gives room for an experiment in which we change the source of volatility. This is done in Figure 2.8. As is evident from that graph, the main effect is in the short end of the risk structure of interest rates.

While it is tempting to think of quadratic variation as realized volatility, it is important to understand the difference between the volatility arising from the diffusion and the volatility arising from the jump part. For a fixed t we have

$$[R]_t = \langle R^c \rangle_t + \sum_{0 \leqslant s \leqslant t} \Delta R_s^2,$$

where R^c is the continuous part of R. Therefore, when we compute $(1/t)[R]_t$ from an approximating sum, we do not get a limit of $\sigma^2 + \lambda E \varepsilon_i^2$ for fixed t and finer subdivisions. When our time horizon is fixed, we will always have the random component $\sum_{0 \leqslant s \leqslant t} \Delta R_s^2$, and if jumps are rare this need not be close to $\lambda E \varepsilon_i^2$.

---

[5]The limit is to be understood in the sense of uniform convergence in probability, i.e. on a finite interval $[0, t]$, if the enemy shows up with small $\epsilon_1 > 0$ and $\epsilon_2 > 0$ then we can choose N large enough so that for $n > N$ the probability of the approximating sum deviating more than ϵ_1 anywhere on the interval is smaller than ϵ_2.

However, as $t \to \infty$ we have

$$\frac{1}{t} \sum_{0 \leqslant s \leqslant t} \Delta R_s^2 \to \lambda E \varepsilon_i^2.$$

This highlights an important difference between diffusion-induced and jump-induced volatility. We cannot obtain the jump-induced volatility, even theoretically, as our observations get closer and closer in time. Observing the whole sample path in $[0, t]$ would allow us to single out the jumps and then obtain $\langle R^c \rangle_t$ exactly. In practice, we do not have the exact jumps, and filtering out the jumps from the volatility based on discrete observations is a difficult exercise. So, while the jump-diffusion model is excellent for illustration and simulating the effects of jumps, the problems in estimating the model make it less attractive in practical risk management.

2.5 Discrete Coupons in a Merton Model

As mentioned earlier we cannot use the Merton model for zero-coupon debt to price coupon debt simply by pricing each component of the bond separately. The pricing of the coupon bond needs to look at all coupon payments in a single model and in this context our assumptions on asset sales become critical.

To understand the problem and see how to implement a pricing algorithm, consider a coupon bond with two coupons D_1 and D_2 which have to be paid at dates t_1 and t_2.

For $t > t_1$, if the firm is still alive and the assets are worth V_t, we can value the only remaining coupon D_2 simply using the standard Merton model, so

$$B(V_t, t) = D_2 p(t, t_2) - P^{\text{BS}}(V_t, D_2, t_2 - t)$$

for $t > t_1$. The situation at date t_1 is more complicated and it critically depends on the assumptions we make on what equity owners, who control the firm, are allowed to do with the firm's assets.

First, assume that equity owners are not allowed to use the firm's assets to pay debt. This means that they have to finance the debt payment either by paying "out of their own pockets" or by issuing new equity to finance the coupon payment. In this simple model with no information asymmetries, it does not matter which option they choose. If they issue M new shares of stock in addition to the (say) N existing shares, they will raise an amount equal to $(M/(M + N))S_{t_1}$, where S_t is the total value of equity at time t. Hence, to finance D_1 they need to choose M so that

$$\frac{M}{M + N} S_{t_1} = D_1,$$

thereby diluting the value of their own equity from S_{t_1} to $(N/(M + N))S_{t_1}$. This dilution causes a fall in their equity value of $S_{t_1} - D_1$, and so if they do not pay D_1 out of their own pockets they lose D_1 through dilution of equity. Hence it does not matter which option we consider. The option to issue new debt is not considered here, where we assume that the debt structure is static. So, think of equity owners as deciding an instant before t_1 whether to pay the coupon at date t_1 out of their own pockets. Paying the coupon will leave them with equity worth $C(V_{t_1}, D_2, t_2 - t_1)$ and hence it is optimal to pay the coupon D_1 if

$$D_1 < C(V_{t_1}, D_2, t_2 - t_1).$$

If this is not true, they will default and debt holders will take over the firm.

Applying this line of reasoning leads to the following recursion when pricing coupon debt assuming no asset sales. Given coupons $D_1, \ldots, D_N$ due at dates $t_1, \ldots, t_N$, we now proceed as follows.

(1) Price debt and equity at dates $t > t_{N-1}$ using the standard Merton setup.

(2) At t_{N-1}, find the value $\bar{V}_{N-1}$ for which $D_{N-1} = C(\bar{V}_{N-1}, t_N - t_{N-1}, D_N)$.

(3) At date t_{N-1}, let

$$S(V, t_{N-1}) = \begin{cases} C(V, D_N, t_N - t_{N-1}) - D_{N-1} & \text{for } V \geqslant \bar{V}_{N-1}, \\ 0 & \text{for } V < \bar{V}_{N-1}, \end{cases}$$

and

$$B(V, t_{N-1}) = \begin{cases} D_{N-1} + V - C(V, D_N, t_N - t_{N-1}) & \text{for } V \geqslant \bar{V}_{N-1}, \\ V & \text{for } V < \bar{V}_{N-1}; \end{cases}$$

this gives us the boundary conditions for debt and equity at date t_{N-1}.

(4) From this we can, at least numerically, value equity right after a coupon payment at date t_{N-2}.

The value $\bar{V}_{N-2}$ is the value for which equity is worth D_{N-2} right after the coupon has been paid at date t_{N-2}.

(5) Use the same procedure then as in (3) to set the boundary conditions at date t_{N-2} and continue backwards to time 0.

This will give us prices of debt and equity using an assumption of no asset sales.

What if asset sales are allowed? In this case we still work recursively backwards but we need to adjust both the default boundary and the asset value. At date $t > t_{N-1}$ we are still in the classical Merton setup. To set the relevant boundary condition for debt and equity at date t_{N-1}, we argue as follows.

If assets are worth more than D_{N-1}, it is never optimal for equity owners to default, since this leaves them with 0. Clearly, it is better to sell D_{N-1} worth of assets to cover the coupon and continue with assets worth $V(t_{N-1}) - D_{N-1}$, and hence equity is worth $C(V_{t_{N-1}} - D_{N-1}, D_N, t_N - t_{N-1})$. They might also consider paying out of their own pockets, but in fact, it is optimal for equity owners to sell assets instead of covering the payment themselves. To see this, note that paying out of their own pockets leaves equity with

$$C(V_{t_{N-1}}, D_N, t_N - t_{N-1}) - D_{N-1},$$

but this is smaller than

$$C(V_{t_{N-1}} - D_{N-1}, D_N, t_N - t_{N-1}),$$

since $C_V < 1$ for all V, and therefore

$$C(V_{t_{N-1}}) - C(V_{t_{N-1}} - D_{N-1}) < D_{N-1}.$$

This is also intuitively obvious, since the payment of the coupon by equity owners alone will benefit both equity and debt, but be an expense to equity only. To write down how to price the securities is a little more cumbersome even if the implementation is not too hard. We leave the details to the reader. The asset value is a geometric Brownian motion between coupon dates, but if an asset sale takes place to finance a coupon, the value drops by an amount equal to the coupon.

All the time, we set the equity equal to zero if asset value at a coupon date falls below the coupon payment at that date, and in that case we let debt holders take over the firm. If the assets are large enough, we subtract the coupon payment in the asset value.

Pricing algorithms are easy to implement in a tree both in the case of asset sales and in the case of no asset sales, but note that only the first model permits a fully recombining tree, since asset value is unaffected by coupon payments. In the model with asset sales, we need to distinguish between the sequence of up-and-down moves, since we subtract an amount from the asset value at coupon dates that is not a constant fraction of asset value.

The assumptions we make on asset sales are critical for our valuation and for term-structure implications. We return to this in a later section. Note that we have only considered one debt issue. When there are several debt issues we of course need to keep track of the recovery assigned to the different issues at liquidation dates.

2.6 Default Barriers: the Black–Cox Setup

We now consider therefore the basic extension of the Merton model due to Black and Cox (1976). The idea is to let defaults occur prior to the maturity of the bond. In mathematical terms, default will happen when the level of the asset value hits a lower boundary, modelled as a deterministic function of time. In the original approach of Black and Cox, the boundary represents the point at which bond safety covenants cause a default. As we will see later, the technique is also useful for modeling default due to liquidity constraints where we approximate frequent small coupon payments by a continuous stream of payments.

First-passage times for diffusions have been heavily studied. If one is looking for closed-form solutions, it is hard to go much beyond Brownian motion hitting a linear boundary (although there are a few extensions, as mentioned in the bibliographical notes). This mathematical fact almost dictates the type of boundary for asset value that we are interested in, namely boundaries that bring us back into the familiar case after we take logarithms. So, in their concrete model, Black and Cox consider a process for asset value which under the risk-neutral measure is

$$dV_t = (r - a)V_t \, dt + \sigma V_t \, dW_t,$$

where we have allowed for a continuous dividend payout ratio of a. The default boundary is given as

$$C_1(t) = C \exp(-\gamma(T - t)).$$

Assume that the bond issued by the firm has principal D and that $C < D$. Note that since $V_t = V_0 \exp((r - a)t - \frac{1}{2}\sigma^2 t + \sigma W_t)$, the default time τ is given as

$$\tau = \inf\{0 \leqslant t \leqslant T : \log V_0 + ((r - a) - \tfrac{1}{2}\sigma^2)t + \sigma W_t = \log C - \gamma(T - t)\}$$
$$= \inf\{0 \leqslant t \leqslant T : \sigma W_t + (r - a - \tfrac{1}{2}\sigma^2 - \gamma)t = \log C - \log V_0 - \gamma T\},$$

i.e. the first time a Brownian motion with drift hits a certain level.

In the Black–Cox model the payoff to bond holders at the maturity date is

$$B(V_T, T) = \min(V_T, D)1_{\{\tau > T\}},$$

corresponding to the usual payoff when the boundary has not been crossed in $[0, T]$. To simplify notation, let the current date be 0 so that the maturity date T is also time to maturity. We let

$$B^{\mathrm{m}}(V, T, D, C, \gamma) = E(\exp(-rT) \min(V_T, D)1_{\{\tau > T\}})$$

denote the value at time 0 of the payoff of the bond at maturity when the face value is D and the function $C_1(\cdot)$ is specified as a function of C and γ as above.

If the boundary is hit before the maturity of the bond, bond holders take over the firm, i.e.

$$B(V_\tau, \tau) = C_1(\tau)1_{\{\tau \leqslant T\}}.$$

With the same conventions as above, we let

$$B^{\mathrm{b}}(V, T, D, C, \gamma) = E(\exp(-r\tau)C_1(\tau)1_{\{\tau \leqslant T\}})$$

denote the value at time 0 of the payoff to the bond holders in the event that the boundary is hit before maturity. We assume that the starting value V is above C_1. We will value the contribution from these two parts separately.

The contribution from the payment at maturity can be valued using techniques from barrier options and here we use the treatment of Björk (1998, Chapter 13, p. 182). Mimicking the expression of the payoff of the bond in the Merton model as a difference between a riskless bond and a put option, we note that the payoff at maturity here is

$$D1_{\{\tau > T\}} - (D - V_T)^+ 1_{\{\tau > T\}}. \tag{2.4}$$

Hence we need to be able to value a "truncated bond" and a "truncated put option," and the technique is available from the results on down-and-out barrier options. The only modification we have to take care of is that the barrier is exponential and that there is a dividend payout on the underlying asset. First, we consider the valuation in the case of a flat boundary and where the drift of the underlying asset is equal to the riskless rate under the risk-neutral measure (i.e. dividends are set to zero). Observe that a put–call parity for barrier options allows us to write

$$D1_{\{\tau > T\}} - (D - V_T)^+ 1_{\{\tau > T\}} = (V_T - D)^+ 1_{\{\tau > T\}} - V_T 1_{\{\tau > T\}}, \tag{2.5}$$

and so we can use price expressions for a barrier call and a contract paying the asset value at maturity if the boundary has not been hit. For these expressions we need to define the value of a contract paying 1 at maturity if the asset value is above L at maturity:

$$H(V, T, L) = \exp(-rT)N\left(\frac{\log(V/L) + (r - \frac{1}{2}\sigma^2)T}{\sigma\sqrt{T}}\right), \tag{2.6}$$

where we assume $V > L$. From Proposition 13.16 and Lemma 13.17 in Björk (1998) we obtain the value BL of the bond payout at maturity if the boundary is flat at the level L (corresponding to $\gamma = 0$ in our model) and there is no dividend payment on the underlying asset (corresponding to $a = 0$ in the model):

$$BL(V, T, D, L)$$
$$= LH(V, t, T, L) - L\left(\frac{L}{V}\right)^{((2r/\sigma^2)-1)} H\left(\frac{L^2}{V}, t, T, L\right)$$
$$+ C^{BS}(V, L, T) - \left(\frac{L}{V}\right)^{((2r/\sigma^2)-1)} C^{BS}\left(\frac{L^2}{V}, L, T\right)$$
$$- C^{BS}(V, D, T) + \left(\frac{L}{V}\right)^{((2r/\sigma^2)-1)} C^{BS}\left(\frac{L^2}{V}, D, T\right),$$

where we have suppressed the riskless rate and the volatility used in the Black–Scholes price of a European call $C^{BS}(V, D, T)$. Now we will use this expression to get the price B^m of the bond payout at maturity of a bond in the Black–Cox model.

The trick is to rewrite the default event and use a different underlying price process. The event of no default can be written as

$$\{\tau > T\} = \{V_t \exp(-\gamma t) > C \exp(-\gamma T) \text{ for all } t \in [0, T]\}$$

and the payoff at maturity as

$$(D - V_T)^+ 1_{\{\tau>T\}} = \exp(\gamma T)(D\exp(-\gamma T) - V_T \exp(-\gamma T)^+)1_{\{\tau>T\}}.$$

Define a new process Y by letting

$$Y_t = \exp(-\gamma t)V_t.$$

Since V has a drift of $r - a$ under the risk-neutral measure Q, the drift of Y is $r - a - \gamma$. To use the formula of Björk (1998) we therefore rewrite to make the riskless discount rate be $r - a - \gamma$. Hence

$$E^Q(\exp(-rT)[D - V_T]^+ 1_{\{\tau>T\}})$$
$$= \exp(-aT)E^Q(\exp(-(r-\gamma-a)T)[D\exp(-\gamma T)-Y_T]^+ 1_{\{Y_t>C\exp(-\gamma T) \text{ for all } t\}})$$

and the expectation is precisely the value of a barrier call option for an underlying asset Y whose drift under the risk-neutral measure is equal to the riskless rate $r - \gamma - a$. The constant lower boundary is $L = C\exp(-\gamma T)$ and the exercise price is $D\exp(-\gamma T)$. The exact same trick can be performed for the truncated stock part and we end up with the following expression for the value of the payment at maturity:

$$B^m(V, T, D, C, \gamma) = BL(V\exp(-\gamma T), T, D\exp(-\gamma T), C\exp(-\gamma T)). \quad (2.7)$$

The second part, i.e. the payout of the option on the barrier, leads us to compute a functional of the form

$$u(0, x) = E_X \int_0^T C\exp(-\alpha s)\varphi_{T,X}(s)\,ds,$$

where $\varphi_{T,X}(s)$ is the first hitting time of a boundary for a Brownian motion with drift and C, α are constants. Had T been ∞, this would just be a Laplace transform of a density (which is known), but the finite boundary T makes things more tricky. For an argument on how to proceed, see Appendix B. Let

$$b = \frac{\log(C/V_0) - \gamma T}{\sigma},$$

$$\mu = \frac{r - a - \frac{1}{2}\sigma^2 - \gamma}{\sigma}$$

and define

$$\tilde{\mu} = \sqrt{\mu^2 + 2\alpha}.$$

Then

$$B^b(V, 0, T, C, \gamma, a) = C \frac{\exp(b\mu)}{\exp(b\tilde{\mu})} \left[N\left(\frac{b - \tilde{\mu}T}{\sqrt{T}} \right) + \exp(2\tilde{\mu}b) N\left(\frac{b + \tilde{\mu}T}{\sqrt{T}} \right) \right]$$

and this completes our derivation of the value of the bond in the Black–Cox model.[6] It is easy to see that the value of equity in the Black–Cox model with no dividends is a simple down-and-out call option. This in turn saves us the computational burden of computing B^b to get the bond value, since we can just determine this value as the difference between asset value and equity.

When $a \neq 0$ the story is different. In this case, V_0 is the present value not only of the pay-offs to debt and equity at maturity but also of the dividend payment flow aV_s, which takes place up to the random time $\min(\tau_b, T)$.

While the existence of a default barrier increases the probability of default in a Black–Cox setting compared with that in a Merton setting, note that the bond holders actually take over the remaining assets when the boundary is hit and this in fact leads to higher bond prices and lower spreads. That is, if we consider a Merton model and a Black–Cox model where the face value of debt is the same in the two models, then the Black–Cox version will have lower spreads, as illustrated in Figure 2.9. This is true because at the boundary the value of the firm's assets is of course $V_t = C \exp(-\gamma(T - t))$ in both models, but in the Black–Cox model this value is entirely transferred to bond holders, whereas in the Merton model, before maturity, a strictly positive part of the asset value lies with shareholders. Or from the equity point of view, the equity owners in Merton's model have a European call option, whereas in the Black–Cox model they have a down-and-out call option with other characteristics being the same.

The fact that credit spreads decrease is of course consistent with the boundary representing a safety covenant and in a diffusion model the boundary makes it impossible to recover less than the value at the boundary. But if instead we make bankruptcy costly to the debt holders, the presence of a barrier will be capable of increasing credit spreads compared with a Merton model. In other words, if we change the recovery assumption at the boundary so that

$$B(\tau) = \delta C_1(\tau) 1_{\{\tau \leqslant T\}},$$

where $\delta < 1$, then the new price is simply

$$B^0 = B^m + \delta B^b.$$

Using an exogenous recovery in a structural model leads to a sort of hybrid form of model in which we focus on modeling asset value but do not distribute all of the asset value to the different parts of the capital structure.

---

[6]The reader should be aware that this is different from the expression obtained in the original paper. Since the analytical derivation is not given in Black and Cox, I have been unable to locate the source of the discrepancy.

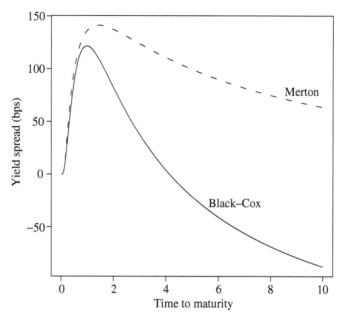

Figure 2.9. A comparison between Merton and Black–Cox. The current level of assets is $V_0 = 120$, asset volatility is 0.2, and the riskless rate is 5%. There is no dividend payout and the Black–Cox boundary has $C = 90$ and $\gamma = 0.02$. Note that despite a higher default probability in the Black–Cox model, the spreads are smaller in the comparable case with no dividend payments on the underlying asset. The smaller spread is due to the favorable recovery from the viewpoint of the bond holders. In fact, when the maturity is long, the default triggering boundary becomes larger than the face value for long time horizons and the payoff to bond holders is therefore larger than face value in some states. This implies negative spreads.

2.7 Continuous Coupons and Perpetual Debt

It is possible to allow for bonds with continuous coupon payments in a Merton or Black–Cox setting. The easiest case to handle is one with asset sales allowed, since payments on coupons then continue until maturity as long as the asset value does not hit zero.

When asset value follows a geometric Brownian motion and we allow for assets to payout an "affine" dividend flow of $aV + d$, we can value a corporate bond G which pays a constant coupon c by solving (numerically) the PDE

$$\tfrac{1}{2}\sigma^2 V^2 G_{VV} + [(r-a)V - (c+d)]G_V + G_t - rG + c = 0.$$

The boundary conditions then depend on which assumptions we make on asset sales. To get analytic solutions for this general case, we assume that the debt is perpetual, so that only changes in the asset value and not the passing of time itself affect the value of the debt.

In this case, the PDE reduces to the ordinary differential equation (ODE)

$$\tfrac{1}{2}\sigma^2 V^2 F_{VV} + [(r-a)V - (c+d)]F_V - rF + c = 0$$

and we then have to supplement with appropriate boundary conditions. Before looking at boundary conditions, an explicit solution to the homogeneous part and then the full ODE must be found, and this is done in Merton (1974) and in greater generality in Black and Cox (1976), who employ a substitution to obtain a differential equation whose solution can be expressed using special functions. We will not dwell on the explicit form of the solution here but instead focus on the boundary conditions employed, since these reveal the assumptions made on asset sales.

The simpler boundary conditions arise when asset sales are permitted. In this case, equity owners will use asset sales to finance the debt payments and therefore the game only stops when asset value hits 0. Letting $G(V)$ denote the value of debt in this case, the relevant boundary conditions are

$$G(0) = 0,$$
$$G_V(V) \to 0 \quad \text{as } V \to \infty.$$

The latter condition is actually equivalent to the requirement that the value of the bond approaches the value of a riskless bond, c/r, as the value of assets goes to infinity.

With no asset sales, we need to decide what is necessary to determine an optimal point for the equity owners to stop paying coupons. The approach taken here closely resembles the approach we will see in the next section. For a given boundary $\bar{V}$ at which the equity owners stop paying coupons, a boundary which would never be above c/r, we obtain the boundary conditions for the value of debt $F(V)$:

$$F(\bar{V}) = \min\left(\bar{V}, \frac{c}{r}\right),$$
$$F(V) \to \frac{c}{r} \quad \text{as } V \to \infty.$$

Now assuming that equity owners will seek to minimize the value of debt—a natural assumption, since in this model this is the same as maximizing the value of equity—they choose the point $\bar{V}$ as a solution to this optimization problem. Plugging the solution to this problem into the boundary condition then gives the solution for the valuation of debt.

The situation here is analogous to the situation considered in the Leland model of the next chapter after the coupon level of the debt issue has been chosen. The refinement of the next section will among other things be to set up a model in which the coupon level is chosen optimally as well. An intermediate case, also studied in Black and Cox (1976), looks at a setup with a safety covenant which terminates the firm when assets hit a given value.

2.8 Stochastic Interest Rates and Jumps with Barriers

We have seen that it is possible to obtain reasonably explicit solutions in some mod-
ifications of the Merton model. In this section we consider what can be done with
stochastic interest rates when there is a default barrier. We also give an analytical
solution in a special case where the assets of the firm can only jump downwards.
This solution is considered since it seems to be a natural way of modeling asset processes for insurance or reinsurance companies, who invest their reserves in products
following an index (say) but who occasionally suffer large insurance losses.

2.8.1 Stochastic Interest Rates and Barriers

It is possible to obtain a closed-form extension of the Black–Cox model to stochastic
interest rates, provided that the bond price processes have deterministic volatility
and the default boundary is picked carefully.

With the same choices as in the Merton model with stochastic interest rates we
let

$$\frac{1}{V_t}\, dV_t = r_t\, dt + \sigma_V(\rho\, dW_t^1 + \sqrt{1-\rho^2}\, dW_t^2)$$

and

$$\frac{1}{p(t,T)}\, dp(t,T) = r_t\, dt + \sigma_P(t,T)\, dW_t^1,$$

where r_t is the stochastic short rate which may well have deterministic drift and
volatility, as in the Hull–White extension of the Vasicek model. Now choose the
default boundary as

$$C_1(t) = \alpha Dp(t,T),$$

where D is the face value of the debt. Assume that the payoff at the default boundary
is a fraction f_1 of the asset value at that point, i.e. $f_1 C_1(t)$. The point of choosing
the bond price $p(t,T)$ as part of the boundary description is that reinvesting the
fractional payout $f_1 C_1(\tau)$ at the boundary when hit at time $\tau < T$ in the riskless
bond and holding it to maturity produces a payoff equal to $f_1\alpha D$, and therefore we
may think of the payoff if the boundary is hit as equivalent to the payoff at maturity T
contingent on the barrier being hit before T. This means that we can treat all payoffs
as occurring at date T and this brings the numeraire-change technique back on track.
If in addition we modify the payoff at maturity to include a fractional bankruptcy
cost of f_2, then the payoff at maturity is given as

$$B(T) = D1_{\{\tau>T\}} + 1_{\{\tau>T,\ V_T<D\}} f_2 V_T + 1_{\{\tau\leqslant T\}} f_1\alpha D.$$

Using the time T bond as numeraire, we let

$$Z_t = \frac{V_t}{p(t,T)}, \quad \text{for } 0 \leqslant t \leqslant T,$$

and note that $Z_T = V_T$. Also note that

$$V_t = C_1(t) \iff Z_t = \alpha D$$

and to value this payoff we use the forward measure Q^T, i.e. the measure under which Z is a martingale, and the value can then be written as

$$B(0, T) = p(0, T)E^{Q^T} B(T).$$

Since the riskless rate is a Gaussian diffusion, $p(0, T)$ has a closed-form solution as in the Vasicek model or the Hull–White extension of the Vasicek model. Hence we need only compute the expectation of $B(T)$ under the forward measure. Under Q^T, Z_t is a martingale and it has a deterministic volatility. All we need to do then is to translate our results for barrier options into the case with 0 drift and a deterministic volatility and this is done simply by changing the timescale. Abstractly, if we define a Brownian motion

$$X_t = \int_0^t \sigma(s) \, dB_s,$$

where $\sigma(\cdot)$ is a deterministic (strictly positive) function, then we can rephrase any question on the joint distribution of X_T and its minimal value m_T on $[0, T)$ as a question on the joint distribution of B and its running minimum on the interval $[0, \int_0^T \sigma^2(s) \, ds]$. Obviously, $X_T \sim N(0, \int_0^T \sigma^2(s) \, ds)$ has the same distribution as $B_{\int_0^T \sigma^2(s) \, ds}$. This gives us the result (see Briys and de Varenne 1997)

$$B(0, T) = Dp(0, T)\left[1 - N(-d_2) + \ell_0 N(-d_1) + \alpha N(-d_6) - \frac{\ell_0}{\alpha} N(-d_5) \right.$$
$$- (1 - f_1)\ell_0 \left(N(-d_3) + \frac{\alpha N(-d_4)}{\ell_0} \right)$$
$$\left. - (1 - f_2)\ell_0 \left(N(d_3) - N(d_1) + \frac{\alpha(N(d_4) - N(d_6))}{\ell_0} \right) \right],$$

where

$$d_1 = \frac{\log \ell_0 + \frac{1}{2}\Sigma(T)}{\sqrt{\Sigma(T)}} = d_2 + \sqrt{\Sigma(T)},$$

$$d_3 = \frac{\log(\ell_0/\alpha) + \frac{1}{2}\Sigma(T)}{\sqrt{\Sigma(T)}} = d_4 + \sqrt{\Sigma(T)},$$

$$d_5 = \frac{\log(V_0/\alpha^2 Dp(0, T)) + \frac{1}{2}\Sigma(T)}{\sqrt{\Sigma(T)}} = d_6 + \sqrt{\Sigma(T)},$$

$$\ell_0 = \frac{V_0}{Dp(0, T)},$$

$$\Sigma(T) = \int_0^T [(\rho\sigma_V + \sigma_P(t, T))^2 + (1 - \rho^2)\sigma_V^2] \, dt.$$

The particular functional form of the boundary is what ensures the analytical solution in this model. In Longstaff and Schwartz (1995a) the same dynamics as above for the firm value and spot rate are taken as given, but here default occurs when V drops to a fixed level K. If default occurs, bond holders receive $(1 - \omega)$ times face value at maturity, hence the payoff is

$$1 - w 1_{\{\tau \leqslant T\}},$$

where τ is the first-passage time of V to K. The value of this is, of course (at time 0),

$$E^Q \left[\exp \left(- \int_0^T rs \, ds \right) (1 - w 1_{\{\tau \leqslant T\}}) \right]$$

$$= p(0, T) - w E^Q \left[\exp \left(- \int_0^T rs \, ds \right) 1_{\{\tau \leqslant T\}} \right]$$

$$= p(0, T) - w p(0, T) Q^T (\tau \leqslant T),$$

where Q^T is the forward measure. The numeraire change helps us to separate the valuation of the bond from the computation of the first hitting time probability, but starting with a constant barrier means that we get a hitting problem involving a stochastic barrier under the forward measure and this requires numerical methods. These methods will benefit from the fact that the transition probabilities are known explicitly for the short rate and the logarithm of asset value. We will return to this when we consider stationary leverage ratios.

Kim et al. (1993) use CIR dynamics for the short rate while keeping the correlation between asset value and interest rates. The dynamics under Q are given as

$$dV_t = (r_t - \gamma)V_t \, dt + \sigma_1 V_t \, dZ_t^1,$$

$$dr_t = \kappa(\mu - r) \, dt + \sigma_2 \sqrt{r_t} \, dZ_t^2,$$

with $dZ_t^1 Z_t^2 = \rho \, dt$. The asset value takes into account a net cash outflow of γV_t per unit of time, independent of capital structure. Shareholders are not allowed to liquidate assets to cover the payment to bond holders, which is assumed to be fixed at c per unit time. Hence default is triggered when cash flows cannot cover coupons, i.e. when $\gamma V_t < c$ (equivalent to $V_t < c/\gamma$). At default, bond holders receive

$$\min(\delta(\tau) B(r; t; c), c/\gamma), \quad \tau = T - t,$$

i.e. either a fraction of an otherwise equivalent treasury bond B, or (if not possible) the remaining assets. At maturity, the assumption $\delta(0) = 1$ ensures the usual payoff equal to the minimum of the principal P and asset value V. The shareholders are paid the difference $\gamma V_t - c$ whenever positive and (if this remains positive so there is no liquidation) they are residual claimants at the end. Due to the CIR dynamics of the short rate, volatility of bonds is no longer deterministic and the numeraire-change technique is not helpful. Kim et al. (1993) therefore solve everything numerically to obtain bond prices. Two of the important conclusions to draw from this model are the following. First, the default triggering boundary has a large effect on yield spreads. But this is mainly due to the fractional recovery, since as we have seen for the Black–Cox model, a boundary triggering default may well serve to lower spread because it transfers assets to debt holders in states where equity would still have positive value in a model with no boundary. Second, stochastic interest rates play a much less significant role. While they (of course) influence both the treasury and the corporate yield structure, they have a small effect on the computed *spreads*.

2.8.2 Jumps and Barriers

Continuous default barriers and jump-diffusions are tough to deal with simultaneously if one wants to obtain closed-form solutions. In Zhou (2001b) a numerical scheme is proposed for dealing with this situation. Here, we briefly mention the powerful analysis in Hilberink and Rogers (2002), which actually allows something very close to closed-form solutions for claims in a setting with perpetual-debt issuance. The model is in fact used to price corporate claims in a model with endogenous default, which we will meet in Chapter 3. Here we merely quote part of the results.

For the methods to work, the model requires that asset value evolves as a jump-diffusion Lévy process with only downwards jumps. This suggests a very natural application to insurance companies suffering occasional large claims from policy holders. While the method works for cases other than than those of exponentially distributed downwards jumps, we write it out here only for that case. Firm assets are assumed to be of the form $V_t = \exp(X_t)$, where, under a risk-neutral measure Q,

$$dX_t = \sigma W_t + bt + J_t,$$

where J_t is a compound Poisson process with downwards jumps which occur at a rate a and which have an exponential distribution with mean c. To obtain a drift rate of assets equal to the riskless rate minus the payout rate δ under Q, use Itô's formula for jumps and check that this requires

$$b = r - \delta - \tfrac{1}{2}\sigma^2 + \frac{a}{1+c}.$$

Let τ_H denote the first time assets hit or fall below a lower boundary at level H. We can develop models for corporate bonds if we are able to evaluate the present value of a linear function of the assets at the default date, the present value of a coupon flow received up to the default date, and the present value of a lump-sum payment (independent of assets) at the default date. Without loss of generality, assume that X starts at x and that the default boundary is 0. Hilberink and Rogers (2002) show

how to obtain an expression up to a Fourier transform of

$$E^x(\exp(-\lambda\tau_0)\exp(\theta X(\tau_0))),$$

which for $\theta = 1$ and $\lambda = r$ gives us the present value of the asset value at the default time. Because of possible "undershoot" this may be strictly below the default barrier. For $\theta = 0$ one gets the present value of a payment of 1 at the default date. And since

$$E\int_0^{\tau_0} \exp(-rs)\,\mathrm{d}s = \frac{1}{r}E(1 - \exp(-r\tau_0)),$$

we automatically cover the case of a continuous coupon paid up until the default date. The expressions for the transforms are given in Hilberink and Rogers (2002), but inversion is not a trivial numerical problem. We will not discuss the numerical issues here.

2.9 A Numerical Scheme when Transition Densities are Known

As we saw from the model with default barriers and stochastic interest rates, it is only by careful choice of default boundaries and interest-rate dynamics that we obtain closed-form solutions in such models. In reality, we want to work with more complicated boundaries—also a point of theoretical interest, as we will see in the next section.

This section presents a numerical scheme for finding a first-passage density of a one-dimensional diffusion process (which in particular is strong Markov, a fact used in the algorithm) when the transition density of the diffusion is known. We present the result abstractly—the following section will show a concrete application.

Given a one-dimensional diffusion process X, we let $f(x, t \mid x_0, 0)$ denote the transition-probability density from x_0 at time 0 to x at time t. We let $g_b(s \mid x_0, 0)$ denote the first-passage time density of X to a boundary at b when the starting point is x_0 at time 0. The key to the numerical scheme for solving for g is to observe that for $x_0 < b < x$ we have the following equation:

$$f(x, t \mid x_0, 0) = \int_0^t g_b(s \mid x_0, 0) f(x, t \mid b, s)\,\mathrm{d}s,$$

which simply states that to go from x_0 to x the process must first cross the boundary and then go from the boundary to the level x. The integral on the right-hand side collects the probabilities of all such paths. Since f is known, we can use this to obtain g numerically. If we integrate both sides with respect to x over $[b, \infty)$ and apply Fubini, then we get

$$P(X_t > b \mid x_0, 0) = \int_0^t g(s \mid x_0, 0) P(X_t > b \mid X_s = b)\,\mathrm{d}s.$$

For a subdivision of the interval $[0, t]$ into n intervals of length Δt, and approximating the integral on the right-hand side using mid-points, we get

$$P(X_{\Delta t} > b \mid x_0, 0) = g(\tfrac{1}{2}\Delta t \mid x_0, 0)\Delta t\, P(X_t > b \mid X_{\Delta t/2} = b),$$

and this determines our first-passage time density at $\tfrac{1}{2}\Delta t$. Approximating over two intervals we get

$$P(X_{2\Delta t} > b \mid x_0, 0) = g(\tfrac{1}{2}\Delta t \mid x_0, 0)\Delta t\, P(X_{2\Delta t} > b \mid X_{\Delta t/2} = b)$$
$$+ g(\tfrac{3}{2}\Delta t \mid x_0, 0)\Delta t\, P(X_{2\Delta t} > b \mid X_{3\Delta t/2} = b),$$

and there is only one unknown $g(\tfrac{3}{2}\Delta t)$ in this equation. This can be continued all the way up to t. The method can be extended to two dimensions: see Collin-Dufresne and Goldstein (2001).

2.10 Towards Dynamic Capital Structure: Stationary Leverage Ratios

The Merton model is static in the sense that it considers a static capital structure. In reality, firms "roll over" debt, i.e. they issue new debt to repay maturing debt and to maintain a desired maturity structure of debt. Ideally, we want to model such decisions as solutions to a dynamic firm-value optimization exercise, but this is only meaningful when the choice of capital structure affects firm value in such a way that an optimization problem can be formulated. This is not possible in the setting of this chapter.[7]

Therefore we consider instead an exogenous assumption on future leverage which takes into account the attempt by a firm to maintain a target leverage ratio. As in Merton (1974) the firm-value process is assumed to follow—under the risk-neutral measure—a geometric Brownian motion:

$$dV_t = (r - \delta)V_t\, dt + \sigma V_t\, dW_t,$$

where δ is the payout rate, r is the risk-free rate, and σ is the volatility, and they are all taken to be constants.

Instead of having a deterministic default boundary as in Black–Cox, the default threshold, k, is modeled dynamically over time:

$$dk_t = \lambda(y_t - v - k_t)\, dt,$$

where $y_t = \log V_t$, and λ and v are constants. The idea is to model default the first time the log-leverage

$$l_t = k_t - y_t$$

___

[7] In fact, for some of our models that involve bankruptcy costs so that the asset value is not distributed solely between shareholders and equity holders, it would be suboptimal for the firm ex ante to issue debt. We ignore this in this chapter and simply take the capital structure as given and analyze its components using contingent-claims analysis.

hits 0. The dynamic adjustment of the default boundary pushes k down when k_t is larger than $y_t - v$, i.e. the log-asset value is less than a distance v away from the default barrier. λ is the speed of this adjustment. In this simple setting, l turns out to be a one-dimensional Ornstein–Uhlenbeck process:

$$dl_t = \lambda(y_t - k_t - v)\,dt - (r - \delta - \tfrac{1}{2}\sigma^2)\,dt - \sigma\,dW_t$$
$$= \lambda(\bar{l} - l_t)\,dt - \sigma\,dW_t,$$

where

$$\bar{l} = \frac{\delta + \tfrac{1}{2}\sigma^2 - r}{\lambda} - v.$$

Default, therefore, is the first time the process l hits 0.

Assume that the recovery is $(1 - \omega)$ at the maturity date, i.e. a recovery of treasury at the default date. Then the price of the zero-coupon bond maturing at date T is

$$B(0, T) = \exp(-rT)(1 - \omega Q(\tau \leqslant T)),$$

where τ is the default time. Hence all we need is the expression for the distribution of the first-passage time τ. Although an analytical expression for this density is available (see the references for more on this), we use the numerical implementation using the explicit transition probability of the Ornstein–Uhlenbeck process. An example of the effect of the assumption of a stationary leverage ratio is shown in Figure 2.10, where we compare yield spreads for parameter values suggested in Collin-Dufresne and Goldstein (2001).

We show the effect on speculative-grade debt and note that the long-run level for the speculative issues is much smaller than a case with a deterministic barrier because leverage is assumed to become lower. The assumption for a target leverage ratio has a significant effect in the long run for investment grade, because leverage will be much higher in the long term.

2.11 Estimating Asset Value and Asset Volatility from Observed Equity Prices

A key problem in the practical application of option-based techniques is the fact that we can rarely observe the asset value, let alone the asset volatility, of a firm. Hence we are left with the need to estimate both quantities from observed equity values, assuming that we know the face value of debt. In principle this looks easy. In the Merton model we have (letting $C = C^{BS}$)

$$S_t = C(V_t, D, \sigma_V, r, T - t),$$

so that, by Itô's formula,

$$dS_t = (\cdots)\,dt + C'(V_t, \sigma_V)\sigma_V V_t\,dW_t,$$

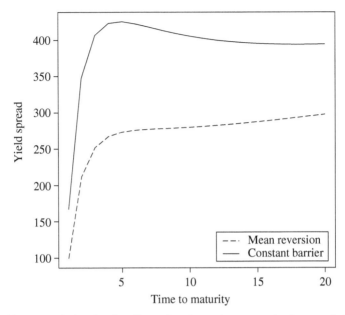

Figure 2.10. A graph showing the effects of stationary leverage ratios for speculative-grade debt. Parameter values are (with the notation of the model) as in Collin-Dufresne and Goldstein, i.e. $r_0 = 0.06$, $\kappa = 0.1$, $\delta = 0.03$, $\sigma = 0.2$, $\lambda = 0.18$, $\nu = 0.5$, $\omega = 0.56$, $\omega_{\text{coup}} = 1$. Initial leverage, i.e. $\exp(l_0)$, is set at 65%.

where we write $(\cdots)$ since only the volatility is of interest right now. Therefore, the volatility of S is

$$\sigma_S(t) = C'(V_t, \sigma_V)\sigma_V \frac{V_t}{S_t}$$

(namely the coefficient in front of the Brownian motion in $(1/S_t)\,dS_t$). Hence, in principle, if we observe equity values and volatility, we have two equations in two unknowns, and can therefore determine σ_V and V by solving the (nonlinear) equations numerically. But note that $\sigma_S(t)$ in this model is not a parameter but a process in itself. If leverage is not high, i.e. if $L_t = V_t/S_t$ is small, then $C'(V_t)$ is very close to 1 and the approximation $\sigma_S(t) = L_t\sigma_V$ works well. If, furthermore, L_t does not vary too much over the observation period, then the stock looks like a Brownian motion, and we can estimate its volatility as we normally would (i.e. when applying Black–Scholes to call options on stocks).

An iterative scheme which seems to work well even when the changes in leverage are significant over the sample period is proposed in Vassalou and Xing (2002).

Assume that we have observed a series of equity prices $S_{t_0}, S_{t_1}, \ldots, S_{t_N}$ and let $V_{t_i}(\sigma)$ denote the value of assets obtained by inverting the Black–Scholes formula for given σ.

The nth step, bringing us from an estimate σ_V^n of asset volatility to an improved estimate σ_V^{n+1}, runs as follows.

(1) Calculate $V_{t_0}(\sigma_V^n), \ldots, V_{t_N}(\sigma_V^n)$ from $S_{t_0}, \ldots, S_{t_N}$ using the inverse of the Black–Scholes formula viewed as a function of the value of the underlying asset.

(2) Estimate σ_V^{n+1} by thinking of $V_{t_0}(\sigma_V^n), \ldots, V_{t_N}(\sigma_V^n)$ as a GBM, i.e. let

$$\sigma_V^{n+1} = \sqrt{\frac{1}{N\Delta t} \sum_{i=1}^{N} \left(\ln\left(\frac{V_{t_i}}{V_{t_{i-1}}}\right) - \bar{\xi} \right)^2},$$

where

$$\bar{\xi} = \frac{1}{N\Delta t} \sum_{i=1}^{N} \ln\left(\frac{V_{t_i}}{V_{t_{i-1}}}\right) = \frac{1}{N\Delta t}[\ln V_{t_N} - \ln V_{t_0}].$$

Using this updated value the procedure continues with σ_V^{n+1} in place of σ_V^n.

As starting value one can use the estimate of equity volatility obtained by viewing equity as a geometric Brownian motion and correcting for leverage. In practice, the convergence is fast and the starting value seems of little importance. The advantage of the method is that it is quickly implemented. Preliminary numerical analysis suggests that the estimator is not exactly identical to the maximum-likelihood estimator (MLE) but it is extremely close. The advantage of the MLE method is that it also gives us an asymptotic variance of the estimators.

We therefore now show how an MLE is carried out in a Merton setting. The method can—at least in principle—be extended to other models with different asset dynamics or where the option-pricing formula which links the price of the unobserved underlying asset value to the observed equity value is different from the Black–Scholes formula. The advantage of the current setting is that it makes it possible to write down the exact likelihood function.

We need the following result from statistics on the distribution of transformations of random variables: let X be a random variable with density on R^n given by the function $f(x_1, \ldots, x_n; \theta)$, where θ is a parameter belonging to some open subset Θ of R^k. In our application, which follows, $\theta = (\mu, \sigma)$, i.e. it consists of the drift and volatility of the underlying asset-value process. Consider a mapping $T : R^n \rightarrow R^n$ (the option-pricing function, working on a vector of asset prices) which depends on θ and write $Y = T(X; \theta)$ as a shorthand for

$$Y = (T_1(X; \theta), \ldots, T_n(X; \theta)).$$

Assume that T is one-to-one and continuously differentiable for every θ and write $T^{-1}(Y; \theta)$ for the mapping, which for fixed θ finds X so that $T(X; \theta) = Y$. Furthermore, we write $J_T(x)$ for the Jacobian of T, which is

$$J_T(x) = \det \begin{pmatrix} \dfrac{\partial}{\partial x_1} T_1(X;\theta) & \cdots & \dfrac{\partial}{\partial x_n} T_1(X;\theta) \\ \vdots & & \vdots \\ \dfrac{\partial}{\partial x_1} T_n(X;\theta) & \cdots & \dfrac{\partial}{\partial x_n} T_n(X;\theta) \end{pmatrix}.$$

With this notation we have that the density of Y is given as

$$g(y;\theta) = f(T^{-1}(y;\theta)) \frac{1}{J_T(T^{-1}(y;\theta))}. \tag{2.8}$$

Here we have divided by the Jacobian of T instead of multiplying by the Jacobian of the inverse transformation, that is, we have used the fact that

$$J_{T^{-1}}(y) = (J_T(T^{-1}(y)))^{-1}.$$

In our example with the Black–Scholes formula we can compute derivatives of the transformation (i.e. the option-pricing formula) explicitly, whereas derivatives of the inverse function would require numerical methods. In both cases we have to invert T using numerical methods.

The case we consider in the following is special in the sense that the transformation has a coordinate-by-coordinate structure in the sense that

$$y_1 = T_1(x_1;\theta), \ldots, y_n = T_n(x_n;\theta),$$

so that the derivatives $(\partial/\partial x_i)T_j(X;\theta)$ are 0 when $i \neq j$. Then the Jacobian in the denominator of (2.8) simply becomes

$$J_T(T^{-1}(y,\theta)) = \prod_{i=1}^n \frac{1}{(\partial/\partial x_i)T_i(T_i^{-1}(y_i,\theta);\theta)},$$

and if we write for simplicity

$$x_i(\theta) = T^{-1}(y_i,\theta),$$

this is just

$$J_T(x(\theta)) = \prod_{i=1}^n \frac{1}{(\partial/\partial x_i)T_i(x_i(\theta);\theta)}.$$

Now consider the process for asset values

$$dV_t = \mu V_t \, dt + \sigma V_t \, dW_t.$$

Since there is no stationary distribution for V, we condition on the starting value v_0. Now the density of V_i given $V_{i-1} = v_{i-1}$ is

$$\phi(v_i \mid v_{i-1}; \mu, \sigma)$$

$$= \frac{1}{\sqrt{2\pi}\sigma\sqrt{t_i - t_{i-1}}} \exp\left(-\frac{[\log v_i - \log v_{i-1} - (\mu - \frac{1}{2}\sigma^2)(t_i - t_{i-1})]^2}{2\sigma^2(t_i - t_{i-1})}\right)\frac{1}{v_i},$$

and with this density in place we can write out the likelihood function for asset value and asset volatility given the observed prices of equity. The likelihood function is given in terms of observed values of equity $s_1, \ldots, s_n$, where $s_i = C(v_i; \sigma, t_i)$ and C_i is the call option price taking into account the remaining maturity at date t_i and suppressing the parameters K, r, and T. We use s_0 as conditioning variable to obtain a fixed value of v_0 which can then be plugged into the likelihood function for asset values. Letting $v_i(\sigma) = C^{-1}(s_i; \sigma)$ we find

$$L(s_1, \ldots, s_n \mid s_0, \sigma, \mu) = \prod_{i=1}^{n} \phi(v_i(\sigma) \mid v_{i-1}(\sigma), \mu, \sigma)\frac{1}{C_i'(v_i(\sigma); \sigma)},$$

and hence the log-likelihood function is

$$\log L(s_1, \ldots, s_n \mid s_0, \mu, \sigma)$$

$$= -\frac{1}{2}n \log 2\pi - n \log \sigma - \frac{1}{2}\sum_{i=1}^{n} \log(t_i - t_{i-1})$$

$$- \frac{1}{2\sigma^2}\sum_{i=1}^{n} \frac{(\log v_i(\sigma) - \log v_{i-1}(\sigma) - (\mu - \frac{1}{2}\sigma^2)(t_i - t_{i-1}))^2}{t_i - t_{i-1}}$$

$$- \sum_{i=1}^{n} \log v_i(\sigma) - \sum_{i=1}^{n} \log N(d_1(\sigma)).$$

Note that given σ, the observed value of S_0 gives a fixed value of v_0, but since we maximize over σ we find V_0 as part of the estimation. Once this value is given, we get a whole sequence of estimated asset values,

$$V_1(\hat{\sigma}), \ldots, V_n(\hat{\sigma}),$$

which are of course only the same as the "true" underlying value when our estimator happens to hit the true value σ. If $\hat{\sigma}$ is different from the true σ, the estimated asset values will either be too high or too low.

The estimator of volatility and underlying asset value works well even for relatively few observations when equity is in perfect agreement with the model option price. Consider a case where we have 50 weekly observations on a firm with an asset volatility of 0.2 and a drift rate of 0.1. The sample path of the true value is

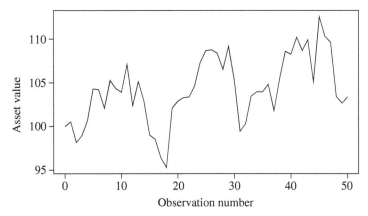

Figure 2.11. Sample path of the firm's asset value in the simulation experiment illustrating estimation of the firm's asset value and asset volatility from equity data. The simulated sample corresponds to 50 weekly observations.

Table 2.3. Estimates of asset value, volatility, and drift based on 50 weekly observations of equity prices assumed to be exact option values with assets as underlying. The true asset value at time 1 is 103.38.

Debt	$\hat{V}_1$	$\hat{\sigma}$	sd($\hat{\sigma}$)	$\hat{\mu}$	sd($\hat{\mu}$)
Face value 30	103.41	0.197	0.025	0.068	0.232
Face value 60	103.45	0.201	0.025	0.049	0.242
Face value 90	103.14	0.219	0.045	0.034	0.239

depicted in Figure 2.11. The maturity of the bond is assumed to be three years, and we are looking at the first year. We consider, for the same sample path, what would happen in three cases of leverage: one with low leverage (face value of debt 30); one with medium leverage (face value 60); and one with high leverage (face value 90). The results in Table 2.3 show the estimates of asset value (at the end of the year), volatility, and drift parameter for the three different cases of leverage. One hundred sample paths have been used to estimate the standard deviations of the estimators, and the estimates themselves are based on the sample path shown in Figure 2.11. As we see, the results for the estimates of firm value and volatility are extremely encouraging. It is remarkable that based on 50 observations, the estimate of the volatility is so accurate. The estimate of the drift, however, has a huge standard deviation. The imprecision of the estimate can be seen from the likelihood function shown in Figure 2.12, which is extremely flat in the direction of the drift parameter. This bad determination of the drift does not hurt us when inverting the observed equity prices to asset values, since the drift does not enter into the option-pricing formula. Hence the estimates of asset value at year 1 are all extremely accurate. But

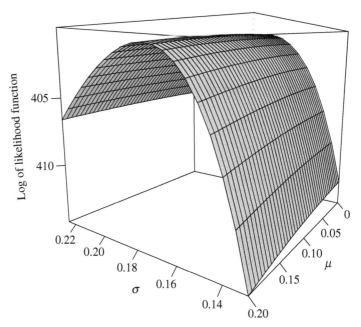

Figure 2.12.   Log-likelihood function. The curvature in the volatility direction gives good information on volatility. The flatness in the drift direction shows poor information on the drift variable.

the drift uncertainty means that one cannot use the estimate of the drift to predict default probabilities unless stronger assumptions are made. We return to this point later.

2.12   On the KMV Approach

The likelihood procedure outlined in the previous section gives us a method for estimating the asset value and asset-value dynamics using the observed equity prices. The procedure may be expanded to a case with a default boundary. We will now look at a practical use of this methodology in default prediction. In any practical use we will have to live with the assumption behind the model being violated. In a sense, the fact that there is an estimation problem is already breaking with the assumption of the option-pricing model that the option can be hedged by trading in the underlying security. If the underlying cannot be observed, how can it be used for hedging? While this is a valid, although technical, argument, it is a problem which is completely dwarfed by other practical issues, which we will model shortly. We could of course also argue that the equity value is an equilibrium price, reflecting information known to analysts and investors, and as such it is the best estimate for the asset value. However, when using the model (or a variation thereof) in practice, it is much better to think of it as a convenient transformation device (as discussed in the introduction). We will now look at how this is used in practice.

Note that if the firm's asset value satisfies

$$V_t = V_0 \exp((\mu - \tfrac{1}{2}\sigma^2)t + \sigma W_t),$$

the probability of finishing *below* D at date T is given as

$$N\left(-\frac{\log(V_t/D) + (\mu - \tfrac{1}{2}\sigma^2)T}{\sigma\sqrt{T}}\right),$$

where N is the cumulative distribution function of the normal distribution. Hence in a perfect world we could define

$$\frac{\log(V) - \log(D) + (\mu - \tfrac{1}{2}\sigma^2)T}{\sigma\sqrt{T}} = \frac{E\log(V_T) - \log(D)}{\sigma\sqrt{T}}$$

as a measure for "distance to default" (DD). In Merton's model this distance could be negative, but for $V_T = D$ it is 0. This measure is of course just another way of stating the default probability, just as the implied volatility of an option is equivalent to the price. An actual test of whether this is a good model for default would then look at how well DD_{Merton} has historically predicted defaults. A simple test would be to group the distances to default into small intervals, small enough to consider the default probability as a constant over the interval but large enough to include enough firms, then the default frequency within each bucket would be a reasonably accurate estimate of the default probability. This would produce an empirical curve. In practice, we would find that the incidence of defaults greatly differs from those predicted by this model. But even if this is true, DD may still be a good way of ranking firms in classes of risk. If this is true, we could compute the distance to default and use the *empirically estimated* default frequency as our estimate of the default probability. This is essentially the philosophy behind the notion of an expected default frequency, as used by Moody's KMV.

While the philosophy of using an empirically estimated connection between distance to default and default probability is clear; in practice, there are a number of difficulties to overcome before this idea can be carried out. These include the following.

- Which option model to use. A company's balance sheet is typically a lot more complicated than is assumed in the Merton model and the Black–Cox model, even if we include differences in seniority. Bonds have covenants and may for example be callable, the firm may issue warrants, and so forth. In empirical studies we often discard from the sample those firms which have a complicated capital structure to get a "clean" dataset. But this of course will not work when we have to deal with concrete cases.

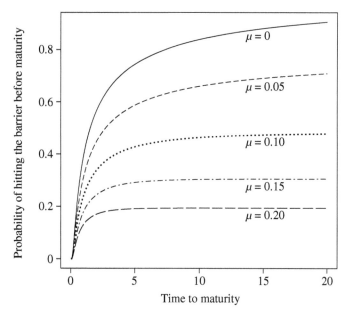

Figure 2.13. Default probability for varying values of the drift as a function of time to maturity. Initial asset value is 120, the default boundary is at 100, and the asset volatility is 20%.

- How to define the default point. It is difficult to know exactly what triggers the default. It is often because the possibility of refinancing "dries up" and there are no liquid assets left. When this occurs exactly is difficult to model.

- Measuring the liabilities, including off-balance sheet commitments, accurately is difficult.

The measure for distance to default actually reported in Crosbie (2002) is

$$DD = \frac{V - D}{\sigma_V V}.$$

The measure does not include the drift of the assets. In theory, the drift of the assets has a large influence on first hitting times. Consider, for example, a firm with an initial asset value of 120, a volatility of 20%, and a constant lower boundary at 100. The effect on the default probability at different time horizons of varying the value of the drift is shown in Figure 2.13. Although the value of the drift seems to affect the default probability greatly, especially near default and for medium to long maturities, the fact that we have such a hard time estimating it accurately may imply that adding it to the model adds almost no information. Also, the effect in the very short term is not large. In fact, as we will see later, it is the volatility alone which determines the default probability in the very short term.

The default point is defined in Crosbie (2002) as

$$0.5 \times \text{long-term debt} + \text{short-term debt},$$

which is an attempt to capture the idea that short-term debt requires a repayment of the principal soon, whereas long-term debt requires only coupon payments to be met. Note that the measure does not take into account the liquidity of assets, although in reality there may be some correction in asset value taking this into account. For more on practical applications, see Crosbie (2002).

2.13 The Trouble with the Term Structure of Credit Spreads: a Structural Viewpoint

The yield on treasury bonds allows us to compare prices of bonds of different maturities. The yield of treasury bonds has the additional advantage of being—at least in principle—model independent. If we have a "spanning" set of treasuries, we can derive prices and yields on zero-coupon bonds.

Since corporate bonds typically have promised payments with the same structure as treasury securities, it is natural to also use yields to compare prices of corporate bonds across maturities and issuers and to compute yield spreads as a measure of discount to (say) credit risk. The yield measure and the whole term-structure machinery are so deeply rooted that one almost forgets the many complicating issues which arise in their use in connection with the modeling of defaultable securities. This section collects some of the many difficulties in structural models. We will see that the notion of a yield (and hence of a term structure and the shape of a term structure) becomes much more model dependent. We will revisit this theme in the section on intensity models.

2.13.1 The Term Structure

For the treasury term structure of zero-coupon yields, the story is straightforward, at least in theory. The price of a treasury security with maturity T is $d(T)$. As a function of T, d is the discount function and from that we compute the price of a coupon bond with coupons $c_1, c_2, \ldots, c_T$ as

$$P^C(T) = \sum_{i=1}^{T} d(i)c_i.$$

Since discount functions are hard to grasp for longer maturities, we compute the yield as the interest rate at which $d(T)$ would have to grow from time 0 to reach 1 at time T, i.e.

$$d(T)(1 + y(T))^T = 1$$

or

$$y(T) = \left(\frac{1}{d(T)}\right)^{1/T} - 1.$$

With continuous compounding we would get

$$y(T) = -\frac{1}{T}\log d(T).$$

The term structure of interest rates is then a function of T.

We typically derive $d(\cdot)$ from coupon bonds using linear algebra to combine bonds to form zero-coupon bonds. From a term structure of yields on par bonds we are thus able to obtain the yields on zero-coupon bonds.

In practice, there are of course difficulties with this approach. Parts of the maturity spectrum we are interested in have "holes" with no or thinly traded issues. Bonds exhibit price differences due to liquidity, due to their role in repo transactions, due to their role as benchmarks, and for a number of other reasons. Still, it seems meaningful to at least try to estimate the yield curve from observed price data and to use that yield curve to price other bonds. The story is a lot less simple with defaultable bonds. To even estimate a yield curve we need more fundamental assumptions and it is not clear that we can price other issues using the same yield curve. Remember that the risk structure of interest rates as derived, for example, in a Merton model, does not provide us with a discount function from which we can price coupon paying corporate bonds. To see this directly, consider a firm with initial value 100 and zero-coupon bonds with a face value of 80 maturing at years 1 and 2. With a volatility of 0.25 and a riskless rate $r = 0.06$, the prices of these bonds are 73.95 and 68.36, and hence their sum is larger than the initial asset value, which cannot be true of course.

As is clear from this, we need of course to take into account the whole capital structure when pricing the individual components. When this is done we run into several modeling issues. I will focus here on the asset-sale assumptions, or the asset-liquidity assumptions.

2.13.2 *The Importance of Asset-Sale Assumptions*

We can change the assumptions on asset sales in all of our models in this book, although the precise way it would influence the dynamics is less clear in some than in others. In most models, permitting asset sales will increase the mathematical complexity. In order not to obscure the central message in the mathematical complications, this section presents the simplest possible example to illustrate the importance of assumptions on asset value. We will focus on two effects: the effect on debt price, and the term-structure effect. As we will see, the effect on the computed term structure of credit spreads is drastic.

Consider a model with three dates, $t = 0, 1, 2$. Assume that the dynamics of the asset value before any sales is modeled as a binomial process with the effect of an up-jump being a price increase by a factor of 1.15 and a down movement causing a decrease by the same factor. The riskless rate is assumed to be 5% per period. Assuming that the asset-value process represents the price of a traded asset, the risk-neutral probability of an up-jump must be

$$q = \frac{1.05 - \frac{1}{1.15}}{1.15 - \frac{1}{1.15}} = 0.643.$$

The initial asset value is 100, and to get a positive probability of default in this simple model we need to consider a firm with extremely high leverage.

To study term-structure effects as well as pricing effects we consider the pricing of a "short" bond maturing at date 1 and a long bond maturing at date 2.

In the case with no asset sales, the model works as explained in the setting of (say) Geske (1977), in which equity owners pay the coupon at time 1 precisely when this coupon is less than the value of the call option that the equity owners retain by paying the coupon. This option is of course the call option on the firm's assets with a strike price equal to the face value of the long bond.

With asset sales permitted, the equity owners will pay the coupon as long as there are sufficient assets to cover the payment, since even if this leaves assets lower, it at least retains an option with a positive value, whereas default leaves equity with nothing.

If there is a default at time 1, it is assumed throughout that bond holders share the remaining asset value proportionally to the face values of their debt, i.e. we are not discounting the face value of the longer debt in the default settlement. This is not unlike what is done in practical bankruptcy settlement.

In the first example the face value of the debt is equal to 45 for the short bond and 65 for the long bond. We would expect the asset-sale restriction to negatively impact equity owners who lose an opportunity to keep their option on the firm's assets alive. Indeed, this is the case. While asset-sale restrictions increase the total debt value by about 1%, equity value is close to losing 20% in value by having asset-sale restrictions.

More significant, perhaps, is the redistribution of wealth between the short and long maturity bonds. When asset sales are permitted, the short bond in essence gains a higher priority than the long bond and it becomes risk free. The long bond becomes fairly risky compared with the short bond and has a yield of 12.5% when asset sales are permitted. Without asset sales, the short bonds becomes very risky, since they are only repaid if there is enough asset value to justify a redemption. The yield on the long bond in this case becomes smaller than that on the short bond.

Table 2.4.   The face value of the short bond is 45 and that of the long bond is 65.

	No asset sales	Asset sales
Price of short bond	39.66	42.86
Yield of short bond	13.5%	5.0%
Price of long bond	55.38	51.32
Yield of long bond	8.3%	12.5%
Total debt value	95.04	94.18
Total equity value	4.96	5.82

Table 2.5.   The face values of both the short bond and the long bond are 50.

	No asset sales	Asset sales
Price of short bond	45.50	47.62
Yield of short bond	10.1%	5.0%
Price of long bond	43.95	41.73
Yield of long bond	6.7%	9.5%
Total debt value	89.35	89.35
Total equity value	10.65	10.65

We can construct the example in such a way that the asset-sale restriction has no effect on equity value (and therefore not on total debt value either), but has a drastic term-structure effect by changing the prices of the short and long bonds drastically.

This is done in the second example where the firm has issued two zero coupons both with a face value of 50. In this case, total debt value remains invariant since in both cases equity owners lose everything if a down jump occurs in the first period. But in the case with asset sales, the short bond is riskless and the long bond has a yield of 9.5%. If we restrict asset sales, the "slope of the yield curve" is inverted and the short bond gets a yield of more than 10%, whereas the long bond has a lower yield of 6.7%.

In practice, the truth is somewhere between the two assumptions, but it seems meaningless to discuss the slope of the yield curve for a speculative-grade issuer without looking at the asset-sale restrictions and also at the liquidity of debt.

2.14   Bibliographical Notes

The basic Merton model (Merton 1974) is of course an application of the Black and Scholes (1973) option-pricing model to corporate debt. This way of naming things is perhaps not historically consistent. Merton also developed the Black–Scholes model, and Black and Scholes had the valuation of corporate liabilities as part of the title of their original paper. But the risk structure of interest rates for zero-coupon debt and the extensions to coupon paying debt are in Merton (1974). The jump-diffusion model for option pricing developed in Chapter X of Merton (1990) can of course be directly applied to corporate bonds as well, and this is what we do here, working however with a more general specification of risk premiums, as done in Chapter 1 of Lando (1994). The model is chosen because of its analytical solution. An alternative to Merton's jump-diffusion model can be found in Zhou (2001b) and we have briefly touched on Hilberink and Rogers (2002) also. Mason and Bhattacharya (1981) also treat jumps.

Geske (1977) develops expressions for the prices of coupon bonds in terms of multivariate normal integrals. These integrals have to be evaluated numerically and it seems easier to solve using a finite-difference scheme directly—a technique which has now become a standard tool of derivative pricing. The first paper to work with a continuous default barrier—interpreted as a safety covenant—was Black and Cox (1976), where both the perpetual-debt case and the finite-horizon case were considered. This work also touches on the issue of optimal capital structure but it does not introduce the trade-off between tax advantage and bankruptcy costs that we will meet in the next chapter. Ho and Singer (1982, 1984) deal with sinking-fund provisions.

Introducing stochastic interest rates complicates things, and the chapter lists two examples where numeraire shift does the job. The simplest possible extension of the Merton model is obtained in Shimko et al. (1993) but a judicious choice of default boundary allowed Briys and de Varenne (1997) to work in a Black–Cox setting with stochastic interest rates. The case with CIR dynamics of the interest rates is treated in Kim et al. (1993). First-passage time densities in general become difficult with stochastic interest rates. The idea of developing an integral equation for first-passage times when the transition densities of the "free" (i.e. nonabsorbed) process are known was used in Buonocore et al. (1987). We follow closely the work of Collin-Dufresne and Goldstein (2001), which among other things clarifies the work of Longstaff and Schwartz (1995a), which uses the same integral equation techniques. This clarification involves a two-dimensional version of the numerical algorithm presented here. Moody's KMV approach is described in Crosbie (2002) (see also Bohn 2000). The maximum-likelihood procedure for estimating a firm's asset value from equity data is discussed in detail in Duan (1994) and Ericsson and Reneby (2001).

The empirical literature on the credit-spread behavior of structural models is large if one includes works which test qualitative predictions of the theory, but it is not that extensive if one looks at testing the precise spread predictions of the models. The problem with testing the concrete predictions of the models is that most models are (deliberate) idealizations of real-world scenarios. For example, there are few firms which issue only zero-coupon bonds, as in the most simple Merton model, and hence one will have to adapt the pricing model to the pattern of coupons observed in practice. It is also true of many bonds that they have covenants or callability features which are not easily priced in the models.

While there is a fairly large literature on the behavior of credit spreads, dating at least back to Fisher (1959), in this section we only treat papers which attempt a literal implementation of an option-based model. To meet this criterion, it must specify asset-value dynamics and values of claims based on such models. Papers analyzing spreads in general are treated in Chapter 5. The list here is far from complete but covers some important works.

The literature which tries to test "structural" models started with the study of Jones et al. (1984), but this is a fairly crude paper in the sense that the sample of bonds is very small. Sarig and Warga (1989) consider a very clean dataset for testing the Merton model since they consider zero-coupon bonds, and they find agreement with qualitative predictions concerning the shape of the term structure for different credit quality, but the precise predictions in terms of spreads are not discussed. Interestingly, Helwege and Turner (1999), also focusing on the slope of the term structure, find that the shape of the term structure for speculative-grade issuers is upward sloping, in contradiction with what a realistic Merton model (even when introducing coupons) would predict. They point to an interesting selection bias when analyzing term structures of credit spreads: within a given credit quality there is a tendency for the stronger credits within that class to issue longer bonds. If the poorer credits are concentrated in the short end and the better ones in the long end, this tends to bias the structure towards being downward sloping. Correcting for this bias, they obtain the result that the speculative curve is upward sloping. The upward-sloping "term structure" of risk-neutral probabilities of default found in Delianedis and Geske (1999) is consistent with this empirical finding.

Papers which actually implement Merton-style models—correcting in various ways for coupons, stochastic interest rates, and compound option effects—include Delianedis and Geske (1999), Eom et al. (2003), and Ericsson and Reneby (2002). Eom et al. (2003) find support, as far as low-risk bonds are concerned, for the classical criticism of the Merton-style models: that they underpredict spreads. They find, however, that correcting for endogeneous defaults along the lines of Geske (1977) produces more realistic credit spreads. They also find that the model of Leland and Toft (1996), with endogenous default boundaries, on average overestimates spreads. Their overall conclusion is that structural models need to raise the spreads on the safe bonds while not touching the spreads on the riskier bonds too much. Delianedis and Geske (1999) extract risk-neutral probability densities from corporate bonds using both a Merton model and a simple version of Geske (1977) and find that changes in the risk-neutral probability lead rating changes. Ericsson and Reneby (2002) also find that endogenous default, future growth of nominal debt, and reorganization costs can help bring the spread predictions in line with observed spreads.

Huang and Huang (2003) consider structural models but are mainly concerned with the default probability assessment of the models and the fraction of bond spreads which can actually be attributed to credit risk. See Elton et al. (2001) for a paper discussing, among other things, tax effects and liquidity effects in credit spreads; and see, for example, Collin-Dufresne et al. (2001) for an analysis of which factors drive credit spreads.

3
Endogenous Default Boundaries and Optimal Capital Structure

One limitation of the option-based pricing approach to modeling equity and corporate bonds is that it only gives us the prices of equity and bonds in a given capital structure. In essence, given a certain level of debt the models tell us how the firm's asset value is split between debt and equity. By assumption, however, the total payoff to equity and debt does not depend on the level of debt and therefore the Modigliani–Miller proposition on capital structure holds. In practice, firms do worry about their capital structure and we need to develop models that explain this.

The most direct way of building models that describe optimal capital-structure choice is to introduce bankruptcy costs and tax advantage to issuing debt. The tax advantage favors higher debt levels, whereas bankruptcy costs push in the opposite direction, since these costs are lost to third parties (lawyers, accountants, courts, etc.) and therefore diminish the value left for equity and debt.

It is easy to build models which capture the trade-off between bankruptcy and tax shield advantages qualitatively. In this section we focus on a class of models which allows us to make more clear-cut quantitative predictions on the chosen level of leverage and on the effects on credit spread for corporate bonds.

The framework provides insights not only into the static choice of capital structure, but also gives us tools to analyze dynamic capital-structure choice, including important features such as maturity choice, callable debt, and strategic models of renegotiation. Including such dynamic features is important for our understanding of the term structure of credit spreads, which we will discuss in a later chapter.

The workhorse of this section is Brownian motion and various present-value functionals of Brownian motion which can be computed explicitly. All of the mathematical formulas that we need for this section are collected in Appendix B. In this chapter we write down every cash flow that has to be priced, but the reader will have to verify that the formulas are correct using the results in the appendix.

3.1 Leland's Model

The following model is presented in Leland (1994) and Leland and Toft (1996). Consider a process for asset value which under the risk-neutral measure Q evolves as

$$dV_t = (r - \delta)V_t\, dt + \sigma V_t\, dW_t.$$

Here δ represents a constant fraction of the asset value available for distribution to debt and equity. Any difference between this payout ratio and the actual cash flow paid as dividends to shareholders is financed by the existing shareholders, or, equivalently, by issuing new equity. r is the riskless rate, which is assumed to be constant in this model.

We follow the convention of Leland and Toft (1996) here, and assume that the drift of the capital-gains process represented by holding V is r, but note that this restriction is only needed if the underlying firm-value process is the price process of a traded asset. Thinking of V as a traded asset will in fact cause problems with the interpretation of the model, as we see below. If this is not the case, we would need either risk-neutrality or other not-too-realistic assumptions to justify this drift restriction.

All the claims that we consider are time homogeneous, i.e. they do not change value as a function of t (but of course vary with V_t). Hence the claims are "perpetual" in the sense that no maturity date is set beyond which the payments terminate. However, payments may still terminate in finite time but the conditions under which this occurs are only linked to conditions on the underlying process V and not to the passing of time itself. Hence we can use all the results of the appendix to price the claims considered.

A good way to think about the model is to imagine an owner in possession of the asset at time 0 and with no debt outstanding. The owner may now issue debt— essentially with the underlying asset as collateral—and he seeks to maximize the amount of money raised by issuing debt (selling corporate bonds) and by keeping the remaining equity.

The debt issued is perpetual with a constant coupon rate of C, meaning that C dollars is being paid every unit of time so that in a time interval Δt the coupon paid is $C\Delta t$ dollars.

The owner's incentive to issue debt stems from a tax advantage to issuing debt, which in this simple model is represented as an additional cash flow of τC dollars per unit of time available for distribution among the firm's claim holders. Here, τ is a tax rate which one thinks of as being related to the tax paid by the company. But the modeling of taxes is not going to be explicit until we consider models based on EBIT (earnings before interest and taxes).

However, to prevent the firm from using only debt financing, there must also be a disadvantage and this disadvantage is the cost of bankruptcy. The equity owners are responsible for paying the coupon flow to the bond holders. Any amount not covered by dividend payout and the tax advantages of debt is to be paid for out of the equity holder's own pockets or by issuing new equity (with a dilution of equity equal to the amount saved by not having to pay from their own pockets). If at some point the equity owners decide that the value of the firm's assets has become too low to justify such a payout, they can choose to stop paying the coupon and hence liquidate the firm. In liquidation, the equity owners get nothing and the debt holders take over the remaining assets after suffering a loss in bankruptcy. To begin with, consider the case where in addition to the coupon rate C, we know the level of assets V_B at which default on the debt is triggered. Let τ_B denote the first time the assets hit V_B.

The value of the tax benefit is then a present discounted value of a flow of size τC lasting until τ_B, the value of the bankruptcy cost is the value of a payment of size αV_B received at τ_B, and the value of debt is a combination of a flow of C received until τ_B and a liquidation payment of $(1 - \alpha)V_B$. The calculations of these values all follow in Appendix B. Let $\mu = r - \delta$ and let

$$\gamma = \frac{\mu - \frac{1}{2}\sigma^2}{\sigma^2} + \sqrt{\frac{(\mu - \frac{1}{2}\sigma^2)^2 + 2\sigma^2 r}{\sigma^2}}.$$

The value $p_B(V)$ of a claim whose only payment is 1 at the default boundary, given that the current level of assets is V, and 0 otherwise (see Appendix B) is given as

$$P_B(V) = \left(\frac{V}{V_B}\right)^{-\gamma}.$$

Therefore, the present value of the bankruptcy costs is

$$BC(V; V_B, C) = \alpha V_B \left(\frac{V}{V_B}\right)^{-\gamma}.$$

We have also seen that the value of a flow of C received up until time τ_B may be expressed as $(C/r)(1 - p_B(V))$. Therefore, the value of the tax advantage associated with the issuing of debt is given as

$$TB(V; V_B, C) = \frac{\tau C}{r}(1 - P_B(V)). \tag{3.1}$$

And combining the two types of payment, the value of debt is simply

$$D(V; V_B, C) = \frac{C}{r}(1 - P_B(V)) + (1 - \alpha)V_B P_B(V),$$

where the first term is the value of the coupon flow paid until the default time τ_B.

We may now define the full value of the part of the firm which is distributed among security holders as

$$v(V; V_B, C) = V + TB(V; V_B, C) - BC(V; V_B, C), \tag{3.2}$$

and since there is only debt and equity we have

$$v(V; V_B, C) = E(V; V_B, C) + D(V; V_B, C).$$

We have determined $D(V; V_B, C)$ and $v(V; V_B, C)$ so $E(V; V_B, C)$ is now simply assumed to be the residual, and note that $E(V_B) = 0$ since, by assumption, the equity owners get nothing in liquidation. One can show that if we assume $\delta > 0$, this equity value is equal to the present value of the cash flow $\delta V_s - (1 - \tau)C$ received (and paid if negative) until τ_B.

The goal of the initial owners of the assets is to choose a level of debt which maximizes the total value $v(V; V_B, C)$, since this is the value of the firm after it has been levered. At first glance, it is easy to see that a lower V_B increases total firm value—since having a lower boundary does not change the current value of V—but decreases the cash outflow to third parties in bankruptcy and increases the present value of the tax subsidy. However, the default point V_B cannot be set by the initial owner. After debt and equity have been issued, it is the equity owners who decide when to default. If V_B is set too low, nothing guarantees that $E(V)$ is nonnegative for $V > V_B$. If V_B is very low, the payment of coupons may simply become too costly compared with the value of future cash flows to equity.

Since equity owners have a limited-liability asset, they would never allow equity value to become negative but would choose to stop paying coupons and force the firm into bankruptcy. Hence a model of rational equity holders should involve a choice of V_B high enough to make sure that $E(V)$ is never negative. So, for a given level of coupons, the default triggering boundary should be set in a manner consistent with equity owners optimizing equity value right after the firm has issued its debt initially. Hence for a given level of coupons we should assume that equity owners choose $V_B^*(C)$ as the optimal default triggering level.

Finding $V_B^*(C)$ is done using a "smooth-pasting" condition. The lowest possible value of V_B consistent with nonnegative equity is where

$$\frac{d}{dV} E(V; V_B, C) \Big|_{V=V_B} = 0.$$

This equation is solved for $V_B = V_B^*(C)$, where

$$V_B^*(C) = \frac{\gamma(1 - \tau)C}{r(1 + \gamma)}. \tag{3.3}$$

Now, plugging this value into the expression for total firm value (3.2) we find the total firm value for a given level of coupons and the optimal default point corresponding to this level.

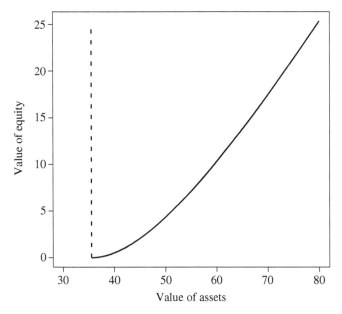

Figure 3.1. The graph shows the value of equity for optimal leverage, i.e. optimal coupon and optimal default boundary. The parameters of the model are $\mu = r = 0.05$, $\sigma = 0.2$, $\tau = 0.35$, $\alpha = 0.5$. For $V = 100$, this implies an optimal coupon of $C^* = 5.22$ and a default boundary (the dotted line) of $V_B^* = 35.53$.

Finally, to find optimal firm value this has to be maximized as a function of C, which can be done analytically by differentiating and setting equal to zero and checking the second-order condition. The solution is

$$C^* = V \frac{r(1+\gamma)}{\gamma(1-\tau)} \left(\frac{(1+\gamma)\tau + \alpha(1-\tau)\gamma}{\tau} \right)^{-1/\gamma}. \tag{3.4}$$

Plugging $V_B(C^*)$ and C^* into (3.2) gives us the firm value for optimal choice of leverage. To summarize, at the initial debt issue the owners choose to maximize firm value. When setting the coupon level they take into account the fact that once debt is issued, equity holders will optimally choose V_B as the default point. Hence, owners rationally predict this behavior and equity holders follow this behavior once debt has been issued. The rational behavior, captured by the smooth pasting condition, shows up in Figure 3.3, which shows the values of debt and of the firm, as functions of coupon, when the default boundary is chosen optimally. Note the smooth pasting of equity near the default point.

It is this endogenous choice of default point which allows for some conclusions which are qualitatively different from those in the classical option-based models, and which makes the reasoning a little more delicate. To understand these, we first look at the comparative statics of the default point, which follow from (3.3).

First, as the coupon is increased, so is the default boundary. This is clear, since coupons are the expense at which the equity owners keep their option alive. The tax subsidy mitigates this effect, so the higher the tax, the lower the default boundary. The default boundary depends on bankruptcy costs in an indirect fashion: for a given coupon, it is independent of bankruptcy costs, but the optimal choice of coupons falls when bankruptcy costs go up, and this in turn lowers the default point. This has consequences for the sensitivity of firm value to bankruptcy costs. Figure 3.2 shows the effects of the two critical variables, the tax rate and bankruptcy costs, which distinguish this model from, say, a Black–Cox model. The figure shows the factor by which firm value is increased, compared with the unlevered case, for different combinations of the tax rate and bankruptcy costs. Note that the increase in firm value which follows from the tax advantage of issuing debt is significant, but note also the relative insensitivity of firm value to bankruptcy costs. Increasing bankruptcy costs lowers the optimal coupon, and this would suggest that the tax advantage is decreased. It is, but the lowering of the default boundary allows the firm to enjoy the tax advantage for a longer period of time, and this counterbalances the reduction in tax advantage.

Some other significant effects of the endogenous default boundary are that near default, higher risk (σ^2) may *increase* the value of debt $D(V)$, a higher coupon may *decrease* $D(V)$, and higher r may *increase* $D(V)$. All of this has to do with the effects of the changes on V_{B}. Having a higher σ^2, r, or C will lower the optimal default point V_{B}, and when the asset value is close to the default point this will make bankruptcy less imminent. This positive effect on $D(V)$ dominates near V_{B}.

It is also interesting to see that debt value has a maximum as a function of the coupon level, defining therefore a "debt capacity" of the firm, i.e. the maximum amount of debt that the firm can raise initially. This is different from the debt value in an optimally levered firm. In Merton's model the firm can raise an amount as close to the firm's asset value as desired by setting a high face value. In this model the debt capacity has a maximum. To find the debt capacity for a given V, find the value of C which maximizes $D(V, C)$ and insert that value into $D(V, C)$. Note that even with $\alpha = 0$, i.e. no bankruptcy costs, we obtain less than 100% leverage simply because there is an implicit bankruptcy cost due to loss of tax shield. Figure 3.2 illustrates this.

3.2   A Model with a Maturity Structure

The model of Leland and Toft contains an additional feature, namely that of analyzing maturity choice. Since the model is still one with time homogeneity, the trick is to split up the continuously paid debt service into a component viewed as a coupon

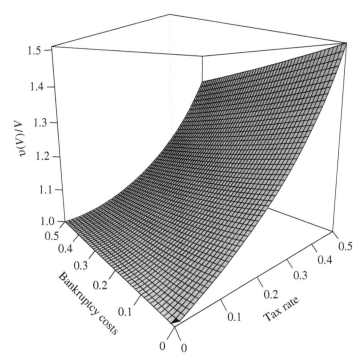

Figure 3.2. The graph shows the relative value of $v(V)$ to V when coupon and default boundary have been chosen optimally. The other parameters of the model are $\sigma = 0.2$, $r = \mu = 0.05$.

payment and another one viewed as a redemption of principal. Only the coupon payment carries a tax advantage. In this setting one thinks of the firm as issuing a continuum of bonds with maturity ranging from 0 to T. As in Leland and Toft (1996) we consider here only the case where the amount of principal is constant and equal to p for each individual bond. To make sense of this we have to think of the bonds in the same way as we think about probability densities. The amount of principal outstanding for bonds with maturities between t and $t + \Delta t$ is equal to $p\Delta t$ and this is the amount of principal that has to be redeemed over a time interval Δt. We consider here a model in which the firm starts out with the maturity structure described above and then issues debt perpetually with time T to maturity. The same bonds give rise to a coupon flow of $c\Delta t$, where c is the coupon rate of each bond. Hence, when choosing a maturity of T, the total amount of principal outstanding is $P := pT$ and the coupon to be paid continuously is $C = cT$. The amount of principal becoming due contributes to a flow of $p = P/T$, and so the total debt service is

$$d = C + (P/T).$$

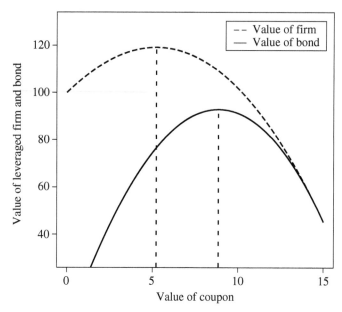

Figure 3.3. The graph shows the value of the firm $v(V)$ and the value of debt as a function of the coupon level when the default boundary has been chosen optimally. The debt capacity is the maximum of the debt value. The coupon for the optimally levered firm is lower than the coupon rate which raises the maximum amount of debt (the debt capacity). To interpret the graph for high coupon levels, think of the current asset level as being low compared with the level of coupons, possibly because the firm has seen a drop in asset value after choosing its capital structure. Note how, for higher coupons, the asset value and the debt value of the firm approach each other smoothly, forcing the value of equity to 0. The parameters of the model are $\sigma = 0.2$, $r = \mu = 0.05$, $\alpha = 0.5$, $\tau = 0.35$, $V = 100$.

Given the tax rules, it is of course optimal to have as much as possible of the debt service viewed as coupon payments, so if c could be chosen freely, the firm would prefer to issue bonds with almost no principal and an extreme coupon rate. In Leland and Toft (1996) this type of behavior is ruled out by assuming that the coupon is set in such a way that the amount of money raised by issuing a new bond is equal to the principal, i.e. that the bond trades at par value.

The explicit formulas can be found in Leland and Toft (1996) with extensions and generalizations in Hilberink and Rogers (2002).

3.3 EBIT-Based Models

Note that there is no inconsistency in having V as the price process of a traded asset and having $E(V)$, $D(V)$, and (hence) $v(V)$ as traded assets. They all have the correct drift under the risk-neutral measure. The problem is the ability to "create" the asset-value process $v(V)$ merely by purchasing V and then using debt issue and equity sale to obtain a package worth $v(V)$. The problem is essentially that one obtains a cash subsidy from issuing debt which increases the total value of the package.

We can get around these problems by using as the underlying state variable a process for the cash flow generation of the firm. This state variable is the EBIT, i.e. earnings before interest and taxes (EBIT), of the firm. The EBIT value does not reflect the value of a traded asset and therefore we are not pricing the cash flows of the different securities from a contingent-claims approach but rather appealing to the existence of equilibrium prices, which can be found as expected discounted values under a pricing measure Q. In this section we suppress references to this measure. Below is a quick outline of this approach for a case where there is dynamic restructuring of the firm's debt both at an upper and a lower boundary. The upper boundary will reflect the owner's ability to call the debt. At the lower boundary the debt holders will take over the firm's assets.

Consider an EBIT process

$$d\xi_t = \mu \xi_t \, dt + \sigma \xi_t \, dW_t.$$

Without loss of generality, assume that $\xi_0 = 1$. We now assume that there is an upper boundary $u > 1$ at which the firm increases its nominal debt and a lower boundary $l \in (0, 1)$ at which the firm is either liquidated or reorganized. We define

$$\tau_u = \inf\{t \geqslant 0 : \xi_t = u\},$$
$$\tau_l = \inf\{t \geqslant 0 : \xi_t = l\},$$
$$\tau = \min(\tau_u, \tau_l).$$

For a starting value $x \in [l, u]$ define the present values

$$P_u(x, u, l) = E_x \exp(-r\tau_u) 1_{\{\tau_u < \tau_l\}},$$
$$P_l(x, u, l) = E_x \exp(-r\tau_l) 1_{\{\tau_l < \tau_u\}},$$

i.e. the present values of receiving 1 when the process ξ, currently at x, hits one boundary without having hit the other first. Also define, for a starting value $x \in [l, u]$,

$$F(x, u, l) = E_x \int_0^\tau \exp(-rs) \, ds,$$

$$G(x, u, l, \delta) = E_x \int_0^\tau \delta \xi_s \exp(-rs) \, ds,$$

i.e. the present values, respectively, of receiving a flow of 1 or $\delta \xi_t$ until one of the boundaries is hit. Equity, debt, and bankruptcy costs are all composed of cash flows of these types in our model. Note that these specifications permit tax deductions from corporate taxes, personal taxes, and tax deductability of interest-rate payments to be accounted for. If the boundaries are known and the cash flows to debt and equity at the boundaries are known, then we can value debt and equity at time 0 using these functions.

Assume that equity receives until τ a dividend payment which is affine in ξ, and equal to $d_0 + d_1 \xi_t$. Let $E(\xi, 1)$ denote the value of equity when dividends are chosen on the basis of $\xi = 1$ and when EBIT has moved to the level ξ. Use the same notation $D(\xi, 1)$ for debt.

Assume that equity receives $E(u, 1)$ if the upper boundary is hit before the lower, and $E(l, 1)$ if the lower boundary is hit first. Likewise, assume that debt receives a constant cash flow C_0 and a given amount $D(u, 1)$ ($D(l, 1)$) at the upper (lower) boundary. Then, clearly, the values of debt and equity at time 0 given the EBIT value $\xi_0 = 1$ are

$$D(1, 1) = D(u, 1)P_u(1, u, l) + D(l, 1)P_l(1, u, l) + C_0 F(1, u, l),$$

$$E(1, 1) = E(u, 1)P_u(1, u, l) + E(l, 1)P_l(1, u, l) + d_0 F(1, u, l) + G(1, u, l, d_1).$$

And we can easily modify the values to take into account that ξ has moved away from 1 simply by noting that this only changes the present-value expressions P_u and P_d:

$$\left.\begin{aligned} D(\xi, 1) &= D(u, 1)P_u(\xi, u, l) + D(l, 1)P_l(\xi, u, l) + C_0 F(1, u, l), \\ E(\xi, 1) &= E(u, 1)P_u(\xi, u, l) + E(l, 1)P_l(\xi, u, l) \\ &\qquad + d_0 F(1, u, l) + G(1, u, l, d_1). \end{aligned}\right\} \quad (3.5)$$

If the values $E(u, 1)$, $E(l, 1)$, $D(u, 1)$, $D(l, 1)$ received at the boundary are fixed in advance, then these values can be computed directly using the expressions for the present-value functions whose expressions are in Appendix B. But for realistic models of dynamic capital structure this is too restrictive. If we want to model a new debt issuance at the upper boundary, then debt and equity holders have a firm which is recapitalized and thus the dividend payments will change. Similarly, at the lower boundary we might have a liquidation value of the firm which is proportional to the firm value as a going concern. Hence, for the model to be realistic, we need to specify continuation values of the firm (and hence for debt and equity) at both boundaries.

We can relate the continuation values to the starting values if we use a geometric Brownian motion model and the scaling properties of the process. Assume that we have settled on some optimal values of u, l, and C_0. Then the firm which starts afresh at either $\xi = u$ or $\xi = l$ will use exactly the same relative numbers we used initially for $\xi_0 = 1$, and hence if starting at u will choose upper and lower boundaries u^2 and lu, a coupon of uC_0, and the dividend to the stock will be $ud_0 + d_1 \xi_t$. All we need do is describe what happens at the boundaries. We show that if we stipulate what happens at the boundaries and use the scaling property of the problem, we can derive closed-form expressions for debt and equity for given boundaries and coupon/dividend levels.

Assume that at the lower boundary the debt holders take over a fraction of the firm's asset value as a going concern, and at the upper boundary old debt holders are paid off (with a call premium), the equity holders retain the residual and immediately issue new debt.

If there is a cost of k per unit of new debt both at the upper and lower boundaries and we force a complete repayment of old debt before new debt is issued, then a recapitalization brings in a total revenue of

$$V(\xi) = E(\xi, \xi) + (1 - k)D(\xi, \xi)$$

whether ξ is u or d and where we here think of equity and debt as newly issued. Now we are in a position to express the payoffs to debt and equity at the two boundaries. If debt has a call premium of λ per unit of principal, and equity gets nothing in bankruptcy, then the cash flow to the old equity owners are

$$E(u, 1) = V(u) - (1 + \lambda)D(1, 1),$$
$$E(l, 1) = 0.$$

The boundary conditions giving the payments to the old debt holders are

$$D(u, 1) = (1 + \lambda)D(1, 1),$$
$$D(l, 1) = \alpha V(l),$$

which reflect the call premium at the upper boundary, and the bankruptcy costs incurred at the lower boundary. Now we can use a scaling argument and say that if coupons, dividends, and boundaries are all scaled versions of those used when EBIT was 1, then we have

$$V(u) = uV(1) = uE(1, 1) + u(1 - k)D(1, 1),$$
$$V(l) = lV(1) = lE(1, 1) + l(1 - k)D(1, 1),$$

and substituting all this into Equations (3.5) for debt and equity value gives two equations in two unknowns for the initial values of debt and equity (where we suppress the arguments of the present-value functionals):

$$(1 - (1 + \lambda)P_u - \alpha l(1 - k)P_l)D(1, 1) - dl P_l E(1, 1) = C_0 F,$$
$$((1 + \lambda)P_u - u(1 - k)P_u)D(1, 1) + (1 - uP_u)E(1, 1) = d_0 F + G.$$

This solves the valuation problem for given boundaries u and l. One then has to optimize both the bankruptcy decision and the call decision to obtain optimal boundaries using smooth pasting conditions (but note that the derivatives can be computed explicitly). Finally, set the optimal coupon level for the debt. This last stage also has to be done numerically. This is the cost of working with upper and lower boundaries: analytical solutions are harder to come by.

3.4   A Model with Strategic Debt Service

Renegotiation of debt contracts in times of financial distress is an important feature of debt markets that has so far not been captured by our models. In the models considered so far, the default boundary is fixed and shareholders do not try to persuade bond holders into renegotiation even if they have a common interest in avoiding the loss associated with bankruptcy costs. Differently stated, our models so far consider no violations of absolute priority: if there is not enough cash or asset value to pay bond holders their contractual amount, they take over the firm and equity is worthless. In practice, absolute priority violations do take place, i.e. we see cases where debt payments are reduced but equity is still "alive" after the restructuring and has a positive value. The model of Anderson and Sundaresan (1996) captures this phenomenon.

To begin with, the model looks like a case of cynical "blackmailing" by the shareholders. They use the threat of bankruptcy to its fullest making sure that bond holders are never offered more than what they would obtain from a liquidation. However, a more precise view on this is that, since bond holders anticipate this type of behavior, the bonds are priced accordingly. Hence the story is really turned around in the sense that the firm has to accept large spreads on its debt (i.e. low value) because bond holders (correctly) anticipate that shareholders in the model are cynical!

The model is a binomial model and runs as follows: V_t denotes the value at time t of the current and future cash flows (i.e. a cum-dividend value) which the firm's assets can generate. This value follows a binomial process in which V_t jumps to $u V_t$ or $d V_t$, where $d = 1/u$. This riskless rate is $r - 1$ and the cash-flow ("dividend") generated at time t by V_t is $f_t = \beta V_t$, where β is the "payout ratio." Assuming that V is a traded asset, this means that there should exist a risk-neutral probability q such that the ex-dividend price at time t is equal to the expected discounted value of the cum-dividend value at time $t + 1$, i.e.

$$(1 - \beta)V_t = \frac{q u V_t + (1 - q)d V_t}{r},$$

which gives us

$$q = \frac{r(1 - \beta) - d}{u - d}.$$

The firm issues debt to finance a project. The amount to be raised is D but we will not be needing that here. The debt calls for a payment of C_t^c in period t up to the maturity T, but only the cash flow f_t is available for coupon payments since we assume that no new debt can be issued, and sale of assets is prohibited. The actual coupon paid (or, rather, proposed by shareholders) is denoted C_t^s, and this is called the debt service. We must have

$$C_t^s \in [0, f_t],$$

and there is no reason to have $C_t^s > C_t^c$ so think of $C_t^s \in [0, \min(f_t, C_t^c)]$.

If full payment of C_t^c is not made at time t, the bond holders have the right to liquidate the firm. If they choose to do this, they receive a payment of

$$\max(V_t - K, 0),$$

where K is the fixed cost of liquidation. These costs will not exceed V_t, i.e. only the firm's assets can and will be used to cover bankruptcy costs.

Shareholders, which we identify with owners, will make sure never to service more debt than is necessary to keep bond holders indifferent between liquidation and continuation (and we assume that when indifferent they choose continuation). Given this policy, we will now solve for debt and equity values "working backwards through the tree."

As usual, things are easy at time T: V_T is observed and the owner selects a debt service C_T^s. If $C_T^s = C_T^c$, then the bond holders are happy and the game ends. If $C_T^s < C_T^c$, the bond holders must decide which is more profitable: liquidation or receiving the reduced coupon. Hence they compare C_T^s with $\max(V_T - K, 0)$. Shareholders know this and therefore squeeze the bond holders to the limit and offer a debt service at T of

$$C_T^s = \begin{cases} C_T^c & \text{if } V_T - K > C_T^c, \\ \max(V_T - K, 0) & \text{otherwise.} \end{cases}$$

Hence the value of the bond at time T is given by

$$B(V_T) = \min(C_T^c, \max(V_T - K, 0)).$$

Equity as usual claims the residual, if any, i.e.

$$S(V_T) = V_T - B(V_T).$$

It is worth noting that even if V_T is big enough to cover C_T^c, equity holders may choose not to pay the coupon. When V_T is only slightly bigger than K, shareholders exploit the low liquidation value and offer a reduced "strategic" debt service.

Now we have to work backwards through the tree taking into account continuation value *and* the limitation on payout imposed by f_t. At time t, V_t is observed. If the chosen debt service C_t^s is equal to C_t^c, there is no liquidation and the game continues. To keep the bond holders from liquidating the firm, it must be the case that the value of C_t^s plus the continuation value is as big as the liquidation value, i.e. if f_t is large enough to permit it, shareholders choose a payment of

$$C_t^s = \min\left(C_t^c, \max\left(0, \max(V_T - K, 0) - \frac{q B(u V_t) + (1 - q) B(d V_t)}{r}\right)\right).$$

This expression takes a little while to internalize. First, note that

$$\max(V_t - K, 0) - \frac{q B(u V_t) + (1 - q) B(d V_t)}{r}$$

is the difference between liquidation value and continuation value for the bond holders. If the liquidation value is smaller than the continuation value, there is no need to offer anything, hence the service is 0. If C_t^c is smaller than what is needed to bring the continuation value up to the liquidation value, then of course choose this since bond holders cannot liquidate if the contractual coupon is paid. If the contractually required coupon is larger than what it takes to make bond holders indifferent between liquidation and continuation, then pay the smaller amount. The value of debt in such a state is then

$$B(V_t) = C_t^s + \frac{1}{r} E(B(V_{t+1}))$$

and equity is

$$S(V_t) = f_t - C_t^s + \frac{1}{r} E(S(V_{t+1})).$$

Now it may happen that f_t is not sufficient to pay the amount C_t^s that we just found. Then we have "forced liquidation" and in this case we assume

$$B(V_t) = \max(0, \min(V_t - K), C_t^c + P_t),$$

i.e. the bond holders receive the promised coupon and the principal if there is enough post-liquidation value to cover this, otherwise they receive the liquidation value. Hence even in forced liquidation there could be something left for equity:

$$S(V_t) = V_t - K - B(V_t),$$

which is always nonnegative and positive if post-liquidation assets are sufficient to cover $C_t^c + P_t$. With these specifications one can work backwards through the tree.

3.5 Bibliographical Notes

The idea of endogenizing the default boundary is in Black and Cox (1976), where a model with perpetual debt is proposed in which debt is perpetual and the equity holders for a given level of coupons decide when to default. The optimality criterion is minimizing the value of the outstanding debt and it is assumed in this case that the assets of the firm cannot be liquidated to finance coupon payments. An early paper studying dynamic capital-structure choice is Brennan and Schwartz (1984), and bankruptcy costs, tax advantage to debt, and callability of debt are included in Fischer et al. (1989). The papers by Kane et al. (1984, 1985) study the issue of how a tax advantage of holding an asset should be reflected in its price. The model of Leland (1994) does not deal with the issue of whether the underlying asset is traded, but if one is willing to live with that it gives a very transparent treatment of the trade-off in dynamic capital-structure choice between the tax advantage of debt and the cost of bankruptcy. This is why the model is emphasized here. An extension which handles finite-maturity structures is presented in Leland and Toft (1996). The problem with assuming a traded underlying asset can be dealt with by working instead with a state variable which does not represent the price process of a traded asset. This is done in, for example, Mella-Barral and Perraudin (1997) and Goldstein et al. (2001), both of which also consider restructuring of the debt. Dynamic models which consider strategic behavior by the shareholders of the firm include the model of Anderson and Sundaresan (1996) presented here, but Mella-Barral and Perraudin (1997) is another example. An attempt at combining the scaling argument of Goldstein et al. (2001) and the strategic considerations is made in Christensen et al. (2002).

There are many extensions of the model presented in Leland (1994). For example, Uhrig-Homburg (1998) considers a distinction between liquidity default and Hilberink and Rogers (2002) extends the model to the case with downward jumps in asset value that we met in Chapter 2 (see also Acharya and Carpenter (2002)). The empirical implications of the models are investigated in Davydenko and Strebulaev (2003).

4
Statistical Techniques for Analyzing Defaults

While the option-based approach provides a consistent way of thinking about default probabilities and prices of corporate bonds, it seems implausible that a single value, the value of the firm's assets, is the sole determinant of default probabilities. We saw, in fact, that the liquidity of assets and restrictions on asset sales were key factors as well. It is not always easy to build full structural models which include all the variables that empirically influence estimated default probabilities. The intensity models that we will turn to later try to include more variables in the default pricing, typically (but not necessarily) at the cost of making their influence exogenously specified. Before we enter into these models it is natural to look at some of the dominating methods used for default probability estimation. As we will see, the most natural statistical framework for analyzing defaults is also the natural framework for linking credit scoring with pricing. The focus of this section is on model structure. No properties of the estimators are proved.

4.1 Credit Scoring Using Logistic Regression

Firm default is an example of a qualitative response—at least if we do not look at the severity of the default in terms of recoveries. We simply observe a firm's characteristics and whether it defaults or not. Logistic regression views the probability of default as depending on a set of firm characteristics (or *covariates*). The actual response depends on a noise variable, just like the deviation of a response from its mean in ordinary regression depends on a noise variable.

Specifically, let Y be the observed status of the firm at the end of some predetermined time horizon. Let $Y = 1$ if the firm has defaulted and 0 otherwise. The assumption in a logistic regression is that for each firm,

$$P(Y = 1 \mid x_1, \ldots, x_k) = p(x_1, \ldots, x_k).$$

The function p of course needs to take values in $(0, 1)$ and this is done typically by using either a *logit* specification or a *probit* specification. In the logit specification, we use the logistic distribution function to specify probabilities, i.e. we assume that

$$P(Y = 1 \mid x_1, \ldots, x_k) = \frac{\exp(\alpha_0 + \beta_1 x_1 + \cdots + \beta_n x_n)}{1 + \exp(\alpha_0 + \beta_1 x_1 + \cdots + \beta_n x_n)}.$$

If we define

$$\text{logit}(x) = \log\left(\frac{x}{1-x}\right),$$

we may write this as

$$\text{logit}(P(Y = 1 \mid x_1, \ldots, x_k)) = \alpha_0 + \beta_1 x_1 + \cdots + \beta_n x_n,$$

where $\alpha, \beta_1, \ldots, \beta_n \in \mathbb{R}$. The model then assumes that the outcomes of different firms are independent. In a probit specification we use the distribution function Φ of a standard normal random variable to transform the regression into the unit interval, i.e. we let

$$P(Y = 1 \mid x_1, \ldots, x_k) = \Phi(\alpha_0 + \beta_1 x_1 + \cdots + \beta_n x_n).$$

We will return to the probit analysis at the end of the chapter. At this point, we will focus on the logit specification because of its connection with discriminant analysis and because we have an interpretation of the β-coefficients in terms of log-odds ratios: if two firms have covariate vectors x^i and x^j and we let p^i and p^j denote their probabilities of default as given by a logit specification, then we have

$$\log \frac{p^i/(1 - p^i)}{p^j/(1 - p^j)} = \beta'(x^i - x^j),$$

where we have $\beta = (\beta_1, \ldots, \beta_k)$ and of course

$$\beta' x^i = \sum_{j=1}^{k} \beta_j x_j^i.$$

If we let y_i denote the response of the ith firm and think of $y_i = 1$ as default, then we may express the likelihood function as

$$L(\alpha, \beta) = \prod_{i=1}^{n} \left(\frac{\exp(\alpha + \beta' x^i)}{1 + \exp(\alpha + \beta' x^i)}\right)^{y_i} \left(\frac{1}{1 + \exp(\alpha + \beta' x^i)}\right)^{1-y_i}$$

$$= \prod_{i=1}^{n} \left(\frac{1}{1 + \exp(\alpha + \beta' x^i)}\right) \exp(\alpha S + \beta' SP),$$

where we define

$$S = \sum_{i=1}^{n} y_i \quad \text{and} \quad SP = \sum_{i=1}^{n} y_i x^i.$$

The computation of the maximum-likelihood estimators of the variables requires numerical methods. In fact, the fact that logistic regression is not used so much in earlier studies related to default risk is probably due to computational limitations. With modern computers and statistical software, the maximization is simple when the number of regressors is not too large.

4.2 Credit Scoring Using Discriminant Analysis

The basic assumption in a discriminant analysis is that we have two populations which are normally distributed with different means. For the purpose of default modeling we think of one group as being the firms which will survive over a relevant period of time and the other group as being those which will default. The normal distributions then are multivariate normals and each component represents a relevant firm characteristic. Hence the logic is somewhat reversed compared with a logistic regression. In a logistic regression, we have certain firm characteristics which influence the probability of default. Given the characteristics, nonsystematic variation determines whether the firm actually defaults or not. In a discriminant analysis, the firms which default are given, but the firm characteristics are then a product of nonsystematic variation.

The essential feature of discriminant analysis that is relevant for our purposes is as follows. Assume that we are given a "training sample"

$$(x_1^0, \ldots, x_N^0) \quad \text{and} \quad (x_1^1, \ldots, x_D^1)$$

consisting of multivariate firm characteristics of N surviving firms and D defaulting firms. Hence, x_1^0 is a vector of firm characteristics for a firm labelled 1 within the group of nondefaulted firms. Faced with a new observation x, our goal is to decide whether this vector of characteristics belongs to a firm which will survive or a firm which will default. We mention here two approaches to making that decision which lead to the same type of discriminant function. One uses a decision-theoretic approach and the other uses a likelihood ratio test. The true population means for the two groups are denoted μ^0 and μ^1 and we denote by Σ the common variance/covariance matrix. We let ϕ_0, ϕ_1 denote the associated multivariate normal densities.

To understand the decision-theoretic approach, assume for a moment that we know the true parameters and that we also know (or are willing to assign) the probability q_i to the event that in the total population, a firm belongs to group i. Furthermore, let $c(0 \mid 1)$ $(c(1 \mid 0))$ denote the cost associated with erroneously assigning a firm to belong to the surviving (defaulting) firms when it is a defaulting (surviving) firm. If our decision rule places a firm in group 0 when its characteristics belong to the set R_0 and to group 1 when its characteristics belong to the complement R_1, then we can compute the probabilities of the possible types of classification. Suppressing the dependence on regions, Let $p(i \mid j)$ denote the probability of assigning a firm to class i when it belongs to j. Then

$$p(i \mid j) = \int_{R_i} \phi_j(x)\, dx, \quad i = 1, 2 \text{ and } j = 1, 2.$$

With this notation, the expected cost of misclassification is

$$q_1 p(0 \mid 1) c(0 \mid 1) + q_0 p(1 \mid 0) c(1 \mid 0).$$

It is shown in Anderson (1984) that the expected cost of misclassification is minimized if one uses a discriminant function of the form

$$d(x) = x' \Sigma^{-1}(\mu^0 - \mu^1) - \tfrac{1}{2}(\mu^0 - \mu^1)' \Sigma^{-1}(\mu^0 - \mu^1)$$

and assigns the firm with characteristics x to group 0 if $d(x) \geqslant \log K$ and to 1 if $d(x) < \log K$, where

$$K = \frac{q_1}{q_0} \frac{c(0 \mid 1)}{c(1 \mid 0)}.$$

Note that if we define $\Sigma^{-1}(\mu^0 - \mu^1)$ to be the column vector d, the criterion amounts to looking at whether the linear function $d'x$ is larger than a certain constant or not. In practical applications of discriminant analysis the parameters of the populations are estimated using the training sample, i.e.

$$\hat{\mu}^0 = \frac{1}{N} \sum_{i=1}^{N} x_i^0, \qquad \hat{\mu}^1 = \frac{1}{D} \sum_{i=1}^{D} x_i^1$$

and

$$\hat{\Sigma} = \frac{1}{N + D - 2} \left(\sum_{i=1}^{N} (x_i^0 - \hat{\mu}^0)'(x_i^0 - \hat{\mu}^0) + \sum_{i=1}^{D} (x_i^1 - \hat{\mu}^1)'(x_i^1 - \hat{\mu}^1) \right).$$

These estimated values are then used in the discriminant function.

A second approach (see Anderson 1984 for details) for classifying a new observation x is to use a maximum-likelihood approach. Given our sample of nondefaulting firms and their characteristics and the new observation x first compute MLEs of μ^0, μ^1 and Σ under the hypothesis that the observation x is added to the sample of nondefaulting firms, and then subsequently compute MLEs under the hypothesis that x is added to the sample of defaulting firms. The decision with the highest likelihood wins. This also results in a linear discriminant function of the same form as above.

The outcome of this exercise is not completely satisfactory in modern risk management in which we want to be able to assign probabilities of default. Our basic setup allows us to say conditionally on default or no default what the distribution of the firm characteristics is. But we really want to do the opposite and assign a default probability to a given set of characteristics. This can be done using the Bayes theorem provided that we know the full joint distribution of our firms, i.e. we know the probability of belonging to group i. As before, let this probability be denoted q_i and let Y be the indicator of default for the firm. Then from the Bayes theorem we have

$$p(x) := P[Y = 1 \mid X = x]$$

$$= \frac{q_1 \phi_1(x)}{q_0 \phi_0(x) + q_1 \phi_1(x)},$$

where ϕ_i is the density of an $N(\mu^i, \Sigma)$ distribution. We can establish an interesting link to logistic regression using this. Note that

$$\frac{p(x)}{1 - p(x)} = \frac{q_1 \phi_1(x)}{q_0 \phi_0(x)}$$

and hence, plugging in the expression for the multivariate normal densities, we find

$$\text{logit}(p(x)) = \text{logit}(q_1) + \left(x - \frac{\mu^1 + \mu^0}{2}\right)' \Sigma^{-1}(\mu^1 - \mu^0)$$

and if we let

$$\alpha = \text{logit}(q_1) - \left(\frac{\mu^1 + \mu^0}{2}\right)' \Sigma^{-1}(\mu^1 - \mu^0)$$

and

$$\beta = \Sigma^{-1}(\mu^1 - \mu^0),$$

we obtain a specification of the default probability given the characteristics of exactly the same form as in the logit model.

Now assume that we are interested in estimating a discriminant function based on a sample. We could then follow two procedures. We could use the information on whether firms default or not conditionally on their covariates and perform a logistic regression with a logit specification as above. This can be viewed as working in a conditional model, taking the regressors as given. We could also view the whole problem as a multiple discriminant problem, estimate the means of the two populations, the common covariance matrix, and the probability of belonging to each category (which is just the frequency of default and nondefault in the sample) and then compute the discriminant function by plugging in the estimates. Efron (1975) argues that since the latter procedure uses a full maximum likelihood as opposed to a conditional, it must be more efficient. But, as he also notes, this is of course only a fair comparison if the true distribution of the covariates is normal, and this is quite a stretch for many covariates that we would consider in default probability estimation. Press and Wilson (1978) give examples of how the discriminant analysis can have problems with robustness compared with the logistic regression when the characteristics are not normally distributed.

While the efficiency depends on model assumptions, a fundamental problem with the discriminant analysis is that the assumption of normality seems unrealistic for many types of characteristics that we observe. Furthermore, it is hard to imagine that if we had a very large sample of firms, we would see a two-point mixture distribution of normals. In practice, characteristics do not follow such a simple distribution. Furthermore, we cannot reasonably make default probability estimates using the model unless we are willing to specify an "overall" default probability rate. And, finally, the model is static and does not include the important information on how long a firm survives with a set of characteristics. All of this can be remedied using methods of survival analysis.

We finish by mentioning an example of a discriminant function reported in Altman (1968), the first work to use this methodology for default prediction. Here, the discriminant function, labeled the Z-score, has the form

$$d(X) = 0.012X_1 + 0.014X_2 + 0.033X_3 + 0.006X_4 + 0.999X_5,$$

where

$$X_1 = \frac{\text{working capital}}{\text{total assets}},$$

$$X_2 = \frac{\text{retained earnings}}{\text{total assets}},$$

$$X_3 = \frac{\text{earnings before interest and taxes}}{\text{total assets}},$$

$$X_4 = \frac{\text{market value of equity}}{\text{book value of total debt}},$$

$$X_5 = \frac{\text{sales}}{\text{total assets}}.$$

Working capital is defined as the difference between current assets (i.e. assets which can be turned into cash within a year) and current liabilities. Note that except for the market value of equity, the quantities are all derived from financial statements. This means that, in practice, the updating of the values will only take place when (say) quarterly reports are published, and since these are published with a time delay, the ratios are not useful for explaining short-term variations of credit spreads. The leverage measure X_4 is a market-based variable but does not include the volatility of assets, in contrast with the distance-to-default measure we saw in Chapter 2. In the study of Altman (1968), a lower threshold of 1.81 is reported below which all firms in the study defaulted and an upper threshold of 2.67 above which all firms survived.

4.3 Hazard Regressions: Discrete Case

The most natural statistical framework for analyzing survival data involves statistical modeling of hazard rates, which are clearly related to conditional default probabilities. We give here the basic setup in discrete time. The theory is perhaps most conveniently stated in continuous time, but the estimators we use when working with continuous-time data are often (but not always) directly seen to be estimators based on a discrete-time hazard regression with small time periods.

Consider a collection of N firms. Assume that the probability of a firm defaulting at date t is $f(t, \theta)$, where $t \in \{1, 2, \ldots\}$ and θ is some parameter. f is assumed to have support on all of $\mathbb{N}$. Assume that we observe the firms up to and including time T. Firms which are still alive at time T are thus (right) censored. We also allow firms to leave the sample before T for reasons other than default. In this case if a firm leaves at date c we interpret this to mean that the firm was known to be alive at c, but nothing is known after this date.

We think of this censoring mechanism as being unrelated to the default event. If, for example, some clairvoyant was able to ask firms to leave the sample one year before they defaulted, we would never see any defaults in the sample.

In the real world, we see nondefaulted firms as part of mergers or target of takeovers, and although in some sectors such activity may be related to an increased default probability, it does not seem to be a big problem in empirical work.

We now let $t_1, \ldots, t_N$ denote the set of dates at which firms leave the sample for any reason. We let $C \subseteq \{1, \ldots, N\}$ denote the set of firms for which the leaving of the sample was due to censoring and let $U = \{1, \ldots, N\} \backslash C$ denote the firms whose leaving dates were an actual default event. If censoring takes place at time t, we assume that we do not know the true status of the firm at time t.

At this point we could write down the likelihood directly as

$$\prod_{i \in U} f(t_i, \theta) \prod_{i \in C} S(t_i, \theta),$$

where $S(t_i, \theta) = \sum_{u \geq t_i} f(u, \theta)$ is the probability of surviving at least until t_i. While this is correct, it turns out that we can get a much clearer sense of the dynamics of the model by looking at the hazards.

Let

$$h(t, \theta) = \frac{f(t, \theta)}{f(t, \theta) + f(t + 1, \theta) + \cdots},$$

i.e. $h(t, \theta)$ is the probability of defaulting at date t given survival up to that time.

Clearly,

$$f(1, \theta) = h(1, \theta),$$
$$f(2, \theta) = h(2, \theta)(1 - f(1, \theta)) = h(2, \theta)(1 - h(1, \theta)),$$

and in general

$$f(t, \theta) = h(t, \theta) \prod_{s < t} (1 - h(s, \theta)).$$

Writing the likelihood in terms of the hazards we then get a factor in the likelihood of

$$h(t_i, \theta) \prod_{s \leqslant t_i} (1 - h(s, \theta)) \quad \text{for each } i \in U,$$

and of

$$\prod_{s < t_i} (1 - h(s, \theta)) \quad \text{for each } i \in C.$$

Now

- let d_t be the number of firms which default at date t; and
- let r_t be the number of firms exposed to default at date t.

Hence r_t is the number of firms which had not left the sample at the time when the defaults and censorings at $t - 1$ were known. Each firm alive at date t contributes a factor $1 - h(t, \theta)$ to the likelihood and the defaulting firms contribute a factor $h(t, \theta)$ each.

So, instead of taking a product over firms, we may instead write

$$\prod_{t=1,\dots,T} h(t, \theta)^{d_t} (1 - h(t, \theta))^{r_t - d_t}.$$

Each factor in this expression can be viewed as the probability of seeing d_t defaults and $r_t - d_t$ nondefaults at time t.[1] A special, nonparametric case is worth mentioning. If we let $h(t, \theta) = h(t)$ be unrestricted, corresponding to a time-dependent hazard, we can maximize the log-likelihood by maximizing each term in the sum:

$$d_t \log h(t) + (r_t - d_t) \log(1 - h(t)),$$

and this gives

$$h(t) = d_t / r_t,$$

which is simply the "occurrence/exposure" ratio, which is a standard variable in all mortality analysis. We will see this quantity reappear several times.

Another possibility, relevant for default studies, is that the hazard is not time dependent but rather depends on firm specific covariates, i.e. instead of writing $h(t, \theta)$ we write $h(x_i)$ for firm i. This corresponds to a case which in essence all

---

[1] Strictly speaking, it is the probability of seeing d_t explicitly designated firms default. The binomial probability would have a binomial coefficient in front, but that will not affect the likelihood.

default prediction is concerned with, namely that of finding default predictors which do not vary over time.

In this case, we could define $d_t(x)$ as the number of defaulting firms at date t having covariate x, and let $r_t(x)$ be the number of firms exposed at date t.

Then our nonparametric estimator of $h(x)$ would just be

$$h(x) = \frac{\sum_{t=1}^{T} d_t(x)}{\sum_{t=1}^{T} r_t(x)}.$$

If time was retained as a covariate, we would use

$$h(t, x) = \frac{d_t(x)}{r_t(x)}.$$

In practice, this type of estimation would be difficult, since it would require exposures (and observations of default) for the different values of covariates.

Hence the feasible solution in practical situations is often to select a parametric model

$$h(t, \theta) = h(x_t, \theta),$$

where $h(t, \theta)$ has some functional form (such as $h(x_t, \theta) = \exp(\theta' x_t)$) in which x_t is the set of covariates at date t.

Shumway (2001) estimates a model in which

$$h(t; x; \theta_1, \theta_2) = \frac{1}{1 + \exp(g(t)\theta_1 + x'\theta_2)},$$

where $g(t)$ is a function of the firm's age (the logarithm for example), and x is a set of covariates.

He finds that the market variables given by market size, its past stock returns, and the idiosyncratic standard deviation are important in predicting failure. In addition to these variables, net income divided by total assets and total liabilities over total assets are viewed as powerful predictors.

4.4 Continuous-Time Survival Analysis Methods

The analysis of default and the link to pricing models is most easily done using the continuous-time version of a hazard rate. Consider a nonnegative random variable τ, which we think of as the default time of some firm. We assume that the distribution of τ has a continuous density function f, so that the distribution function F and the survival function S are related as follows:

$$P(\tau \leqslant t) = F(t) = 1 - S(t) = \int_0^t f(s) \, ds. \tag{4.1}$$

The hazard rate h is defined as

$$h(t) = \frac{f(t)}{1 - F(t)} = \frac{f(t)}{S(t)} = -\frac{d}{dt} \log S(t),$$

i.e.

$$S(t) = \exp\left(-\int_0^t h(s)\, ds \right).$$

The functions F and S are of course each complete descriptors of the distribution of any real-valued random variable, and if f and h exist, so are they. The hazard function is of particular interest in default modeling because of its link to conditional default probabilities, which is similar to the link we saw in the discrete-time case. Note that

$$P(\tau \leqslant t + \Delta t \mid \tau > t) = \frac{P(\tau \leqslant t + \Delta t, \tau > t)}{P(\tau > t)}$$

$$= 1 - \exp\left(-\int_t^{t+\Delta t} h(s)\, ds \right),$$

and therefore

$$\lim_{\Delta t \downarrow 0} \frac{1}{\Delta t} P(\tau \leqslant t + \Delta t \mid \tau > t) = h(t),$$

so $h(t)\Delta t$ is approximately the conditional probability of a default in a small interval after t given survival up to and including t. Note that it is a conditional default probability which we can compute already at time 0.

Now we consider the continuous-time analogue of the discrete-time hazard analysis. We focus on three specifications: a fully parametric, a semi-parametric, and a nonparametric one.

In the parametric case we consider a model in which the density of the default time of a firm is given as

$$f(t; \theta) = h(t; \theta) \exp\left(-\int_0^t h(s; \theta)\, ds \right),$$

where h is a nonnegative integrable function for all t. Again under an assumption of independent censoring[2] we arrive at a likelihood expression

$$\prod_{i=1}^N h(t_i; \theta)^{\alpha_i} \exp\left(-\int_0^{t_i} h(s; \theta)\, ds \right),$$

where t_i is the time at which the firm leaves the sample. If leaving is due to censoring, we let $\alpha_i = 0$, otherwise $\alpha_i = 1$. Note the analogy with the discrete-time

---

[2] In fact, more general patterns of censoring are allowed while preserving this likelihood (see Andersen et al. 1993).

case. Except for very simple cases, the maximum has to be found using numerical techniques.

The more interesting and useful specification is one in which the population of firms is nonhomogeneous and we characterize the dependence of default rates by some firm characteristics or covariates. A popular form is the Cox proportional-hazards model in which we let the hazard of default be specified as

$$\lambda_i(t) = \lambda_0(t) \exp(\beta_0' z_i(t)),$$

where $\lambda_0(t)$ is nonnegative for all t and where $z_i(t)$ is a set of firm characteristics. The exponential is chosen to make sure we have a positive intensity—any other positive function could be used. $\lambda_0(t)$ is a "baseline" hazard, i.e. a hazard which applies if the firm has 0 exposure to covariates.

This is a convenient specification for applications. The baseline intensity captures common variations in the default intensity which we do not try to model. For example, in a default study in which we are studying the effect of a particular accounting variable, we may want to test the influence without explicitly modeling the dependence on business-cycle variables. Still, we can get a nonparametric estimate for λ_0.

But first we estimate β using the so-called partial-likelihood function

$$L(\beta) = \prod_{i=1}^{N} \prod_{0 \leqslant s \leqslant t} \left[\frac{Y_i(s) \exp(\beta' z_i(s))}{\sum_{j=1}^{N} Y_j(s) \exp(\beta' z_j(s))} \right]^{\Delta N_i(s)}, \qquad (4.2)$$

where

$$\Delta N_i(s) = \begin{cases} 1 & \text{if firm } i \text{ is observed to default at time } s, \\ 0 & \text{otherwise}, \end{cases}$$

and

$$Y_i(s) = \begin{cases} 1 & \text{if firm } i \text{ has not defaulted or been censored strictly before } s, \\ 0 & \text{otherwise}. \end{cases}$$

The somewhat complicated-looking expression (4.2) is actually very simple. The double product contains as many factors as there are observed default times. A default time t_i of firm i contributes the factor

$$\frac{\exp(\beta' z_i(t_i))}{\sum_{j=1}^{N} Y_j(s) \exp(\beta' z_j(t_i))}$$

to the expression. Firms which are censored (either due to survival past T or because of "real" censoring) do not contribute a factor, but do cause the denominator to change when they leave the sample.

It is far beyond the scope of this presentation to discuss what a partial likelihood function is and why it is used. Here we will just note the following: the contribution to the partial likelihood made by firm i defaulting at date t_i is a conditional probability. It is the probability that given a default at date t_i, out of the firms which remain in the sample at that date, it is firm i which defaults. It is straightforward to check that the common baseline intensity (viewed as deterministic) cancels out here. There is an example of this computation in the section on first-to-default swaps, where we will see that with stochastic covariates this does not hold. It is also clear that we are certainly not maximizing the full likelihood, since that would have to address $\lambda_0(t)$. This baseline intensity is, however, nonparametric and it therefore requires some nonparametric technique to obtain it from data. We therefore finish this overview by looking briefly at nonparametric techniques for intensity modeling. These techniques provide useful diagnostics to risk managers and regulators interested in getting a good overview of the performance of (say) a rating system.

4.4.1 Nonparametric Techniques

When estimating continuous distributions, it is straightforward to write down a non-parametric estimator for the distribution function (namely the empirical distribution function) but it requires smoothing techniques to obtain a probability density. We are typically more interested in densities since they typically give us a better view of the properties of a distribution. The same is true of hazard rates: we can write down a natural estimator for the integrated hazard, but we then need smoothing techniques to obtain the hazard itself, which is a much more natural object to look at.

The analogue for integrated intensities of the empirical distribution function, allowing for censored observations, is the Nelson–Aalen estimator. We start by considering a sample of firms with the same default intensity. Let

$$Y(t) = \sum_{i=1}^{N} Y_i(t)$$

denote the number of firms at risk of defaulting at date t. The Nelson–Aalen estimator for the cumulative intensity is then defined as

$$\hat{A}(t) = \sum_{\{i:T_i \leqslant t\}} \frac{1}{Y(T_i)},$$

where T_i is the default date of firm i. Returning briefly to the proportional hazard model we may obtain an estimate for the cumulative baseline hazard by plugging our estimate of β into

$$\hat{A}_0(t) = \sum_{t_i \leqslant t} \frac{1}{\sum_{j=1}^{N} Y(t_i) \exp(\hat{\beta}' z_j(t_i))}.$$

A smoothed version of the intensity is provided by the estimator

$$\hat{\lambda}_b(t) = \frac{1}{b} \sum_{\{i:T_i \leqslant t\}} K\left(\frac{t - T_i}{b}\right) \frac{1}{Y(T_i)}, \tag{4.3}$$

where K is a bounded function which is 0 outside $[-1, 1]$, bounded on $[-1, 1]$, and integrates to 1 over this interval; b is the bandwidth and it determines how far away from t that a default will influence the intensity estimate at t. Typical choices for K are the uniform kernel

$$K_U(x) = \tfrac{1}{2} \qquad \text{for } -1 \leqslant x \leqslant 1,$$

and the Epanechnikov kernel

$$K_U(x) = \tfrac{3}{4}(1 - x^2) \quad \text{for } -1 \leqslant x \leqslant 1.$$

The choice of b is a question of optimal bandwidth selection. While there are criteria for this, it is often visual inspection which allows the statistician to come up with a reasonable b. The trade-off is really one between bias and variance. If b is small, the estimator is better at picking up local changes in the intensity but the variance is also big. Large b will give more bias, since observations "far away" from the point we are interested in are allowed to influence the estimator. But larger b will decrease the variance, since it takes more occurrences to move the estimator. An alternative to the estimator (4.3) is to use smoothing of the occurrences and smoothing of the exposures separately. In this case,

$$\hat{\lambda}_b(t) = \frac{\sum_{i=1}^{N}(1/b)K((t - t_i)/b)}{\sum_{i=1}^{N}\int_0^t (1/b)K((t - s)/b)Y_i(s)\, ds},$$

which is a smoothing method that is more robust to sudden shifts in the number of exposures. As seen in Figure 4.1, the two methods are almost equivalent when looking at defaults from the B category over a 20 year period.

4.5 Markov Chains and Transition-Probability Estimation

Markov chains are the critical modeling tool whenever a discrete credit-rating system plays an important role in the problem formulation. The most prominent rating systems are of course those provided by the major rating agencies such as Moody's and Standard & Poor's, but in the risk-management process of banks, internal rating systems which classify the credit quality of borrowers and counterparties are equally important. The primary aim of these systems is to give a simple, yet accurate, assessment of the credit quality of borrowers, contract counterparties, issuers of guarantees, etc.

Understanding the behavior of both public ratings and internal rating systems involves studying migration dynamics. The most important goal is of course to

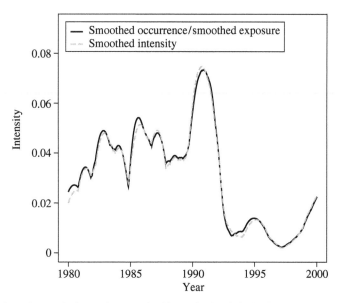

Figure 4.1. The graph shows the smoothed intensity for defaults from rating category B in the period between 1980 and 2000 using rating and default data from Moody's. The firms considered are US corporates. The bandwidth is 1.5 years, and both the version smoothing the intensity directly and the version computing a smoothed occurrence and dividing by a smoothed exposure are shown.

see how well the rating system predicts defaults and if the system is consistent in some sense. That is, if there is a stated goal with the ratings, can we see, based on historical behavior, that this goal seems to be satisfied. This question is of interest both to managers and to supervisors.

When analyzing rating histories, in practice one inevitably discovers non-Markov properties. Naturally, this leads one to consider whether the analysis using Markov chains is, in fact, the right framework to use. The key point here is that the Markov formulation serves as an important baseline case compared with which we formulate deviations. It is natural to investigate ratings for non-Markov properties by looking at the specific tests against a Markov hypothesis. One example is the mover–stayer analysis, which is essentially a model for a heterogeneous population consisting of two types: one type which moves according to a Markov process, and one which stays fixed. Another example tests whether the previous rating of a chain matters in determining the current migration out of a state. This can be analyzed by enlarging the state space into a pair of ratings in which one coordinate corresponds to the previous rating and the other coordinate is the current rating. The test is then whether or not the rating transition probabilities depend on the first coordinate of the state. Furthermore, a number of summary statistics which are informative turn out to be maximum-likelihood estimates under a Markov assumption. Knowing in which model a statistic is actually a maximum-likelihood estimate is important in understanding the statistic. Appendix C lays out the (very few) analytical tools for Markov chains that are needed for this section.

The most important aspect of this section is to illustrate the significant advantages obtained by estimating, whenever possible, the dynamics of a continuous-time chain instead of a discrete-time chain. The estimator based on continuously observed data is easy to implement and understand, it gives better estimates for rare event transitions, and it permits a simple bootstrapping procedure to determine approximate confidence sets for the transition probabilities for any time horizon. But before we can do this, we need to know the discrete-time story.

4.5.1 Estimation of Discrete-Time Markov Chains

Consider a sample of N firms whose transitions between different states are observed at discrete dates $t = 0, \ldots, T$. We assume that the transitions of different firms are independent.

Now introduce the following notation.

- $n_i(t)$ is the number of firms in state i at date t.
- $n_{ij}(t)$ is the number of firms which went from i at date $t - 1$ to j at date t.
- $N_i(T) = \sum_{t=0}^{T-1} n_i(t)$ is the total number of firm exposures recorded at the beginnings of the transition periods.
- $N_{ij}(T) = \sum_{t=1}^{T} n_{ij}(t)$ is the total number of transitions observed from i to j over the entire period.

We perform all of the analysis by conditioning on the initial state.

It is clear that the probability of observing a particular path $x_0, x_1, \ldots, x_T$ of one firm is

$$p_{x_0, x_1} p_{x_1, x_2} \cdots p_{x_{T-1}, x_T}.$$

Assuming that rating migrations are independent across firms, we get products of the individual likelihoods and hence the complete likelihood function takes the form

$$\prod_{(i,j)} p_{ij}^{N_{ij}(T)},$$

where of course $p_{ij}^0 = 1$. Therefore, the log-likelihood is

$$\sum_{(i,j)} N_{ij}(T) \log p_{ij}.$$

Since we have the restriction $\sum_{j=1}^{K} p_{ij} = 1$ for every i, we have to maximize

$$\sum_{(i,j)} N_{ij}(T) \log p_{ij} \quad \text{subject to} \quad \sum_{j=1}^{K} p_{ij} = 1.$$

Solving this is a standard Lagrange multiplier exercise and one arrives at

$$\hat{p}_{ij} = \frac{N_{ij}(T)}{N_i(T)}$$

for all $i, j \in K$.

Note the similarity with a multinomial estimator: we estimate the probability of going from i to j by counting the total number of exposures $N_i(T)$ in state i and computing the fraction of those which went to j. For this reason we will refer to this estimator as the multinomial estimator.

It is clear that by adding observations across time periods, this estimator implicitly uses an assumption of time-homogeneity. Why is it not exactly a multinomial estimator? The number of firm exposures $N_i(T)$ in each category is random. Hence the standard deviation of the estimator, which would be true if we counted N_i as being fixed, does not really hold here.

Note that if $N_i(T)$ was fixed, an estimate for the variance of our estimator would be

$$\sigma^2(\hat{p}_{ij}) = \frac{1}{N_i(T)} \hat{p}_{ij}(1 - \hat{p}_{ij}).$$

The importance of this homogeneous Markov specification is that it serves as a useful benchmark for testing various alternatives to this assumption, such as time variation and dependence on previous states.

4.5.2 A Mover–Stayer Model

The mover–stayer assumption is that the j-year transition matrix $P(0, j)$ has the form

$$P(0, j) = SI + (I - S)M^j,$$

where

- I is the $K \times K$ identity matrix,
- M is a transition matrix ($K \times K$ of course),
- $S = \text{diag}(s_1, \ldots, s_K)$, and
- s_i is the fraction of "stayers" in state i at time 0.

Note that as "movers" move in and out of state i, the proportion of firms in state i that are stayers changes. Following Frydman (1984), the maximum-likelihood estimators of M and S are as follows. To alleviate the notational burden, we omit T from our "counters" and let

$$N_i = N_i(T),$$
$$N_{ii} = N_{ii}(T).$$

Finally, we let n_i denote the number of firms which stay continuously in state i throughout the period, and we let $n_i(0)$ denote the number of firms in state i at time 0.

First, we set up an equation for m_{ii}:

$$[N_i - Tn_i(0)]m_{ii}^{T+1} + [Tn_i(0) - N_{ii}]m_{ii}^T + [Tn_i - N_i]m_{ii} + N_{ii} - Tn_i = 0.$$

The solution of this is $\hat{m}_{ii}$.

Now we get the off-diagonal elements by computing for the ith row starting with $k = 1$ (or $k = 2$ when $i = 1$) as follows:

$$\hat{m}_{ik} = \frac{n_{ik}(1 - \hat{m}_{ii} - \sum_{r=1, r\neq i}^{k-1} \hat{m}_{i,r})}{\sum_{r=k, r\neq i}^{k} n_{ir}}.$$

Hence this works through a row using the previous estimators in the recursion.

Finally, we obtain the MLE of s_i as

$$\hat{s}_i = \begin{cases} \dfrac{n_i - n_i(0)\hat{m}_{ii}^T}{n_i(0)(1 - \hat{m}_{ii}^T)} & \text{if } n_i - n_i(0)\hat{m}_{ii}^T > 0, \\ 0 & \text{otherwise.} \end{cases}$$

If T is large (or if we have many firms), we may approximate the MLE by

$$\hat{m}_{ii} = \frac{N_{ii} - Tn_i}{N_i - TN_i} \quad \text{and} \quad \hat{s}_i = \frac{N_i}{n_i(0)}$$

and then use the recursion above for the off-diagonal elements of M.

Note that $\hat{s}_i$ has a very natural interpretation. If a firm is a mover, it will eventually move away from any nondefault state and hence the fraction of remaining firms after T periods is a good estimate of the stayer fraction when T is large. With this in mind we can correct the estimate for the one-period probability of "staying in i" by subtracting out the stayers both from the occurrences and the exposures. This explains the $\hat{m}_{ii}$ estimate.

The mover–stayer analysis has proven useful for studying consumer credits where there seems to be a part of the population which is of "nondefaulting" type. One might contemplate using it as a diagnostic for internal rating systems, possibly as a way of checking whether the system is being carefully monitored or whether certain credits are "forgotten" possibly because they are small and therefore not carefully monitored. However, filtering out the stayers from the movers requires either a very large sample, or a long sampling period. If, for example, 10% of a population in a rating are expected to leave the class every year, then after 20 years we would still expect to see 12% of the initial population left in the state even when they were all movers.

4.5.3   Estimating the Generator of a Continuous-Time Chain

Most internal rating systems will of course reveal the date at which a rating transition occurs, and it is also possible to obtain the data from rating agencies. Using these data improves estimates significantly.

Assume that we have observed a collection of firms between time 0 and time T. To estimate the elements of the generator under an assumption of time-homogeneity we use the MLE (see, for example, Küchler and Sørensen 1997)

$$\hat{\lambda}_{ij} = \frac{N_{ij}(T)}{\int_0^T Y_i(s)\,\mathrm{d}s}, \tag{4.4}$$

where $Y_i(s)$ is the number of firms in rating class i at time s and $N_{ij}(T)$ is the total number of transitions over the period from i to j, where $i \neq j$. The interpretation of this estimator is straightforward: the numerator counts the number of observed transitions from i to j over the entire period of observation; the denominator has the number of "firm-years" spent in state i. Any period a firm spends in a state will be picked up through the denominator. In this sense all information is being used.

4.5.4   Estimates for Probabilities of Rare Transitions: a Simple Example

Now we illustrate the estimator both through a simple example and on our dataset. The simple example will explain the basic idea of the procedure. The application on our dataset will test the practical significance of using the continuous-time technique.

Consider a rating system consisting of two nondefault rating categories A and B and a default category D. Assume that we observe over 1 year the history of 20 firms, of which 10 start in category A and 10 in category B. Assume that over the year of observation, one A-rated firm changes its rating to category B after one month and stays there for the rest of the year. Assume that over the same period, one B-rated firm is upgraded after two months and remains in A for the rest of the period, and a firm which started in B defaults after six months and stays there for the remaining part of the period. In this case we have, for one of the entries,

$$\hat{\lambda}_{\mathrm{AB}} = \frac{N_{\mathrm{AB}}(1)}{\int_0^1 Y_{\mathrm{A}}(s)\,\mathrm{d}s} = \frac{1}{9 + \frac{1}{12} + \frac{10}{12}} = 0.100\,84.$$

Proceeding similarly with the other entries (and noting that the state D is assumed to be absorbing and that each diagonal element is minus the sum of the nondiagonal elements of the same row) we obtain the estimated generator

$$\hat{\Lambda} = \begin{pmatrix} -0.100\,84 & 0.100\,84 & 0 \\ 0.104\,35 & -0.208\,68 & 0.104\,35 \\ 0 & 0 & 0 \end{pmatrix}.$$

From this, we obtain the MLE of the 1-year transition matrix as

$$\widehat{P(1)} = \begin{pmatrix} 0.9087 & 0.086\,57 & 0.004\,75 \\ 0.0895 & 0.816\,07 & 0.094\,34 \\ 0 & 0 & 1 \end{pmatrix}.$$

Had we instead used a cohort method the result would have been

$$\widehat{P(1)} = \begin{pmatrix} 0.90 & 0.10 & 0 \\ 0.10 & 0.80 & 0.10 \\ 0 & 0 & 1 \end{pmatrix}.$$

As we see, the traditional method does not capture default risk in category A simply because there is no firm defaulting directly from A. Note that the continuous-time method produces a strictly positive estimator for default from A over 1 year despite the fact that no firm in the sample defaults in 1 year from A. This is appropriate because the probability of migrating to B and the probability of default from B are clearly both positive. As a side remark, note that in a classical cohort analysis the firm upgraded from B does not provide more information than the upgrade. Here, it matters exactly when the upgrade took place, and the six months spent in A with no further change contributes information to the estimate of the transition intensity from rating class A. In the next section we will use this method on real data from Moody's.

4.6 The Difference between Discrete and Continuous: an Example with Real Data

The example in the previous section was of course stylized, and it is interesting to see what difference the alternative techniques make on real data. The following gives an indication of how the discrete-time methods and the continuous-time methods work on Moody's data for US corporate issuers in the period 1997–2001. Based on these data, we estimate the generator using the MLE and get from this the 1-year transition-probability estimate based on the empirical generator. Now compare this with the estimator we would have obtained by using the multinomial, discrete-time estimator. The results are shown in Tables 4.2–4.4. There are two observations we will stress here.

- First, all zeros in the multinomial method are replaced by nonzeros when we use the exponential of the generator. For example, the probability of going from Aa to speculative grade is roughly 3 basis points in the continuous-time setting, whereas it is estimated to be 0 in the discrete-time case. But note that the sign is not unambiguous. The multinomial method has a larger probability of having an A-rated firm default within a year.

Table 4.1. The last years of the rating history of the Bethlehem Steel Corporation, which filed for Chapter 11 on 15 October 2001. This type of rating history illustrates the difference between a multinomial method and a generator method, as explained in the text.

Date	Rating
29 May 1998	Ba3
27 December 2000	B2
31 January 2001	Caa1
1 October 2001	Caa3
15 October 2001	Default
16 October 2001	Ca

- The second observation is the large difference between the 1-year default probability from Caa. This difference is caused by rating histories similar to that experienced by Bethlehem Steel corporation in 2000 and 2001. The history is shown in Table 4.1. The multinomial will only pick up a transition from B to default, and not capture the short period in Caa. The short stay in this low category of course contributes to a large intensity estimate.

The generator has an additional appealing feature, which should make its calculation useful to risk managers. It shows the type of direct transitions that took place in the period. Zeros in the generator means that no direct transition between the relevant states has been observed. We note that transitions more than two categories away are rare.

4.6.1 Confidence Sets for Default Probabilities in Rating Models

Using the estimate of the generator is convenient not only for obtaining estimates of probabilities of rare events but also for getting meaningful confidence sets. The trouble with obtaining meaningful confidence sets can be understood as follows: if someone throws a coin 10 times and obtains 0 heads, the maximum-likelihood estimator for the probability of obtaining heads is 0. We may obtain a confidence set for the estimate by asking how high p (the probability of obtaining heads) could be without us being able to reject it (at the 5% level, for example) based on the outcome that we observed. We are able to compute this limit explicitly in this example. However, in the problem we are interested in, namely looking at rare transitions, there are many parameters and we are not able to simply formulate a confidence set for our parameter of interest. When this is the case, one often resorts to asymptotic methods, using the approximating limiting normal distribution to build confidence sets. But since we are by definition mainly interested in the rare events, asymptotics is bound to fail here. We therefore choose to use bootstrap methods instead of building (one-dimensional) confidence sets for 1-year transition probabilities.

Table 4.2. The generator estimated for the senior unsecured US issuers in the Moody's database for the period 1 January 1997 to 31 December 2001.

	Aaa	Aa	A	Baa	Ba	B	Caa	D
Aaa	−0.116 959	0.096 319	0.020 640	0	0	0	0	0
Aa	0.014 020	−0.116 165	0.100 142	0.002 003	0	0	0	0
A	0.002 781	0.042 825	−0.148 496	0.100 666	0.002 225	0	0	0
Baa	0.001 090	0.002 180	0.068 131	−0.165 150	0.085 573	0.005 996	0.001 635	0.000 545
Ba	0	0	0.006 767	0.143 236	−0.278 577	0.121 807	0.003 384	0.003 384
B	0	0.001 023	0.003 070	0.015 349	0.065 489	−0.317 213	0.207 724	0.024 558
Caa	0	0	0	0	0	0.043 140	−0.471 457	0.428 317
D	0	0	0	0	0	0	0	0

Table 4.3. The estimated 1-year transition-probability matrix $P = \exp(\Lambda^*)$ based on the generator estimated for the period 1997–2001 for the US data.

	Aaa	Aa	A	Baa	Ba	B	Caa	D
Aaa	0.890 255	0.086 193	0.022 366	0.001 129	0.000 052 4	0.000 003 82	0.000 000 773	0.000 000 359
Aa	0.012 615	0.892 832	0.088 104	0.006 133	0.000 286	0.000 023 4	0.000 004 95	0.000 002 36
A	0.002 753	0.037 812	0.866 873	0.086 560	0.005 360	0.000 493	0.000 100	0.000 050 0 0
Baa	0.001 052	0.003 225	0.058 826	0.855 795	0.069 110	0.008 832	0.002 029	0.001 131
Ba	0.000 078 8	0.000 365	0.009 686	0.116 332	0.764 724	0.091 264	0.011 344	0.006 206
B	0.000 001 89	0.000 909	0.003 175	0.015 930	0.049 378	0.734 295	0.140 670	0.055 625
Caa	0.000 000 245	0.000 001 74	0.000 058 2	0.000 294	0.001 000	0.029 196	0.627 044	0.342 391
D	0	0	0	0	0	0	0	1

Table 4.4. The 1-year transition probabilities for the period 1 January 1997 to 31 December 2001 estimated by the multinomial method.

	Aaa	Aa	A	Baa	Ba	B	Caa	D
Aaa	0.841772	0.088608	0.012658	0	0	0	0	0
Aa	0.005874	0.888399	0.070485	0.002937	0	0	0	0
A	0.002165	0.028571	0.864502	0.063636	0.003896	0.001299	0.001299	0.000433
Baa	0.001596	0.001197	0.042282	0.861588	0.042282	0.008775	0.001596	0.001994
Ba	0	0	0.004061	0.104569	0.699492	0.061929	0.006091	0.006091
B	0	0.000804	0.000804	0.008039	0.040193	0.713826	0.097267	0.062701
Caa	0	0	0	0	0	0.029255	0.667553	0.210106

We proceed along the lines of what is often called a parametric bootstrap as follows.

(1) Estimate Λ from our sample of issuers over a chosen time horizon (5 years, say). Call this estimate Λ^*.

(2) Simulate a large number of 5-year histories for the same number of issuers in each rating category using Λ^* as the data-generating parameter.

(3) For each history, compute the estimator $\hat{\Lambda}^*$ and $\exp(\hat{\Lambda}^*)$.

(4) For the parameter of interest (such as a particular default probability), compute the relevant quantiles.

For a given parameter, this gives us a confidence set for that parameter. If we use 95% as our confidence set, we could expect to see 95% of our estimates of that parameter in the confidence interval. Of course, this only holds "marginally." It would of course be extremely rare to see all parameters outside their confidence sets at once. But it is very difficult to report simultaneous confidence intervals for high-dimensional parameter sets. The confidence sets thus obtained are actually too narrow in that they do not take into account the variation in Λ^*. (They are based only on data simulated using Λ^* as the true generator.)

Note that we would have been unable to bootstrap the cohort estimators, since the parameter estimates that are 0 will produce 0 occurrences in the simulated histories as well. Simulating 5-year histories based on a generator (estimated from the data) produces very different distributions for the cohort estimator than would be obtained from a simulation based on the multinomial estimator. In Figure 4.2 we show an example of bootstrapped confidence sets where the histories have been simulated using the generator.

4.7 A Word of Warning on the Markov Assumption

The generator estimator we have applied to the data is more efficient in that it uses all available information. But one should note at the same time that the interpretation of the output depends on the Markov assumption. There are several reasons why the Markov assumption is difficult to maintain in practice. First, business cycles have an effect on rating transitions as documented, for example, in Nickell et al. (2000). Such effects do not rule out that transitions could be Markovian after conditioning on the state variables, but of course time-homogeneity is certainly too much to hope for over different cycles. Based on a shorter time span of data, it may be a good local approximation. Second, it is a stated objective of the rating agencies to seek estimates which are "through-the-cycle" and hence try to separate changes in conditions with long-term implications from changes that are deemed temporary. This could also have an effect on the Markov property. Third, there is a reluctance in

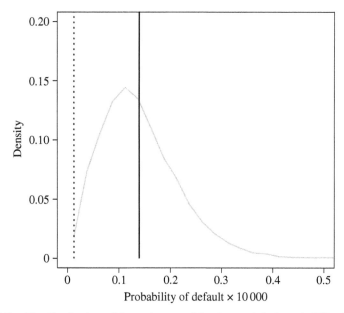

Figure 4.2. The distribution of the estimator of the 1-year default probability for rating category A using cohort analysis and using the exponentiated generator. The estimate of the generator is based on a 5-year dataset. The "true value" is the 1-year transition probability obtained by exponentiating the estimated generator. The distribution based on 25.000 simulations of 5-year histories is seen to be reasonable around the value for the simulated generator, whereas the cohort estimator is 0 for most samples (94%) and roughly 0.005 (outside the graph) for the remaining cases. (Solid black line, the "true" 1-year default probability; solid grey line, 1-year default probability estimate from generator simulation; dotted black line, 1-year default probability estimate from cohort simulation.)

the rating agencies both to multi-notch downgrades and to rating reversals. Both have a tendency to make the rating process deviate from the Markovian case. Imagine, for example, that the condition of a firm has deteriorated drastically. A reluctance towards multi-notch downgrades then leads to successive downgrades with shorter holding times in the intermediate states than the typical firms in these classes.

The average intensities over a 25-sample period for US corporates rated by Moody's illustrate the non-Markov effects at play here. Consider, for example, as shown in Figures 4.3 and 4.4, the smoothed upgrade and downgrade intensities from the class Baa1 over the entire period. The intensities are estimated as functions of time spent in a state and, more notably, divided into strata according to whether Baa1 was reached through a downgrade or an upgrade.

As evidenced by the graphs, there is a significant momentum effect both for downgrades and for upgrades. The firms which are downgraded into Baa1 have an upgrade intensity which is roughly six times smaller than that of firms which were

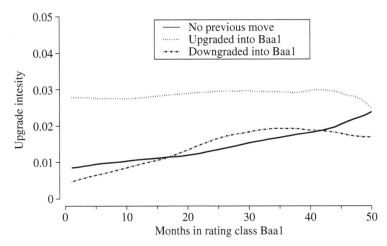

Figure 4.3. Smoothed upgrade intensities from Baa1 as a function of time in state and for different entries into the class. The no-information case typically covers cases where Baa1 is the first recorded rating class.

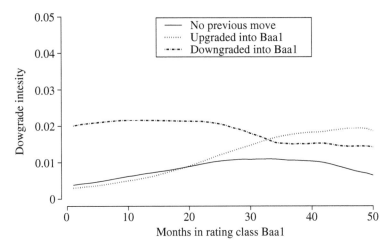

Figure 4.4. Smoothed downgrade intensities from Baa1 as a function of time spent in the state and for different entries into the class. The no-information case typically covers cases where Baa1 is the first recorded rating class.

upgraded into the class. This effect seems to persist for very long periods of time. The downgrade intensity is also much higher for firms downgraded into Baa1 than for firms upgraded into the class, but the tendency is slightly less persistent from a rough inspection.

Inspired by these graphs, we present a simple illustration of how the generator estimator may perform poorly at assessing a default probability if the Markov assumption is violated. We consider a sample of 100 firms initially rated A and 100 firms initially rated B, and we work only with these two "official" nonde-fault categories. In the specification of the evolution, however, we add an "excited" state B* which firms enter into when downgraded into the B rating. We think of this excited state as having a larger default intensity and a smaller upgrade intensity than the "normal" state. Firms may, however, after a certain period become "normalized" and move to category B. In the real world we would look for the indicator "on review for further downgrade" as a way of distinguishing between the two categories B and B*. If the transition is not observed, we are facing an estimation problem involving a "hidden" Markov chain. For the point of this example, we compare the statistical analysis performed by not distinguishing between the two B classes with the one where the two are being recorded as separate states. Clearly, the first case will serve as the case with a violation of the Markov property, which is a consequence of the collapsing of two states in the richer state space.

Assume that we follow the histories of the firms for 2 years. The firms which experience rating changes have their histories listed in Table 4.5. The firms listed A1–A10 are firms which start in rating class A and the firms B1–B15 start in B. A1, for example, then jumps to B* after two months and it stays in this new category for 21 months before falling back to the "normal" B state. We now compare the 1-year transition estimates based on the continuous-time estimator with the classical multinomial estimator, both in the Markovian case, where the full state space is observed, and in the non-Markovian-case, where only the unstarred categories are observed.. For the sake of clarity we list the matrices as tables so that we can keep track of the varying state space. First, we estimate the generator matrix and find the result shown in Table 4.6. We then take the exponential of this matrix to obtain the continuous-time estimate of the 1-year transition probabilities. The result is reported in Table 4.7. Note the very small (0.08%) probability of default from A. Now look at the multinomial estimator, which only sees the states at the beginning and the end of the year. This estimator is shown in Table 4.8. This estimate captures the firms which experienced a downgrade to the B category and then (as part of the momentum effect) continued down to default. Therefore it obtains a much higher default probability of about 0.50% from the category A. This effect is not captured by the generator, since after a firm is downgraded into B it becomes part of the overall mass of B-rated firms, and its contribution to the default rate from B is diluted by the large population of B-rated firms with no momentum towards the default state.

If we add the excited state B* thus transforming it into a Markovian system, the generator estimator regains its advantage. In this case we obtain the estimate of the generator shown in Table 4.9 and this gives us the estimate of the 1-year transition probabilities listed in Table 4.10. Now compare this with the multinomial estimator, which gives us Table 4.11.

Table 4.5. Stylized examples of rating histories of firms which change rating during a 2-year period. The remaining 90 A-rated firms and 85 B-rated firms stay in their initial category throughout the period.

Firm	Time in state	New state	Time in state	New state	Time in state
A1	1	B*	2	B	21
A2	3	B*	3	B	18
A3	5	B*	4	B	15
A4	7	B*	1	B	16
A5	9	B*	4	D	—
A6	11	B*	13	—	—
A7	13	B*	5	B	6
A8	15	B*	8	D	—
A9	17	B*	3	B	4
A10	19	B*	5	—	—
B1	3	D	—	—	—
B2	6	D	—	—	—
B3	9	D	—	—	—
B4	15	D	—	—	—
B5	18	D	—	—	—
B6	1	A	23	—	—
B7	3	A	21	—	—
B8	5	A	19	—	—
B9	6	A	18	—	—
B10	8	A	16	—	—
B11	9	A	15	—	—
B12	14	A	10	—	—
B13	15	A	9	—	—
B14	16	A	8	—	—
B15	18	A	6	—	—

Table 4.6. The estimator of the generator disregarding the excited state.

State	A	B	D
A	−0.0499	0.0499	0
B	0.0519	−0.0882	0.0363
D	0	0	0

Focusing again on the probability of default, the generator-based estimate is roughly eight times larger than the one obtained when leaving out the excited state, and it is about 60% larger than the discrete-time estimator, which includes the excited state. The reliable performance of the cohort estimator in the non-Markov case is

Table 4.7. The 1-year transition probabilities obtained by
exponentiating the generator in Table 4.6.

State	A	B	D
A	0.9525	0.0466	0.0009
B	0.048	0.918	0.0344
D	0	0	1

Table 4.8. The estimate of the 1-year transition probabilities using the
multinomial estimator and still disregarding the excited state.

State	A	B	D
A	0.95	0.045	0.005
B	0.0508	0.9184	0.0305
D	0	0	1

Table 4.9. The estimate of the generator including the excited state.

State	A	B	B*	D
A	−0.0499	0.0499	0	0
B*	0	−2	1.5	0.5
B	0.0530	0	−0.0794	0.0265
D	0	0	0	0

partly due to the fact that in this example it is fortunate to actually capture a default
within a year of an initially A-rated firm.

Understanding the mechanics of this example allows one to understand the huge
discrepancies between default probabilities from junk categories like Caa or B estimated by the different methods.

4.8 Ordered Probits and Ratings

The estimation of transition probabilities directly using hazard-rate regressions on
transition intensities is a powerful tool for analysis. There is another method, the
ordered probit method, which we will mention here since that has also been used
for analyzing changes in rating regimes. To understand the ordered probit analysis,
consider first a probit analysis involving two rating classes numbered 0 and 1. We
can think of 0 as default and 1 as no default. A variable z_i, which we can naturally
think of as the log-asset value, determines whether firm i is in default or not. We do
not, however, observe this value. We do, however, observe a variable (which can be

Table 4.10. The estimate of the 1-year transition probabilities obtained by exponentiating the generator estimate.

State	A	B	B*	D
A	0.952	0.021	0.0202	0.0071
B*	0.0215	0.1356	0.6158	0.2271
B	0.0496	0.0007	0.924	0.0256
D	0	0	0	1

Table 4.11. The estimate of the 1-year transition probabilities obtained by the multinomial discrete-time method.

State	A	B	B*	D
A	0.95	0.015	0.03	0.005
B*	0	0.5	0	0.5
B	0.0513	0	0.923 08	0.0256
D	0	0	0	1

a vector) x_i which is related to the unobserved z_i:

$$z_i = \alpha + \beta x_i + \epsilon_i,$$

where α, β are constants and ϵ_i is a random normal variable with mean 0 and variance σ^2. We also observe the rating η^i of the firm, which is related to an unobserved threshold z_0, so that

$$\eta^i = \begin{cases} 1 & \text{if } z_i > z_0, \\ 0 & \text{if } z_i \leqslant z_0. \end{cases}$$

It is easy to check that

$$P(\eta^i = 1) = P(z_i > z_0)$$
$$= \Phi\left(\frac{\alpha - z_0}{\sigma} + \frac{\beta}{\sigma} x_i\right),$$

and we see that we cannot hope to identify more than two parameters

$$\alpha' = \frac{\alpha - z_0}{\sigma} \quad \text{and} \quad \beta' = \frac{\beta}{\sigma},$$

i.e. we arrive at the probit model

$$P(\eta^i = 1) = \Phi(\alpha' + \beta' x_i).$$

Note the similarity between α' and a distance-to-default measure. The ordered probit method is a direct extension of this model to several categories, so that instead of two rating levels we have K levels and hence $K - 1$ thresholds, $z_1, \ldots, z_{K-1}$, and

$$P(\eta^i = 0) = \Phi(\beta' x_i),$$
$$P(\eta^i = 1) = \Phi(z_1 + \beta' x_i) - \Phi(\beta' x_i),$$
$$\vdots$$
$$P(\eta^i = K) = 1 - \Phi(z_{K-1} + \beta' x_i)$$

employed, for example, in Nickell et al. (2000) and Blume et al. (1998). Both the thresholds and the regression coefficients β have to be estimated.

4.9 Cumulative Accuracy Profiles

An important step in all statistical modeling is to use misspecification tests to see if the proposed model seems reasonable. If the data do not seem to fit the model or satisfy the model assumptions, we cannot believe the tests. The literature on this is of course an integral part of the literature on the various statistical techniques described above, and we will not attempt to review it here.

A much harder problem in statistics is to compare models which are not nested, so that we cannot test one against the other. How would one, for example, compare a logistic regression model to a continuous-time survival analysis model? An obvious answer is to compare the predictions made by the models. A typical procedure is to estimate the parameters of each model on one-half (say) of the data, and then see how they perform on the remaining half. This still leaves the question of how we compare the quality of the predictions. A tool for doing this is the so-called cumulative accuracy profile, which we now discuss.

A credit risk model produces an estimate of the default risk of a firm. The estimate may be a probability of default or some measure of distance to default (like KMV's distance-to-default or Altman's Z-score) which ranks the firms according to their default risk. A cumulative accuracy profile compares the performance of the different rankings produced by the models, on a single data set. Assume that every firm in a sample has been given a score at the beginning of the observation period and assume that a low score means a high risk of default. We then record whether the firms in our sample defaulted or not over the observation period. The cumulative accuracy profile is constructed as follows. For $x \in [0, 1]$, let $c(x)$ denote the fraction of the defaulted firms whose risk score placed them in the lowest x percentile of issuers among *all* issuers. In other words, if $c(0.1) = 0.5$, it means that half of the defaults in the sample occurred among the 10% of the firms deemed by the risk score to be the most risky.

If we knew precisely the identity of the firms which default, we would rank them to be the most risky and the CAP curve would then display perfect foresight. In this case, if a fraction p of firms defaulted in the total population, we would have $c(p) = 1$, since all the defaulted firms then occupied the lowest p percentile of scores. At the other extreme is a case in which a score, completely unrelated to default risk, is assigned to the firms. If the sample of firms is large, the CAP curve will then be close to the 45° line. Note that this only holds true for the case with many firms. For small samples we could have CAP curves below the 45° line. With reasonable sample sizes and a reasonable model, this should not be a problem.

Another important feature to note for the CAP plot is that the performance of a model is intimately linked to the initial distribution of issuers. If the issuers are close in characteristics, it will be hard—even for the best model—to separate. Hence it only makes sense to compare CAP curves for different models on the same sample. The deviation from the 45° line is not only a function of the model's ability to separate but also on the composition of the firms' characteristics, i.e. the quality of the sample. We end this chapter with an illustration of this point.

Assume that a model correctly assigns a default probability of $p(x)$ to a firm whose score is x, and assume that the distribution of firm scores in the sample is given by a density function $f(x)$. Assume without loss of generality that 0 is the lowest possible score. We think of the sample size as being very large, so that the fraction of firms with characteristics in the interval $[x, x + dx]$ is given by (or very well approximated by) $f(x) \, dx$. Let $y(x)$ denote the x percentile of the risk score, meaning that a fraction x of the firms have risk scores below $y(x)$. The CAP curve will now be given as follows (still assuming a very large sample):

$$c(x) = \frac{\int_0^{y(x)} p(x) f(x) \, dx}{\int_0^{\infty} p(x) f(x) \, dx}.$$

The denominator counts the fraction of the total population of firms which default, the numerator counts the fraction of the total population which default starting from a risk score in the lowest x percentile. In Figure 4.5 we illustrate the significance of the assumptions that we make about the distribution $f(x)$. We do this by choosing the default probability $p(x)$ to be the probability that a geometric Brownian motion, starting at level $100 + \Delta V$, hits the level 100 within 1 year. The drift is chosen to be 0.1 and the volatility is 0.2. Since all firms have the same volatility, we can think of ΔV as a measure of distance to default. We now compare two distributions of initial distance: one is a uniform distribution on the interval $[10, 150]$ and the other is a less-dispersed uniform distribution on the interval $[24.1, 64.1]$. As we see, the large sample CAP curve for the more-dispersed population is much higher than that for the less-dispersed population. Hence one needs to be careful comparing CAP curves across populations. For more on model validation, see Sobehart et al. (2000).

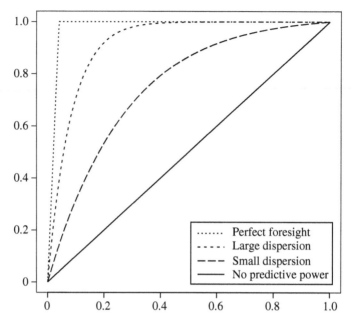

Figure 4.5. The graphs illustrate the effect of the dispersion of credit scores for the cumulative accuracy profiles. The model considered views the distance of the firm value to a default boundary as the credit score. The firm value is assumed to follow a geometric Brownian motion with a volatility of 0.2 and a drift equal to 0.1. In the large-dispersion case, the initial sample of firms is assumed to have a uniform distribution of credit scores on the interval [10, 150], signifying starting values of the firm value ranging from 110 to 250 and a default boundary at 100. The small-dispersion case uses a uniform distribution on the interval [24.1, 64.1] set to make the total default frequency of both populations roughly equal to 4.1%. We show the CAP curve one would obtain with very large samples in the two cases. Also shown are the perfect foresight curve corresponding to a default frequency of 4.1% and the curve one would obtain for a model with no predictive power.

4.10 Bibliographical Notes

The works of Beaver (1966) and Altman (1968) were among the first to study the power of financial ratios in predicting defaults. Altman (1968) employs a discriminant analysis which continues to be applied in financial institutions. The power of modern-day computing has moved empirical studies towards logistic regression or hazard regressions, which is a more natural framework for formulating the default probability as a function of key ratios. I learned about the connection between logistic regression and discriminant analysis from Efron (1975) and Anderson (1984). An extensive study using logistic regression can be found in Bernhardsen (2001).

For examples of the use of hazard regressions, see Shumway (2001) and Hillegeist et al. (2002). Also, the modern techniques of survival analysis seem ideally suited for studying default probabilities and default intensities dynamically. An overview with a very detailed reference list can be found in Andersen et al. (1993). The smoothed intensity (4.3) in Section 4.5 was proposed by Ramlau-Hansen (1983) and the robustness issue is dealt with in Nielsen and Tanggaard (2001).

The statistical analysis of rating migrations has a long history as well. For example, the issue of rating drift is studied in Altman and Kao (1992a,b) and Fons and Kimball (1991), although some of the definitions of drift should be modified as discussed in Lando and Skødeberg (2002) and Skødeberg (1998). The cyclicality and sensitivity of ratings to business-cycle indicators is discussed in Lucas and Lonski (1992), Nickell et al. (2000), and Bangia et al. (2002), and theoretical explanations for non-Markov effects are addressed in Löffler (2002, 2003). Nonparametric analysis of non-Markov effects is carried out in Fledelius et al. (2004) and the significance of non-Markov effects for default probabilities and their confidence sets is analyzed in Christensen et al. (2004). For a study on the role of watchlists and outlooks in reducing non-Markov effects, see Cantor and Hamilton (2004). The mover–stayer analysis is based on Frydman et al. (1985).

For monographs on survival analysis, see, for example, Cox and Oakes (1984) and Andersen et al. (1993). Ordered probits are used in Nickell et al. (2000), discussing sensitivity of rating transitions to business-cycle indicators, and in Blume et al. (1998), discussing whether rating agencies became stricter in the 1990s.

Some examples of default studies are Fons and Kimball (1991), Fons et al. (1991), and Carty (1997). For practical issues of ratings and capital adequacy, see Carey and Treacy (2000) and Carey and Hrycay (2001).

5

Intensity Modeling

In the option-based models studied so far, the default event is defined in terms of the process modeling the assets of an issuer. Default is triggered when assets, or some function thereof, hit (or fall below) some boundary. We now move to a different class of models, the intensity models, which model factors influencing the default event but typically (but not necessarily) leave aside the question of what exactly triggers the default event.

There are two main reasons why intensity models are important in the study of default risk. First, intensity models clearly seem to be the most elegant way of bridging the gap between credit scoring or default prediction models and the models for pricing default risk. If we want to incorporate into our pricing models not only the firm's asset value but other relevant predictors of default, we could turn to the default prediction models and ask which covariates are relevant for predicting default. To turn this into a pricing model we need to understand the dynamic evolution of the covariates and how they influence default probabilities. The natural framework for doing this is the intensity-based models which link hazard regressions with standard pricing machinery.

Second, the mathematical machinery of intensity models brings into play the entire machinery of default-free term-structure modeling. This means that econometric specifications from term-structure modeling and tricks for pricing derivatives can be transferred to defaultable claims. Furthermore, some claims, such as basket default swaps, whose equivalent is not readily found in ordinary term-structure modeling, also turn out to be conveniently handled in this setting.

In ordinary term-structure modeling, our ignorance of what truly governs the dynamics of interest rates is often hidden in an "exogenous" specification of (say) the short rate. This use of exogenous specifications will be transferred into the default-risk setting, where most models use exogenously given specifications of the intensity of default. The mathematical structure for ordinary term-structure modeling easily allows, however, for the short rate to depend on multidimensional state variable processes and even to depend on observable state variable processes. It is mainly the trouble of specifying good models for this dependence which forces us to use exogenous specifications. In this category we include specifications that use observable quantities (such as yields and volatilities) from the structure that we are trying to model as state variables. The same then becomes true of intensity models of default. As our knowledge of good predictors of default improves, we can hope to build better models for credit spreads and default intensities which do not just rely on exogenous specifications of the default, but actually include more fundamental variables. There are not many models around (yet) which do that convincingly. The machinery of this section should be useful for trying to build such models.

Having stressed the similarity between ordinary term-structure modeling and the modeling of defaultable bonds, it is important to understand the differences as well. The two most important differences are the specifications of risk premiums and the recovery assumptions. The reason for the similarity between the price of a default-free bond and a defaultable bond in an intensity model is the similarity between the expected value of the discount factor and the survival probability. However, because the default intensity is linked to a jump process (which the short rate is not), there is a richer set of risk premiums, so by using only the specification of risk premiums that works for short-rate models, one is leaving out the important notion of event risk, which must be addressed. Understanding the structure of risk premiums is important if we ultimately want to link the default prediction models with pricing models. If we estimate a hazard function which links certain dynamic covariates with default probabilities and we specify the dynamic evolution of the covariates, when is it the case that the empirically estimated hazard function can be used for pricing, possibly adjusting for risk premiums in the covariates? This is an important question for any attempt to infer default probabilities from observed prices.

A second important difference between defaultable bond pricing and treasury-bond pricing is the fact that recovery assumptions enter prominently into the pricing of defaultable bonds. We will spend some time studying the role of different recovery assumptions.

The presentation of intensity models will focus almost exclusively on the construction using a setting of doubly stochastic Poisson processes or Cox processes. While this is not the most general setting, it is by far the most convenient to work with in practical pricing problems.

There is of course some loss of generality using defaults modeled as Cox processes, and this loss of generality is mainly apparent when modeling multiple defaults by the same firm or defaults of strongly interlinked companies. We will see an example of how this loss of generality manifests itself. As will be argued in Chapter 9, a simultaneous strong change in a common state variable controlling default intensities of several firms can induce high levels of interdependence even while preserving the structure of Cox processes. Hence, for practical modeling purposes the machinery of this chapter will take the modeler a long way towards constructing realistic models that are analytically tractable.

From a modeling perspective, one may wonder if the analytical tractability of intensity models comes at too high a price, namely by giving up the explicit description of default as the first hitting time of a firm's asset value. We will see that in fact intensity models arise naturally in a structural model if we add the realistic feature that the asset value or the distance of the asset value to the default boundary cannot be observed perfectly. This simple complication has the additional advantage that variables correlated with asset value have predictive ability simply by virtue of being correlated with the true value. Hence even in models where perfect observation of the asset value would make the asset value a sufficient predictor of default, the imperfect information causes additional variables to increase our predictive ability.

5.1 What Is an Intensity Model?

To better understand what the intensity model tries to achieve, let us briefly recall the notion of a hazard rate and its link to conditional default probabilities.

Let τ be a positive random variable whose distribution can be described in terms of a hazard function h, i.e.

$$P(\tau > t) = \exp\left(-\int_0^t h(s)\,ds\right).$$

Then, as noted in Section 4.4,

$$\lim_{\Delta t \downarrow 0} \frac{1}{\Delta t} P(\tau \leqslant t + \Delta t \mid \tau > t) = h(t),$$

so $h(t)\Delta t$ is approximately the conditional probability of a default in a small interval after t given survival up to and including t. Note that this is a conditional default probability which we can compute for all t at time 0, since the only reason that this conditional default probability changes with t is the passing of time itself.

In real modeling situations there are factors other than the passing of time which affect the default probability of a firm that has managed to survive up to time t. If the firm survives between time 0 and time t, we normally have access to information at time t which is not available at time 0. Hence we want to be able to build models in which we can condition on a more general information set $\mathcal{F}_t$ so that, loosely speaking,

$$P(\tau \leqslant t + \Delta t \mid \mathcal{F}_t) \approx 1_{\{\tau > t\}} \lambda(t)\Delta t, \tag{5.1}$$

where $\mathcal{F}_t$ contains information on the survival up to time t and λ is a process which is adapted to (in fact predictable with respect to) the filtration $\mathbb{F}$. The problem, of course, is that this loosely formulated desire does not serve as a definition and it is therefore impossible to build rules of computation on it. We therefore need to turn to a more technical definition.

5.2 The Cox Process Construction of a Single Jump Time

The construction we will be using throughout is well known from the theory of stochastic processes under the name of "Cox processes" or "doubly stochastic Poisson processes." This construction obtains an intensity of default which is governed by "exogenous" state variables.

We assume, from now on, that a probability space $(\Omega, \mathcal{F}, Q)$ is given. It is convenient to think of Q as a pricing measure, i.e. a risk-neutral (or martingale) measure which exists in an arbitrage-free economy. All securities are then priced as expected discounted values under this measure. The particular choice of Q depends among other things on our assumptions on risk premiums, but in practical modeling the structure of risk premiums is almost always chosen so that we arrive at the structure presented in this chapter. Until we discuss the structure of risk premiums, where we explicitly need to distinguish between the physical measure P and the pricing measure Q, the expectations we compute are under the measure Q.

A process X of state variables with values in $\mathbb{R}^d$ is defined on the probability space. Let $\lambda : \mathbb{R}^d \longrightarrow R$ be a nonnegative (measurable) function. The goal is to construct a jump process N_t with the property that $\lambda(X_t)$ is the $\mathcal{F}_t$-intensity of N. We focus only on the first jump time τ of this process. Let $(\mathcal{G}_t)_{t \geqslant 0}$ denote the filtration generated by X, i.e. $\mathcal{G}_t = \sigma\{X_s; 0 \leqslant s \leqslant t\}$. Let E_1 be an exponential random variable with mean 1, which is independent of $(\mathcal{G}_t)_{t \geqslant 0}$.

Let $\mathcal{F}_t = \mathcal{G}_t \vee \mathcal{H}_t$, where $\mathcal{H}_t = \sigma\{N_s; 0 \leqslant s \leqslant t\}$, i.e. $\mathcal{F}_t$ contains the information in both X and the jump process. Define

$$\tau = \inf \left\{ t : \int_0^t \lambda(X_s)\, ds \geqslant E_1 \right\}.$$

As we will see in the following section, this definition of the default time τ will capture the idea that $\lambda(X)$ is a stochastic (pre-default) intensity for the jump time τ. The workable definition of this is that $1_{\{\tau \leqslant t\}} - \int_0^t \lambda(X_s) 1_{\{\tau \geqslant s\}}\, ds$ is an $\mathcal{F}_t$-martingale. We will show this in the next section along with some other useful computational results. Before these more technical results, however, we explain why the construction is so useful.

Consider a zero-coupon bond issued by a risky firm at time 0. Assume that the maturity of the bond is T and that under the risk-neutral probability measure Q, the default time τ of the issuing firm has an intensity $\lambda(X_t)$, where the setup is precisely as above. Assume also that there is a short-rate process $r(X_s)$ such that default-free zero-coupon bond prices can be computed as

$$p(0, t) = E \exp \left(-\int_0^t r(X_s)\, ds \right),$$

where t is the maturity date of the bond. (More generally, of course, $p(t, T) = E(\exp(-\int_t^T r(X_s)\, ds) \mid \mathcal{F}_t)$.) The price of the risky bond at time 0 is then, assuming zero recovery,

$$
\begin{aligned}
v(0, t) &= E\left[\exp\left(-\int_0^T r(X_s)\,ds \right) 1_{\{\tau > T\}} \right] \\
&= E\left[E\left[\exp\left(-\int_0^T r(X_s)\,ds \right) 1_{\{\tau > T\}} \,\middle|\, \mathcal{G}_T \right] \right] \\
&= E\left[\exp\left(-\int_0^T r(X_s)\,ds \right) E[1_{\{\tau > T\}} \mid \mathcal{G}_T] \right] \\
&= E\left[\exp\left(-\int_0^T r(X_s)\,ds \right) \exp\left(-\int_0^T \lambda(X_s)\,ds \right) \right] \\
&= E\left[\exp\left(-\int_0^T (r + \lambda)(X_s)\,ds \right) \right],
\end{aligned}
$$

i.e. the short rate has been replaced by the intensity-adjusted short rate $(r + \lambda)(X_s)$. To see that $E[1_{\{\tau > T\}} \mid \mathcal{G}_T] = \exp(-\int_0^T \lambda(X_s)\,ds)$ note that

$$
\begin{aligned}
Q(\tau > T \mid \mathcal{G}_T) &= Q\left(\int_0^T \lambda(X_s)\,ds < E_1 \,\middle|\, \mathcal{G}_T \right) \\
&= \exp\left(-\int_0^T \lambda(X_s)\,ds \right)
\end{aligned}
$$

because, when $\mathcal{G}_T$ is known, so is $\int_0^T \lambda(X_s)\,ds$; and because E_1 is independent of $\mathcal{G}_T$.

The example can easily be modified to cover a contingent claim with a *promised* payment of $f(X_T)$ and an *actual* payment of $f(X_T)1_{\{\tau > T\}}$. The key simplification that we obtain is that we replace the complicated random variable $f(X_T)1_{\{\tau > T\}}$ in our valuation formula with the often much simpler $f(X_T)$ at the cost of modifying the short rate. This simple example shows that the framework obviously holds promise for getting analytically tractable prices of defaultable contingent claims.

To make the framework operational, we need to settle the following three technical issues.

(1) Check that the construction really does make λ a stochastic (pre-default) intensity.

(2) Extend the result to a dynamic version, which updates the information as time proceeds.

(3) Extend the method to other types of promised payments.

To solve these issues, we need some technical results first.

5.3   A Few Useful Technical Results

This section provides a useful tool for showing the general expressions for the price of the derivatives examined above. The setting is exactly as in Section 5.2. We have already derived the fundamental identity

$$Q(\tau > t) = E \exp\left(- \int_0^t \lambda(X_s)\, ds \right), \tag{5.2}$$

which can be obtained by simple conditioning. But we also want to handle conditional expectations of relevant functions at arbitrary dates. If we are standing at time t and τ has not yet occurred, then the probability of default before $T > t$ is a function of the state variables, and hence $\mathcal{G}_t$ contains all the information we need.

A formal statement of this is as follows. Let $Z \in \mathcal{F}$ and (to make sure the conditional expectations exist) assume $E|Z| < \infty$. Then there exists a $\mathcal{G}_t$-measurable random variable Y_t such that

$$1_{\{\tau>t\}} E[Z \mid \mathcal{F}_t] = 1_{\{\tau>t\}} Y_t.$$

We will not give a proof here. From this one can show that

$$1_{\{\tau>t\}} E[Z \mid \mathcal{F}_t] = 1_{\{\tau>t\}} \frac{E[Z 1_{\{\tau>t\}} \mid \mathcal{G}_t]}{E[1_{\{\tau>t\}} \mid \mathcal{G}_t]}, \tag{5.3}$$

replacing again the total history $\mathcal{F}$ with the history of the state variable process.

The technical result (5.3) is the essential ingredient of the proofs, and we start by looking at dynamic versions of the survival probability in (5.2).

5.3.1   Dynamic Survival Probabilities

To get a dynamic version of (5.2) we proceed as follows: first note that

$$Q(\tau > T \mid \mathcal{F}_t) = 1_{\{\tau>t\}} E(1_{\{\tau>T\}} \mid \mathcal{F}_t),$$

so that using (5.3) gives us

$$Q(\tau > T \mid \mathcal{F}_t) = 1_{\{\tau>t\}} \frac{E(1_{\{\tau>T\}} \mid \mathcal{G}_t)}{E(1_{\{\tau>t\}} \mid \mathcal{G}_t)}.$$

Now,

$$E(1_{\{\tau>T\}} \mid \mathcal{G}_t) = E(E(1_{\{\tau>T\}} \mid \mathcal{G}_T) \mid \mathcal{G}_t)$$

$$= E\left[\exp\left(- \int_0^T \lambda(X_s)\, ds \right) \Big| \mathcal{G}_t \right]$$

$$= \exp\left(- \int_0^t \lambda(X_s)\, ds \right) E\left(\exp\left(- \int_t^T \lambda(X_s)\, ds \right) \Big| \mathcal{G}_t \right),$$

and therefore, using this for $T = t$ also, we obtain

$$Q(\tau > T \mid \mathcal{F}_t) = 1_{\{\tau > t\}} E\left[\exp\left(-\int_t^T \lambda(X_s)\,ds\right) \,\Big|\, \mathcal{G}_t\right].$$

This result will help us prove the martingale property of the Cox process specification.

5.4 The Martingale Property

If we let $N_t = 1_{\{\tau \leqslant t\}}$, then (using the fact that $1_{\{\tau = t\}}$ has probability 0) we find, using the dynamic result from the last section, that

$$E[N_t - N_s \mid \mathcal{F}_s] = 1_{\{\tau > s\}}\left(1 - E\left[\exp\left(-\int_s^t \lambda_u\,du\right) \,\Big|\, \mathcal{G}_s\right]\right).$$

We want to show that the martingale property of

$$M_t = N_t - \int_0^t \lambda_u 1_{\{\tau > u\}}\,du,$$

i.e. that $E(M_t - M_s \mid \mathcal{F}_s) = 0$. Having computed $E(N_t - N_s \mid \mathcal{F}_s)$ we now consider

$$E\left[\int_0^t \lambda_u 1_{\{\tau > u\}}\,du - \int_0^s \lambda_u 1_{\{\tau > u\}}\,du \,\Big|\, \mathcal{F}_s\right] = E\left[\int_s^t \lambda_u 1_{\{\tau > u\}}\,du \,\Big|\, \mathcal{F}_s\right].$$

Noting that

$$1_{\{\tau > s\}} \int_s^t \lambda_u 1_{\{\tau > u\}}\,du = \int_s^t \lambda_u 1_{\{\tau > u\}}\,du,$$

the useful technical result (5.3) gives us

$$E\left[\int_s^t \lambda_u 1_{\{\tau > u\}}\,du \,\Big|\, \mathcal{G}_s\right] = 1_{\{\tau > s\}} \frac{E[\int_s^t \lambda_u 1_{\{\tau > u\}}\,du \mid \mathcal{F}_s]}{E[1_{\{\tau > s\}} \mid \mathcal{G}_s]}. \qquad (5.4)$$

Now note that

$$E\left[\int_s^t \lambda_u 1_{\{\tau > u\}}\,du \,\Big|\, \mathcal{G}_s\right] = \int_s^t E[\lambda_u 1_{\{\tau > u\}} \mid \mathcal{G}_s]\,du$$

$$= \int_s^t E[E[\lambda_u 1_{\{\tau > u\}} \mid \mathcal{G}_T] \mid \mathcal{G}_s]\,du$$

$$= \int_s^t E\left[\lambda_u \exp\left(-\int_0^u \lambda_v\,dv\right) \,\Big|\, \mathcal{G}_s\right]du$$

$$= E\left[\int_s^t \lambda_u \exp\left(-\int_0^u \lambda_v\,dv\right)du \,\Big|\, \mathcal{G}_s\right]$$

$$= E\left[\int_0^t -\frac{\partial}{\partial u}\exp\left(-\int_0^u \lambda_v\,dv\right)du \,\bigg|\, \mathcal{G}_s\right]$$

$$= E\left[\exp\left(-\int_0^s \lambda_v\,dv\right) - \exp\left(-\int_0^t \lambda_v\,dv\right)\,\bigg|\, \mathcal{G}_s\right],$$

and hence we can rewrite (5.4) as

$$1_{\{\tau>s\}}\frac{E[\exp(-\int_0^s \lambda_v\,dv) - \exp(-\int_0^t \lambda_v\,dv)\,|\,\mathcal{G}_s]}{\exp(-\int_0^s \lambda_v\,dv)}$$

$$= 1_{\{\tau>s\}}\left(1 - E\left[\exp\left(-\int_s^t \lambda_v\,dv\right)\,\bigg|\,\mathcal{G}_s\right]\right)$$

and this gives us the martingale result.

5.5   Extending the Scope of the Cox Specification

With these technical results in place, we are ready to extend the scope of the model setup. In default modeling we will be concerned with pricing cash flows which in one way or another are tied to the random variable τ. The pricing formulas that we obtain are easy to recognize as simple extensions of those obtained when τ has a deterministic intensity. Assume therefore for a moment that the intensity $\lambda(s)$ is deterministic (and therefore equal to the hazard rate) so that $Q(\tau > t) = \exp(-\int_0^t \lambda(s)\,ds)$. Then, with the relevant integrability assumptions on the functions g and h, we have the following expressions:

$$E\exp(-rT)1_{\{\tau>T\}} = \exp\left(-\int_0^T (r + \lambda(s))\,ds\right),$$

$$E\left(\int_0^T \exp(-rt)g(t)1_{\{\tau>t\}}\,dt\right) = \int_0^T \exp\left(-\int_0^t (r+\lambda(s))\,ds\right)g(t)\,dt,$$

$$E\exp(-r\tau)h(\tau)1_{\{\tau\leqslant T\}} = \int_0^T \exp\left(-\int_0^t (r+\lambda(s))\,ds\right)\lambda(t)h(t)\,dt.$$

Pricing at time t, one obtains the expression

$$E\left(\exp\left(-\int_t^T r(X_s)\,ds\right)f(X_T)1_{\{\tau>T\}}\,\bigg|\,\mathcal{F}_t\right)$$

$$= E\left[\exp\left(-\int_t^T (r+\lambda)(X_s)\,ds\right)f(X_T)\,\bigg|\,\mathcal{G}_t\right]1_{\{\tau>t\}},$$

so that all we need is the state variable information (and the information that default has not yet occurred) to compute the price of a defaultable claim. Two more "building blocks" can be priced using this framework, and with these blocks we have a very flexible collection of tools.

First consider a claim paying $g(X_s)1_{\{\tau>s\}}$ continuously until default or until the maturity date T in the case of no default. For this we find (assuming maturity T)

$$E\left[\int_t^T g(X_s)1_{\{\tau>s\}}\exp\left(-\int_t^s r(X_u)\,du\right)ds\,\bigg|\,\mathcal{F}_t\right]$$
$$= 1_{\{\tau>t\}}E\left[\int_t^T g(X_s)\exp\left(-\int_t^s (r+\lambda)(X_u)\,du\right)ds\,\bigg|\,\mathcal{G}_t\right]. \quad (5.5)$$

Another piece is a payment at the (random) default date (again T is expiration)

$$E\left[\exp\left(-\int_t^\tau r(X_u)\,du\right)h(X_\tau)1_{\{t<\tau\leqslant T\}}\,\bigg|\,\mathcal{F}_t\right]$$
$$= 1_{\{\tau>t\}}E\left[\int_t^T h(X_s)\lambda(X_s)\exp\left(-\int_t^s (r+\lambda)(X_u)\,du\right)ds\right]. \quad (5.6)$$

When X is a diffusion process, we sometimes have closed-form solutions for these expressions or we can express the expectations as solutions to a partial differential equation, which can then be solved numerically.

5.6 Recovery of Market Value

Now we consider a special recovery assumption that provides an extension of the convenient pricing formulas developed so far. The extension requires a fairly extensive stochastic calculus apparatus, so we focus on three more intuitive explanations instead.

Consider the price process of a defaultable contingent claim V promising a payoff of $f(X_T)$ at T. The claim is said to have a (fractional) recovery of market value (RMV) of δ at a default time τ if the amount recovered in the event of default is equal to

$$h(\tau) = \delta V(\tau-)\quad\text{for }\tau\leqslant T,$$

where $V(\tau-)$ is the value of the claim just prior to default and $\delta \in [0, 1)$. We work with a constant δ here since this assumption is often made in practical applications.

With this recovery assumption, we have that the price at t of the defaultable contingent claim, if there has not been a default at date t, is

$$V(t) = E_t\left[\exp\left(-\int_t^T (r+(1-\delta)\lambda)(X_s)\,ds\right)f(X_T)\right]. \quad (5.7)$$

Note the special case $\delta = 0$, leading us back to the case from the previous section. We now give three arguments in support of this result.

5.6.1 A Discrete-Time Argument

This argument follows Duffie and Singleton (1999a). Consider a discrete-time setting in which

- λ_s is the probability of defaulting in $(s, s + 1]$ given survival up to time s;
- r_s is the (continuously compounded) rate between s and $s + 1$; and
- δ is the fractional recovery received at time $s + 1$ in the event of a default in the time interval $(s, s + 1]$.

Using our general discrete-time pricing framework (Appendix A) we have, given that the claim is alive at t,[1]

$$V(t) = \lambda_t \exp(-r_t) E_t[\delta V(t + 1)] + (1 - \lambda_t) \exp(-r_t) E_t[V(t + 1)]$$

$$\text{for } t < T$$

$$\equiv \exp(-R_t) E_t[V_{t+1}],$$

where we have defined

$$\exp(-R_t) = \lambda_t \exp(-r_t)\delta + (1 - \lambda_t) \exp(-r_t).$$

Iterating this expression gives us

$$V(t) = \exp(-R_t) E_t[\exp(-R_{t+1}) E_{t+1}(V_{t+2})]$$
$$= E_t[\exp(-(R_t + R_{t+1})) V_{t+2}],$$

and continuing on

$$V(t) = E_t\left[\exp\left(- \sum_{i=0}^{T-t-1} R_{t+i} \right) f(X_T) \right],$$

since $V(T) = f(X_T)$ by definition. Now, moving from a period of length 1 to one of length Δt, but keeping the annual rates, we have

$$\exp(-R_t \Delta t) = \lambda_t \Delta \exp(-r_t \Delta t)\delta + (1 - \lambda_t \Delta t) \exp(-r_t \Delta t).$$

For small Δt, $\exp(-R_t \Delta t) \approx 1 - R_t \Delta t$ and $\exp(-r_t \Delta t) \approx 1 - r_t \Delta t$, which gives us

$$1 - R_t \Delta t \approx \lambda_t \delta \Delta t(1 - r_t \Delta t) + (1 - \lambda_t \Delta t)(1 - r_t \Delta t),$$

and matching Δt terms on both sides gives us

$$R_t \approx r_t + (1 - \delta)\lambda_t,$$

as was to be shown.

---

[1]Note that $V(\tau-)$ is a limit from the left and therefore may be viewed as the value of the claim had there been no default. In the discrete-time setting this value is represented by $V(t + 1)$.

5.6.2 *Repeated Fractional Recovery of Par at Maturity*

This argument is due to Schönbucher (1998). What we show here is that a seemingly different recovery assumption produces the same formula and then we realize that the recovery assumption is really that of fractional recovery. Returning to the continuous-time setting, assume that, in the event of default, the payment of the defaultable claim is reduced to a fraction δ of the original payment at maturity. Hence, if there is a default, the promised payment is reduced from $f(X_T)$ to $\delta f(X_T)$. Assume that there may be repeated defaults in the interval $[0, T)$ and that every time a default occurs, the promised payment is reduced by a factor of δ at maturity. In our Cox process setting, this implies that the price at time t if no default has occurred yet is

$$V(t) = \sum_{k=0}^{\infty} E_t\left(\exp\left(-\int_t^T r(X_s)\,ds \right) \delta^k f(X_T) 1_{\{N_T=k\}} \right),$$

where N_T counts the number of defaults at time T. Conditioning (as usual) on the evolution of X up to T, we note that

$$\sum_{k=0}^{\infty} E_t[\delta^k f(X_T) 1_{\{N_t=k\}} \mid (X_t)_{0 \leqslant t \leqslant T}]$$

$$= \sum_{k=0}^{\infty} \delta^k \frac{(\int_t^T \lambda(X_s)\,ds)^k}{k!} \exp\left(-\int_t^T \lambda(X_s)\,ds \right) f(X_T)$$

$$= f(X_T) \exp\left(-\int_t^T \lambda(X_s)\,ds \right) \exp\left(\delta \int_t^T \lambda(X_s)\,ds \right)$$

$$\times \sum_{k=0}^{\infty} \frac{(\int_t^T \delta\lambda(X_s)\,ds)^k}{k!} \exp\left(-\int_t^T \delta\lambda(X_s)\,ds \right)$$

$$= f(X_T) \exp\left(-\int_t^T ((1-\delta)\lambda(X_s))\,ds \right),$$

and therefore

$$V(t) = E_t\left[\exp\left(-\int_t^T (r + (1-\delta)\lambda)(X_s)\,ds \right) f(X_T) \right],$$

and this is of course the same formula as in the case of fractional recovery. This is because the recovery assumption made here in fact implies fractional recovery. To see this, note that the price conditionally on k defaults having occurred is just

$$\delta^k V(t),$$

and hence the price drops by a factor δ every time a default occurs. When we consider time-dependent (or even stochastic) recovery rates, we need to be careful. To make the approach above produce the right result, we need to assume that the recovery rate at the first default is also used on all subsequent defaults. Hence if δ_{τ_1} is used at the first default, the same quantity should be used on the subsequent defaults.

5.6.3   Recovery of Market Value and Thinning

If N is a Cox process with intensity λ, we define a thinning of this process as follows. Let $\tau_1, \tau_2, \ldots$ be the jump times of N and consider a sequence of independent Bernoulli variables $Y_1, Y_2, \ldots$ all with $P(Y_i = 1) = \delta$. The thinning N^Y of N is then given by

$$N_t^Y = \sum_{i=1}^{\infty} 1_{\{\tau_i \leq t\}} 1_{\{Y_i = 0\}},$$

i.e. we delete a jump every time $Y_i = 1$.

Receiving a fraction δ at default of the pre-default value $V(\tau-)$ has the same expectation as receiving 0 with probability $1 - \delta$ and $V(\tau-)$ with probability δ. Since receiving $V(\tau-)$ is equivalent to a cancellation of the default event, we note that this formulation of recovery is equal to a zero-recovery assumption in a thinned default-event process. The thinning rate is $1 - \delta$ and hence we can use our zero-recovery formulation with the intensity $(1-\delta)\lambda(X_s)$, and this brings us back to (5.7).

5.7   Notes on Recovery Assumptions

The assumed form of recovery is important for term structures of credit spreads, and we focus here on three ways of measuring recovery used in the literature for corporate bonds. As a useful reference point, we consider in Figure 5.1 the evolution of the price of a corporate bond issued by Enron over a 1-year period around the default date, which in Moody's database is recorded as 3 December 2001. Note how the decline in credit quality is composed of many consecutive jumps. The three recovery assumptions are as follows.

(1) **Recovery of face value.** This measures the value to the investors as a fraction of face value. This is the closest we come to legal practice, in the sense that debt with the same priority is assigned a fractional recovery depending on the outstanding notional amount but not on maturity or coupon. It is also the measure typically used in rating-agency studies. It is not equal to the drop in price unless the bond trades at par. One only needs a post-default market price to estimate the quantity. In Moody's these data are set 30 days after the default date. In mathematical terms, the formula for a bond price is not quite as pretty as in the case of recovery of market value, since we have to compute an integral of the form (5.6).

(2) **Recovery of market value.** This measures the change in market value at the time of default. This has economic meaning since this is the loss in value associated

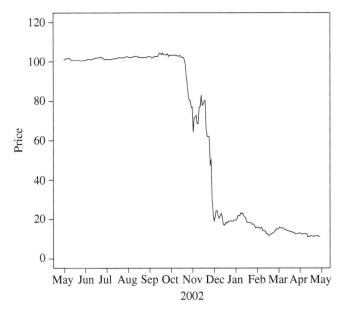

Figure 5.1. The price of an Enron Corporation bond issued in 1997 and with maturity data 15 November 2005. The coupon rate was 6.625%. The Chapter 11 filing was recorded on 3 December 2002. (Source: Datastream.)

with default. Here we need prices both before and after the default date, and in empirical measurement the pre-default price would be the hardest to define if one has the literal interpretation of a single drop in mind. For ex-ante pricing purposes, the approximation invoked in viewing the default event as a simple drop instead of a dragged out event is probably not serious. As we have seen, this quantity is extremely convenient to work with for modeling purposes.

(3) Recovery of treasury. Under this assumption, the corporate bond in default is replaced with a treasury bond with the same maturity but a reduced payment. This could, from an economic point of view, be seen as a more sophisticated approach than recovery of face value, since it at least tries to correct for the fact that amounts of principal with long maturity should be discounted more than principal payments with short maturity.

One could, as a purely mathematical statement, say that one assumption can always be expressed in terms of another, and therefore they are all equivalent. But that of course ignores the fact that once we have assumed a particular type of recovery, we often assume that it is constant (or use the mean recovery for valuation). And it matters for pricing which recovery rate we keep constant.

A final note concerns the ease with which we extract implied default probabilities from prices. This extraction is critically linked to the recovery assumptions. An advantage of the recovery of treasury approach is that is permits (at least with an assumption of independence between the short rate r and the default intensity λ) an immediate expression for implied survival rates. If we work with a constant and known recovery of market value, we cannot (even in the case of independence between bond markets and default) in general infer the implied default probability from a bond without having a specification for the evolution of λ.

For a zero-coupon bond with maturity T and fractional recovery δ, we have

$$v(0, T) = p(0, T) E \exp\left(- \int_0^T \lambda_s (1 - \delta) \, ds \right)$$

$$= p(0, T) E \left(\left(\exp\left(- \int_0^T \lambda_s \, ds \right) \right)^{1-\delta} \right),$$

but the $(1 - \delta)$th moment does not give us the implied default probability

$$E \left(\exp\left(- \int_0^T \lambda_s \, ds \right) \right)$$

unless we know more about λ.

In the recovery of treasury setting (with independence) between r and λ we have

$$E \exp\left(- \int_0^T \lambda_s \, ds \right) = \frac{v(0, T) - \delta p(0, T)}{(1 - \delta) p(0, T)},$$

which is very convenient to work with but which may give problems with real data, since the right-hand side need not be a number between 0 and 1.

5.8 Correlation in Affine Specifications

We have now seen how the intensity setting links up the modeling of defaultable claims with ordinary term-structure modeling. If we work with intensities which are independent of interest rates, we can then specify a model for the default-free term structure and add a model of defaultable bond prices to this model. We do, however, want to incorporate dependence between interest rates and default intensities and in this section we summarize some of the problems in doing this if one wants to maintain tractability of the model.

When we model the joint behavior of interest rates and default intensities, the two obvious strategies for incorporating dependence are to use correlated Brownian motions as drivers of the processes or to have an intensity function depend on the interest rate. To illustrate the two approaches in their simplest form, the choice is between correlation through the noise term,

$$dr_t = \kappa_r (r_t - \theta_r) \, dt + \sigma_r \, dW_t^1,$$

$$d\lambda_t = \kappa_\lambda (\lambda_t - \theta_\lambda) \, dt + \sigma_\lambda (\rho \, dW_t^1 + \sqrt{1 - \rho^2} \, dW_t^2),$$

or correlation through affine dependence,

$$dr_t = \kappa_r(r_t - \theta_r)\, dt + \sigma_r\, dW_t^1,$$
$$\lambda(t) = \alpha + \beta r_t.$$

The trade-off we have to make can be summarized as follows. In Gaussian models we can model both positive and negative correlation between interest rates and intensities and we can do it both by using correlated noise or by using affine dependence. However, we have to accept that interest rates and intensities can become negative. In a model where agents cannot hold cash except in the money-market account, negative interest rates are consistent with no arbitrage.

Negative intensities do not make sense, however, and we must then view the expressions as giving an analytical approximation to a setting in which the default intensity is set to zero whenever the intensity process becomes negative. For short horizons this is usually not a problem.

If we are concerned with obtaining positive rates and intensities, while having tractable models, we can look towards the CIR-type specifications in affine models or the closely related quadratic Gaussian models. In the CIR class we cannot obtain negative correlation through the driving Brownian motions and still stay within the affine class. Even positive correlation is problematic.

Positive affine dependence works easily. If we are willing to accept negative rates, we may also specify an intensity function which depends negatively on r, but this may cause problems with infinite expectation. The dependence cannot be too large. Again, such negative dependence can induce negative intensities, and we must resort to the analytical approximation argument once more.

Finally, in the quadratic Gaussian model we can obtain correlation with a desired sign but only in a subdomain of the driving state variables.

This section is not a detailed mathematical treatment of these issues. The biographical notes contain references to detailed accounts, which should be easier to approach keeping the following examples in mind.

5.8.1 *Correlation in the Gaussian Models*

The Gaussian models are easy to work with. Any specification of the short rate and the intensity as affine functions of a Gaussian state variable diffusion gives expressions for bond prices which have closed-form solutions.

Whether they are meaningful depends on the probability of the intensities becoming negative. It is typically a problem for small spreads (in the high-credit-rating categories) that the absolute size of the spread is small compared with the volatility, and therefore a Gaussian specification will often produce parameters which leave a large probability of negative intensities.

5.8.2   *Correlation and the CIR Process*

The following "dead end" is perhaps illustrative. Assume that we try the following setup:

$$dr_t = \kappa_r(\theta_r - r_t)\,dt + \sigma_r\sqrt{r_t}\,dW_t^1,$$

$$d\lambda_t = \kappa_\lambda(\theta_\lambda - \lambda_t)\,dt + \sigma_\lambda\sqrt{\lambda_t}(\rho\,dW_t^1 + \sqrt{(1-\rho^2)}\,dW_t^2),$$

where $\rho \in [-1, 1]$ and W^1, W^2 are independent Brownian motions. The diffusion terms may then be written as

$$\begin{pmatrix} \sqrt{r_t} & 0 \\ 0 & \sqrt{\lambda_t} \end{pmatrix} \begin{pmatrix} \sigma_r & 0 \\ \sigma_\lambda\rho & \sigma_\lambda\sqrt{(1-\rho^2)} \end{pmatrix} \begin{pmatrix} dW_t^1 \\ dW_t^2 \end{pmatrix},$$

which is the same as

$$\begin{pmatrix} \sigma_r\sqrt{r_t} & 0 \\ \sigma_\lambda\rho\sqrt{\lambda_t} & \sigma_\lambda\sqrt{(1-\rho^2)}\sqrt{\lambda_t} \end{pmatrix} \begin{pmatrix} dW_t^1 \\ dW_t^2 \end{pmatrix}.$$

If we let

$$\Sigma = \begin{pmatrix} \sigma_r\sqrt{r_t} & 0 \\ \sigma_\lambda\rho\sqrt{\lambda_t} & \sigma_\lambda\sqrt{(1-\rho^2)}\sqrt{\lambda_t} \end{pmatrix},$$

then the off-diagonal entry of $\Sigma\,\Sigma^{T}$ is equal to

$$(\Sigma\,\Sigma^{T})_{12} = \sigma_r\sigma_\lambda\rho\sqrt{\lambda_t}\sqrt{r_t}$$

and this means that the model is not affine. So, even if the processes r and λ are CIR processes, if $\rho \neq 0$, they are not jointly affine.

Note that if we try to put the correlation in front instead,

$$\begin{pmatrix} \sigma_r & 0 \\ \rho & \sigma_\lambda \end{pmatrix} \begin{pmatrix} \sqrt{r_t} & 0 \\ 0 & \sqrt{\lambda_t} \end{pmatrix},$$

this does give affine entries in $\Sigma\,\Sigma^{T}$ but the problem here is controlling the processes under the square root sign. If λ is close to zero (say), its volatility must die out in order for the positive drift to be able to keep the process positive.

But if $\sqrt{r_t}$ is positive, then λ's volatility is affected by shocks to the r-process as well and this means that λ cannot be guaranteed to stay positive and hence the solution to the SDE is not well defined.

Because of this, the typical way to obtain correlation using CIR processes is to let r_t be a CIR process, and specify the default intensity as

$$\lambda(r_t) = \alpha + \beta r_t + s_t,$$

where α and β are constants, and r_t and s_t are independent CIR processes.

If β is positive, this is unproblematic. If β is negative, we cannot guarantee positive intensities and, in fact, the expectation $E\exp(-\int_0^t \beta r_s\,ds)$ for β negative need not be finite if β is large enough.

5.8.3 *Correlation in the Quadratic Gaussian Models*

In a quadratic Gaussian model, we can obtain negative instantaneous correlation between positive processes, at least in part of the domain of the processes.

Consider the following example:

$$dX_{1t} = a_1(b_1 - X_{1t})\,dt + \sigma_1\,dW_t^1,$$

$$dX_{2t} = a_2(b_2 - X_{2t})\,dt + \sigma_2\rho\,dW_t^1 + \sigma_2\sqrt{1-\rho^2}\,dW_t^2,$$

where a_1 and a_2 are positive constants.

Then, letting

$$Y_{1t} = X_{1t}^2 \quad \text{and} \quad Y_{2t} = X_{2t}^2,$$

we have two positive processes and it is tempting to conclude that if ρ is negative they have negative instantaneous correlation.

By Itô's formula, we have, worrying only about the volatility term,

$$dY_{1t} = (\cdots)\,dt + 2X_{1t}\sigma_1\,dW_t^1,$$

$$dY_{2t} = (\cdots)\,dt + 2X_{2t}(\rho\sigma_2\,dW_t^1 + \sqrt{1-\rho^2}\sigma_2\,dW_t^2),$$

and from this we see that

$$d\langle Y_1\rangle_t = 4X_{1t}^2\sigma_1^2\,dt,$$

$$d\langle Y_2\rangle_t = 4X_{2t}^2\sigma_2^2\,dt,$$

$$d\langle Y_1, Y_2\rangle_t = 4X_{1t}X_{2t}\rho\sigma_1\sigma_2\,dt.$$

This means that the instantaneous correlation of Y_1 and Y_2 is

$$\text{corr}(dY_{1t}, dY_{2t}) = \rho\frac{X_{1t}}{\sqrt{X_{1t}^2}}\frac{X_{2t}}{\sqrt{X_{2t}^2}},$$

so that the instantaneous correlation is ρ when the underlying state variables X_{1t} and X_{2t} have the same sign and $-\rho$ when they have opposite signs.

Hence if we want negative correlation $\rho < 0$, this can be ensured by setting the mean reversion level to be positive and the variance to be small enough that the processes stays positive with high probability. In other words, if Y_{1t}^2 and Y_{2t}^2 are the interest rate and an intensity, we have ensured positivity by squaring the Gaussian, and we have obtained negative correlation with a high probability.

We could obtain the same instantaneous correlation ρ everywhere by letting

$$dY_{1t} = (\cdots)\,dt + 2|X_{1t}|\sigma_1\,dW_t^1,$$

$$dY_{2t} = (\cdots)\,dt + 2|X_{2t}|(\rho\sigma_2\,dW_t^1 + \sqrt{1-\rho^2}\sigma_2\,dW_t^2).$$

This would not change the marginal distributions of Y_1 and Y_2, but it does change the joint distribution and sends us outside the quadratic class.

5.9   Interacting Intensities

The fundamental relationship between the survival probability and the $\mathcal{F}$-pre-default intensity, which holds in a Cox setting

$$Q(\tau > T) = 1_{\{\tau > t\}} E \exp\left(-\int_t^T \lambda_s \, ds \,\middle|\, \mathcal{G}_t \right),$$

is a primary motivation for using this setup.

In this section we look at an example where the above result does not hold. The example still permits explicit calculations and it is therefore a useful starting point for understanding the technical issues addressed in the literature of handling common jumps in state variables and jump processes associated with default.

Consider two issuers, firms A and B. Define τ^i as the default time of issuer i and let $N_t^i = 1_{\{\tau^i \leqslant t\}}$. Assume that the pre-default intensities of A and B are

$$\lambda_t^A = a_1 + a_2 1_{\{\tau^B \leqslant t\}},$$
$$\lambda_t^B = b_1 + b_2 1_{\{\tau^A \leqslant t\}}.$$

For the sake of some of the explicit calculations below, assume that the numbers a_1, a_2, b_1, and b_2 are all different. This setup corresponds to a situation in which the default of one firm affects the default intensity of the other firm. If, for example, $a_2 > 0$, then the default of firm B increases the intensity of A's default from a_1 to $a_1 + a_2$. If $a_2 = b_2 = 0$, we are back to a case with default times which are independent exponential distributions.

It is possible to analyze the problem using abstract compensator theory, but the simple structure of the problem can be made transparent in a simple Markov chain setting. Consider a four-state Markov chain in continuous time whose state space is $\{(N, N), (D, N), (N, D), (D, D)\}$, where "N" signifies nondefault and "D" is default and the first coordinate refers to issuer A and the second to B. We can then reformulate the analysis by looking at the generator:

$$\Lambda = \begin{pmatrix} -(a_1 + b_1) & a_1 & b_1 & 0 \\ 0 & -(b_1 + b_2) & 0 & b_1 + b_2 \\ 0 & 0 & -(a_1 + a_2) & a_1 + a_2 \\ 0 & 0 & 0 & 0 \end{pmatrix}.$$

Because of the simple upper triangular structure of the generator it is easy to compute its matrix exponential. Clearly, the eigenvalues of Λ are just its diagonal elements. Letting

$$D = \begin{pmatrix} -(a_1 + b_1) & 0 & 0 & 0 \\ 0 & -(b_1 + b_2) & 0 & 0 \\ 0 & 0 & -(a_1 + a_2) & 0 \\ 0 & 0 & 0 & 0 \end{pmatrix}$$

and relying on the assumption of distinct parameter values,

$$
B = \begin{pmatrix}
1 & \dfrac{a_1}{a_1 - b_2} & \dfrac{b_1}{b_1 - a_2} & 1 \\
0 & 1 & 0 & 1 \\
0 & 0 & 1 & 1 \\
0 & 0 & 0 & 1
\end{pmatrix},
$$

we have

$$
\Lambda = BDB^{-1}.
$$

In fact, B^{-1} is also easy to compute as

$$
B^{-1} = \begin{pmatrix}
1 & \dfrac{-a_1}{b_2 - a_2} & \dfrac{b_1}{a_2 - b_1} & 1 + \dfrac{b_1}{b_1 - a_2} + \dfrac{a_1}{a_1 - b_2} \\
0 & 1 & 0 & -1 \\
0 & 0 & 1 & -1 \\
0 & 0 & 0 & 1,
\end{pmatrix}
$$

and hence we can compute all relevant transition probabilities:

$$
P(t) = B \begin{pmatrix}
\exp(-(a_1 + b_1)t) & 0 & 0 & 0 \\
0 & \exp(-(b_1 + b_2)t) & 0 & 0 \\
0 & 0 & \exp(-(a_1 + a_2)t) & 0 \\
0 & 0 & 0 & 1
\end{pmatrix} B^{-1}.
$$

In particular, this gives us the marginal probability of A being in default before t:

$$
Q(\tau^A \leqslant t) = P_{12}(t) + P_{14}(t),
$$

where we have added the case where B has not defaulted and where both have defaulted. Simple computation gives us

$$
Q(\tau^A \leqslant t) = \frac{a_2 - a_2 \exp(-(a_1 + b_1)t) + b_1[\exp(-(a_1 + a_2)t) - 1]}{a_2 - b_1}.
$$

The important thing to note is that this expression does *not* depend on b_2. This is intuitively clear. b_2 only takes effect after the default of A and from that time it controls the waiting time for B to follow A in default. In other words, changing b_2 will only serve to move probability mass between $P_{12}(t)$ and $P_{14}(t)$ but will not alter the sum.

Had we tried to compute

$$
E \exp\left(-\int_0^t \lambda_s^A \, ds\right) = E \exp\left(-\int_0^t (a_1 + a_2 1_{\{\tau^B \leqslant s\}}) \, ds\right),
$$

we would obtain an expression that does depend on b_2, since the distribution of τ^B obviously depends on b_2 and this enters into the expression.

By observing that

$$
\int_0^t (a_1 + a_2 1_{\{\tau^B \leqslant s\}})\, ds = \begin{cases} a_1 t & \text{on } \{\tau^B \geqslant t\}, \\ a_1 t + a_2(t - \tau^B) & \text{on } \{\tau^B < t\}, \end{cases}
$$

it follows that

$$
E \exp\left(- \int_0^t \lambda_s^A\, ds \right)
$$

$$
= Q(\tau^B \geqslant t)\exp(-a_1 t) + \exp(-a_1 t)\int_0^t \exp(-a_2(t - s))Q(\tau^B \in ds), \quad (5.8)
$$

and all of these expressions can be obtained from the explicit results. Since $Q(\tau^B \leqslant t)$ depends on b_2 in the same way as $Q(\tau^A \leqslant t)$ depends on a_2, it is clear that the expression above depends on b_2 and therefore does not give us the right expression.

Only in the special case where we modify the setup letting $b_2 = 0$, i.e. where we let

$$
\lambda_t^B = b_1,
$$

will we get

$$
Q(\tau^A > t) = E \exp\left(- \int_0^t (a_1 + a_2 1_{\{\tau^B \leqslant t\}})\, ds \right),
$$

as you can verify by letting $b_2 = 0$ in (5.8).

5.10   The Role of Incomplete Information

Intensity models are frequently criticized for having too little "economic content." Even if they are acknowledged by most to be convenient for econometric specification of models and for building derivative pricing models, the fact that the default triggering event is not explicitly modeled is seen as a weakness by some. However, as one will see below, intensity models are fully consistent with a "structural" (option-based) approach in models where bond holders have incomplete information about the asset value of the firm. This is true even when the asset-value process has no jumps.

We start by describing a mathematical result which is central to this idea. Let τ denote the first time the asset-value process V hits the boundary $\underline{v}$ and assume that V is modeled as a diffusion process. We noted in Chapter 3 that

$$
\lim_{h\downarrow 0} \frac{Q_{v_0}(\tau \leqslant h)}{h} = 0, \quad (5.9)
$$

where Q_{v_0} is the probability conditional on $V_0 = v_0$, and we assume that $v_0 > \underline{v}$. It is this fact, and not just the fact that $Q_{v_0}(\tau \leqslant h) \to 0$, which causes yield spreads to be 0 in the short end for diffusion-based models.

Now assume that we do not know the starting point of the firm's assets and that we represent our uncertainty of the starting point through a density function $f(x)$ whose support is on $(\underline{v}, \infty)$, since we know that the firm has not yet defaulted. The analogue of (5.9) is then

$$\lim_{h\downarrow 0} \frac{1}{h} \int_{\underline{v}}^{\infty} Q_x(\tau \leqslant h) f(x) \, dx,$$

and moving $1/h$ inside the integral sign followed by ruthless interchange of limit and integration would suggest that this goes to 0 since the integrand, as noted in (5.9), converges pointwise in x to 0. Therefore one would be tempted to conclude that even assuming that the asset-value process is an unknown distance away from default does not help bring about nonzero spreads in the short end. However, the interchange of limit and integration leading to that conclusion is indeed ruthless and serves as a good illustration of why measure theory has a dominated convergence theorem.

If we assume that

$$\lim_{x\downarrow \underline{v}} f(x) = 0$$

and that the right derivative exists at $\underline{v}$, denoted $f'(\underline{v})$, then in fact

$$\lim_{h\downarrow 0} \frac{1}{h} \int_{0}^{\infty} Q_x(\tau \leqslant h) f(x) \, dx = \tfrac{1}{2}\sigma^2(\underline{v}) f'(\underline{v}), \qquad (5.10)$$

where $\sigma^2(\underline{v})$ is the squared diffusion coefficient (assumed to satisfy Lipschitz conditions) of V at the boundary. This can be proved directly and it can be shown that this limit is indeed the default intensity (see the bibliographic notes). Here we give a discrete-time argument in support of the result: consider the binomial approximation of the problem in Figure 5.2. The process is a binomial approximation over a short time period of a Brownian motion with zero drift. The barrier is at 0, and the only way the process can reach the barrier is by starting at the level nearest the boundary. The probability of starting here is approximately the density multiplied by the grid size. Now the probability of hitting default is the probability of starting at the lowest grid point and moving down. We therefore get an approximation of the intensity by considering $\tfrac{1}{2} f(\sigma\sqrt{h})\sigma\sqrt{h}/\sqrt{h}$, and the limit of this as $h \to 0$ is precisely $\tfrac{1}{2}\sigma^2 f'(0)$.

One might wonder if the assumptions on the density f are reasonable. As an indication of why they are indeed plausible, consider the conditional density at time t of a log-asset-value process

$$Z_t = z_0 + mt + \sigma B_t$$

which started at $z_0 = \log v_0$, is known not to have hit $\underline{z} := \log \underline{v}$, but has otherwise not been observed between date 0 and date t. Let $\tau(\underline{z})$ denote the first time that the

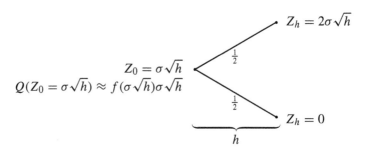

Figure 5.2.   A binomial argument supporting the limit result (5.10).

lower boundary is hit by Z. Define the distance between the starting point and the barrier as

$$d = z_0 - \underline{z},$$

and now, using the results on Brownian hitting times from the appendix, we have

$$P(\tau(\underline{z}) > t) = \Phi\left(\frac{d + mt}{\sigma\sqrt{t}}\right) - \exp\left(\frac{-2md}{\sigma^2}\right)\Phi\left(\frac{mt - d}{\sigma\sqrt{t}}\right). \qquad (5.11)$$

Again from results in the appendix and some tedious calculations we obtain the density of log-assets given that Z has not hit $\underline{z}$ between time 0 and time t to be

$$f(z) = \frac{1}{P(\tau(\underline{z}) > t)}\left[\frac{1}{\sigma\sqrt{t}}\phi\left(\frac{d + mt}{\sigma\sqrt{t}}\right) - \exp\left(\frac{-2md}{\sigma^2}\right)\frac{1}{\sigma\sqrt{t}}\phi\left(\frac{mt - d}{\sigma\sqrt{t}}\right)\right], \qquad (5.12)$$

and this density is indeed 0 at the boundary $\underline{z}$ and has a right derivative at the boundary which is different from 0, and both of these properties are preserved, of course, in the transformation from log-assets to assets. There are analytical results extending this result to diffusions. Hence it is natural when there is a lag in the knowledge of the true asset value and when it is only known that a boundary has not been hit to get densities satisfying the assumptions. This extends to wider classes of diffusion process. The problem now is to set up a model which, from sensible assumptions, produces a density function f. We will see two (related) ways of doing this. One is fairly realistic but requires some computation, the other is somewhat unrealistic but is very simple from a computational point of view. In both approaches we will assume that the default boundary is known, and this requires a few comments first. It would be straightforward to adapt a Black–Cox model to the setting with unknown starting point and obtain explicit solutions for debt value by simply integrating the relevant-value expressions with respect to the density of the initial starting point. The problem lies in justifying the boundary. If it is set by some covenant and we assume that only insiders (equity owners) can observe the asset value, then certainly with asset sales permitted they have no incentives to reveal to the outside bond holders that the default triggering boundary has been reached. If insiders are paying the coupon "out of their own pockets" (i.e. possibly by issuing new equity and diluting), there may well be an endogenously determined default boundary which is above the covenant value. In fact, even if the endogenously determined boundary is below the one set by the covenant, there is no reason why the insiders would respect the covenant. Hence it requires a model with endogenous default to make sure that the default boundary is set in such a way that it is consistent with the incentives of the "insiders," who observe the asset value perfectly to default. Such a model is set up in Duffie and Lando (2001) building on the Leland model. Here everybody knows the parameters of the asset-value process and the value of the assets at the time at which the firm chose its capital structure. This capital structure is chosen optimally but after it has been chosen, the debt holders receive only partial information about the true value of assets (but still know the parameter values of the process). Insiders, thought of as owners of private, nontraded equity, service the coupons. As part of the initial choice of capital structure a level of asset value is determined at which the equity owners will stop paying the coupon on the debt.

Now let us look at two ways of obtaining a model for the uncertainty of asset value. In the simplest approach, the incomplete information arises simply from a fixed time lag l between the current value of assets and the asset value known to outsiders. In other words, when the true asset value is Z_t, the outsiders know only the value Z_{t-l} and that the asset value has not hit zero between time $t - l$ and time t. To analyze this problem, consider first the hazard rate associated with the hitting time distribution (5.11). This can be computed directly as

$$\lambda(t) = \frac{-(\mathrm{d}/\mathrm{d}t)P(\tau(\underline{z}) > t)}{P(\tau(\underline{z}) > t)}.$$

This differentiation looks ugly, but there are many simplifications, and the final result is

$$\lambda(t) = \frac{\dfrac{d}{\sqrt{2\pi}\sigma t^{3/2}}\phi\left(\dfrac{mt+d}{\sigma\sqrt{t}}\right)}{\Phi\left(\dfrac{d+mt}{\sigma\sqrt{t}}\right) - \exp\left(\dfrac{-2md}{\sigma^2}\right)\Phi\left(\dfrac{mt-d}{\sigma\sqrt{t}}\right)}. \tag{5.13}$$

In passing, note the following. The distribution for the first hitting time has a hazard rate. If no information other than the initial state of the process is known as time passes, this also becomes the (deterministic) pre-default intensity process for the counting process, which jumps to 1 at default. The value of the hazard rate is 0 at time 0, and is strictly positive thereafter. If, however, the information of current asset value is updated, the "instantaneous hazard" remains 0 as long as the firm's assets are away from the boundary. Then there is no intensity for the first hitting time.

Returning to the expression for the hazard rate, we have a situation in which the distance to the default barrier is $d = z_0 - \underline{z}$. Now define a dynamic version of this:

$$d(t) = z_t - \underline{z}.$$

We can then obtain a stochastically varying hazard rate by assuming that at time t there is perfect information on the asset value at time $t - l$, where l is a fixed lag, but the only additional information at time t is that the process has not hit $\underline{z}$. We can then apply the formula above directly to obtain

$$\lambda(t) = \frac{\dfrac{d(t-l)}{\sqrt{2\pi}\sigma l^{3/2}}\phi\left(\dfrac{ml + d(t-l)}{\sigma\sqrt{l}}\right)}{\Phi\left(\dfrac{d(t-l) + ml}{\sigma\sqrt{l}}\right) - \exp\left(\dfrac{-2md(t-l)}{\sigma^2}\right)\Phi\left(\dfrac{ml - d(t-l)}{\sigma\sqrt{l}}\right)}. \qquad (5.14)$$

This is a very simple way of having a stochastically varying default intensity, but it of course carries the unpleasant assumption that the lagged asset value and the default intensity (and hence the spread in the short end) are perfectly correlated. It also does not capture the arrival of lumpy information about the firm at discrete-time intervals. This is possible at the cost of larger computational efforts, though. The technical problem is to work with an extended version of the conditional distributions of a Brownian motion where we condition not only on the process not having hit the boundary but also on noisy signals of the firm's assets. This is done in Duffie and Lando (2001) and we briefly outline the idea here. Consider a log-asset value starting at z_0. Assume that at time t we observe the logarithm of the asset value plus a noise term, i.e. we observe

$$Y_t = Z_t + U_t,$$

where U_t is normally distributed. The goal then is to find the conditional distribution of Z_t given Y_t, and the fact that the process Z has not hit a lower boundary $\bar{v}$ in the time interval $[0, t]$. Call the hitting time of the boundary τ. The critical quantity to obtain is

$$b(x \mid Y_t, z_0, t)\, dx := P(\tau > t \text{ and } Z_t \in dx \mid Y_t, Z_0 = z_0), \quad x > \bar{v}.$$

Once we have this, we can integrate out x to get

$$P(\tau > t \mid Y_t, Z_0 = z_0) = \int_{\bar{v}}^{\infty} b(x \mid Y_t, z_0, t)\, dx,$$

and then apply the Bayes rule to obtain the desired density of Z_t given the noisy information and that Z_t has not hit the lower boundary:

$$g(x \mid y, z_0, t) = \frac{b(x \mid y, z_0, t)}{\int_{\bar{v}}^{\infty} b(x \mid Y_t, z_0, t)\, dx}.$$

Obtaining b is the harder part. It requires first calculating the conditional probability of Z not hitting the boundary given that the log-asset value starts at z_0 and ends up at z_t. This quantity depends only on volatility and time, and not on drift, and is given as

$$\psi(z_0, z_t, \sigma\sqrt{t}) = 1 - \exp\left(-\frac{2z_0 z_t}{k^2}\right).$$

With applications of the Bayes rule one can then show that

$$b(x \mid Y_t, z_0, t) = \frac{\psi(z_0 - \bar{v}, x - \bar{v}, \sigma\sqrt{t})\phi_U(Y_t - x)\phi_Z(x)}{\phi_Y(Y_t)},$$

where ϕ_U, ϕ_Z, and ϕ_Y are densities for U, Z, and Y, respectively. The fact that all of this only involves exponential functions allows one to compute an explicit expression for b. We refer to Duffie and Lando (2001) for details. Note that once we have the density g, the default intensity of the firm evolves deterministically over time until the next accounting report (or other information on the firm's assets) arrives. One obtains this intensity simply by mixing the hazard rate of the first hitting distribution over g.

5.11 Risk Premiums in Intensity-Based Models

Understanding the structure of risk premiums in intensity models is critical for understanding the pricing formula and the current econometric literature. This is inevitably technical, but the equivalence result given below is in fact refreshingly concrete compared with some of the more abstract equivalence theorems for semimartingales that we will touch upon in Appendix D. To make its implications concrete, we illustrate the effect on a term structures of various risk premium assumptions.

5.11.1 An Equivalence Result

The following equivalence result is from Kusuoka (1999). For definitions of process properties see Appendix D. Let $(\Omega, \mathcal{F}, P)$ be a complete probability space. For a given time horizon T, let $(\mathcal{G}_t)_{t\in[0,T]}$ be a filtration generated by a d-dimensional Brownian motion W such that the following martingale representation holds: any P-square-integrable martingale Z can be obtained as a stochastic integral with respect to W, i.e.

$$Z_t = Z_0 + \int_0^t f(s)\,dW(s)$$

for some predictable process f. Also defined on the probability space is a collection of "default times," i.e. random variables $\tau_1, \ldots, \tau_N$ taking values in $[0, \infty)$, whose distributions are continuous and who have no common jumps, i.e. $P(\tau_k = \tau_l) = 0$,

$k \neq l$. We associate with each default time a counting process jumping to 1 at the default time, i.e.

$$N_k(t) = 1_{\{t \geq \tau_k\}}, \quad t \in [0, T], \ k = 1, \ldots, N,$$

and the information contained in the state variables and from observing the jumps if they occur is

$$\mathcal{F}_t = \mathcal{G}_t \vee \sigma\{N_k(t), \ k = 1, \ldots, N\}.$$

This filtration is assumed to be right-continuous. Now we assume that intensities of the jump processes exist, i.e. that there exists $(\mathcal{G}_t-)$ progressively measurable processes $\lambda_k : [0, T] \times \Omega \to \mathbb{R}, \ k = 1, \ldots, N$, such that

$$M_k(t) = N_k(t) - \int_0^t (1 - N_k(s))\lambda_k(s) \, ds$$

are martingales under P with respect to $(\mathcal{F}_t)$. This filtration is assumed to be right-continuous and a subtle assumption made in Kusuoka (1999) is that *any* $P - \mathcal{F}_t$-martingale is a $P - \mathcal{G}_t$-martingale. The setting we have laid out so far encompasses that of Cox processes, and this assumption can be shown to mean that we can in fact always represent the processes using the Cox process technique. This, however, leads us into territory we do not want to cover here, but see the references for more on this topic.

Now comes the result which lays out the possible structure of risk premiums. Assume that Q is equivalent to P on $(\Omega, \mathcal{F})$. Define the density process

$$\rho_t = E^P\left[\frac{dQ}{dP} \,\Big|\, \mathcal{F}_t\right], \quad t \in [0, T],$$

and assume that $\log \rho_t$ is locally bounded. Then there are predictable processes $\beta : [0, T] \times \Omega \to \mathbb{R}^d$ and $\kappa_k : [0, T] \times \Omega \to \mathbb{R}, \ k = 1, \ldots, N$, such that

$$\rho_t = 1 + \int_0^t \rho_{s-}\left[\beta(s) \, dW(s) + \sum_{k=1}^N \kappa_k(s) \, dM_k(s)\right],$$

and under Q

$$\tilde{B}(t) = B(t) - \int_0^t \beta(s) \, ds$$

is a d-dimensional $Q - \mathcal{F}_t$-Brownian motion and

$$\tilde{M}_k(t) = N_k(t) - \int_0^t (1 - N_k(s))(1 + \kappa_k(s))\lambda_k(s) \, ds, \quad k = 1, \ldots, N,$$

are $Q - \mathcal{F}_t$-martingales. Hence the intensities under Q have changed by a (stochastic) factor $(1 + \kappa_k)$.

Why is this statement so important? It says that (ignoring the condition that ρ is locally bounded, which is a small technicality) we know exactly what can happen to our driving processes under an equivalent change of measure. Essentially, the drift of the Brownian motion can change and the drift change may be a function of jump times. Also, each intensity process of the jump times can change and the factor by which it changes is a positive process which can depend on the diffusion and on the jumps of other processes. This last part is crucial. While the equivalent change of measure cannot introduce simultaneous jumps (they would then also have to exist under P), it is possible to have a jump in the intensity of one process caused by a jump in intensity of another process under Q, even if this effect is not there under P.

5.11.2 The Implications for Expected Returns

The technical result from the last section allows us to illustrate the significance of the risk premium in a corporate bond through a simple example. Assume that our model for the default of a single issuer is given as follows under the real-world measure P:

$$dr_t = \kappa(\bar{r} - r_t)\,dt + \sigma_r\sqrt{r_t}\,dW_t^1,$$
$$d\lambda_t = \gamma(\bar{\lambda} - \lambda_t)\,dt + \sigma_\lambda\sqrt{\lambda_t}\,dW_t^2,$$
$$\tau = \inf\left\{t \geqslant 0 : \int_0^t \lambda_s\,ds \geqslant E_1\right\},$$

where W^1, W^2 are independent Brownian motions, and E_1 is exponentially distributed and independent of (r, λ). We write $N_t = 1_{\{\tau \leqslant t\}}$ and

$$\mathcal{G}_t = \sigma\{r_s, \lambda_s : 0 \leqslant s \leqslant t\},$$
$$\mathcal{F}_t = \sigma\{r_s, \lambda_s, N_s : 0 \leqslant s \leqslant t\},$$

so $M_t \equiv N_t - \int_0^t \lambda_s\,ds$ is a martingale. Now assume the following structure for the evolution under the equivalent measure Q,

$$dr_t = (\kappa\bar{r} - (\kappa - \psi_r^\sigma)r_t)\,dt + \sigma_r\sqrt{r_t}\,d\tilde{W}_t^1,$$
$$d\lambda_t = (\gamma\bar{\lambda} - (\gamma - \psi_\lambda^\sigma)\lambda_t)\,dt + \sigma_\lambda\sqrt{\lambda_t}\,d\tilde{W}_t^2,$$

and assume that under Q, $\tilde{W}_t^1$ and $\tilde{W}_t^2$ are independent, and

$$M_t = N_t - \int_0^t \mu\lambda_s 1_{\{N_s=0\}}\,ds$$

is a martingale. μ, ψ_r, and ψ_λ are prices of risk which we now interpret. Consider a bond with maturity T and payoff $1_{\{N_T=0\}}$, i.e. a zero-coupon bond with zero recovery in the event of default. By independence of r and λ under Q we may write the price of this bond as

$$v(t,T) = 1_{\{N_t=0\}} E_t^Q \left(\exp\left(-\int_t^T r_s \, ds \right) \right) E_t^Q \left(\exp\left(-\int_t^T \lambda_s \, ds \right) \right)$$

$$= 1_{\{N_t=0\}} \exp(A^r(T-t) - B^r(T-t)r_t) \exp(A^\lambda(T-t) - B^\lambda(T-t)\lambda),$$

where A^r, B^r, A^λ, and B^λ are the functions associated with the affine representation of bond prices in the CIR model.

We can now complete the following program (but we will not do so in details here).

- Use Itô's formula to derive a stochastic differential equation for $v(t,T)$ under Q and under P.

- Compute $(1/v(t-,T)) \, dv(t,T)$ by pre-multiplying $1/v(t-,T)$ on both sides of the stochastic differential equation.

- Make sure, by writing N_t as $dN_t = dM_t + \mu \lambda_t 1_{\{N_t=0\}} \, dt$, that the coefficient in front of dt captures the drift, i.e. the remaining expressions (integrals with respect to $d\tilde{W}_t^1$, $d\tilde{W}_t^2$, and dM_t) are martingales.

- Do the same under P to obtain the drift of the return process under P.

- We know that the drift under Q must be $r_t \, dt$, so if we subtract the expression for the drift under Q from that under P we have the excess return.

If we let μ_v denote the drift rate under P of the corporate bond, we obtain the following expression for the excess return:

$$\mu_v(t) - r_t = B_r \sigma_r \psi_r r_t + B_\lambda \sigma_\lambda \psi_\lambda \lambda_t + (\mu - 1)\lambda_t 1_{\{N_t=0\}}$$

$$= B_r \sigma_r \sqrt{r_t} \psi_r \sqrt{r_t} + B_\lambda \sigma_\lambda \sqrt{\lambda_t} \psi_\lambda \sqrt{\lambda_t} + (\mu - 1)\lambda_t 1_{\{N_t=0\}}.$$

The excess return has three components: the bond has interest-rate risk; the volatility due to this component is $B_r \sigma_r \sqrt{r_t}$; and *each* unit of volatility is rewarded with a factor risk premium of $\psi_r \sqrt{r_t}$. The same is true for the fluctuation in the default-risk factor, whose contribution to volatility (of diffusion type) is given by $B_\lambda \sigma_\lambda \sqrt{\lambda_t}$ and this is rewarded by $\psi_\lambda \sqrt{\lambda_t}$. Finally, the jump component contributes positively to excess return if $\mu > 1$.

If $\psi_\lambda > 0$ but $\mu = 1$, then risk associated with fluctuations in the default intensity carries a risk premium, but the default event itself does not. This is consistent with the default event risk being diversifiable (see Jarrow et al. 2003). If $\psi_\lambda = 0$ and $\mu > 1$, the risk associated with the default event carries a risk premium, but the fluctuations in default risk do not. To see the significance of the different assumptions about risk premiums consider Figure 5.3. Here we have assumed that the short rate and the

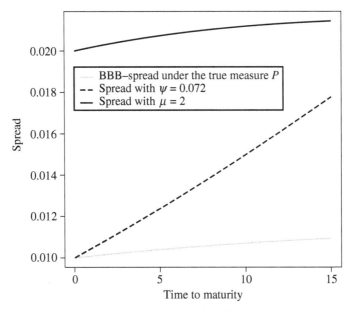

Figure 5.3. The term structure of credit spreads for different assumptions about risk premiums. The solid grey line corresponds to the spread computed using the "true" intensity process with mean reversion level 0.016, mean reversion coefficient 0.03, volatility 0.0286, and a starting level of 0.01 for the intensity. This is roughly comparable with a Baa/BBB default intensity. The event risk premium is set at $\mu = 2$, and the associated yield spread is shown as the solid black line. Here we assume no compensation for default-risk variation. The dashed black line assumes no event risk compensation, but the value of ψ_λ, the risk premium for variations in default risk, is set at -0.0072.

default intensity are independent of each other, and that the default intensity follows a CIR process under P with parameters given in the caption.

We compare the effects on the spread curve of the different assumptions on risk premiums. The lowest spread curve corresponds to a case of risk neutrality, i.e. one with no risk premiums. A risk premium on variations in default risk, but no event risk premium, leaves the short end of the yield curve identical to the risk-neutral curve, but at longer maturities, the difference is pronounced. A risk premium on the default event shifts the entire spread curve upwards compared with the risk-neutral curve.

There is one final remark that is important in this context. The situation in which the yield spread in the short end becomes identical to that under a risk-neutral pricing (i.e. one using the empirical measure) hinges on the assumption that the driving factors are diffusion processes. If the state variable process has a jump component which captures the risk of an overall increase in default risk due to a market-wide event, then a risk premium on this jump component (which is not related to the actual defaults of individual firms) will push even the short spreads higher than those obtained using a risk-neutral calculation. Hence one *can* have a risk premium on overall variation in default risk only and still obtain a difference in the short end between empirical default probabilities and those implied by market prices. However, the driving factors must then have jump components. The presence of such a market-wide factor seems like a very plausible explanation for the discrepancy between short-end default probabilities and actual spreads.

5.11.3 On Diversifiable Default Risk and Market-Implied Default Probabilities

The default intensity of firms in intensity models typically plays the role of a latent variable which we cannot observe—a role similar to that of the short rate in the classical models of the term structure. By methods outlined in the next section, if we propose an intensity model for corporate bond prices, we can use filtering techniques to estimate from bond prices the evolution of the intensity. To keep the argument simple, we assume in this section that prices have no liquidity component. The joint inversion of prices to latent variables and the time-series evolution of the latent variable determine the evolution of the latent variable process λ under the risk-neutral measure Q and the real-world measure P. In a CIR setting, for example, we would end up with estimates for the parameters in the joint specifications:

$$d\lambda_t = \kappa(\theta - \lambda_t)\,dt + \sigma\sqrt{\lambda_t}\,dW_t \quad (P),$$

$$d\lambda_t = (\kappa + \psi)\left(\frac{\kappa\theta}{\kappa + \psi} - \lambda_t\right)dt + \sigma\sqrt{\lambda_t}\,d\tilde{W}_t \quad (Q).$$

The risk parameter ψ could then, in analogy with the riskless rate, be thought of as a risk premium for variations in default risk. It would be tempting to then conclude that the empirical default probability, as derived from bond prices, is equal to

$$P(\tau > t) = E \exp\left(-\int_0^t \lambda(s)\,ds\right).$$

But this is only true if there is no event risk premium. Only if there is no event risk premium can we say that the intensity process λ is also the compensating P intensity of the default jump process under P. If there is event risk, we have to correct for this as well. In fact, if there is a component of event risk, we have no guarantee that the parameter ψ describes the risk premium for variations in default risk correctly.

Similarly, going in the other direction, we could envisage modeling the default intensity as a function of underlying state variables X. If we worked with an equity-based model, the state variable might be only equity. Combined with estimated volatilities and default boundaries we could translate a short-term default probability (obtained, say, from some measure of distance to default) into an empirical default intensity from the usual approximation over short time intervals:

$$P(\tau \in (t, t + \Delta t] \mid \tau > t) = \lambda(X_t)\Delta t.$$

Since we can estimate the risk premium associated with equity from market data on equity, it would seem natural to use the evolution of the process $\lambda(X_s)$ under the risk-neutral measure Q to determine the prices of corporate bonds. Such a link is only valid if there is no default-event risk premium.

Understanding the market prices of risk fully in intensity-based models requires a pairing of empirical default data or default intensities with pricing intensities. Only then can we separate risk premiums for event risk from variations in default risk and obtain correct estimates for both.

5.12 The Estimation of Intensity Models

In this section we outline a technique for estimating the parameters of intensity models for bond prices which exploits the similarities between ordinary term-structure modeling and the modeling of credit-risky bonds. The purpose of the outline is to give a fairly precise description of what it takes to estimate an intensity model, but for an actual implementation one should consult the references given in the notes. The critical additional components that need to be estimated in a model of credit risk are the default intensity and possibly a recovery rate.

Ideally, we would estimate the default intensity and recovery rates from extensive histories of defaults and recoveries on bonds. There are several practical problems with this: the number of defaults that we have actually observed makes the estimation difficult. Indeed, if we were to include relevant predictors of default, as a true extension of credit scoring, we would need occurrence/exposure ratios for a high-dimensional grid, and as mentioned earlier this is not easy to handle. We may also argue that it is precisely the difficulties in obtaining all the information for each issuer which makes intensity models popular, since we can specify a process which aggregates the default risk into a single process without decomposing this process into various dependencies. And finally, often we deal with credit-related interest rates, like the LIBOR rates we will encounter in the section on swaps, where it would be very unclear how to estimate the credit spread from actual defaults.

This leads us to specify the default intensity as a latent variable and observed through a pricing function. The default intensity is a continuous-time process, but of course we observe prices only at discrete-time points.

The Kalman filter is a standard tool for estimating latent-factor models for the term structures of government bonds and for corporate bonds. While the word "filtering" leads one to focus on the estimation of the underlying variable, this is not the central focus in our econometric applications. In essence, here is what the Kalman filter helps us to do. Imagine a statistical model indexed by a parameter ψ. For each value of ψ we know the distribution of a vector of random variables $(X_1, \ldots, X_n, Y_1, \ldots, Y_n)$. We observe only the Y-variables. For each value of the parameter, we can integrate out the X-variables from the distribution to get a marginal distribution of

$(Y_1, \ldots, Y_n)$ given ψ, i.e. if we insert the observed values of Y, we have the likelihood function evaluated at ψ. It is the computation of the likelihood function for a particular ψ which is obtained by the Kalman filter. As a byproduct of the computation, we obtain least squares estimates of the latent variables for each ψ. Maximizing the likelihood over ψ is difficult and note that the recursion we now describe for computing the value at a single point must be run until a maximum is found. Once the maximum is found, we have estimates for the latent variable.

Abstractly, the setup is as follows. The latent variables are modelled as a Markov process X whose evolution is described through a family of transition densities

$$P(X_k \in dx_k \mid X_{k-1} = x_{k-1}; \psi),$$

where the dependence on the parameter vector ψ is apparent. The state variables may be the default intensities themselves or the intensities may be functions of the state variables.

We observe prices collected in a vector process Y, which is of the form

$$Y_k = z(X_k; \psi) + \varepsilon_k.$$

Exactly as in our example where we estimated a firm's value, the parameter vector ψ determines both the evolution of the state variables and the prices we observe. Hence it enters into the pricing equation and into the transition densities.

The Kalman filter recursions work on a particular structure for the latent and the observed variables. More precisely, consider the following system:

$$Y_k = A_k(\psi) + B_k(\psi)X_k + \varepsilon_k \qquad \text{(observation)},$$
$$X_k = C_k(\psi) + D_k(\psi)X_{k-1} + u_k \quad \text{(state)},$$

where

$$\varepsilon_k \sim N(0, H_k(\psi)) \quad \text{and} \quad u_k \sim N(0, Q_k(\psi)).$$

Here, H_k and Q_k are variance/covariance matrices of the appropriate dimension. Typically, the matrix H_k is assumed to be of the form $\sigma^2 I$. In the observation equation, the matrices A_k and B_k are derived from the pricing equations for bonds, which express the yields of bonds as functions of the underlying state variables. The cleanest case is in an affine model for zero-coupon bond prices, where yields are affine functions of the state variables. The matrices C_k and D_k can be computed explicitly in the case of Gaussian diffusions by looking at the transition densities over discrete-time intervals. If the process is not Gaussian, but still Markov, we can still, for affine processes, compute conditional means and variances of the process over a discrete period and these means and variances are then used in a Gaussian approximation of the transition densities.

It is worth pointing out that all the distributions given in the system refer to the evolution under the physical measure P. The "martingale" measure Q is a helpful device for calculating the values of z at a particular point in time, but this is only relevant for computing the function z and hence for determining the coefficients in the observation equation. Some of the parameters in the vector ψ may enter the state variable evolution only, similar to the role of the drift in the firm-value evolution in the option-based approach, and some may also enter in the pricing equation (as with the volatility) and it is possible for parameters to be only part of the pricing function (a market price of risk, for example).

As mentioned above, the Kalman filter is a method for computing the likelihood function and for obtaining best (mean squared error optimal) estimates for the state variables. For it to work, we must assume a starting value of X equal to $\hat{x}_0$ and an associated variance matrix $\hat{\Sigma}_0$. While we do not know these values, the traditional approach is to choose these from the unconditional distribution of X_0 given the parameter.

The Kalman recursions start by assuming that an estimate of $\hat{x}_{k-1}$ has been computed with associated mean squared error matrix $\hat{\Sigma}_{k-1}$. From these values the best prediction of X_k based on observations up to time $k - 1$ is

$$\hat{x}_{k|k-1} = C_k + D_k \hat{x}_{k-1}$$

and

$$\hat{\Sigma}_{k|k-1} = D_k \hat{\Sigma}_{k-1} D_k' + Q_k.$$

Now include information on y_k to obtain

$$\hat{x}_k = E[X_k \mid \mathcal{F}_k] = \hat{x}_{k|k-1} + \hat{\Sigma}_{k|k-1} B_k' F_k^{-1} V_k,$$
$$\hat{\Sigma}_k = \Sigma_{k|k-1}^{-1} - \Sigma_{k|k-1}^{-1} B_k' F_k^{-1} B_k \Sigma_{k|k-1}^{-1},$$

where

$$V_k = y_k - (A_k + B_k \hat{x}_{k|k-1}),$$
$$F_k = \mathrm{cov}(V_k) = B_k \hat{\Sigma}_{k|k-1} B_k' + H_k,$$

and with n observations we end up with the (log)likelihood function

$$\log L(\psi \mid y_1, \ldots, y_n) = \sum_{k=1}^{n} (-\tfrac{1}{2} N_k \log(2\pi) - \tfrac{1}{2} \log |F_k| - \tfrac{1}{2} V_k' F_k^{-1} V_k),$$

where $N_k = \dim(V_k)$.

This completes the computation of the likelihood for a single ψ. A nontrivial part of the estimation is now to maximize this likelihood over ψ. The Kalman filter is ideally suited for a Vasicek-type model (where the transition equations are Gaussian) for zero-coupon bonds. In this case the price function is exponential-affine, and the yields are therefore affine functions of the state variables. Assuming

Gaussian observation errors, we end up in exactly the same framework in which the filter is formulated above. In practice, the filter must be extended to handle at least two complications.

(1) The yield of a coupon bond is not an affine function of the state variable. This is handled in practice by letting the price function be approximated by a first-order Taylor approximation around the estimated state

$$z(X_k; \psi) \approx z(\hat{x}_{k|k-1}; \psi) + z'(\hat{x}_{k|k-1}; \psi)(X_k - \hat{x}_{k|k-1}).$$

(2) If we have a CIR model for the state variable, the evolution of the state does not conform to the format above, since the variance matrix is then state dependent. In practice, since the variance matrix is allowed to be time varying in the filter, we replace the state by its estimated value and substitute into the expression for the variance matrix.

5.13 The Trouble with the Term Structure of Credit Spreads: the Reduced-Form Viewpoint

The main advantage of intensity models is the ease with which they are adapted to analyze aggregate measures of risk. In Chapter 7 we will set up a model for analyzing the role of credit risk in swap spreads and we will relate it to broad measures of credit risk as contained in indexes of yield spreads. The analysis of these quantities is conveniently carried out in an intensity setting. The intensity setting also has advantages in the setting for pricing credit derivatives, and that is also a topic of later chapters.

But let us also keep in mind some of the problems one has to remember when analyzing term structures of defaultable bonds. The first warning is of course that we should be careful whenever we price coupon bonds. The analogy with the treasury-bond modeling of the whole setup makes it tempting to price using a term structure of zero-coupon bonds as we do with treasuries. This can only be justified if we consider "small" debt issues or derivatives which do not change the underlying capital structure.

An intensity model implicitly assumes Poisson-type arrivals of defaults. Defaults are often recorded at coupon dates, since this is the day a payment is missed. This introduces a degree of predictability into the default event. While this is often brought up as an argument against intensity models, it may not be too serious a problem. At some point as we get closer to the coupon date, refinancing opportunities dry up and it is clear to investors that there is no hope of the firm repaying its debt. The event which makes it clear to investors that there is no hope may well come as a surprise and it is this date that is reflected in market prices, not the "legal" default date.

5.14 Bibliographical Notes

The first models I met which addressed pricing of corporate bonds using intensities were working paper versions of Jarrow and Turnbull (1995) and Madan and Unal (1998). This led to work presented in Lando (1994) on how to specify and calibrate different rating-based models and how to use the Cox process setup to dispense with the assumption of independence between the riskless rate and the default intensity. Parts of this work were later published with extensions in Jarrow et al. (1997) and Lando (1998). At the same time, the model of Duffie and Singleton (1999a) was developed. The theoretical presentation of the basic setup builds largely on these works. But the result on conditional expectations that I learned from Elliott et al. (2000) facilitates the derivations. Other early works on intensity modeling include Artzner and Delbaen (1995), Schönbucher (1998), Duffie et al. (1996), and Arvanitis et al. (1999),

A classic reference for studying intensities is the book by Brémaud (1981), and other useful sources are Grandell (1976, 1991). The new book by Bielecki and Rutkowski (2002) contains a detailed discussion of intensity modeling of default risk. See also Belanger et al. (2001), Elliott and Jeanblanc (1998) and Elliott et al. (2000). Papers addressing cases where the Cox setting is no longer valid include Kusuoka (1999), Duffie et al. (1996), Jarrow and Yu (2001), and Collin-Dufresne et al. (2003a).

For more on the structure of affine models, see Dai and Singleton (2000). The case with (local) negative correlation in the quadratic setting was learned from Duffie and Liu (2001). We have emphasized the connection with the class of affine models. For links to Heath–Jarrow–Morton (HJM) modeling, see Schönbucher (1998), Duffie and Singleton (1999a), and Bielecki and Rutkowski (2002).

Preliminary results on diversifiable default risk are in Lando (1994). Diversifiability and the structure of risk premiums is a topic studied in Jarrow et al. (2003), Kusuoka (1999), and El Karoui and Martellini (2002). Gordy (2003) also uses diversifiability arguments in his work on capital charges for loan portfolios driven by a single systematic risk factor.

The section on incomplete information draws on the work by Duffie and Lando (2001), which first showed a sense in which a diffusion-based, structural model has an intensity representation if there is noisy information about the firm's assets. They also derived an algorithm for updating information about a firm's assets given noisy information at fixed dates and survival. For a multivariate extension of the result on the computation of the intensity in this model, see, for example, Song (1998). For an empirical investigation of the central conclusion that accounting information matters, see Yu (2003). A fixed time lag is used in Collin-Dufresne et al. (2003b). Incomplete information with an unobserved default boundary is treated for example in Finger (2002) and Giesecke (2003), and—modeling creditor races—in Lambrecht and Perraudin (1996).

The extended Kalman filter was employed for defaultable bonds in Duffee (1999) and examples of its use for estimating bond-pricing models can be found in many sources. For more on the use of the Kalman filter for estimating affine term-structure models, see, for example, Chen and Scott (2003), de Jong (2000), Duan and Simonato (1999), Geyer and Pichler (1999), and Lund (1997). The book by Harvey (1990) remains the classical reference for the Kalman filter.

There are many papers on credit-spread estimation whose conclusions are central to our understanding of the empirical performance of intensity-based models, but there are not that many papers which implement and test the intensity-based framework using the original formulation. In Duffie and Singleton (1997) the intensity model of default with fractional recovery is used to analyze the term structure of swap spreads. While it is a reduced-form setting, the paper's main conclusions are related to swap spreads. The first paper to truly test a reduced-form specification of defaultable bonds is Duffee (1999), who specifies a two-factor model for the treasury-bond evolutions and a one-factor firm-specific intensity process and estimates using a Kalman filter technique, as described in this chapter. His conclusion is that the intensity models seem capable of fitting term-structure evolutions for corporate bonds. An empirical analysis of event risk premiums is taken up by Driessen (2002), where it is found that there is an event risk premium by comparing the empirical default rates with corporate bond spreads. Duffie et al. (2003) analyze an intensity-based model on Russian bonds around the crisis in 1998. Jarrow (2001) is concerned with estimating an intensity models with covariates based on market prices.

There is also empirical work focusing on recovery rates or, equivalently, loss given default. For more on this, see, for example, Acharya et al. (2003), Altman et al. (2002), Bakshi et al. (2001), Guha (2002), Gupton and Stein (2002), and Schuermann (2003).

6

Rating-Based Term-Structure Models

6.1 Introduction

In December 2001, Moody's conducted a survey to determine the extent to which companies have rating triggers contained in on- and off-balance sheet financial arrangements. Focusing mainly on companies rated Ba1 or higher, Stumpp and Coppola (2002) in their report on the survey found that out of 771 issuers rated Ba1 or higher who responded (the response rate was 97.6%) to the survey, 675 had rating triggers in some of their financial arrangements. So, rating triggers seem to be the rule rather than the exception.

Rating triggers can be of many types (see Stumpp and Coppola (2002) for an excellent survey) but the most prevalent are provisions which require the issuer of debt to post some sort of (extra) collateral as a security enhancement if ratings deteriorate or a *pricing grid* which, for example, links the coupon payments on a bond issue, the rate paid on a bank credit line, or the payment on a swap contract to the rating of a company. Interestingly, the survey found that companies with ratings closer to speculative-grade ratings are more likely to have rating triggers in their balance sheets. This raises the difficult issue of "feedback" effects where the downgrade impacts a company negatively, thus pushing the company further into distress. We will not consider models for such "feedback" behavior here. Our focus will be on models that allow us to incorporate the ratings of issuers directly into the pricing of securities.

Apart from rating triggers, ratings are also used as a (crude) way of aggregating corporate bond prices. Even if ratings are not sufficient to price a bond, any attempt to obtain a benchmark term structure for corporate bonds needs to pool different bonds and rating is a natural place to start. If we want to model the credit spreads for such indices or compare individual bonds with the index, it is natural to look at rating-based models, i.e. models which incorporate information on credit migrations into bond prices.

6.2 A Markovian Model for Rating-Based Term Structures

A good place to start is to set up a model for corporate bond prices that is based on ratings. It is by no means our final model, since it is clear that ratings remain a crude measure of credit quality. Although rating agencies have access to a lot of information on individual companies, their ratings are (deliberately) not changed often, and hence the rating is by its very definition only a rough aggregation of credit information. Nevertheless, to have an idea of how we can calibrate a model to take into account ratings and to account for risk premiums in a consistent fashion, it is a useful place to start, and we will build generalizations later.

The model we are about to see is really only a model of spreads and hence it can be combined with any model of the term structure that one prefers. This is achieved by assuming independence between the default event and the short rate (which we only really need under the pricing measure but think of as holding under the physical measure as well).

As always we denote the short-rate process by r and assume that treasury bonds are priced under some martingale measure as

$$p(0, t) = E^Q \left(\exp \left(- \int_0^t r_s \, ds \right) \right) \quad \text{all } t.$$

Next, consider an issuer of a corporate bond (zero coupon) whose default probability is given as $Q(\tau < t)$ for all t under Q. If we assume that in the case of default, the bond pays out δ at maturity instead of the promised payment 1, and if we assume that τ *is independent of* r under Q, then the price of the corporate bond is

$$
\begin{aligned}
v(0, t) &= E^Q \left[\exp \left(- \int_0^t r_s \, ds \right) [1_{\{\tau > t\}} + \delta 1_{\{\tau \leqslant t\}}] \right] \\
&= p(0, t) E^Q [1_{\{\tau > t\}} + \delta 1_{\{\tau \leqslant t\}}] \\
&= p(0, t) [Q(\tau > t) + \delta Q(\tau \leqslant t)] \\
&= p(0, t) [\delta + (1 - \delta) Q(\tau > t)].
\end{aligned}
$$

The idea now is to make $Q(\tau > t)$ depend on the rating of the issuer, i.e. to simply change the formula above into

$$v^i(0, t) = p(0, t)[\delta + (1 - \delta) Q^i(\tau > t)], \tag{6.1}$$

where "i" refers to the rating at time 0, and Q^i means the probability of survival past t (under Q) for a company starting out in category i. It would be tempting to simply use the empirical transition probabilities as reported by the major rating agencies. This temptation quickly disappears when one tries to do it. As shown in Figure 6.1 the spreads obtained are far too small for a high rating category, even if we use a recovery rate of 0, which produces the maximal spread for a given default probability. The same is true in the short end of Baa, as shown in Figure 6.2, whereas, as shown in Figure 6.3, the spread in B is far off, particularly in the long end. There are many reasons for this discrepancy, some of which are related

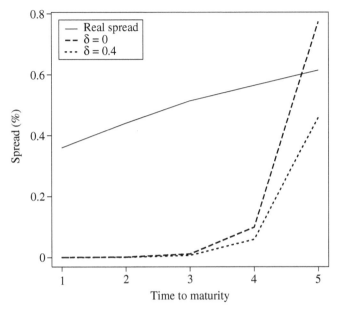

Figure 6.1.   The observed zero-coupon spread for the Aa category and
the implied spread using delta values of 0 and 0.4, respectively.

to differential tax treatment of corporate bonds and treasury bonds, differences in
liquidity, and the effects of specialness in the repo market for treasury securities, to
which we will return in Chapter 8. At this point we ignore such effects and treat the
spread as a credit risk-related spread. Even then, from a theoretical perspective, we
would also expect to see risk premiums in the market associated with default risk
and this in particular implies that spread computed essentially under a risk-neutrality
assumption (assuming that the recoveries are known) must be smaller than observed
spreads.

Given the discrepancy, we look for a sensible specification of the transition probabilities of ratings. This turns the model into a calibration device by using it the
other way around: observe bond prices of zero-coupon bonds $v^i(0, t)$ for each ratings category i and different maturities and try to infer $Q^i(\tau > t)$ from this. These
probabilities could then be used to price credit derivatives. A first idea would then
be to model the rating migration as a Markov chain under Q with parameters varying freely subject only to the constraint that the matrix is a transition-probability
matrix. In theory, it is possible with enough maturities observed for each rating
category to infer all the parameters of the transition matrix Q if the Markov chain
is time-homogeneous (under some technical conditions) under the pricing measure.
To see this, let δ be a known recovery. Let $q_i^{imp}(t)$ denote the implied probability of
default before time t for a firm rated i today, based on observation of the price of a

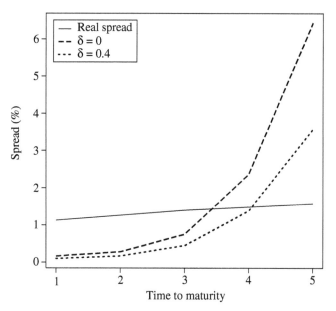

Figure 6.2. The observed zero-coupon spread for Baa-rated US industrials and the implied spread using delta values of 0 and 0.4, respectively. Based on data from CreditMetrics' homepage, September 2002.

zero-coupon bond maturing at t, and using the pricing Equation (6.1). Hence

$$1 - q_i^{\text{imp}}(t) = \frac{v^i(0, t) - (1 - \delta)p(0, t)}{p(0, t)(1 - \delta)}$$

for $i = 1, \ldots, K - 1$ and $t = 1, 2, \ldots, T$. Now we are trying to find a matrix

$$Q = \begin{pmatrix} q_{1,1} & \cdots & q_{1,K} \\ \vdots & \ddots & \vdots \\ q_{K-1,1} & \cdots & q_{K-1,K} \\ 0 & \cdots & 1 \end{pmatrix}$$

so that $(Q^t)_{i,K} = q_i^{\text{imp}}(t)$. Let $s^i(t, u)$ denote the probability of surviving past time u given a (nondefault) rating of i at time t under the dynamics given by Q. Note that under a time-homogeneity assumption we must have

$$s^i(0, t) = \sum_{j=1}^{K-1} q_{i,j} s^j(1, t) = \sum_{j=1}^{K-1} q_{i,j} s^j(0, t - 1),$$

and using this identity for maturities $2, \ldots, K - 1$ and adding the requirement $q_{i,1} + \cdots + q_{i,K} = 1$, we get the following system of equations for each (non-

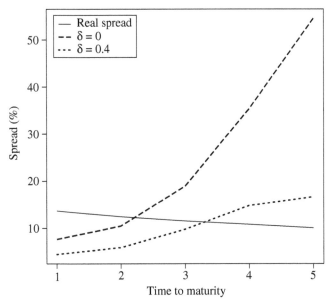

Figure 6.3. The observed zero-coupon spread for B-rated US industrials and the implied spread using delta values of 0 and 0.4, respectively. Based on data from CreditMetrics' homepage, September 2002.

default) rating i

$$
\begin{pmatrix}
1 - s^i(0,1) \\
s^i(0,2) \\
\vdots \\
s^i(0,t_{K-1}) \\
1
\end{pmatrix}
=
\begin{pmatrix}
0 & \cdots & 0 & 1 \\
s^1(0,1) & \cdots & s^{K-1}(0,1) & 0 \\
\vdots & \ddots & \vdots & \vdots \\
s^1(0,t_{K-2}) & \cdots & s^{K-1}(0,t_{K-2}) & 0 \\
1 & \cdots & 1 & 1
\end{pmatrix}
\begin{pmatrix}
q_{i,1} \\
\vdots \\
q_{i,K}
\end{pmatrix},
$$

and hence, in principle, plugging in the implied values

$$ s^i(0,t) = 1 - q_i^{\mathrm{imp}}(t) $$

and solving this system should allow us to determine $q_{i,1}, \ldots, q_{i,K}$.

In practice, this does not work: the homogeneity assumption is much too strong and we will find $q_{i,1}, \ldots, q_{i,K}$ which are not even a probability vector. Even if we succeed, we have no guarantee that plugging the probabilities into the formula

$$ v^i(0,t) = \delta p(0,t) + (1-\delta) p(0,t) Q^i(\tau > t) $$

will match observed bond prices, since only information about the bond from a particular rating class is used to infer what the corresponding row in the transition matrix is. This is unsatisfactory since the whole idea of building a consistent term-structure model across ratings should be to take into account the prices of bonds in adjacent rating classes as well.

So, instead of using a homogeneous chain, we could try, at the other extreme, to match prices using a nonhomogeneous Markov chain, so that

$$Q^i(\tau > t) = 1 - (Q(0,1)Q(1,2)\cdots Q(t-1,t))_{i,K},$$

but this would add $(K-1)^2$ new parameters for each time period and there is no hope of recovering those from market prices.

Therefore, the procedure we will adopt in this section is to let P be a "base matrix" that is possibly, but not necessarily, equal to the empirical 1-year transition probabilities. For $\theta \in \mathbb{R}^{K-1}$ let $Q(\theta)$ denote a modification of P depending on θ. The idea is to let the implied transition-probability matrix over t periods be given as a nonhomogeneous Markov chain in which each one-period transition matrix is a modification of P using the low-dimensional parameter θ. In short, find a sequence of parameters $(\theta_1, \ldots, \theta_t)$, and define

$$Q(0,t) = Q(\theta_0)Q(\theta_1)\cdots Q(\theta_{t-1}) \tag{6.2}$$

such that, for all t, the implied default probabilities of the bonds maturing at t match the default probabilities in $Q(0,t)$. The whole computation we have to go through is then evident from the following description of how to get the first two values θ_0 and θ_1.

(1) Assume known recovery for all bonds.
(2) Observe $v^i(0,1)$, $v^i(0,2)$ for $i = 1, \ldots, K-1$. Compute the implied default probabilities $Q^i(\tau \leqslant 1)$, $Q^i(\tau \leqslant 2)$ for $i = 1, \ldots, K-1$.
(3) Letting $Q(\theta)$ be a modification of the empirically observed transition matrix P (or some other "base matrix") depending on $\theta \in \mathbb{R}^{K-1}$, find θ_0 such that $[Q(\theta_0)]_{ik} = Q^i(\tau \leqslant 1)$, $i = 1, \ldots, K-1$.
(4) Find θ_1 such that

$$(Q[\theta_0]Q[\theta_1])_{iK} = Q^i(\tau \leqslant 2), \quad i = 1, \ldots, K-1.$$

The critical question is how to choose the base matrix and the functional form of $Q(\theta)$, i.e. how the modification of P depends on θ.

One possibility is to use the following modification in discrete time:

$$q_{ij}(\theta) = \begin{cases} \theta_i p_{ij} & \text{for } i \neq j, \\ 1 - \sum_{j \neq i} \theta_i p_{ij} = 1 - \theta_i(1 - p_{ii}) & \text{for } i = j. \end{cases}$$

This numerical scheme can be seen as a discrete-time approximation to a row-wise adjustment of the generator, a point we now explain. Assume that Θ is a diagonal matrix with $\theta_1, \ldots, \theta_{K-1}, 0$ in the diagonal. Let Λ denote the generator of a continuous-time Markov chain describing the actual transition probabilities, i.e. $P(\Delta t) = \exp(\Lambda \Delta t)$. Then a possible modification of $P(\Delta t)$ would be the one obtained by multiplying the generator by Θ, thus obtaining a "row-wise" adjustment of the generator matrix where the ith row is multiplied by θ_i, i.e.

$$Q(\Delta t) = \exp(\Theta \Lambda \Delta t),$$

and this would always produce a transition matrix as long as Θ is positive. Hence even large adjustments would be permissible, although it would in practice be a problem if the empirical generator matrix had zeros in the default column (as may well happen for top categories), since then the multiplication would have to be very large, giving an unreasonably low holding time in the state under Q. But there would be no problem with the resulting matrix not being a transition matrix. Now consider the discrete-time approximations

$$P(\Delta t) = I + \Lambda \Delta t,$$
$$Q(\Delta t) = I + \Theta \Lambda \Delta t = I + \Theta (P(\Delta t) - I),$$

and note that this is exactly the scheme proposed above. For large discrepancies between prices observed in the market and those obtained by using an empirical transition matrix, large adjustments are necessary, and then it is not a very stable method. The problem is that if, for example, at time 1 the default probability in category i as read from the base matrix (which could be the matrix of empirical transition probabilities) is much smaller than the implied default probability from observed bond prices for rating class i, then the ith coordinate of the parameter θ must be large. More precisely, it must be the ratio of the implied default probability to the empirical default probability. If this ratio is large, then the multiplication of the other elements of the matrix by θ_i may result in numbers outside the unit interval. This then makes the resulting matrix useless. The stability can be greatly improved by replacing the column of actual default probabilities in the empirical transition matrix with average implied default probabilities computed over a long time interval. Then Θ only measures deviations from the long-term average, but the "base" matrix P is no longer an empirical transition-probability matrix.

This deficiency can also be fixed by using the following modification instead:

$$q_{ij}(\theta) = \begin{cases} \theta_i \, p_{ij} & \text{for } i \neq K, \\ 1 - \theta_i (1 - p_{iK}) & \text{for } i = K, \end{cases}$$

which turns out to be more stable in practice. Having calibrated, one can in principle price derivatives. If the derivatives are priced in the initial term structure, there will

Table 6.1. Par bond yields for US industrial firms divided according to Moody's rating and time to maturity in years. Data source: CreditMetrics' homepage, September 2002.

	1	2	3	5
Treasury	0.0153	0.0172	0.0202	0.0263
Aaa	0.0179	0.0203	0.0238	0.0308
Aa	0.0189	0.0216	0.0253	0.0323
A	0.0214	0.0244	0.0287	0.0364
Baa	0.0266	0.0298	0.0341	0.0417
Ba	0.0953	0.0905	0.0885	0.0904
B	0.1519	0.1422	0.1368	0.1296
Caa	0.2453	0.2372	0.2202	0.2113

be no difference in prices as the calibration method is changed; otherwise the method does make a difference. This means that we need economic arguments or empirical guidance as to how to choose the calibration method. There is little research in this direction. The stable method above has the economic shortcoming of being able to assign nonzero default probabilities under one measure and zero probabilities under what should be the equivalent measure. This is not a serious objection though, as we can just estimate the transition probabilities using the continuous-time method presented in Chapter 4 to ensure strictly positive transition probabilities for the empirical matrix. A more serious objection is that the stable method either moves probability mass to the default state at the cost of all other categories or removes probability mass from the default state and adds it to the other categories. This gives an odd interpretation of risk premiums, as one could, for example, see very large positive risk premiums for default but very large negative risk premiums for downgrade to speculative grade. This would make little sense economically and could lead to strange prices for products linked to downgrade to speculative-grade ratings.

6.3   An Example of Calibration

We now work through the algorithm on a specific set of data from CreditMetrics' homepage. We stress that this is only for illustration. There are many reasons why the data need to be handled with great care. Most importantly the prices are not actually prices at which bonds traded but are based on polling of dealers on how they would price a bond issued with a specific maturity. The (index of) par bond yields on 30 September 2002 for US industrials are given in Table 6.1. We translate this into zero-coupon yields (using simple linear interpolation to get the 4-year yield), which gives us the figures shown in Table 6.2. The 1-year transition matrix for the same period, estimated using the generator method, is given in Table 6.3.

Table 6.2. Zero-coupon yields of the Moody's rating categories 30 September 2002.

	1	2	3	4	5
Treasury	0.0153	0.017 216	0.020 274	0.023 449	0.026 625
Aaa	0.0179	0.020 324	0.023 904	0.027 572	0.031 241
Aa	0.0189	0.021 629	0.025 418	0.029 094	0.032 769
A	0.0214	0.024 437	0.028 854	0.032 922	0.036 990
Baa	0.0266	0.029 848	0.034 286	0.038 330	0.042 373
Ba	0.0953	0.090 284	0.088 178	0.089 339	0.090 500
B	0.1519	0.141 517	0.135 603	0.131 455	0.127 308
Caa	0.2453	0.236 247	0.215 720	0.210 540	0.205 359

Again, whether this is a reasonable matrix to use for calibration is not the issue here. We work with this to illustrate the procedure.

We now wish to find a matrix of transition probabilities $\tilde{\phi}$ such that for a given recovery of treasury, δ, we can match the observed prices

$$v^i(0, t) = \delta p(0, t) + (1 - \delta)p(0, t)Q^i(\tau > t)$$

for each maturity $t = 1, \ldots, T$ and each rating class $i = \text{Aaa}, \ldots, \text{Caa}$. First, based on observed yields we compute the 1-year implied default probabilities. This gives us

$$q^{\text{imp}}(1) = \begin{pmatrix} 0.995\,743 \\ 0.994\,111 \\ 0.990\,046 \\ 0.981\,655 \\ 0.878\,268 \\ 0.802\,356 \\ 0.692\,176 \end{pmatrix}.$$

We then find θ_i^0 such that

$$q_{iK}^{\text{imp}} = 1 - \theta_i^0(1 - q_{iK}),$$

where q_{iK} is the actual default probability shown in the last column of Table 6.3. Solving these equations gives the following result:

$$\theta^0 = \begin{pmatrix} 0.995\,743 \\ 0.994\,115 \\ 0.990\,120 \\ 0.983\,258 \\ 0.887\,066 \\ 0.862\,827 \\ 1.045\,694 \end{pmatrix}.$$

Table 6.3. One-year transition matrix based on data of US senior unsecured debt issuers represented in the Moody's database. The generator behind this matrix was estimated for the period 1 January 1999 to 1 January 2002.

	Aaa	Aa	A	Baa	Ba	B	Caa	D
Aaa	0.924 928	0.048 130	0.025 504	0.001 372	0.000 059	0.000 006	0.000 001	0.000 001
Aa	0.018 147	0.895 159	0.079 680	0.006 682	0.000 289	0.000 031	0.000 008	0.000 004
A	0.003 585	0.035 883	0.862 686	0.091 728	0.005 276	0.000 619	0.000 147	0.000 074
Baa	0.001 453	0.003 730	0.052 676	0.856 051	0.070 451	0.011 102	0.002 907	0.001 631
Ba	0.000 091	0.000 386	0.007 656	0.098 518	0.753 156	0.113 161	0.017 113	0.009 919
B	0.000 028	0.001 354	0.002 964	0.011 392	0.020 296	0.726 653	0.167 228	0.070 085
Caa	0.000 000 345	0.000 025	0.000 053	0.000 208	0.000 392	0.027 709	0.633 542	0.338 070

Table 6.4. The risk premiums obtained by using the calibration method proposed in Kijima and Komoribayashi (1998).

	θ^0	θ^1	θ^2	θ^3	θ^4
Aaa	0.995 743	0.995 635	0.991 099	0.993 393	0.993 214
Aa	0.994 115	0.991 876	0.991 080	0.991 666	0.992 118
A	0.990 120	0.986 970	0.981 965	0.979 441	0.974 171
Baa	0.983 258	0.988 054	0.989 603	1.002 311	1.014 263
Ba	0.887 066	0.900 117	0.907 670	0.855 529	0.777 953
B	0.862 827	0.913 885	0.947 784	1.078 748	1.281 998
Caa	1.045 694	0.995 219	1.015 081	0.784 027	0.352 169

The other elements of $Q(\theta)$ are then fixed by letting

$$q_{ij}(\theta) = \theta_i^0 q_{ij}, \quad i \neq K.$$

With this implied matrix $Q(\theta)$ we then turn to the 2-year implied default probabilities. We find

$$q^{\mathrm{imp}}(2) = \begin{pmatrix} 0.989\,862 \\ 0.985\,633 \\ 0.976\,589 \\ 0.959\,366 \\ 0.784\,096 \\ 0.656\,793 \\ 0.461\,739 \end{pmatrix}.$$

Now we wish to find a $\theta^1 \in \mathbb{R}^{K-1}$ such that

$$[Q(\theta^0)Q(\theta^1)]_{,K} = q^{\mathrm{imp}}(2).$$

Hence we have

$$[Q(\theta^1)]_{i,K} = ([Q(\theta^0)]^{-1} q^{\mathrm{imp}}(2))_i.$$

The entire procedure results in the premiums shown in Table 6.4.

6.4 Class-Dependent Recovery

In the model we have just seen the recovery rate is set initially, and for simplicity of exposition it is set equal for all rating classes. Of course, it is a simple matter to make the recovery rate a function of some particular bond characteristics like seniority or initial rating. It may be more realistic to have a recovery rate which depends on the rating class prior to default. If, as is the case with Moody's ratings, the grade reflects the recovery expectation in the event of default, then it is clear that we need to take into account the rating prior to default. The trick of enlarging the state space is generally convenient, if some very simple path-dependent property is to be kept track of while preserving the tractability of the Markovian framework. It is easy to think of other applications, for example in connection with bonds with step-up provisions, where current rating is not enough to determine the next coupon payment.

To illustrate the idea, consider a rating system with three nondefault classes A, B, and C and an absorbing default state which we denote D. To keep track of the default state, we actually enlarge the absorbing state into three distinct absorbing states DA, DB, and DC. A firm defaulting from category i will then drop into Di, for $i = $ A, B, C. Hence if the generator in the original setup is equal to

$$\lambda = \begin{pmatrix} -\lambda_A & \lambda_{AB} & \lambda_{AC} & \lambda_{AD} \\ \lambda_{BA} & -\lambda_B & \lambda_{BC} & \lambda_{BD} \\ \lambda_{CA} & \lambda_{CB} & -\lambda_C & \lambda_{CD} \\ 0 & 0 & 0 & 0 \end{pmatrix},$$

then the extended generator needed to keep track of the pre-default rating is

$$\Lambda^e = \begin{pmatrix} -\lambda_A & \lambda_{AB} & \lambda_{AC} & \lambda_{A,DA} & 0 & 0 \\ \lambda_{BA} & -\lambda_B & \lambda_{BC} & 0 & \lambda_{BD} & 0 \\ \lambda_{CA} & \lambda_{CB} & -\lambda_C & 0 & 0 & \lambda_{CD} \\ 0 & 0 & 0 & 0 & 0 & 0 \\ 0 & 0 & 0 & 0 & 0 & 0 \\ 0 & 0 & 0 & 0 & 0 & 0 \end{pmatrix}.$$

To illustrate this, consider a generator of the form

$$\Lambda = \begin{pmatrix} -0.1 & 0.08 & 0.01 & 0.01 & 0 & 0 \\ 0.06 & -0.15 & 0.07 & 0 & 0.02 & 0 \\ 0.05 & 0.1 & -0.25 & 0 & 0 & 0.1 \\ 0 & 0 & 0 & 0 & 0 & 0 \\ 0 & 0 & 0 & 0 & 0 & 0 \\ 0 & 0 & 0 & 0 & 0 & 0 \end{pmatrix}.$$

The 1-year transition-probability matrix corresponding to this generator is given by $P(1) = \exp(\Lambda)$, which equals

$$\begin{pmatrix} 0.907\,240 & 0.071\,174 & 0.010\,794 & 0.009\,524 & 0.000\,740 & 0.000\,528 \\ 0.054\,546 & 0.865\,776 & 0.057\,710 & 0.000\,282 & 0.018\,607 & 0.003\,079 \\ 0.044\,642 & 0.083\,774 & 0.781\,875 & 0.000\,232 & 0.000\,889 & 0.088\,587 \\ 0 & 0 & 0 & 1 & 0 & 0 \\ 0 & 0 & 0 & 0 & 1 & 0 \\ 0 & 0 & 0 & 0 & 0 & 1 \end{pmatrix}.$$

The interpretation of the probabilities of going from A to the BD category is that the issuer which is now in A will be in state B before defaulting. Hence for the short time horizon this is a small value compared with the probability of a direct default. For long time horizons, the probability of defaulting from a given category will be almost independent of the starting category.

The technique of enlarging the state space is a flexible tool which often allows simple "toy" extensions of models. Expanding on the example above we may use the existing extensions to model post-default migration between different categories. If we have different recovery rates depending on whether we default from A, B, or C, we can incorporate migration between the states AD, BD, and CD to capture variation in post-default prices. In real markets, a defaulted bond often trades after a default has been declared, and the market price then reflects the market's opinion of expected recovery.

Let us define a block structure such that

$$\Lambda = \begin{pmatrix} \Lambda_{11} & \Lambda_{12} \\ 0 & \Lambda_{22} \end{pmatrix},$$

where Λ_{11}, Λ_{12}, and Λ_{22} are 3×3 matrices. A model with post-default recovery migration would then work with a matrix Λ_{22} different from 0.

As a final generalization we could include random recovery by letting Λ_{12} have nonzero elements everywhere. This would capture three possible recovery levels. For example, letting

$$\Lambda_{12} = \begin{pmatrix} 0.007 & 0.002 & 0.001 \\ 0.005 & 0.01 & 0.005 \\ 0.02 & 0.03 & 0.05 \end{pmatrix}$$

and letting $\delta_A = 0.5$, $\delta_B = 0.4$, and $\delta_C = 0.3$ would allow for three levels and the A-rated firm would have a post-default recovery expectation (right after default has been declared) of 0.5 with probability $0.007/0.01 = 70\%$. Of course, we could expand the set of possible recoveries to a much finer grid. The pricing formula can easily incorporate a recovery which depends on pre-default rating as follows:

$$v^i(0, t) = p(0, t)\left(\sum_{k=A,B,C} \delta_k p_{i,Dk}(t) + \sum_{k=A,B,C} p_{ik}(t) \right),$$

where the first term in the sum is the value of payment in the three default states and the remaining term is the value of the (full) payment in the default-free states.

6.5 Fractional Recovery of Market Value in the Markov Model

Consider the setup in which we have a rating process η described by a generator Λ, but we assume a fractional recovery of market value δ instead of a recovery of treasury. We now show that pricing a bond assuming fractional recovery δ of market value when the generator for the rating process (including default) is Λ is equivalent to pricing assuming zero recovery and using a modified generator Λ^δ given as

$$\lambda_{iK}^\delta = (1-\delta)\lambda_{iK}, \quad i=1,\ldots,K-1,$$
$$-\lambda_i^\delta = -\lambda_i + \delta\lambda_{iK}, \quad i=1,\ldots,K-1,$$
$$\lambda_{ij}^\delta = \lambda_{ij}, \quad i \neq j, \ j \neq K.$$

The modified generator simply changes the values in the default column to the recovery-adjusted values and then changes the diagonal to make sure that row sums are still zero.

The key to this equivalence is the following equivalence between looking at an absorption time of a Markov chain and the first jump of a Cox process. More precisely, the distribution of the first time a Markov chain with generator Λ hits an absorbing state K is the same as the distribution of the first jump time of a Cox process whose intensity is $\lambda(\tilde{\eta}_t) = \lambda_{\tilde{\eta}_t K}$. Here, $\tilde{\eta}_t$ is a Markov chain on $\{1,\ldots,K-1\}$ with generator Γ, where

$$\gamma_{ij} = \lambda_{ij}, \quad i,j=1,\ldots,K-1, \ i \neq j,$$
$$-\gamma_i = -\lambda_i + \lambda_{iK}, \quad i=1,\ldots,K-1.$$

With this in mind we now compare the price of a bond with a fractional recovery of δ using Λ and a bond with zero recovery computed using Λ^δ instead.

For the fractional recovery of δ using Λ, we first consider the Cox-process representation of the first absorption time of η by letting

$$\lambda(\nu_t) = \lambda_{\nu_t K}.$$

Here, the generator of ν is Γ as defined above, i.e. it is equal to the upper left $(K-1) \times (K-1)$ submatrix of Λ except in the diagonal, where

$$-\gamma_i = -\lambda_i + \lambda_{iK}.$$

Now, using the fractional recovery pricing formula we have

$$v(0,t) = p(0,t)E\exp\left(-\int_0^t (1-\delta)\tilde{\lambda}(\nu_s)\,ds\right)$$
$$= p(0,t)E\exp\left(-\int_0^t (1-\delta)\lambda_{\nu_s K}\,ds\right),$$

where the dynamics of ν on $\{1,\ldots,K-1\}$ are generated by Γ.

Now consider instead zero recovery using the modified generator Λ^δ. Let the associated Markov chain on $\{1,\ldots,K\}$ be η^δ. Again, we construct the Cox-process representation of the absorption time of η^δ by letting ν^δ be a Markov chain on $\{1, \ldots, K-1\}$ controlling the default intensity

$$\tilde{\lambda}(\nu_t^\delta) = (1-\delta)\lambda_{\nu_t^\delta K}.$$

Here, ν^δ has a generator Γ^δ equal to the upper left $(K-1) \times (K-1)$ corner of Λ^δ except in the diagonal, where

$$\begin{aligned} -\gamma_i^\delta &= -\lambda_i^\delta + (1-\delta)\lambda_{iK} \\ &= -\lambda_i + \delta\lambda_{iK} + (1-\delta)\lambda_{iK} \\ &= -\lambda_i + \lambda_{iK}, \quad i = 1, \ldots, K-1. \end{aligned}$$

Now the zero-recovery pricing formula says that

$$\begin{aligned} \frac{v(0,t)}{p(0,t)} &= E \exp\left(-\int_0^t \lambda(\nu_s^\delta)\,ds\right) \\ &= E \exp\left(-\int_0^t (1-\delta)\lambda_{\nu_s^\delta K}\,ds\right), \end{aligned}$$

and since ν^δ has the same generator as $\tilde{\eta}$, we have established the formula.

In summary, in a rating-based model where the generator is Λ and where there is fractional recovery of pre-default market value, a zero-coupon bond can be priced using zero recovery and the modified generator Λ^δ. The key to understanding this is to express the absorption times in both Markov chains as the first jump time of the associated Cox process. This carries over to the models of the next section as well.

6.6 A Generalized Markovian Model

The Markovian model presented in the last section makes some simplifying assumptions that have empirical consequences that are not plausible. By using only ratings as the relevant predictor of default, the model does not explain variations in credit spreads between different issuers of the same credit quality—a deviation which can be large in practice. Also, the nonhomogeneous Markov chain assumption implies that bond prices evolve deterministically between ratings changes. Clearly, we need a generalization which incorporates state dependence in transition rates and risk premiums, thus allowing for stochastic changes in credit spreads between ratings transitions. In this section, we will see how the Markovian model can be generalized to incorporate random transition rates and random default intensities. We will start with a fairly general model and then impose special structure for computational reasons and derive a model which is easy to implement.

In addition to a process modeling the rating migration, we now have a state variable process X that performs the same role that we saw in the section on Cox processes. We will specify the intensity matrix as depending on this state variable. First, define the matrix

$$
a_X(s) = \begin{pmatrix}
-\lambda_1(X_s) & \lambda_{12}(X_s) & \lambda_{13}(X_s) & \cdots & \lambda_{1K}(X_s) \\
\lambda_{21}(X_s) & -\lambda_2(X_s) & \lambda_{23}(X_s) & \cdots & \lambda_{2K}(X_s) \\
\vdots & \vdots & \ddots & \cdots & \vdots \\
\lambda_{K-1,1}(X_s) & \lambda_{K-1,2}(X_s) & \cdots & -\lambda_{K-1}(X_s) & \lambda_{K-1,K}(X_s) \\
0 & 0 & \cdots & \cdots & 0
\end{pmatrix}
$$

and assume that the functions λ_{ij} are all nonnegative and that

$$
\lambda_i(X_s) = \sum_{j=1,\ j\neq i}^{K} \lambda_{ij}(X_s), \quad i = 1, \ldots, K - 1.
$$

It is not necessary that the random entries $a_X(s)$ are written as functions of state variables, but we choose this formulation since this is the interesting one to work with in practice. We could of course also include time as one of the state variables. Heuristically, we think of, say, $\lambda_1(X_s)\Delta t$ as the probability that a firm in rating class 1 will jump to a different class or default within the (small) time interval Δt.

With the definition of $a_X(s)$ we can construct, for a given sample path of X, an intensity measure $A_X(\cdot)$ by integrating each coordinate of a_X with respect to time. As noted in Appendix C, this intensity measure corresponds to a nonhomogeneous Markov chain, and the transition probabilities of this Markov chain satisfy the equation

$$
\frac{\partial P_X(s,t)}{\partial s} = -a_X(s)P_X(s,t).
$$

We think of this Markov chain as describing the evolution of a rating process that is conditional on a particular path of the process X. To get unconditional transition probabilities we then need to take the expectation of these transition probabilities over the distribution of X. Our concern here is that the expected value of the conditional transition matrix has a closed-form solution. The problem is that the solution of the equation in the time-inhomogeneous case is typically *not* equal to

$$
P_X(s,t) = \exp\left(\int_s^t a_X(u)\,\mathrm{d}u \right),
$$

which is most easily seen by recalling that when A and B are square matrices, we only have

$$
\exp(A + B) = \exp(A)\exp(B)
$$

when A and B commute. Hence if we looked at integrated intensity measures for adjacent intervals which do not commute, then we would not get the fundamental transition semigroup property of the postulated transition probabilities.

The way to ensure that the intensity measures for different intervals do commute is to make sure that they have a common basis of eigenvectors, i.e. to assume that the time-dependent generator matrix has a representation

$$a_X(s) = B\tilde{\mu}(X_s)B^{-1},$$

where B is a $K \times K$ matrix whose columns are then K eigenvectors of $a_X(s)$, and where $\tilde{\mu}(X_s)$ is a diagonal matrix with diagonal elements that is well behaved enough to ensure that the product is indeed an intensity measure. This is a restrictive assumption that says that the family of generators has a common set of eigenvectors regardless of how the state variable process evolves. If this is true, then defining the diagonal matrix

$$E_X(s,t) = \begin{pmatrix} \exp\left(\int_s^t \mu_1(X_u)\,du\right) & 0 & \cdots & 0 \\ 0 & \ddots & \cdots & 0 \\ \vdots & \cdots & \exp\left(\int_s^t \mu_{K-1}(X_u)\,du\right) & 0 \\ 0 & \cdots & 0 & 1 \end{pmatrix},$$

we have

$$\frac{\partial P_X(s,t)}{\partial s} = B(-\tilde{\mu}(X_s))E_X(s,t)B^{-1}$$

$$= -B\tilde{\mu}(X_s)B^{-1}BE_X(s,t)B^{-1}$$

$$= -a_X(s)P_X(s,t)$$

and, hence, remembering that we have conditioned on the sample path of X, $P_X(s,t)$ is the transition matrix of a time-inhomogeneous Markov chain on $\{1, \ldots, K\}$. There are several problems with this formulation. There are no nice conditions which ensure that the modified matrix remains a generator. Furthermore, the assumption that the eigenvectors of $a_X(s)$ exist and are not time varying is a strong assumption and it does not have a clear probabilistic or statistical interpretation so we do not really know what it means to modify the eigenvalues as above.

We therefore consider a special case which poses no problems of that kind. Assume that a $K \times K$ generator is given and that it permits a diagonalization

$$\Lambda = BDB^{-1},$$

where $D = \text{diag}(d_1, \ldots, d_{K-1}, 0)$ is a diagonal matrix of eigenvalues. Let μ be a *scalar-valued* positive function defined on the state space of the state variable X, and define the local intensity as

$$a_X(s) = \Lambda\mu(X_s) = BD\mu(X_s)B^{-1},$$

which corresponds to considering a one-dimensional scalar multiple of the generator. Also, define the $K \times K$ diagonal matrix

$$E_X(s, t) = \text{diag}\left(\exp\left(d_1 \int_s^t \mu(X_u)\, du \right), \ldots, \exp\left(d_{K-1} \int_s^t \mu(X_u)\, du \right), 0 \right).$$

Then we have $P_X(s, t) = B E_X(s, t) B^{-1}$ and hence we can compute the unconditional "migration" matrix $P(s, t)$ as the expected value of $P_X(s, t)$. Note that the family of migration matrices is not a family of transition matrices, since they do not satisfy the Markov semigroup property. But calculations are still simple with the proposed structure. To price bonds we need to be able to calculate the survival probability conditionally on a starting state i. One may show that

$$1 - P_X(s, t)_{iK} = \sum_{j=1}^{K-1} \beta_{ij} \exp\left(d_j \int_0^t \mu(X_s)\, ds \right),$$

where

$$\beta_{ij} = -b_{ij} b_{jK}^{-1}.$$

Now consider, for example, a bond, currently rated i, maturing at date T. Then given zero recovery in default, the price of the bond is (assuming that the short rate is a function of the state variable as well)

$$v^i(t, T) = E\left(\exp\left(-\int_t^T r(X_s)\, ds \right)\left(1 - P_X(t, T)_{i,K} \right) \,\middle|\, \mathcal{G}_t \right)$$

$$= \sum_{j=1}^{K-1} \beta_{ij} E\left(\exp\left(\int_t^T d_j \mu(X_s) - r(X_s)\, ds \right) \,\middle|\, \mathcal{G}_t \right),$$

and as long as $\mu(X_s)$ belongs to the affine class or the quadratic models, this is a sum of easy-to-compute terms.

6.7 A System of PDEs for the General Specification

We pay a price to retain closed-form or nearly closed-form solutions in the setup of conditional Markov chains given above. Either we have to rely on a stochastic modification of each of the eigenvectors, which makes it complicated to ensure that the generator property of the modified matrix is preserved, or we have to use a one-dimensional modification that corresponds to randomly speeding up and slowing down the clock of rating transitions. As long as the modifying process is positive, we are sure to retain the generator property of the modified matrix. But we might want to, for example, twist the default intensities for different categories while keeping the transition rates between nondefault states fixed. This would correspond to modifying the generator in the default column by some stochastic factors and then adjusting the diagonal to retain row sums of zero. This kind of modification requires us to be able to solve rating-based models with stochastic intensities numerically, and in this section we derive the relevant equation in a simple setting. The derivation can easily be extended to cases with two counterparties by working with a large Markov chain of pairwise ratings, but we just indicate the simple case here.

We consider a claim which pays off $d(T, r, i)$ at maturity when the state variable (here, the short rate) is r and the rating of the issuer or reference credit is given by i. Let $f(t, r, i)$ denote the corresponding price at time t of the contingent claim. We model the rating process η as a continuous-time Markov chain with a finite state space $\mathcal{K} = \{1, \ldots, K\}$ which includes the default state K. The generator of the Markov chain is denoted Λ. In this simple example, the payoff in default is made at maturity. If the chain defaults before that, it is modeled as absorbed in the default state until maturity, and in this case the claim becomes a riskless bond whose only price variation is due to fluctuations in r. But note that, in fact, nothing in our derivation of a system of PDEs for f requires the interpretation of K as an absorbing default state.

Define

$$\mathcal{D}f = \frac{\partial}{\partial t}f + \mu\frac{\partial}{\partial r}f + \tfrac{1}{2}\sigma^2\frac{\partial^2}{\partial r^2}f. \tag{6.3}$$

By Itô's lemma for processes with jumps (see Appendix D) we have

$$f(t, r_t, \eta_t) - f(0, r_0, \eta_0)$$
$$= \int_0^t \mathcal{D}f(s, r_s, \eta_s)\, ds + \sum_{0 < s \leqslant t} (f(s, r_s, \eta_s) - f(s, r_s, \eta_{s-})) + M_t,$$

where M_t is a local martingale and we assume that there is enough regularity that this is a true martingale. This is something one has to check for each application. We now almost have the drift of the process, except that we need to write the sum of jumps as the sum of a martingale and a drift term. As usual, this drift term is a product of an intensity of jumps and a mean jump size, both of which are stochastic. More specifically,

$$\sum_{0 < s \leqslant t} (f(s, r_s, \eta_s) - f(s, r_s, \eta_{s-}))$$

$$= \int_0^t \left(\lambda_{\eta_s} \sum_{l \in \mathcal{K}\backslash\{\eta_s\}} \frac{\lambda_{\eta_s, l}}{\lambda_{\eta_s}}(f(s, r_s, l) - f(s, r_s, \eta_s)) \right) ds + M_t^*$$

$$= \int_0^t \left(\sum_{l \in \mathcal{K}\backslash\{\eta_s\}} \lambda_{\eta_s, l}(f(s, r_s, l) - f(s, r_s, \eta_s)) \right) ds + M_t^*$$

$$= \int_0^t (\Lambda\bar{f}(s, r_s))_{\eta_s}\, ds + M_t^*.$$

Here, $\bar{f}(t, r)$ is the K-dimensional column vector whose ith element is $f(t, r, i)$, and $(\Lambda \bar{f}(s, r_s))_{\eta_s}$ denotes the η_sth element of the vector $\Lambda \bar{f}(s, r_s)$. Also, in the last equality we use the fact that a diagonal element of Λ is minus the sum of the off-diagonal elements in the same row. We can now write the differential of f as

$$\mathrm{d}f(t, r_t, \eta_t) = (\mathcal{D} f(t, r_t, \eta_t) + (\Lambda \bar{f}(t, r_t))_{\eta_t})\, \mathrm{d}t + \mathrm{d}\tilde{M}_t, \qquad (6.4)$$

where $\tilde{M}_t$ is a local martingale. Under the pricing measure, the drift of this price process must be equal to $r_t f(t, r_t, \eta_t)$ and this implies that $\bar{f}(t, r)$ must solve the system of PDEs

$$\mathcal{D} \bar{f}(s, r) + \Lambda \bar{f}(s, r) - r_s \bar{f}(s, r) = 0, \qquad (6.5)$$

and from the lumpy dividend paid at time T we have the boundary condition

$$f(T, r, i) = d(T, r, i).$$

This gives the steps one has to go through to get the system of partial differential equations representing the valuation of the rating-contingent claims. It is straightforward to extend this to claims which pay out dividends at intermediate times. In this book we will not use an implementation of this system, but use only our simple workhorse model defined earlier.

6.8 Using Thresholds Instead of a Markov Chain

An alternative to the Markov chain modeling of defaultable claims is the use of threshold crossings of diffusion processes to represent changes in credit quality. Working within an affine framework makes it possible to develop reasonably explicit formulas for prices of rating-dependent payoffs. Given a state-variable process (which may well be multidimensional)

$$\mathrm{d}X_t = \mu(X_t)\, \mathrm{d}t + \sigma(X_t)\, \mathrm{d}W_t,$$

assume that there exist a rating function $v : \mathbb{R}^d \to [0, \infty)$ and $K - 1$ thresholds $0 < \gamma_1 < \cdots < \gamma_{K-1}$.

Define the rating at time t to be i if and only if $v(X_t) \in [\gamma_{i-1}, \gamma_i)$, $i = 1, \ldots, K - 1$. Denoting the default time by τ and assuming that the default intensity is $\lambda(X_t)$, the probability of being in state i at time t is given as

$$
\begin{aligned}
P(\eta_t = i) &= P(v(X_t) \in [\gamma_{i-1}, \gamma_i) \text{ and } \tau > t) \\
&= E[E(1_{\{v(X_t) \in [\gamma_{i-1}, \gamma_i)\}} 1_{\{\tau > t\}} \mid X)] \\
&= E\left[1_{\{v(X_t) \in [\gamma_{i-1}, \gamma_i)\}} \exp\left(-\int_0^t \lambda(X_s)\, \mathrm{d}s \right) \right],
\end{aligned}
$$

and of course the probability of default before t is

$$P(\tau < t) = 1 - E \exp\left(- \int_0^t \lambda(X_s)\, ds \right).$$

A natural candidate for a rating function is of course the default intensity itself. This would correspond to the modeling assumption that ratings reflect default intensities over short time horizons. This is typically not consistent, though, with the stated goal of rating agencies to rate—at least partially—"through the cycle", i.e. to let ratings reflect a long-horizon perspective. The formulation above fortunately allows for a separation of the default intensity and the rating function, since ν may be chosen to depend solely on the state variables.

When the process of state variables falls within the class of generalized affine models or quadratic jump-diffusions, then we may calculate prices up to Fourier transforms explicitly using the methods laid out in Duffie et al. (2000). To see this, consider a particular case where the rating function is linear in the state variables, the state variable is an affine process, and the intensity and short-rate processes are affine. Then the function giving the value of a payment conditional on the rating finishing below a given boundary y is

$$G_{0,b}(y) = E\left[\exp\left(- \int_0^T R(X_s)\, ds \right) 1_{\{bX_T \leqslant y\}} \right],$$

where $R(X_s) = r(X_s) + \lambda(X_s)$. It follows from Duffie et al. (2000) that the Fourier–Stieltjes transform of G is given by

$$\mathcal{G}_{0,b}(v; X_0; T) = \psi(ivb, X_0, 0, T)$$

where

$$\psi(u, x, t, T) = E\left(\exp\left(- \int_0^T R(X_s)\, ds \right) \exp(uX_T) \,\middle|\, \mathcal{F}_t \right).$$

This transform can, for affine jump-diffusions, be computed by solving ordinary differential equations. Prices can then be found by inverting this transform numerically. In Appendix E this procedure is made completely explicit up to a simple univariate integral but this explicit solution only works when the driving state variable is one dimensional. For this to be useful, one has to work with a model in which the short rate and the default intensity are independent, and then let the rating be a simple function of the default intensity. An alternative is to let the same state variable control the short rate, the rating, and the default intensity, but this is not very appealing from an economic point of view. Working with the independence assumption, assume that the reference issuer has rating i at time T if the default intensity λ_T is in the interval $(\gamma_{i-1}, \gamma_i]$. Then with the pre-default intensity process λ as driving state variable, we can compute the value of a claim paying 1 contingent upon no default and the rating being i. Using the notation of Appendix E this becomes

$$p(0, T)E\left(\exp\left(-\int_0^T \lambda_s \, ds \right) 1_{\{\lambda_T \in [\gamma_{i-1}, \gamma_i)\}} \right)$$
$$= G(T, \lambda_0, 1, \gamma_i) - G(T, \lambda_0, 1, \gamma_{i-1})$$

and this can be computed explicitly (up to an integral) using the results in Appendix E.

6.9   The Trouble with Pricing Based on Ratings

It is hard to ignore the ratings process when someone asks you to price the step-up provision on a corporate bond. We have now seen the kind of model structures which are useful for pricing corporate bonds and derivatives with rating-related risk. Our workhorse model will appear again later when analyzing swap contracts. But before continuing on, let us consider one of the problems one faces in practical implementation when valuing rating triggers present in telecommunication bonds, for example.

In the modeling assumptions, we are assuming that each rating category has associated with it a (possibly risk-adjusted) default intensity. This intensity and the migration between states determines the prices of the bonds. The same is true for models in which we assume that rating changes are triggered when the default intensity or a probability of default passes certain thresholds. In reality, however, the rating process is to some extent disconnected from the default intensity process. If we view, for example, the expected default frequency (EDF) process as an indicator of the default intensity, then we can see in Figure 6.4 that the default intensity is much more volatile than the actual ratings. If a rating change occurred every time the EDF passed a certain fixed threshold, then one would see a much more volatile rating process. Hence the dynamics of the rating implied by EDF changes is inappropriate to use as a measure for the actual rating, which determines the cash flows for (say) a bond with a step-up provision.

The idea of calibrating a rating-based model to an existing term structure and then pricing derivatives is nice from a theoretical viewpoint but hard to implement in practice. The biggest problem is probably that every company has characteristics not captured by the rating class. So, if one tries to compensate for this by choosing a clever adjustment of the generator, then one can only use the bonds of the particular issuer for calibration and often there are too few bonds to do this properly.

6.10   Bibliographical Notes

The rating-based calibration methods outlined in this chapter are based on Lando (1994), which contains the continuous-time part of the model published in Jarrow

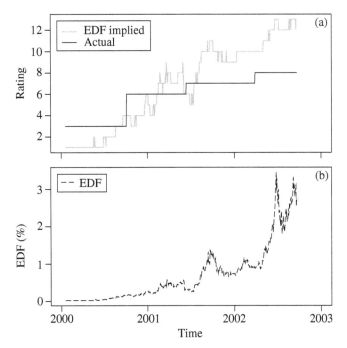

Figure 6.4. (a) The actual rating by Moody's of Deutsche Telekom since 1 January 2002 compared with a (rough) estimate of the rating corresponding to the EDF. The translation from EDF to rating uses an informal scale close to that shown in KMV publications. (b) The actual EDF's development over the same period of time.

et al. (1997) and an extension to stochastic spreads. An early extension involving stochastic recovery rates was introduced in Das and Tufano (1996). The paper by Fons (1994) studies term-structure implications of rating-dependent default probabilities. The method of modifying the eigenvalues of the generator stochastically was introduced in Lando (1994, 1998) and was also studied in Arvanitis et al. (1999). It seems more desirable to work either with a scalar modification (which will be used for illustration later, in the chapter on swaps) or to modify only the default intensities stochastically. The latter method requires numerical computation but it can be handled in a finite system of PDEs with as many equations as there are rating categories. An application of this can be found in Huge and Lando (1999) (see also Becherer 2001). It is also possible to discretize rating-based models using trees, even if the computational cost can be quite high if one insists on fitting the initial term structure of each class of debt. For more on this, see Acharya et al. (2002). Kijima and Komoribayashi (1998) noted that the discrete-time calibration method employed in Jarrow et al. (1997) is unstable and proposed instead the method discussed in this chapter. The idea of adjusting the generator by a diagonal matrix is used in Lando (1994). The practical application of rating-based pricing is difficult, but it seems hard to get around it when studying, for example, the rating-dependent step-up clauses contained in bonds. For more on this, see Lando and Mortensen (2003). The threshold argument using the technology of Duffie et al. (2000) is used in Huge (2000). We have not looked at the forward-rate formulation with different rating classes here. For more on this, see Bielecki and Rutkowski (2002).

7
Credit Risk and Interest-Rate Swaps

An interest-rate swap is a contract by which the parties agree to exchange a constant, fixed payment stream for a variable payment stream. The variable payment stream, the so-called floating leg of the contract, is typically linked to three- or six-month LIBOR rates, an interbank deposit rate which will be defined below. The fixed leg is typically set so that the contract has zero initial value and the size of this fixed leg is referred to as the swap rate. The actual dollar size of the payments is computed from a notional value of the contract, but in interest-rate swaps this notional value is only for calculation purposes: it is never exchanged.

The market for interest-rate swaps has reached an enormous size. Current estimates in Bank of International Settlements (2003) are that the size of the euro swap market by the end of 2002 had an outstanding notional amount of $31.5 trillion, and that the corresponding amount for the dollar market was $23.7 trillion. This is of course an enormous amount but it tends to exaggerate the size of the cash flows involved since it is common practice in the swap markets to close out positions by taking new offsetting positions in swaps instead of getting out of the existing swaps.

Still, the volume is large, and it is partly a reflection of the fact that swap markets are increasingly supplementing government bonds for hedging and price discovery in fixed-income markets. This leads to the natural question of whether swap curves are replacing yield curves on government bonds as "benchmark" curves. A benchmark curve is a curve against which prices of other securities are measured, but it is also a natural question to think of whether the swap curve is a better measure of the riskless rate. Whether we use swap curves as benchmarks or even consider using them as proxies for a riskless rate, we need to understand their meaning and their dynamics.

In this chapter we focus on understanding the relationship between swap pricing and credit risk. Credit risk enters in two ways. First, since the contract is typically an over-the-counter instrument (i.e. the counterparty is not an organized exchange), there is counterparty credit risk in the contract. And second, the floating rate on which the contract is based is the so-called LIBOR rate, which is sensitive to, among other things, changes in credit quality. We start out by defining the LIBOR rate.

7.1   LIBOR

The LIBOR rate is an average of rates which a selected group of "contributor banks" are offering on interbank deposits "of reasonable size" made in the London interbank market. As stated in the definition of LIBOR on the British Bankers' Association's homepage:

> The BBA LIBOR is the most widely used benchmark or reference rate for short-term interest rates. It is compiled by the BBA and released to the market at about 11.00 each day. LIBOR stands for the London Interbank Offered Rate and is the rate of interest at which banks borrow funds from other banks, in marketable size, in the London interbank market.

Hence it is the contributor bank who quotes a rate at which it thinks it could borrow in the interbank market if the bank itself went out and asked for a loan. Each contributor bank is asked for rates on deposits of certain maturities ranging from an overnight rate up to a 12-month rate. The lowest and the highest quartile contributed rates are then removed before computing the average of the remaining quotes. Currently, dollar LIBOR rates will be based on the middle 8 quotes out of a sample from 16 contributor banks. The ratings of the contributor banks are typically within the Aa categories in the Moody's system. Since a deposit in the interbank market is subject to credit risk if the receiving bank defaults, the deposit rate must be set high enough to compensate the depositor for the risk of default.

7.2   A Useful Starting Point

It is useful to see how a swap rate is set in an idealized, default-free setting where the floating rate is derived from the shortest-maturity treasury zero-coupon bond. This is not a typical construction but it will highlight the problems faced when looking at "real" interest-rate swaps.

Let $p(s, t)$ denote the price at date s of a zero-coupon bond maturing at date t, where $s \leqslant t$. Consider an interest-rate swap with maturity date T in which party A pays to B a fixed amount c_T at every date $t = 1, \ldots, T$ and B pays to A the amount

$$\rho_t = \frac{1}{p(t-1, t)} - 1 \tag{7.1}$$

at dates $t = 1, \ldots, T$. The floating rate is thus set as the yield on the zero-coupon bond maturing in the next period. Hence the net payment from A to B is $c_T - \rho_t$ at date t. The swap rate c_T is set such that the value of the contract initially is 0. We use the subscript T because this rate will depend on the maturity of the contract. More surprisingly, at least until you see the argument below, the rate is a function of observable prices at date 0 only.

It is not surprising that the value of the fixed payment is a function of the given zero-coupon prices and is simply equal to

$$c_T \sum_{i=1}^{T} p(0, i).$$

The value of the floating payment is $1 - p(0, T)$, as follows from the following argument. Note that 1 unit invested at time 0 in a short bond will generate a payment of $1/p(0, 1)$ at date 1. Reinvesting the amount 1 and keeping $(1/p(0, 1)) - 1$ as a dividend will generate the first floating payment. This strategy can be continued until maturity T, where the payment is $\rho_{T-1} + 1$. Hence an initial investment of 1 will generate the cash flow of the floating side plus a zero-coupon bond with maturity date T. This shows that the value of the floating side of the swap must be $1 - p(0, t)$.

We are now in a position to find the swap rate by equating the value of the floating and the fixed payments to obtain

$$c_T = \frac{1 - p(0, T)}{\sum_{i=1}^{T} p(0, i)}.$$

Note that c_T is also a solution to the equation

$$c_T \sum_{i=1}^{T} p(0, i) + p(0, T) = 1, \tag{7.2}$$

which shows that it is the same as a par bond yield, namely the coupon required on a bullet bond to give it par value initially. Hence in this setting the swap rate is "model free." It does not depend on which particular model generated the prices of the zero-coupon bonds. The swap curve becomes a par bond yield curve and is therefore simply another way of expressing the term structure of interest rates. Furthermore, the swap rate can be computed by computing the value of each leg of the swap separately.

7.3 Fixed–Floating Spreads and the "Comparative-Advantage Story"

In the setting above it is hard to see any reason for the existence of swaps. We now take a closer look at a classical argument for the existence of interest-rate swaps that is often seen in textbooks, namely the comparative-advantage story. This story is compelling, but anyone versed in no-arbitrage theory will inevitably feel suspicious about it. In this section we present the comparative-advantage argument first without reference to the size of the spreads involved. Then we explain how the fundamental setup for the argument can be obtained even in an arbitrage-free setting, and exactly why there is no advantage after all. Hence, if there is to be an advantage, it must be due to institutional frictions, tax differences, and information asymmetries.

It is important to note that while the floating–fixed spreads needed to set up the relevant trading strategy can exist in theory even in arbitrage-free and frictionless markets, they are extremely small for typical model settings.

To understand the setting, we first introduce the notion of floating–fixed spreads. Consider a defaultable issuer whose zero-coupon bond term structure is given by the prices $v(0, t)$, $t = 1, \ldots, T$. We will use this structure to price "small" additional contracts in an existing term structure, as discussed in Chapter 1. In particular, we will use the term structure to value coupon bonds issued by the firm by summing the values of the coupons separately.

For a given issuer, we define the "fixed spread" $S(T)$ at maturity T as a "par bond spread," i.e. the spread the issuer must pay over the fixed treasury par rate $c(T)$ to obtain the par value of a bullet bond. We can use the term structure of corporate debt to find $S(T)$ by setting the present value of the coupons and the principal equal to 1, i.e. by solving

$$(c(T) + S(T)) \sum_{i=1}^{T} v(0, i) + v(0, T) = 1.$$

This gives us

$$S(T) = \frac{1 - v(0, T) - c(T) \sum_{i=1}^{T} v(0, i)}{\sum_{i=1}^{T} v(0, i)}.$$

Note that this quantity is a function only of the initial defaultable term structure.

Now consider a floating-rate bond issued by a defaultable firm. The promised coupon at time t is $\rho_{t-1} + s(T)$ for $t = 1, \ldots, T$, where ρ_t is the riskless treasury rate defined in (7.1), and the promised principal payment at date T is 1. We then define the floating-rate spread $s(T)$ as the constant, but maturity-dependent, spread that the issuer has to pay to get this floating-rate bond valued at par.

If we let $v_T(\rho)$ denote the value of the promised floating payments $\rho_0, \ldots, \rho_{T-1}$, then setting the value of the floating-rate bond equal to 1 gives us

$$s(T) = \frac{1 - v(0, T) - v_T(\rho)}{\sum_{i=1}^{T} v(0, i)}.$$

The value of $v_T(\rho)$ is model dependent and it depends, among other things, on the correlation between the short rate used for discounting and the default event. Nevertheless, quotes on the floating spread are sometimes available in the market, for example, through the asset swap market.

$s(T)$ and $S(T)$ are different in general and we define the floating–fixed spread as

$$\Delta(T) = s(T) - S(T).$$

For treasuries it is of course 0, since both $s(T)$ and $S(T)$ are 0.

Table 7.1. The cash flows for the party that obtains a floating-rate loan and pays a fixed rate on the swap contract.

Source of cash flow	Cash flow paid by riskless party
Interest on loan	ρ_t
Fixed payment on swap	$c(T) - \frac{1}{2}\Delta(T)$
Floating payment on swap	$-\rho_t$
Total	$c(T) - \frac{1}{2}\Delta(T)$

Table 7.2. The cash flow for the party that obtains a floating-rate loan and receives a fixed rate on the swap contract.

Source of cash flow	Cash flow paid by risky party
Interest on loan	$c(T) + S(T)$
Floating payment on swap	ρ_t
Fixed payment on swap	$\frac{1}{2}\Delta(T) - c(T)$
Total	$\rho_t + S(T) + \frac{1}{2}\Delta(T)$

The fact that the spread is not 0 for corporate issuers and may be different for different credit quality issuers gives rise to the classical scenario in which we can seemingly use swaps to get "cheaper" financing. To understand the argument better, consider just one risky and one default-free party. Since the floating–fixed spread is, by definition, 0 for a default-free issuer, all we need to assume is that the floating–fixed spread is positive for our risky issuer. In analogy with the classical "comparative-advantage" argument in international trade, we may argue that the risky issuer is "less disadvantaged" in the fixed-rate market, since the spread paid here is smaller than the spread paid in the floating-rate market. Hence there seems to be an advantage in letting the risky party borrow fixed and letting the default-free party borrow floating, and then "trading" coupons through a swap agreement.

Now assume the following.

- The risky party borrows 1 at the fixed rate $c(T) + S(T)$.

- The riskless party borrows 1 at the floating rate ρ.

- The two parties enter into a swap in which the riskless party pays $c(T) - \frac{1}{2}\Delta(T)$ fixed and receives ρ floating.

The total coupon flows for each party are shown in Tables 7.1 and 7.2.

Clearly, during the life of the swap the riskless borrower now pays a smaller fixed rate than he could have obtained directly. Remarkably, the total payment for the

Table 7.3. Prices and par bond yields in a four-period
model with interest-rate dynamics specified below.

Maturity date	Zero-coupon bond price	Par bond yield
1	0.9524	0.05
2	0.9023	0.052 65
3	0.8501	0.055 42

risky party is smaller as well! To see this, note that

$$\rho_t + S(T) + \tfrac{1}{2}\Delta = \rho_t + \tfrac{1}{2}(2S(T) + s(T) - S(T))$$
$$= \rho_t + \tfrac{1}{2}(s(T) + S(T))$$
$$< \rho_t + s(T)$$

since $s(T) > S(T)$. Therefore, we have a situation in which, seemingly, both parties
have received cheaper funding than they would otherwise be entitled to.

What we show next is that it is possible to construct the scenario above in an
arbitrage-free setting and that the cheaper financing in this case is indeed an illusion.
The source of the illusion is easy to see—once you see it.

The point can be made very clear in a simple model if we allow a few simplifying
assumptions:

- there is just one credit-risky counterparty;
- the swap contract terminates at default with no settlement payment; and
- the underlying corporate bond prices are zero-recovery prices.

Once the source of the confusion is understood in this example it is easily understood
in examples with more complicated recovery structures.

Consider a three-period model in which we construct an arbitrage-free term-
structure model as explained in Appendix A. Hence we take as given a short-rate
process r with starting value $r_0 = 0.05$. The dynamics under the equivalent martingale measure are specified as follows:

$$Q(r_t = ur_{t-1} \mid r_{t-1}) = 0.7,$$
$$Q(r_t = dr_{t-1} \mid r_{t-1}) = 0.3,$$

where

$$u = 1.2 \quad \text{and} \quad d = 0.9.$$

With these dynamics, the prices of default-free zero-coupon bonds and par bond
yields are given in Table 7.3.

Now assume also that there is a defaultable issuer in the model whose probability
of defaulting is 0.02 in period 1, 0.03 in period 2, given survival in period 1, and 0.04

in period 3, given survival in period 2. The default event is independent of the short rate. It is then straightforward to verify that (remember we assume zero recovery)

$$s(3) = 0.032\,07, \qquad S(3) = 0.031\,93,$$

and therefore

$$\Delta = s(3) - S(3) = 0.000\,14 = 1.4 \text{ bp}.$$

Note that the floating–fixed spread is tiny at 1.4 basis points; a point we will return to shortly. Even if the spread is tiny, though, it is nice to understand exactly why even this tiny spread does not actually deliver cheaper financing to any of the parties.

The key to understanding this is to look at the consequences for the riskless borrower (and party to the swap) of an early termination of the swap due to default. We assume that the parties have seized the opportunity to enter into a swap in which the riskless borrower takes a floating-rate loan and swaps into a fixed-rate loan, whereas the risky party enters into a fixed-rate loan and swaps into a floating-rate loan. If the risky party defaults between period t and $t + 1$ (so that default has occurred at time $t + 1$ but not at date t), the riskless party has no payment from the swap counterparty at date $t + 1$ and therefore has to pay r_t at this date on his own loan.

To evaluate what this situation means, we could ask what rate the riskless borrower would have to pay on a loan with the same cash flow as that obtained by taking a floating-rate loan and swapping with a risky counterparty into a fixed-rate loan. We therefore calculate the fixed rate $c(\tau)$ that the riskless borrower has to pay on a loan which is switched into a floating-rate loan at the date of the default of the risky party. This fair fixed rate, which can be computed directly in a tree, is

$$c(\tau) = 0.055\,28.$$

Clearly, the loan is effectively shorter, and therefore the rate reflects the upward-sloping yield curve and is therefore smaller than $c(3)$. Note that, in fact,

$$C(3) - c(\tau) = 1.4 \text{ bp} = \Delta.$$

Hence, it takes a reduction in the fixed payment of Δ to make the fixed borrower accept a loan on which there is the risk of being switched into a floating-rate loan at the default date of the riskless borrower. This means that the "cake" Δ which can be distributed between the riskless borrower and the risky borrower by entering into the swap has to be given entirely to the riskless borrower to make the package fairly priced. Hence there is no advantage left for the risky borrower and the riskless borrower is given exactly the terms that he would be able to get anyway in the market.

As a final note, it is worth emphasizing that in textbooks, floating–fixed spreads of (say) 1% are often used to illustrate the "comparative-advantage" story. It is almost impossible to generate spreads of this size in realistic arbitrage-free models of the term structure of interest rates and corporate spreads. This issue is studied in Duffie and Liu (2001), where the conditions under which floating–fixed spreads exist, their signs and magnitudes under different assumptions on the slope of the term structures of riskless bonds and corporate bonds and under different correlation assumptions are studied. Typical spreads in the cases studied are up to a few basis points. Therefore, the small spread in our illustrative example is no coincidence.

It is worth emphasizing that there could potentially be frictions in the market which would cause real advantages to exist, perhaps most likely in the currency swap market where companies in different countries have the potential for exploiting differences in taxation, etc. The example above serves as a general warning that it takes a careful analysis to really make sure that there are real gains to be made from entering a swap sold on a "cheap-financing" argument.

7.4 Why LIBOR and Counterparty Credit Risk Complicate Things

In reality, the swap curve is a much more complicated object to analyze and in this chapter we focus on two important reasons for this. First, as already mentioned, the floating rate that is typically paid on plain vanilla interest-rate swaps is LIBOR and this is a rate which closely resembles the rate at which an AA party can borrow in the short term. Hence the underlying floating rate is sensitive not only to the general fluctuations in risk-free interest rates but also to the perceived credit quality of AA corporates, most notably banks.

In fact, to see how the credit risk in LIBOR deposits affects the valuation of swaps, consider the following strategy.

- Enter as a fixed-rate receiver into a swap contract with maturity T and a notional amount of \$1. Assume that the swap rate is $c(T)$.

- Invest \$1 for six months at the LIBOR rate beginning at time 0. Renew the investment every six months at the prevailing LIBOR rate $L(t, t + 0.5)$ finishing six months before swap maturity T.

As shown in Table 7.4 the promised payment of this strategy is easily seen to be a bullet bond with coupon equal to $c(T)$. Since the initial value of the strategy is 1 and assuming that the credit quality of the counterparty to the swap is AA, then a superficial argument will say that the swap rate $c(T)$ must be equivalent to a par bond yield on an AA credit quality bond. There are at least two problems with this argument that highlight the issues dealt with in this chapter.

First of all, the argument does not deal with the actual settlement in the event of a default of the swap counterparty (or for that matter of the LIBOR deposit). If the counterparty to the swap contract defaults, the settlement payment will depend

Table 7.4. Net promised cash flow when repeatedly lending out \$1 at the six months LIBOR rate and entering a swap contract with notional principal \$1.

$t=0$	$t=\frac{1}{2}$	$t=1$	$\cdots$	$t=T-1$	$\cdots$	$t=T-\frac{1}{2}$	$t=T$
-1	$L(0,\frac{1}{2})$	$L(\frac{1}{2},1)$	$\cdots$	$L(T-1,T-\frac{1}{2})$	$\cdots$		$1+L(T-\frac{1}{2},T)$
0	$c(T)-L(0,\frac{1}{2})$	$c(T)-L(\frac{1}{2},1)$	$\cdots$	$c(T)-L(T-1,T-\frac{1}{2})$	$\cdots$		$c(T)-L(T-\frac{1}{2},T)$
-1	$c(T)$	$c(T)$	$c(T)$	$c(T)$	$\cdots$	$c(T)$	$1+c(T)$

on the value of the contract at the default date. Think of the pre-default value of the swap as the value that the swap would have had the counterparty not defaulted. The settlement payment could then depend on the sign of this value seen from the nondefaulting party. If the swap contract has positive value to the nondefaulting party, he only receives a fraction of the value, whereas if the contract has negative value, the nondefaulting party must pay this value in full to the defaulting party.

Secondly, even disregarding counterparty risk on the swap contract, the strategy above generates a fixed cash flow every period which is contingent upon no default on the six month LIBOR deposit. This deposit is renewed every period and therefore carries the default risk associated with a refreshed AA credit quality. The corresponding AA par bond yield applies to a bond issued by a firm initially rated AA but with the potential for experiencing downgrades in the future.

This point will be very clear in Section 7.8. First, we need to clear our conscience by at least laying out a framework for taking full account of counterparty credit risk and then seeing that for symmetric default risk and with netting provisions we can actually ignore counterparty credit risk and instead proceed with linear pricing using the riskless rate to discount the swap payments.

7.5   Valuation with Counterparty Risk

As we have seen, an interest-rate swap involves an exchange of payments from two counterparties. Pricing swaps, and in particular finding the fair swap rate that gives the contract zero value at inception, is simplified tremendously if one simply prices the fixed-rate leg and the floating-rate leg separately. Later on, this is in fact exactly what we are going to do, but this section demonstrates that it requires a justification to do so and outlines the results normally used to justify the procedure.

The difficulty lies in the treatment of default. While the difficulty can be illustrated with just one defaultable party, the general framework for setting up two-sided default is useful, since that allows one to investigate a notion of "symmetric" credit risk.

If one idealizes the swap contract and assumes either that the parties to the contract both terminate their payments at the default date regardless of the market value, or that both parties keep paying their side of the contract until their own default or maturity arrives, then we can value each leg separately. In the first case, we have to use a default time which is the minimum of two default times, and in the second case, we simply discount both sides of the swap using the (possibly different) discount curve relevant for each side.

However, in practice, the payment in default depends in a nonlinear fashion on the market value of the contract at the default time, and this, in theory, precludes pricing each leg separately. If the swap contract has positive value for the nondefaulting party to the contract, then the defaulting party pays a fraction of that amount. If the value is negative to the nondefaulting issuer, the defaulting issuer receives the full market value of the swap in default.

Assume that there are two counterparties A and B to the contract and let a (possibly multidimensional) state variable process be denoted X. The intensity of default for firm i is denoted $\lambda^i(X_t)$ and as usual we let $\lambda^i(X_{t-})$ denote the left limit of this process at t, i.e. the value it has before a possible jump at time t. Let $S(t, X_t)$ denote the value at time t of the swap contract as seen by A. The cash flow received by A is exactly the negative of the cash flow received by B so the value of the contract seen by B is simply $-S(t, X_t)$. Let

$$\tau = \min(\tau^A, \tau^B) \tag{7.3}$$

denote the time of the first default. Using a fractional recovery of pre-default value of ϕ_t^i for $i = $ A, B, we can summarize the payment at default as a function of the value of the underlying swap as follows. If B defaults first (before the maturity of the swap) the payment to A is

$$
\begin{array}{ll}
S(\tau-, X_{\tau-}) & \text{if } S(\tau-, X_{\tau-}) < 0, \\
\phi_{\tau-}^B S(\tau-, X_{\tau-}) & \text{if } S(\tau-, X_{\tau-}) > 0.
\end{array}
$$

If A defaults first (before the maturity of the swap), the payment to A is

$$
\begin{array}{ll}
\phi_{\tau-}^A S(\tau-, X_{\tau-}) & \text{if } S(\tau-, X_{\tau-}) < 0, \\
S(\tau-, X_{\tau-}) & \text{if } S(\tau-, X_{\tau-}) > 0.
\end{array}
$$

If S is negative, it means that A makes a payment to B, of course.

In terms of continuous-time arbitrage pricing technology, here is how we would price the swap. If we think of a security as a claim to a cumulative (actual) dividend process D (which for defaultable securities may be different from the promised dividend process), then in a no-arbitrage setting (see, for example, Duffie 2001), the price of the security satisfies

$$S_t = E_t^Q \left(B_{t,T} S_T + \int_t^T B_{t,s} \, dD_s \right). \tag{7.4}$$

If the contract we are pricing has a maturity of T, then we are left with the expression

$$S_t = E_t^Q \int_t^T B_{t,s} \, dD_s, \tag{7.5}$$

but note that by the definition of the swap contract the cumulative dividends depend, through the settlement provisions, on the future values of S and also on the random default time. A key result stated for two-sided default problems in various forms in Duffie and Huang (1996) and Duffie et al. (1996) tells us how to find S in terms of a pre-default process V and how to compute V as a function of *promised* cash flows, i.e. the cash flow paid if there is no default before expiration.

Define

$$V(t, X_t) = E_t^Q \left[\int_t^T -R(s, V_s, X_s) V(s, X_s) \, ds + dD_s^p \right], \qquad (7.6)$$

where D_t^p is the *promised* cumulative dividend received by A up to time t and

$$\left. \begin{aligned} R(t, v, x) &= r(x_t) + s^A(t, x) 1_{\{v<0\}} + s^B(t, x) 1_{\{v>0\}}, \\ s^i(t, x) &= (1 - \phi^i) \lambda^i(x), \end{aligned} \right\} \qquad (7.7)$$

where $r(x_t)$ is the riskless short rate. Assume that

$$\Delta V(\tau, x_\tau) \equiv V(\tau, x_\tau) - V(\tau-, x_{\tau-}) = 0$$

almost surely. This means that the default event is not occurring at the same time (with positive probability) as an event which would have caused a jump in the state variable, and thus would have caused either the discount factor or the default intensities to jump as well. Then the result of Duffie and Huang (1996) implies that the swap price is given as

$$S(t, x_t) = V(t, x_t) 1_{\{t<\tau\}}, \qquad (7.8)$$

and the solution to (7.6) is

$$V_t = E_t^Q \left[\int_t^T \exp \left[-\int_t^s R_u \, du \right] dD_s^p \right]. \qquad (7.9)$$

Hence the equation which gives us the swap price as an expected discounted value of actual cash flows has been translated into an expression involving an expected, discounted value of promised cash flows, but with a more complicated discount factor.

In Duffie and Huang (1996) the state variable is the riskless rate, and the default intensities are chosen as affine functions of the short rate. Huge and Lando (1999) uses the same framework but allows the state variable to now involve a risk-free rate and a state variable that takes account of the joint rating of the two counterparties. This allows one to model, for example, the effect of rating triggers in swaps. Both works consider, to facilitate computation, a case where the floating-rate payment is determined on the actual payment date and not, as is usually the case, six months before the payment date. This approximation has very little effect on the issues dealt with when analyzing the effect of counterparty default risk.

To give an example of the type of results obtained in this setting, consider the following simple example from Huge and Lando (1999). Include as a state-variable process the rating of each of the swap counterparties and assume that the rating

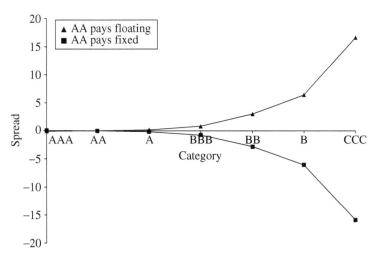

Figure 7.1. Swap spreads in basis points when the initial rating of one counterparty is fixed to AA and the rating of the other counterparty varies. The case in which AA pays fixed and the case in which AA pays floating are both considered. (Reprinted with permission from Huge, B. and D. Lando. 1999. Swap pricing with two-sided default in a rating-based model. *European Finance Review* 3:239–268.)

evolutions of the counterparties are independent and that each is governed by a continuous-time Markov chain with the generator used in Jarrow et al. (1997). This generator has very small default intensities in the top categories and fairly high default intensities in the speculative grade, so the results are for illustration only. Assume a fractional recovery in default of 0.4, and let the riskless rate follow a Vasicek process:

$$dr_t = 0.15(0.05 - r_t)\,dt + 0.015\,dW_t.$$

Since we are mainly worried about the spread due to counterparty risk, we assume that the floating rate is linked to the riskless short rate, and to simplify the numerical calculations we assume that the settlement dates are equal to the payment dates. Figure 7.1 shows the spread on the fixed-rate payment of the swap as the credit rating of the counterparty varies. We consider cases where either the rating of the fixed payer or the rating of the floating payer is fixed at AA. In the case where the fixed-rate payer has an AA rating, the swap spread becomes negative since the promised floating-rate payment by definition is independent of credit quality and the fixed-rate payer therefore has to pay less than the riskless rate to give the contract zero value. Figure 7.1 shows that the credit quality has to be very asymmetric to produce significant effects on the fair swap rate. Rather than measuring the asymmetry in terms of ratings, it is natural to measure it in terms of yield spreads on corporate bonds, which is what is done in Figure 7.2.

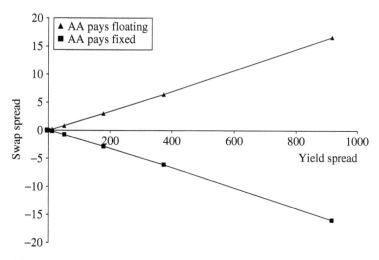

Figure 7.2. Swap spreads in basis points as a function of corporate bond yield spread in basis points for each category. Notice the almost linear relationship. (Reprinted with permission from Huge, B. and D. Lando. 1999. Swap pricing with two-sided default in a rating-based model. *European Finance Review* 3:239–268.)

One should not conclude that counterparty risk does not affect the value of a swap. It is worth remembering that a 5 bp spread on a swap contract with a notional amount of $100 million, say, means an additional semiannual payment of $25 000, which is not insignificant compared with a net payment on the swap of (say) $250 000 at a date where the floating rate is settled 0.5% below the fixed rate. But for symmetric or mildly asymmetric (say within investment grade) credit risk the effect is indeed small. The conclusion from all this is that we are probably not making a huge mistake by assuming, for contracts with symmetric credit quality, that the swap contract can be viewed as being struck between default-free counterparties. This means that the valuation is back to basics, where we discount back the legs on the swap separately and find the swap rate by equating the two present values. Having reached this conclusion, another argument speaks in favor of ignoring counterparty credit risk altogether.

7.6 Netting and the Nonlinearity of Actual Cash Flows: a Simple Example

All pricing rules that we are using in this book are linear pricing rules. Whenever a price is "nonlinear" in some sense (and it is a good rule of thumb when the term "nonlinear" is used to always have it clarified what is nonlinear in what), we can understand the source of the nonlinearity by looking at the actual cash flows.

As a naive example, the price of a corporate bond in the Merton model is obviously nonlinear in face value. But that is simply a consequence of the fact that the actual cash flow to a bond with a face value of $2D$ (say) is not twice the cash flow of a bond with face value D. However, despite this nonlinearity, calculating prices as expected discounted cash flows still implies that prices are linear in actual cash flows. And, more importantly for this section, the cash flow of the bond is independent of the composition of the portfolio of whoever buys it. The same is true in the analysis of counterparty risk in swaps where the option-like payoff profiles in event of default cause a nonlinearity of actual cash flows as a function of promised cash flows, but the pricing is of course still linear in actual cash flows.

When netting agreements are in place between two counterparties, the *actual* cash flow of a swap contract critically depends on the existing portfolio of contracts between the counterparties. Since the actual cash flow that the swap adds to a portfolio can depend on who buys it, the contract may have different value to different buyers, even if the buyers agree on state prices. The following example is probably the simplest possible illustration of that.

We consider two periods. There is a state variable, the interest rate, which can either go up or down. In each case, our issuer can default or survive. This gives rise to four states. We consider a default-free counterparty G (G for government) entering into swap agreements with the firm F. Swap A requires G to pay 1 to F if r goes down, whereas F will pay 1 to G if r goes up. The event of default only affects G in the up-state. Here G will receive a recovery of $\delta < 1$. Assume that the interest rate is 0 and that the risk-neutral probability of r going up is $\frac{1}{2}$ and the probability of a default being ε and assuming default and r to be independent.

The price is then easily seen to be

$$\delta_{\mathrm{A}} = \tfrac{1}{2}(\delta - 1)\varepsilon \qquad (7.10)$$

for the default-free buyer of this security. The swap B with the opposite payoff, i.e. a promised payoff of 1 in the down-state and -1 in the up-state (seen from G), would of course command the same price given our assumptions on state prices. This applies to the contracts seen in isolation. If G is already a counterparty to F with the swap A and is then offered the additional contract B, then if a netting agreement is in place, the total position will become riskless. Thus the position has value 0, and the riskless buyer would be interested in offering a price for B, despite it having a negative price seen in isolation. The setup is summarized in Table 7.5, where all prices are seen from G's perspective.

We have added a final column depicting what B adds to a portfolio which already contains A: a cash flow different from "B actual" seen in isolation.

7.7 Back to Linearity: Using Different Discount Factors

The essence of the research on counterparty credit risk is that the complicated computations can be avoided as long as the credit risk of the two parties is (reasonably)

Table 7.5. The effect of a netting provision on the actual cash flow provided by an offsetting swap. Superscript "p" means promised, "a" actual, so B^a is the actual cash flow of B as a stand alone contract. The values of contracts are as seen from the riskless party G.

State	State price	A^p	A^a	B^p	B^a	A + B net	B's added cash flow
r_{up}, no default	$\frac{1}{2}(1-\varepsilon)$	1	1	-1	-1	0	-1
r_{up}, default	$\frac{1}{2}\varepsilon$	1	δ	-1	-1	0	$-\delta$
r_{down}, no default	$\frac{1}{2}(1-\varepsilon)$	-1	-1	1	1	0	1
r_{down}, default	$\frac{1}{2}\varepsilon$	-1	-1	1	δ	0	1
Price	—	—	$\frac{1}{2}(\delta-1)\varepsilon$	—	$\frac{1}{2}(\delta-1)\varepsilon$	0	$\frac{1}{2}(1-\delta)\varepsilon$

symmetric. And, in practice, the posting of collateral and netting agreements bring us into the symmetric case even when there are large differences in credit quality between the parties to the swap.

The symmetry argument naturally gives us a justification for discounting each leg of a swap contract at the riskless rate. Since symmetry is the critical assumption, we can assume that both parties are default free, and then the "nonlinearity" (of actual payoffs as a function of promised payoffs) which arises due to the typical settlement rule at default does not play any role since default never happens.

It is also a reasonable approximation to say that as long as we preserve the symmetry by discounting both sides of the swap with the same discount factor, the fair swap rate that we compute is close to the true swap rate obtained by looking at the cash flows completely rigorously. It is not completely rigorous since the moment that we introduce discounting at a rate different from the risk-free rate we have to argue that it is OK to price the separate legs independently, i.e. that the nonlinear settlement payment does not play a role at default.

In this section we present three different ways of discounting that are all employed in the literature and we will see that each rule is useful in understanding the position of the swap curve relative to the particular curve used for discounting.

Before we define some important rates, there is a general result on discounting a stream of floating payments which is useful. Assume that R is a stochastic process (adapted to some filtration $\mathbb{F}$) which we think of as a, possibly default-adjusted, short rate. Let Q be the probability measure defining the distribution of R. Let

$$v(t, T) = E_t^Q \exp\left(-\int_t^T R(s)\,ds\right). \tag{7.11}$$

This is interpreted as a zero-coupon bond price corresponding to the discount process R. Also, let

$$Y^1(t) = \frac{1}{v(t, t+1)} - 1. \tag{7.12}$$

The interpretation of this is the "in arrears" payment made at time t based on the one-period short rate at time $t - 1$. The key identity we will need is

$$\sum_{i=1}^{m} E^Q\left(\exp\left(-\int_0^i R(s)\,ds\right)Y^1(i-1)\right) = 1 - v(0, m). \qquad (7.13)$$

We have already seen a version of this in the "useful starting point case" in Section 5.2. There we gave an economic argument, but it is nice to have a purely mathematical version of the theorem that does not require an analysis of trading strategies. The proof is just an application of conditional expectations:

$$E^Q\left(\exp\left(-\int_0^i R(s)\,ds\right)\left(\frac{1}{v(i-1, i)} - 1\right)\right)$$

$$= E^Q\left(\exp\left(-\int_0^{i-1} R(s)\,ds\right)\left(\frac{1}{v(i-1, i)} - 1\right)E_{i-1}^Q\exp\left(-\int_{i-1}^i R(s)\,ds\right)\right)$$

$$= E^Q\left(\exp\left(-\int_0^{i-1} R(s)\,ds\right)\left(\frac{1}{v(i-1, i)} - 1\right)v(i-1, i)\right)$$

$$= E^Q\left(\exp\left(-\int_0^{i-1} R(s)\,ds\right)(1 - v(i-1, i))\right)$$

$$= v(0, i-1) - v(0, i).$$

Now apply this result to every term in the sum and the result follows. The reader will easily modify the proof to be able to handle, for example, semiannual payments based on the corresponding definition of the short rate, so that, for example,

$$Y^{0.5}(t) = \frac{1}{v(t, t+0.5)} - 1.$$

The following discussion critically depends on distinguishing the following discount rates.

- $r(t)$ is the riskless short interest rate used for pricing government debt. We will return to the issue of liquidity later. Hence

$$p(t, T) = E_t^Q \exp\left(-\int_t^T r_s\,ds\right)$$

is the price at time t of a riskless zero-coupon bond with maturity T.

- $R_0^{AA}(t)$ is the recovery-adjusted short rate at time t of a particular issuer whose credit quality at time 0 is AA. Hence this rate is the relevant rate for discounting bonds from this issuer at time 0 for all maturities since the dynamics includes possible deterioration in credit quality. In other words,

$$v_0^{AA}(0, T) = E_0^Q \exp\left(-\int_0^T R_0^{AA}(s)\,ds\right) \qquad (7.14)$$

is the price at time 0 of a risky zero-coupon bond from this issuer.

- $R^{AA}(s)$ is the recovery-adjusted short rate of an issuer in class AA at time s. Consider a bond issued by an AA credit quality firm with a credit trigger that, in case of a change of rating to a nondefault category, transfers the commitment to repay the bond over to a new AA issuer. If the issuer goes directly from AA to default, the bond is in default. $R^{AA}(s)$ is the rate which would be relevant for pricing such a bond. We define

$$B(0, T) = E_0^Q \exp\left(-\int_0^T R^{AA}(s)\, ds\right) \tag{7.15}$$

to be the price of this artificial bond.

We now consider a swap contract with maturity T whose fixed leg is $c(T)$ and whose floating payment is given by the six-month LIBOR rate $Y_L^{0.5}$. It is useful to think of this short LIBOR rate as being well approximated by the six-month yield implied by AA corporate debt, so that

$$Y_L^{0.5}(t) = \frac{1}{v_t^{AA}(t, t + 0.5)} - 1, \tag{7.16}$$

but we will mention this hypothesis of homogeneous LIBOR and AA credit quality when we need it. Even when this assumption is not being made it is understood in the following that there is a credit-related spread on the short LIBOR rate which reflects the underlying credit quality of the contributor banks. Recall the result from the idealized setting of Section 8.2 in which the swap rate was equal to the par rate on a riskless bond. With semiannual payments, and introducing a superscript "r" for riskless, the expression (7.2) reads

$$c_T^r = \frac{1 - p(0, T)}{\sum_{i=1}^{2T} p(0, 0.5 * i)}, \tag{7.17}$$

and the par rate on AA bonds is

$$c_T^{AA} = \frac{1 - v_0^{AA}(0, T)}{\sum_{i=1}^{2T} v_0^{AA}(0, 0.5 * i)}. \tag{7.18}$$

Choosing different discount rates to value the swap will allow us to compare the swap rate with each of these par rates. First, consider the valuation of the LIBOR swap by discounting both legs of the swap by the riskless rate, consistent with a view that counterparty risk in a swap is irrelevant, at least when credit risk is symmetric. In this case we get the swap rate defined as the solution to

$$c(T) = \frac{\sum_{i=1}^{2T} E_0^Q[\exp(-\int_0^i r(s)\, ds) Y_L^{0.5}(i - 1)]}{\sum_{i=1}^{2T} p(0, 0.5 * i)}.$$

Analytical expressions for the discounted value—at the riskless rate—of the LIBOR rate require something like an affine setting. In the next section we will see how this can be done. The important thing to note here is that the fair swap rate has a denominator which is the same as in the expression for the riskless par rate (7.17), but that the numerator must be larger since we are discounting short-term LIBOR rates, which are definitely larger than the riskless short-term rates, by the risk-free rate. Hence the swap rate must be larger than the government par rates. The slope of the swap curve relative to the government curve will depend, among other things, on the expectations of future LIBOR paths.

We could also appeal to the symmetry of credit risk and argue, a bit loosely, that the discount rate might as well be the AA rate. Assuming homogeneous credit quality, or more precisely that the LIBOR six-month rate is equivalent to the six-month corporate AA rate, we obtain

$$c(T) = \frac{\sum_{i=1}^{2T} E_0^Q [\exp(-\int_0^i R_0^{AA}(s) \, ds) Y_L^{0.5}(i-1)]}{\sum_{i=1}^{2T} v_0^{AA}(0, 0.5 * i)}.$$

This time we note that the denominator is the same as the denominator in the expression (7.18) for AA par rates. However, the numerator must be smaller than the numerator in the expression for the AA par rate, since the floating payments of the swap are linked to the refreshed quality AA/LIBOR rate. If we were to use the result (7.13) in the hope of getting the same numerator in the swap rate as in the AA par rate, we would have to have a floating-rate payment in the swap that increased when the credit quality decreased. We conclude that the swap curve must be below the AA curve for maturities longer than six months, at which maturity they are equal, by definition, in this example.

If we want to use the result (7.13) to get a simple expression for the numerator, we may use the refreshed credit quality discount factor on both sides and obtain

$$c(T) = \frac{1 - B(0, T)}{\sum_{i=1}^{2T} B(0, 0.5 * i)}.$$

Since these bond prices are not observable in the market, one may instead use swap data and imply out these rates and think of them as swap zero rates. We will return to this later.

To see an illustration of the conclusions drawn so far, consider the historical evidence presented in Figures 7.3–7.5. In Figure 7.3 average yields between six months and seven years for US treasuries, dollar swaps, and AA corporate bonds (financials and banks) are shown. The average is computed over a 6-year period. Consistent with our theory, the swap rate is squeezed in between the government and corporate AA curve. The corporate AA curve is further from the swap curve at the long end—and this is also consistent with our theory, as we will see in greater detail in the next section.

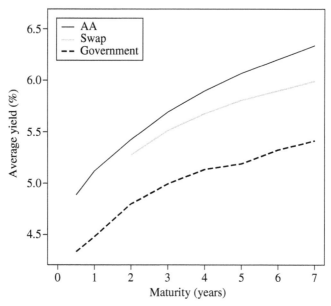

Figure 7.3.   Average term structures of US Treasury and AA par yields and swap rates
for the period 20 December 1996 to 14 February 2003. Source: Bloomberg.

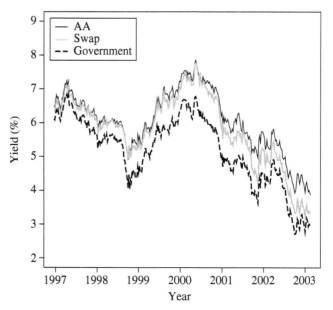

Figure 7.4.   Five-year AA and US Treasury par yield and swap rate. US data from
20 December 1996 to 14 February 2003. Source: Bloomberg.

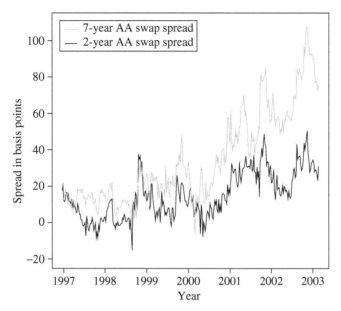

Figure 7.5. Spread between the 2- and 7-year AA par yield and swap rate. US data from 20 December 1996 to 14 February 2003. Source: Bloomberg.

Of course, taking the raw average is a very crude statistic and it is comforting therefore to see, in Figure 7.4, that over the sample period, the 5-year swap rate is squeezed in between the 5-year treasury and AA corporate par yields. We also see in Figure 7.5, which shows the spread between the AA rate and the swap rate at maturities of two and seven years, that the prediction that the spread between the AA rate and swaps tends to increase with maturity has been satisfied almost all of the time. Below we focus on discounting with the riskless rate in a more concrete model to see how the corporate bond and swap spreads could be related in a simple model.

7.8 The Swap Spread versus the Corporate-Bond Spread

It is useful to see a concrete model in which the difference between the swap rates, the corporate AA rate, and the riskless rate is explicitly modeled. This section presents a simple model in which explicit solutions can be obtained using affine machinery and where we can take into account both the stochastic variation in the six-month LIBOR rate and the possible deterioration of credit quality through rating downgrades of a particular issuer. The model can easily be extended to include more factors to better capture slope effects of the term structure, for example.

We consider a rating-based model such as the one presented in Chapter 6. The dynamics of the riskless rate r and a stochastic spread factor μ are given under our

Table 7.6. Base generator matrix (corresponding to the value 1 of the stochastic spread factor). The default intensities are recovery adjusted, as explained in Chapter 6.

$\tilde{\Lambda}$	AAA	AA	A	BBB	SG	D
AAA	−0.1026	0.0847	0.0122	0.0007	0	0.0050
AA	0.0157	−0.1346	0.1090	0.0028	0.0011	0.0060
A	0.0010	0.0267	−0.1102	0.0678	0.0057	0.0090
BBB	0.0009	0.0024	0.0669	−0.1540	0.0723	0.0115
SG	0	0.0004	0.0066	0.1220	−0.1512	0.0222
D	0	0	0	0	0	0

pricing measure Q as

$$dr_t = \kappa_r(\theta_r - r_t)\,dt + \sigma_r\sqrt{r_t}\,dW_t^r \qquad \text{with } r_0 = 0.0375,$$
$$d\mu_t = \kappa_\mu(\theta_\mu - \mu_t)\,dt + \mu_\lambda\sqrt{\mu_t}\,dW_t^\mu \qquad \text{with } \mu_0 = 1,$$

where the Brownian motions W^r and W^μ are independent and

$$\kappa_r = 0.1, \qquad \theta_r = 0.05, \qquad \sigma_r = 0.0671,$$

and

$$\kappa_\mu = 0.022, \qquad \theta_\mu = 1, \qquad \sigma_\mu = 0.175.$$

The "stochastic generator" at time t is given as $\Lambda\mu_t$, where the generator Λ is as specified in Table 7.6.

Let η_t denote the value of the rating at time t of a firm rated AA at time 0. We have collapsed speculative-grade (SG) categories into one SG category for simplicity of exposition. Using a finer grid of ratings in the speculative grades will not change the results. The default-adjusted short rate of this firm at time t is given as

$$R_0^{AA}(t) = r_t + \Lambda_{\eta(t),D}\mu_t.$$

The computation of treasury-bond prices is a standard application of the CIR model. We then compute zero-coupon prices of the AA bonds by evaluating (7.14) using the machinery of Chapter 6, and then use (7.18) to get par bond yields.

To value the floating payment from the swap explicitly using the affine framework we need to make one approximation. Instead of defining the six-month LIBOR rate at time t as in (7.16), we use instead the approximation

$$Y_{0.5}^{AA}(t) = \frac{1}{E_t^Q \exp(-\int_t^{t+0.5} R^{AA}(s)\,ds)} - 1, \tag{7.19}$$

i.e. we use a zero-coupon bond based on the refreshed LIBOR rate. This is equivalent to assuming that the issuer only moves from AA directly to default and not through intermediate downgrades. The difference in six-month rates that one would obtain by including possible downgrades in the price of a six-month bond amounts to 0.8 bp for the chosen parameters. This is acceptable in light of the advantage of obtaining an explicit expression for the value of the floating payment.

To see that we end up with an affine expression, define the coefficients α^λ and β^λ as the coefficients in an affine representation

$$S^\lambda(t, T) \equiv E_t^Q \exp\left(-\int_t^T \lambda_{AA}\mu_s \, ds\right) = \exp(-\alpha^\lambda(T - t) - \beta^\lambda(T - t)\mu_t),$$

where we suppress the state variable dependence of S^λ. Note that due to the independence assumption, the price of an (artificial) bond whose default-adjusted rate corresponds to refreshed AA credit quality can then be expressed as

$$B^{AA}(t, T) \equiv E_t^Q \exp\left(-\int_t^T R^{AA}(s) \, ds\right) = p(t, T)S^\lambda(t, T).$$

We can then compute the value at time 0 of the floating payment made at time t_i settled on the basis of the rate at $t - 1$ (say) as follows. As usual, $p(t, T) = E^Q \exp(-\int_t^T r_s \, ds)$ and therefore

$$
\begin{aligned}
v^{fl}(0, t_i) &= E^Q \exp\left(-\int_0^{t_i} r_s \, ds\right)\left(\frac{1}{B^{AA}(t_{i-1}, t_i)} - 1\right) \\
&= E^Q \exp\left(-\int_0^{t_{i-1}} r_s \, ds\right)\frac{1}{B^{AA}(t_{i-1}, t_i)}p(t_{i-1}, t_i) - p(0, t_i) \\
&= p(0, t_{i-1})\frac{1}{p(t_{i-1}, t_i)S^\lambda(t_{i-1}, t_i)}p(t_{i-1}, t_i) - p(0, t_i) \\
&= p(0, t_{i-1})E^Q \exp(\alpha^\lambda(t_i - t_{i-1}) + \beta^\lambda(t_i - t_{i-1})\mu(t_{i-1})) - p(0, t_i),
\end{aligned}
$$

and the expression for the functional $E^Q \exp(\alpha^\lambda(t_i - t_{i-1}) + \beta^\lambda(t_i - t_{i-1})\mu(t_{i-1}))$ can be found in closed form using the term-structure toolbox in Appendix E. Note that we got some extra simplification due to the independence assumption, but this is not necessary of course, if one is willing to venture into multivariate affine processes. Note, also, that the above machinery translates directly into a setting in which the affine process has jumps and independence is preserved. The results from Appendix E can be used to obtain a closed-form solution in this case.

The fair swap rate in the model is then the fixed payment which equates the present value of the floating-rate payments with the present value of the fixed payments. Discounting both sides using the riskless rate and assuming semiannual payments, we obtain a fair swap rate of

$$C^S(T) = \frac{\sum_{i=1}^{2T} v^{fl}(0, 0.5 * i)}{\sum_{i=1}^{2T} p(0, 0.5 * i)}.$$

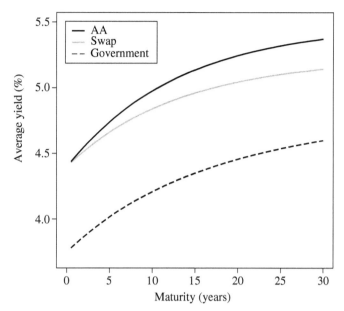

Figure 7.6.   Government and AA par yield curves and
swap curve for the model in Section 7.8.

As shown in Figure 7.6 this simple model produces exactly the kind of pattern that
has been observed empirically with swap rates close to AA rates in the short end
(in the model these two rates are equal by definition when the time to maturity is
six months) and increasing spread between AA rates and the swap rate as maturity
grows.

7.9   On the Swap Rate, Repo Rates, and the Riskless Rate

In the models presented so far, the bond prices computed from the short-rate process r
have been referred to as treasury securities. This follows the tradition in finance
of identifying "riskless" rates with yields on government bonds. However, newer
research argues that the government rate is not the right proxy to use for the riskless
rate. This is particularly true for the so-called on-the-run treasuries in the US market,
which are the most recently issued government bonds. These bonds are heavily
traded and are used in both long and short positions. A short position may be taken
for hedging the interest-rate risk of a trade. If an investor views a corporate bond
as underpriced because the market overestimates the default risk of the issuer, but
the same investor has plenty of interest-rate risk already, he may want to buy the
corporate bond and hedge the interest-rate risk of the bond through a short position
in a government bond. The easiest way of shorting a bond is to obtain the bond
through a so-called reverse repo. A repo transaction is a collateralized loan in which

a borrower delivers a collateral, typically a government bond, and receives a loan, which is typically of short duration (less than six months, often as short as one day or a week). The borrower can choose among a variety of "general collateral" (GC) and the rate at which one can borrow in the repo market using general collateral is called the GC repo rate. This rate is often viewed as a good proxy for the riskless rate—a point we will return to below.

While the repo market thus seems driven by the need to borrow cash in the short term, it has an equally important function in allowing agents to obtain a security as collateral by lending liquidity. If a particular government bond is particularly in demand as collateral (perhaps because many investors wish to use it for short selling), then agents may offer to lend cash in a repo at rates lower than the GC repo rate to try and attract other agents who are willing to post the particular bond as collateral. In this case the particular bond is said to be "special." In this case, an owner of the bond can obtain an extra dividend by lending the bond out for a period and receiving a loan at a rate below the prevailing market rate. On-the-run treasury securities are often "special" and therefore owners of such bonds receive an extra dividend from their ownership of the bond—a dividend in addition to the stipulated coupons. This dividend raises their price, thus lowering the rate—essentially sending the rate below "the riskless rate."

Grinblatt (2001) argues that this convenience yield from holding government bonds explains the difference between swap rates and treasury rates. His starting point is a comparison of two trading strategies.

Strategy G invests $1 at time 0 in an on-the-run government bond maturing at date T. We assume that the bond trades at par and denote the semiannual coupon on the bond $C_T/2$.

Strategy L invests $1 at time 0 in a six-month LIBOR money-market account. After six months the interest is taken out, and the $1 is reinvested for another six months at the then prevailing six-month LIBOR rate and so forth. In short, $1 is rolled over in six-month LIBOR until time T. This rolling over is combined with the purchase at time 0 of a zero present-value swap with maturity T, which requires payment of six-month LIBOR (in arrears) and delivers the fixed swap rate $S_T/2$ semiannually.

The cash flow, disregarding any convenience yield, from Strategy G is −$1 at time 0, $2T$ semiannual fixed payments each of size $C_T/2$, and the $1 principal at maturity. The cash flow, disregarding credit risk in the LIBOR money-market account and swap counterparty credit risk, is similar to the cash flow of Strategy L except for the fact that the semiannual payments are the larger amount $S_T/2$. Grinblatt (2001) argues that the difference between these two coupons must be due to a convenience yield from holding the government bond. More specifically, he models the convenience yield from holding a government bond as a stochastic process, and the difference between the fixed rate of the government bond and the swap rate is then the present value of that convenience yield.

He (2001) takes a different path and models the GC repo rate as the riskless rate by which we discount cash flows and argues that the spread between treasuries and swaps is explained by the "short-term financing spread," i.e. the difference between the GC repo rate and the six-month LIBOR rate.

7.10 Bibliographical Notes

For an early primer on swap valuation, see Sundaresan (1991) and references therein. A nice recent overview of the role of swap curves as benchmark curves is found in Bank of International Settlements (2001). The literature on default risk in swaps is becoming fairly extensive. The focus in this chapter has been on pricing in the intensity-based setting, but the first to study systematically the default risk in swaps from a structural perspective were Cooper and Mello (1991) and Rendleman (1992). Other early papers focusing on credit risk in swaps are Wall and Pringle (1988), Solnik (1990), Sorensen and Bollier (1984), and Litzenberger (1992).

An example of a paper focusing on the comparative-advantage idea are Bicksler and Chen (1986), who assume that institutional barriers allow for a genuine comparative advantage to be present. Of course, an analysis in a fully specified structural model is capable of revealing the source—in an arbitrage-free setting—of a perceived but illusory comparative advantage, but the point was given stronger emphasis in Artzner and Delbaen (1990) and Turnbull (1987). The example in this chapter is inspired by Artzner and Delbaen (1990), but constructed to give what I think is the "minimal" illustration of the main idea.

The argument that in arbitrage-free models using realistic parameters for the relevant rates, floating–fixed spreads are vanishingly small, is presented in Duffie and Liu (2001).

The first treatment of the effect of counterparty credit risk in swaps analyzed in a reduced-form setting was given in Duffie and Huang (1996), who also study the effects of netting, and this framework was extended in Huge and Lando (1999) to take into account rating changes. This allows one to analyze the effect of credit triggers in swap contracts. Jarrow and Turnbull (1997) analyze two-sided default risk in a discrete-time, finite-state-space model. Hübner (2001) considers a method for pricing with asymmetric default risk which avoids the use of recursive methods.

The valuation model of Section 7.8 is very much inspired by Collin-Dufresne and Solnik (2001) and Duffie and Liu (2001) but the modeling of the possible decline in credit quality takes advantage of the affine rating-based model presented in Chapter 6.

An early empirical work on swaps is Sun et al. (1993), where is it shown that counterparty credit quality does have an effect on quoted swap rates. This paper also investigates the relationship between treasury yields, swap rates, and corporate par bond yields. Other empirical work includes Brown et al. (1994) and Minton (1997). The first empirical paper on swaps to take advantage of intensity-based models is Duffie and Singleton (1997). Newer works in this area include Liu et al. (2002) and He (2001).

8

Credit Default Swaps, CDOs, and Related Products

The market for credit derivatives is seeing rapid growth. According to a 2002 survey by the British Bankers' Association (BBA), the estimated size of the market by the end of 2002 was set at almost $2 trillion and the BBA expects the size of the market to reach $5 trillion by the end of 2004.

In this chapter we present the most important vehicles for transferring credit risk, namely variations of the default swaps and a class of asset-backed securities broadly referred to as Collateralized Debt Obligations (CDOs). In the BBA survey, so-called single-name default swaps accounted for almost half of the market volume in credit derivatives and almost a quarter of the volume was in "portfolio products/Collateralized Loan Obligations (CLOs)." This chapter will look at these most important classes of credit derivatives. The main purpose is to understand the fundamental structure of these instruments and how they interact.

We will also consider a few basic issues in building pricing models, but one should be aware that this area—as with corporate bonds in general—is rich in institutional detail. Hence the models tend to deal with stylized versions. As always, one hopes that the stylized structures overcome enough of the most important obstacles in modeling to make it relatively straightforward to build on the basic structures to accommodate particular institutional features. We will not derive more than a few analytical formulas. For multi-name contracts one usually ends up having to simulate the models anyway. We focus therefore on some basic calculations which are helpful for the simulations. Once simulations are called for, the worry then becomes what kind of correlation structure to impose, and this is the topic of the next chapter.

8.1 Some Basic Terminology

The market for credit risk transfer is rich with institutional details and we will not attempt to go into a lot of detail here. Rather, this section serves as an introduction to the most important structures and hints at their definitions and uses.

8.1.1   The Single-Name Credit Default Swap (CDS)

The most important instrument in the credit derivative market is the credit default swap, which essentially provides insurance against the default of an issuer (the reference credit) or on a specific underlying bond (the reference security). In its most basic form the buyer of the protection pays an annual (or semiannual) premium until either the maturity of the contract or default on the reference entity, whichever comes first. If a default occurs, the seller of the protection compensates the buyer for the loss on the reference security by either paying the face value of the bond in exchange for the defaulted bond (physical settlement) or by paying an amount of cash which compensates the buyer of the protection for the difference between the post-default market value of the bond and the par value (cash settlement). The post-default market value is determined based on polling of dealers. In the case of a physical settlement, the protection seller often has a "wildcard" option to deliver one of several bonds from the defaulted issuer. Some cash-settled contracts have a settlement amount which is fixed in advance. This less-common contract is often referred to as a "digital" or "binary" default swap. Typically, the underlying credit of a default swap is a rated firm with publicly traded debt or a sovereign entity. The market for CDSs on firms is quickly outgrowing that for sovereigns.

8.1.2   Basket Default Swaps and first m-of-n-to-Default Swaps

A more advanced type of CDS is a so-called "first-to-default" or "basket default" swap, which insures the protection buyer against the first default in a group of issuers. As an alternative to buying credit protection on each single name, it is of course a lot less expensive but also covers only a fraction of the portfolio credit risk. For portfolios containing many names, this may provide too little insurance and a popular extension of the basket credit derivative insures not only the first default but the first m defaults in a defined group of n issuers, and these are referred to as "first-m-of-n" default swaps. And as a final example of a basket structure, the swap may cover defaults on a fixed interval, say defaults from the fifth to the tenth out of a group of (say) 50 issuers. These contracts resemble stop-loss contracts and "layers" in the traditional reinsurance business. The most important difference is the extent to which the underlying risk is traded in other markets. For most CDS contracts there is a market for the underlying corporate bonds, and, additionally, the risk of the underlying names is often traded in equity markets. For the more exotic basket structures mentioned here, the single-name CDS market becomes the reference market.

8.1.3   Collateralized Debt Obligations

We saw in Chapter 2 how equity, senior debt, and junior debt issued by a firm could be viewed as different claims to the underlying asset value of the firm. In essence, the claims are repackaged claims to the firm's assets. If instead of a firm's assets we consider a repackaging of a portfolio of securities, we have an example of the design of an asset-backed security through the process of tranching. The most naive example would run as follows. Consider a pool of 50 zero-coupon loans maturing in one year. Assume that the face value of each loan is 1 and that there is zero recovery on the loans in the event of default. Now consider three securities: the equity tranche, the junior (or mezzanine) tranche, and the senior tranche with face values (say) 5, 35, and 10, respectively. The senior tranche will be repaid the full face value of 10 in one year as long as there are no more than 40 defaults in the underlying pool of loans. If more than 40 defaults occur within a year, the senior tranche will receive the entire cash flow of the pool of loans, and the junior and equity tranches will get nothing. If less than 40 defaults occur, the junior tranche will receive, up to a limit of 35, the cash flow from what is left after the senior tranche has been paid. And finally, the equity tranche is repaid whatever is left after the senior and junior tranches have been paid off. Equity therefore will only receive 5 if no defaults occur and it will get nothing if 5 or more defaults occur. This is the basic idea of a Collateralized Debt Obligation (CDO). The proceeds from selling the different tranches cover the purchase of the underlying assets.

In practice, the definition of a CDO can be much more complicated, but the example explains the basic idea of repackaging the risk profile of the underlying pool of assets into securities having different degrees of seniority in their claims to the underlying assets. Here is a quick summary of some of the main features and types of CDO and the way they are put to use. We will briefly discuss some of the main modeling issues later, but since all of this really focuses on correlation structures, we postpone some of the more modeling-related issues to Chapter 9.

CDOs are often divided into CLOs (Collateralized Loan Obligations), where the underlying assets are bank loans, and CBOs (Collateralized Bond Obligations), where the underlying assets are bonds. CLOs are used as a vehicle for banks to reduce credit exposure and hence reduce capital requirements. The bank is then referred to as the originator of the CLO.

Rather than the bank securitizing the loans or bonds directly, a special entity called an SPV (Special Purpose Vehicle) is created which is legally separated from the bank. The assets (i.e. the loans or the corporate bonds) are sold to the SPV, which gets the funds from issuing the tranched securities. For the bank to get capital relief it must be clear that the assets that are sold off no longer contribute to the overall risk of the bank. The SPV is the way of ensuring this.

With CLOs, the actual monitoring of the loans remains with the bank, and in order to reduce the moral hazard problems it is therefore standard practice for the bank to hold the equity portion of the CLO. In this way the bank will be the first to suffer if loans are not monitored properly.

This retention of equity is key for understanding the notion of regulatory capital arbitrage, whose proliferation is one of the major motivations behind the new Basel II Accord. Returning to our stylized example above, if the bank retains an equity tranche of 5, it will, under the current rules, have reduced its capital requirement by a factor of 10, since it has replaced a total face value of 50 with one of 5. If the default probability is not too large, say 2%, and we do not assume some drastic correlation between the loans, then the distribution of the (dollar) loss arising from holding the equity piece is virtually indistinguishable from that of holding the entire loan portfolio. They will only differ in the unlikely case of more than 5 defaults. Hence the reduction by a factor of 10 in the capital requirement is not associated with any significant reduction of the risk of loss. Of course, the maximal loss that can be suffered has been reduced by a factor of 10, but capital requirements are not based on maximal losses in a world where banks are allowed to have significant leverage.

CBOs are often used by asset managers to repackage bonds (often in the lower parts of the credit risk spectrum) and to sell claims to the package that match particular demands for leverage. When used by asset managers, the CBOs are typically "managed", i.e. the proceeds from coupons and recovery payments in default are actively reinvested. CLOs are often static with strict rules on how the proceeds can be reinvested. The requirement may be OECD government bonds.

One of the most complicated problems arising in the analysis of (and hence in the regulatory treatment of) CDOs is the prioritization schemes used to allocate cash flows from defaulted issuers during the lifetime of the CDO. The analogy to our contingent-claims analysis is whether firms are allowed to sell assets to pay coupons and dividends to bond holders and shareholders.

Typically, the tranches in a CDO have a promised coupon flow during the life of the CDO and not just at a fixed maturity date, as in the stylized example. The question is to what extent the SPV can use proceeds from defaulted issues to pay coupons on sub-senior tranches. One can imagine that even if the flow of funds is sufficient to pay for coupons for all tranches in the early stages, a surprising number of defaults towards the end of the life of the CDO threatens the full repayment of the senior tranche. By retaining funds in special accounts, one can make sure that nothing is paid to sub-senior tranches unless there is full repayment of principal to the senior tranche.

The timing of defaults alone creates path dependence in the total value of the assets underlying the CDO. The prioritization schemes seen in practice introduce heavy path dependence into the valuation of the individual tranches. The complexity of the prioritization schemes is a good reason for worrying about efficient simulation techniques. The dependence between the different issues in the pool is another central worry of the modelling efforts.

8.1.4 Credit-Linked Notes

In a default swap, the buyer of protection is exposed to the risk of default of the protection seller. If there is a credit event on the reference security and the protection seller defaults, the protection buyer may not receive the promised compensation. Note that the seller can, in principle, sell protection without coming up with any funds and we therefore refer to the default swap transactions as "unfunded" transfers of credit risk.

The credit-linked note (CLN) is a "funded" alternative to this construction. Here the protection seller buys a bond, called a CLN, from the protection buyer and the cash flow on this bond is linked to the performance of a reference issuer. If the reference issuer (or a group of issuers) defaults, the payment to the CLN owner is reduced. Hence the default protection is funded, in the sense that the protection seller, by paying for the CLN, has provided funds initially.

This is an attractive instrument for laying off credit risk to smaller investors who do not have sufficient funds or credit quality to sell default protection. As buyers of CLNs they can sell protection even in small portions. There is no risk of nonperformance of the protection sellers since they have "paid up front," i.e. they have funded the credit risk transfer. Of course, the owners of the CLNs are exposed to default risk both from the CLN issuer and from the reference issuer. They may not get the promised payments on the CDS if the CLN issuer defaults, and they will suffer a reduction of the repayment of the CLN if the reference issuer defaults. Only the buyer of protection has no counterparty credit risk in the CLN transaction.

8.1.5 The Synthetic CDO

An important addition to the CDO market is the so-called synthetic CDO, in which there are no assets transferred from the originator to the SPV, but where the SPV sells default protection to the originator through default swaps. A stylized version is as follows. The originator buys default swaps from the SPV. The SPV structures CLNs whose payouts are linked to the underlying credits of the default swaps. The proceeds from the note sales are invested into (say) government bonds. When defaults happen and the accumulated premium payments from the default swaps are not sufficient to fund the settlement payments, the government bonds are used to finance the settlement and the buyers of the CLNs see their payments reduced.

With this brief outline of the basic terminology, we are ready to go into more of the modeling details.

8.2 Decomposing the Credit Default Swap

For the purposes of hedging default swaps and for understanding their role in creating synthetic CDOs, we focus here on an approximate decomposition of the default

Table 8.1. Cash flow from a c-FRN and a floater in the case of no default. The cash flow is an annuity, as are the payments on a (sold) CDS if there is no default.

Time	$t = 0$	$t = 1$	$\cdots$	$t = T - 1$	$t = T$
Long c-FRN	-1	$r_0 + c(T)$	$\cdots$	$r_{T-2} + c(T)$	$1 + r_{T-1} + c(T)$
Short floater	1	$-r_0$	$\cdots$	$-r_{T-2}$	$-(1 + r_{T-1})$
Total	0	$c(T)$	$\cdots$	$c(T)$	$c(T)$

swap into a long position in a default-free floating-rate note and a short position in a floating-rate note with a fixed spread, which we will denote by c-FRN. We think of the default swap as referencing a single issuer.

A default-free floating rate is a bond which pays the short rate r_t at time $t + 1$ until maturity T, where the payment is $1 + r_{T-1}$. Clearly, such a bond can be created by investing 1 at time 0 in the bond maturing at time 1, and continuing to reinvest 1 in each period in the short bond until the desired maturity. Hence the (ex-coupon) price of such a bond is 1 at all coupon dates.

A floating-rate note with maturity T and a constant spread (c-FRN) is a bond issued by the reference issuer with a coupon which pays the floating rate plus a fixed spread $c(T)$ that is large enough to make the bond trade at par initially. Assume that the recovery value at the default date per unit of principal is $\delta(\tau)$.

What we claim is that, at least approximately, the cash flow of the default swap as seen from the protection seller is equal to a long position in a c-FRN combined with a short position in a default-free floating-rate note. To see the near equivalence we look at the payments resulting from this position in a scenario with no default and in a scenario with default before maturity. We make several simplifying assumptions— the most important being that the coupon dates of the bond match the premium payment dates of the swap. We also assume that if a default occurs, the settlement payment is made to the protection buyer at a coupon date following the default with no consideration of accrued interest. As seen in Tables 8.1 and 8.2, this strategy produces a cash flow which is very similar to that of a written default swap, i.e. a swap in which protection against default has been sold off. This contract delivers a premium and requires payment of a compensation payment in default, and with some simplifying assumptions this is what happens in the strategy above. What separates it from the payment on the default swap is, of course, the small interest payment from the floater liquidated at the default date. It is not hard to make a small correction for this payment in practical pricing. We also note that we must assume that the default swap has premium payments at the coupon dates of the bonds and that the settlement payment in default is made at the coupon date. One would have to correct for this in concrete modeling situations of course.

Table 8.2. Cash flow from a long c-FRN and a short position in a floater in the case of default at time τ, where the position in the default-free floater is liquidated. The payment matches that of a sold CDS, except for the floating-rate piece received at the default time.

Time	$t = 0$	$t = 1$	$\cdots$	τ	$t > \tau$
Long c-FRN	-1	$r_0 + c(T)$	$\cdots$	$\delta(\tau)$	0
Short floater	1	$-r_0$	$\cdots$	$-(1 + r_{\tau-1})$	0
Total	$c(T)$	$c(T)$	$\cdots$	$(\delta(\tau) - 1) - r_{\tau-1}$	0

It is clear that the default swap premium is reasonably thought of as a credit spread. In the idealized setting of the example, it is almost identical to a spread on a floating-rate bond. But it is also clear that differences between spreads on bonds and default swaps can be traced back to the simplifying assumptions in this example. For example, if a financial institution has sold a default swap, it would often try to hedge by taking the opposite position by shorting the c-FRN and buying the riskless floater. Shorting corporate bonds is typically done by obtaining the security in a reverse repo transaction—that is, a transaction in which cash is lent out and the security is obtained as collateral—and then selling the security. But to get the bond through the repo market may be costly (by requiring the provision of a loan at a very low interest rate) and this implicit cost of hedging may make the default swap more expensive. However, as we will see in the section on CDOs, there are other ways for the seller of default protection to get rid of the default risk through asset securitization.

Another decomposition would seem obvious to try: combine the purchase of a fixed-rate corporate bond with the purchase of a CDS with physical settlement. At first glance, this should produce a riskless bond. If there is no default, the bond pays 1 at maturity and we have had a fixed net coupon flow equal to the difference between the coupon on the corporate bond and the CDS premium. If there is default, we receive the face value of the bond in exchange for the defaulted bond, producing a cash flow of 1 at the default time. Hence we are at least close to a fixed-rate default-free bond, except for the fact that we receive the notional value at a random date. But this suggests that the CDS premium is equal to the difference in coupon (again up to small differences due to accrued interest payments, etc.) of the corporate bond and a treasury security with a randomized time to maturity.

We might try a further refinement. A combination of a fixed coupon and receiving 1 at a random time does not give us a recognizable riskless rate, but if instead the rate had been a floating rate, the combination of a floating rate and 1 being received at a random time is very close to a riskless floater. Now introduce a swap contract which is not only cancellable, but is in fact automatically cancelled at the time of default of the reference security. Then buying the bond, the default protection, and entering

Table 8.3. Cash flow from an asset swap with no default on the bond. The cash flow is the combined flow of a long bond and an off-market swap exchanging the floating payment $r_t + a$ for the fixed payment C. Note that the final result is a c-FRN.

Time	$t = 0$	$t = 1$	$\cdots$	$t = T - 1$	$t = T$
Long bond	-1	C	$\cdots$	C	$1 + C$
Swap/pay fixed	0	$r_0 + a - C$	$\cdots$	$r_{T-2} + a - C$	$r_{T-1} + a - C$
Total	-1	$r_0 + a$	$\cdots$	$r_{T-2} + a$	$1 + r_{T-1} + a$

into the cancellable swap produces exactly a floating-rate flow and a payment of 1 at a random date—and this would have a contract value of 1. The forced cancellation is artificial in this example. If we leave the cancellation out, we are naturally led to the final example of an important contract in credit risk transfers: the so-called asset swap.

8.3   Asset Swaps

The c-FRN, which we saw in the first decomposition of the default swap, is close to what can be obtained by buying a fixed-rate corporate bond and swapping the fixed rate with a floating rate using an ordinary interest-rate swap. The only difference is that the swap would typically continue even after a default of the bond. The combination of a bond purchase and a swap of the fixed rate with a floating rate is available through what is known as an asset-swap package. This package is of interest to an investor who thinks that a (fixed-rate) credit-risky coupon bond is undervalued but who is not interested in taking in more interest-rate risk.

Below we will consider three maturity dependent rates: a corporate bond coupon rate; an asset-swap rate; and a swap rate. Instead of referring to these as $C(T), a(T)$, and $c^s(T)$, we will just write C, a, and c^s, but keep in mind that these quantities depend on the chosen maturity. Consider a risky fixed-rate bullet bond with maturity T, which pays C per period. The buyer of the asset swap receives, until maturity of the construct, the cash flow of the underlying bond (including the recovery value at default) and pays C on the swap part while receiving the floating rate plus a fixed spread a, called the asset-swap spread. Note that C is not equal to the swap rate for maturity T. The swap is an example of an "off-market" swap, where the fixed coupon is different from the market swap rate. The payoffs in the cases of no default and default are shown in Tables 8.3 and 8.4.

The asset-swap spread a is set such that the initial value of the package is 1, regardless of the market value of the bond. To find the fair value of a we proceed as follows. Let $v(0, t)$ denote the value of a maturity-t zero-coupon bond from the same issuer as in the asset swap, and let $v^C(0, t)$ denote the value of the bullet

Table 8.4. Cash flow from an asset swap when there is default at data τ. Note that the swap continues after the default.

Time	$t = 0$	$t = 1$	$\cdots$	τ	$\tau < t \leqslant T$
Long bond	-1	C	$\cdots$	$\delta(\tau)$	0
Swap/pay fixed	1	$r_1 + a - C$	$\cdots$	$r_{\tau-1} + a - C$	$r_{t-1} + a - C$
Total	-1	$r_0 + a$	$\cdots$	$\delta(\tau) + r_{\tau-1} + a - C$	$r_t + a - C$

loan with maturity t and coupon rate $C(t)$. As usual, $p(0, t)$ denotes the value of a riskless bond. We are ignoring the credit risk of any of the parties to the asset swap and focus therefore only on the default risk of the underlying reference issuer. Define the value of a riskless annuity paying 1 in each period and a similar annuity issued by the reference issuer of the asset swap:

$$A(T) = \sum_{t=0}^{T} p(0, t), \qquad A^C(T) = \sum_{t=0}^{T} v(0, t).$$

Clearly, the value of the payoffs on the corporate bond is equal to $CA^C(T) + v(0, T)$. The value of the interest-rate payment is a little more subtle. The asset-swap buyer is paying $C - a$ to receive the floating rate. If the market swap rate c^s is different from this quantity, then the swap in the asset swap does not have initial value 0. It has a positive value if the asset-swap buyer pays a lower fixed rate than the market swap rate. The difference is $c^s - (C - a)$ and the value of this cash flow is $(c^s + a - C)A(T)$, since the swap always runs to maturity. We are now in a position to find the asset-swap spread: to have a value of 1 initially, we must have

$$v^C(0, T) + (c^s + a - C)A(T) = 1,$$

i.e.

$$a = \frac{1 - v^C(0, T)}{A(T)} + C - c^s.$$

Note that when the underlying bond is priced at par, this reduces to

$$a = C - c^s,$$

and it is then a spread between the fixed coupon on a par bond (i.e. a par bond yield) and the swap rate. In this case, a is clearly a credit spread.

When the underlying bond is not at par, the asset-swap spread must also reflect this. If we think of the underlying bond as a bullet bond paying C each period until maturity and $1 + C$ at maturity, then expressing the price of the corporate bond as

$$v^C(0, T) = CA^C(T) + v(0, T),$$

we find that

$$a = \frac{1}{A(T)}[1 - v(0, T) + C(A(T) - A^C(T))] - c^s.$$

Now, if we ask for the same credit quality, what happens to the asset-swap spread when we lower the coupon of the underlying bond? The lowering of coupon has no effect on the value of the principal $v(0, T)$, since we are assuming that the credit quality remains fixed, but since $A(T) > A^C(T)$, lowering the coupon while holding the credit quality fixed will produce a lower asset-swap spread.

8.4   Pricing the Default Swap

The basic decompositions above are useful for conceptual purposes but they hinge on types of instruments which are not typically traded. In this section we go back to a more fundamental approach and try pricing the CDS from the fundamental cash flows: that is, finding the premium payment which makes the CDS have zero value at inception. The value is computed using information on the default intensity and the recovery in default.

Regardless of recovery assumptions, the present value of the premium payments is easily handled. Assume that the reference bond has coupon dates $1, \ldots, T$ and matures at date T. Assume that the recovery on the bond per unit face value is δ in default so that the protection seller pays $1 - \delta$ in default. One can change recovery assumptions to fractional recovery or recovery of treasury, but we illustrate using this assumption and refer to our earlier discussion of various recovery assumptions.

We want to find the fair swap premium $c^{ds}(T)$ on a CDS with maturity T and assume that we can model the default intensity of the underlying reference security as a Cox process with intensity process λ.

Since the protection buyer pays a constant premium $c^{ds}(T)$ until maturity T or default, whichever comes first, it is easy to find the value π^{pb} of this leg of the swap:

$$\pi^{pb} = E \sum_{i=1}^{T} \exp\left(-\int_0^i r_s \, ds\right) 1_{\{\tau > i\}} c^{ds}(T)$$

$$= c^{ds}(T) E \sum_{i=1}^{T} \exp\left(-\int_0^i (r_s + \lambda_s) \, ds\right)$$

$$= c^{ds}(T) \sum_{i=1}^{T} v^0(0, i),$$

with the notation $v^0(0, i)$ for a risky zero-coupon bond with zero recovery.

The value π^{ps} of the payment made by the protection seller is a little more technical if we insist on settling everything at the exact default time τ. Using the basic Cox process machinery again we find

$$\pi^{\text{ps}} = E\left[\exp\left(-\int_0^\tau r_s\,ds\right)1_{\{\tau\leqslant T\}}(1-\delta)\right]$$

$$= (1-\delta)E\int_0^T \lambda_t\exp\left(-\int_0^t(r_s+\lambda_s)\,ds\right)dt$$

$$= (1-\delta)\int_0^T E\left[\lambda_t\exp\left(-\int_0^t(r_s+\lambda_s)\,ds\right)\right]dt.$$

To obtain a further simplification, we assume independence (under the martingale measure) between the default intensity and the short-rate process, the expression reduces to

$$\pi^{\text{ps}} = (1-\delta)\int_0^T E\left[\exp\left(-\int_0^t r_s\,ds\right)\right]E\left[-\frac{\partial}{\partial t}\exp\left(-\int_0^t \lambda_s\,ds\right)\right]dt$$

$$= \int_0^T p(0,t)\left(-\frac{\partial}{\partial t}S(0,t)\right)dt$$

$$= (1-\delta)\int_0^T \hat{\lambda}(t)S(0,t)p(0,t)\,dt,$$

where $\hat{\lambda}$ is the hazard rate (not the stochastic intensity) of the survival distribution, i.e.

$$S(0,t) \equiv E\exp\left(-\int_0^t \lambda_s\,ds\right) \equiv \exp\left(-\int_0^t \hat{\lambda}_s\,ds\right).$$

This hazard can be obtained analytically in the class of affine jump-diffusion processes with the exponentially distributed jumps described in Appendix E.

All in all we find, by equating the values π^{pb} and π^{ps}, that

$$c^{\text{ds}}(T) = \frac{(1-\delta)\int_0^T \hat{\lambda}(t)S(0,t)p(0,t)\,dt}{\sum_{i=1}^T v^0(0,i)}$$

$$= \frac{(1-\delta)\int_0^T \hat{\lambda}(t)S(0,t)p(0,t)\,dt}{\sum_{i=1}^T p(0,i)S(0,i)}.$$

The integral appears, of course, since we are considering the settlement exactly at the default date. If instead we define the settlement as taking place on the same days as the swap payments, and we let

$$\hat{Q}(\tau = i) = Q(\tau \in (i-1,i]) = S(0,i-1) - S(0,i),$$

then (still assuming independence) we obtain the swap premium in a form only involving a finite sum (as with our interest-rate swap expressions):

$$c^{\text{ds}}(T) = \frac{(1-\delta)\sum_{i=1}^T p(0,i)\hat{Q}(\tau=i)}{\sum_{i=1}^T p(0,i)S(0,i)}.$$

In this case the default swap curve obtained by considering $c^{\mathrm{ds}}(T)$ as a function of T could be used to derive implied default probabilities.

8.5   Some Differences between CDS Spreads and Bond Spreads

One of the promising prospects of a liquid CDS market is that it will provide us with better information on the term structure of credit risk for specific issuers. First of all, issuing a CDS on a particular firm does not change the capital structure of the firm and hence it is reasonable to assume that the price behaves linearly in the underlying amount insured over much wider intervals. This means that traditional term structure mathematics, in which we price a coupon bond by adding the values of the relevant zero-coupon bonds, can reasonably be assumed to apply to default swap contracts. Also, the maturities of CDS swaps can be chosen independently from the maturity structure of debt chosen by the firm. This means that, in principle at least, it is possible to have a full term structure of credit spreads derived from the CDS prices even for names with very few bonds outstanding.

But there are differences between default swaps and bonds that are likely to be reflected in the corresponding spreads as well. Let us first look at some arguments in favor of why CDS spreads should be larger than comparable bond spreads.

An important difference between the two types of contract is the definition of a credit event. The International Swap and Derivatives Association (ISDA) standard documentation for default swaps includes restructuring as a credit event—even if the restructuring causes no loss for the bond holders. At first glance this ought not make a difference. If bond holders do not view the restructuring as a loss, prices will reflect this, and there will be no loss for the protection sellers in receiving the nondefaulted bonds. But this only holds if the bonds are traded at par value. Long-dated bonds with a low coupon may trade significantly below par—perhaps because there has been a gradual decline in credit quality since issuance—and the protection buyer may then exercise the delivery option and deliver these long-dated bonds at a price below par and receive full par value in return, even if there was no loss associated with the event which permitted the protection buyer to deliver the reference bond and receive the notional value in return. This has led to reconsideration of the definition of a credit event in the standard documentation and to a reconsideration of the wildcard option. This tendency for the CDS to have a wider definition of default than that of the rating agencies would tend to increase the CDS premium compared with the bond spread. The same is true of the delivery option, which means that the protection seller does not know which bond is delivered and is likely to price the contract using an unfavorable choice. A further argument could be that the CDS buyer—in contrast with the owner of a reference bond—has no influence through covenants on the decisions made by the issuer. And finally, the costs of shorting bonds through a reverse repo would also contribute to a larger CDS spread.

On the other hand, a desire of hedge funds and insurance companies to sell CDS contracts as a way of obtaining "unfunded" exposure to credit risk could lower CDS spreads. At this point, there is little empirical evidence but it is rapidly becoming available. Some references are listed in the bibliographical notes.

8.6 A First-to-Default Calculation

This type of construct is easy to handle in an intensity-based setting.

Recall the following property of the minimum of N exponential variables. If $\tau_1, \ldots, \tau_N$ are independent exponentials with parameters $\lambda_1, \ldots, \lambda_N$, then

$$\tau^* = \min_{i=1,\ldots,N} \tau_i$$

is exponentially distributed with parameter

$$\lambda^* = \lambda^1 + \cdots + \lambda^N.$$

This follows simply from the fact that

$$P(\tau^* > t) = P(\tau_1, \ldots, \tau_N > t)$$

$$= \prod_{i=1}^{N} P(\tau_i > t)$$

$$= \exp\left(-\sum_{i=1}^{N} \lambda^i t\right) = \exp(-\lambda^* t).$$

An application of the Bayes rule gives us that the distribution of the identity of the first firm to default is independent of the default time:

$$P(\tau^* = \tau^i \mid \tau^* = t) = \lambda^i / \lambda. \tag{8.1}$$

We now see how these results play out in the Cox process setting, where we have conditional independence of the issuers' default times. As usual we let $G_T = \sigma\{X_s : 0 \leqslant s \leqslant t\}$, where X is a process of state variables, and define

$$\tau_i = \inf\left\{t > 0 : \int_0^t \lambda^i(X_s)\,ds > E_i\right\}$$

for N intensity functions $\lambda^i(\cdot)$ and N independent exponential variables $E_1, \ldots, E_N$ with mean 1. Note that with τ^* defined as above, we get

$$P(\tau^* > t) = E[P(\tau^* > t) \mid G_T]$$

$$= E\left(\prod_{i=1}^{N} \exp\left(-\int_0^t \lambda^i(X_s)\,ds\right)\right)$$

$$= E\exp\left(-\int_0^t \lambda^*(X_s)\,ds\right),$$

where

$$\lambda^*(\cdot) = \sum_{i=1}^{N} \lambda^i(\cdot).$$

Hence the intensity of the first default time is just the sum of the individual intensities even in this setting with random intensities. Note that we rely on the property of no simultaneous jumps. If one exponential drives several jump times, then the intensity of the first to default will be smaller than the sum of the marginal intensities. Just think of a case with two issuers driven by the same exponential variable.

This means that the value of the premium payment of the protection buyer can be valued exactly as in the (single-issuer) credit default swap. But this does not finish the job of valuing the swap. To find the level of premium payment which gives the construct zero value initially, we need to look at the value of the payment of the protection seller. Had this payment been independent of which issuer defaults first, we would again have been able to simply use the result from the single-name default swap. But we need to be able to handle an issuer-dependent recovery, and this is how we proceed: in addition to the default time τ^* let K denote the identity of the firm which defaults first, i.e. K can take on the values $1, 2, \ldots, N$ (or 0 if no firm defaults). We need the probability of the event that $\tau^* \in (t, t + dt)$ and $K = i$, conditionally on X:

$$P(\tau^* \in dt, \ K = i)$$

$$= P(\tau_i \in dt; \ \tau_j > t, \ j \neq i)$$

$$= \lambda^i(X_t) \exp\left(-\int_0^t \lambda^i(X_s)\, ds\right) \prod_{j \neq i} \exp\left(-\int_0^t \lambda^j(X_s)\, ds\right) dt$$

$$= \lambda^i(X_t) \exp\left(-\int_0^t \lambda^*(X_s)\, ds\right) dt. \tag{8.2}$$

In passing, this result gives us the analogue of (8.1), i.e. the probability that it is firm i which defaults given that the first default occurs at time t:

$$P(K = i \mid \tau^* = t) = \frac{E(\lambda^i(X_t) \exp(-\int_0^t \lambda^*(X_s)\, ds))}{E(\lambda^*(X_t) \exp(-\int_0^t \lambda^*(X_s)\, ds))}.$$

This is useful when simulating defaults, as we shall see later. Here we only need (8.2) to obtain the value of the premium payment on a first-to-default swap. Let

$$h(i, t, X_t) 1_{\{t \leqslant T\}}$$

denote the payment at time t to the default protection buyer if $\tau^* = t$ and the identity of the defaulting firm is i. Then the value of the commitment by the protection seller is

$$
\pi^{ps} = E\left[\exp\left(-\int_0^{\tau^\star \wedge T} r_s \, ds \right) h(K, \tau^\star, X_{\tau^\star}) 1_{\{\tau^\star \leqslant T\}} \right]
$$

$$
= E\left[E \exp\left(-\int_0^{\tau^\star \wedge T} r_s \, ds \right) h(K, \tau^\star, X_{\tau^\star}) 1_{\{\tau^\star \leqslant T\}} \,\Big|\, G_T \right]
$$

$$
= E\left(\sum_{i=1}^N \int_0^T \exp\left(-\int_0^t r_s \, ds \right) h(i, t, X_t) \lambda^i (X_t) \exp\left(-\int_0^t \lambda^* (X_s) \, ds \right) dt \right)
$$

$$
= \sum_{i=1}^N \int_0^T E \exp\left(-\int_0^t (r_s + \lambda^* (X_s) \, ds) \right) h(i, t, X_t) \lambda^i (X_t) \, dt.
$$

Again, affine state variables and affine intensities help us obtain analytically tractable solutions. But note that the sum of the intensities λ^* looks deceptively simple. If the intensity processes are all functions of the same underlying univariate process, then the sum of the intensities is univariate still, but if there are idiosyncratic components to each intensity in the sum, then we end up with a multivariate affine problem. A way of getting a one-dimensional problem even with idiosyncratic components in each firm's intensity is treated later when we discuss CDOs.

A key concern when pricing basket products is correlation. Later, when we consider CDOs, we will get a better understanding of what correlation does for the different tranches in a CDO, and the conclusions we draw for equity tranches allow us to say something about first-to-default also.

8.7 A Decomposition of *m*-of-*n*-to-Default Swaps

The *m*-of-*n*-to-default swap is a complicated product and it is not an instrument in which closed-form solutions seem easy to come by. Since the hedging of such instruments is often done through the single-name credit default swap market, we consider here a decomposition of an *m*-of-*n* to default swap into a portfolio of first-to-default swaps under an assumption of no simultaneous defaults.

A simple example illustrates the idea: consider a first-2-of-3-to-default swap which compensates the buyer for the first two defaults among a list of three issuers. Let the payment at default date τ for issuer i be denoted $1 - \delta^i(\tau)$. We claim that a first-2-to-default swap can be replicated through a portfolio consisting of one first-to-default swap on firms $(1, 2)$, one first-to-default swap on firms $(1, 3)$, one first-to-default swap on firms $(2, 3)$, and a short position in a first-to-default swap on firms $(1, 2, 3)$. Consider what happens if firm 1 defaults first and then firm 2 defaults (at dates τ_1 and τ_2). The cash flows on the dates τ_1 and τ_2 is illustrated in Table 8.5, which is clearly the payoff we seek to replicate. It is straightforward to check that this is also true for the case of zero or one default and for any combination of default events. More generally, it can be shown that an *m*-of-*n*-to-default swap can be recursively decomposed into a portfolio of first-to-default contracts.

Table 8.5. The decomposition of a first-2-of-3-to-default
swap into a portfolio of first-to-default swaps.

	τ_1	τ_2
Long (1,2)	$\delta(\tau_1)$	0
Long (1,3)	$\delta(\tau_1)$	0
Long (2,3)	0	$\delta(\tau_2)$
Short (1,2,3)	$-\delta(\tau_1)$	0
Total	$\delta(\tau_1)$	$\delta(\tau_2)$

Let $U^{m,n}(t)$ denote the price at time t of an m-of-n default contract. Let $U_K^{m-1,n-1}$ denote the price of a first-$(m-1)$-of-$(n-1)$ contract in which issuer K is not among the reference securities. We then have the recursive relationship

$$U^{m,n}(t) = \frac{1}{m-1}\left(\sum_{K=1}^{n} U_K^{m-1,n-1}(t) - (n-m)U^{m-1,n}(t) \right).$$

For a proof, see Huge (2000).

In practice, when n is 50 and m is, say, 10, running through the recursion is not feasible. We then have to resort either to Monte Carlo simulation or to simpler "binomial" methods, as in the next chapter.

8.8 Bibliographical Notes

The main sources for this section are Duffie (1999a,b) and Schönbucher (2000). The recent book by Schönbucher (2003) contains a lot of material on credit derivative modeling. I have also benefited much from BIS (2003) and Rule (2001). The application of the Cox setting of Lando (1998) to the case of Gaussian processes can be found in Kijima (2000) and Kijima and Muromachi (2000). The reader can find a detailed discussion of simulation of intensity models in Duffie and Singleton (1999b).

An early overview is presented in Das (1995) and a model is provided in Longstaff and Schwartz (1995b), whereas Das and Sundaram (2000) contains explicit ways of first calibrating a tree model in a forward-rate setting (sacrificing recombining trees) and then pricing default swaps. For more on pricing, see also Gregory and Laurent (2003a) and Hull and White (2001a,b).

For more on the differences between default-event definitions in bond markets and CDS markets, see BIS (2003) and Tolk (2001). Some empirical work related to credit default swap pricing is beginning to emerge (see, for example, Cossin et al. 2002; Houweling and Vorst 2002). The decomposition of the m-of-n default swap is from Huge (2000).

9

Modeling Dependent Defaults

Modeling dependence between default events and between credit quality changes is, in practice, one of the biggest challenges of credit risk models. The most obvious reason for worrying about dependence is that it affects the distribution of loan portfolio losses and is therefore critical in determining quantiles or other risk measures used for allocating capital for solvency purposes. As a direct consequence of the importance of managing the risks of large loan portfolios, a huge market for asset securitization, such as various types of CDOs, has emerged. This market in turn relies heavily on the market for default swaps (for example in generating synthetic CDOs) and default swaps often have a basket structure with many underlying reference names. For pricing and understanding the risk of tranches of CDOs and for understanding the pricing of basket default swaps, effort is focused on methods for modeling "correlation" (which is often used as a general name for dependence). Briefly stated, the credit risk of individual issuers is priced in the market through corporate bonds or single-name default swaps. In this sense, the "marginal" credit risk of each issuer in a pool is well determined. What affects the pricing of the tranches and the basket structures is therefore the varying correlation assumptions imposed on the models. Modeling various correlation structures that work with given marginal characteristics is a central focus of this chapter. A second worry in default swap valuation is whether the credit quality of the protection seller is heavily correlated with that of the underlying reference securities.

Finally, dependence modeling is necessary in trying to understand the risk of simultaneous defaults by, for example, financial institutions. Such simultaneous defaults could affect the stability of the financial system with profound effects on the entire economy. Avoiding such breakdowns is a major motivation behind regulation. Many of the models presented below allow such dependence, but the parameter specification for such models is often somewhat arbitrary and must be seen mainly as a tool for conducting various forms of stress testing. We finish the chapter by looking at network dependence, which is a first step toward modeling simultaneous defaults from more fundamental quantities.

9.1   Some Preliminary Remarks on Correlation and Dependence

Just as variance is one of the first quantities we think of as a measure of risk, the simple measure for dependence among random variables is correlation. Recall that the correlation between two random variables X and Y with finite variances is defined as the quantity

$$\rho(X, Y) = \frac{\text{Cov}(X, Y)}{\sigma(X)\sigma(Y)},$$

where $\sigma(X)$ is the standard deviation of X and

$$\text{Cov}(X, Y) = E(X - EX)(Y - EY)$$

is the covariance between X and Y. In brief, the correlation is the covariance between X and Y when we scale both variables down to having unit variance. It takes on a powerful meaning for normal random variables due to the fact that if (X_1, X_2) is bivariate normal with mean vector (μ_1, μ_2) and covariance matrix

$$\Sigma = \begin{pmatrix} \sigma_1 & \rho\sigma_1\sigma_2 \\ \rho\sigma_1\sigma_2 & \sigma_2 \end{pmatrix},$$

then from the expression for the conditional mean of X_1 given $X_2 = x_2$ we have

$$\frac{E(X_1 \mid X_2 = x_2) - \mu_1}{\sigma_1} = \rho\frac{x_2 - \mu_2}{\sigma_2}.$$

Hence, measured on the scale of the marginal standard deviations, if X_2 is one standard deviation away from μ_2, then X_1 is expected to be ρ standard deviations away from its mean μ_1. In this setting the correlation has a very clear meaning. In the context of default modeling, correlation is often used also for default-event indicators of the form $X = 1_{\{\tau_i \leqslant t\}}$, where τ_i is the default time, i.e. variables which are 1 if the firm defaults and 0 otherwise. In this context the measure is not very useful, since it is very hard to assign any meaning to the measure. It is also used when X and Y are survival times, but since survival times are not generally modeled as normal random variables, the correlation is not that useful in this case either. Furthermore, as we will see, just as variance is an incomplete description of the risk of an asset, so is correlation an incomplete description of the dependence among random variables. Therefore the focus of this chapter is not so much on understanding what the correlation is in different models but rather on specifying full models for the dependence structure and then analyzing the full distributions of default. Another benefit of having full models is that we know what we are estimating when we estimate correlations. Here is an example of what I mean by this.

Based on n independent realizations of the same variables $x_1, \ldots, x_n$ and $y_1, \ldots, y_n$, we define the sample correlation as the quantity

$$\hat{\rho}(X, Y) = \frac{\dfrac{1}{n-1} \displaystyle\sum_{i=1}^{n}(x_i - \bar{x})(y_i - \bar{y})}{\sqrt{\dfrac{1}{n-1} \displaystyle\sum_{i=1}^{n}(x_i - \bar{x})^2} \sqrt{\dfrac{1}{n-1} \displaystyle\sum_{i=1}^{n}(y_i - \bar{y})^2}}.$$

Computation of this quantity is often done for example for return series and for changes in asset values. One often hears the assertion (which may well be true) that correlation increases when prices go down, and the evidence is the sample correlation. It is worth keeping in mind that the correlation structure of a model can be constant over time and still one can see changes in the sample correlation. If, for example, there is a large but rare common jump component in asset values, the sample correlation will increase when jumps occur even if the correlation structure (as measured for example by joint quadratic variation) is stationary.

The mechanisms for obtaining dependence are all versions of (and possible mixtures of) three themes.

- Default probabilities are influenced by common background variables which are observable. As in all factor models, we then need to specify the joint movement of the factors and how default probabilities depend on the factors.

- Default probabilities depend on unobserved background variables, and the occurrence of an event causes an updating of the latent variables, which in turn causes a reassessment of the default probability of the remaining events.

- Direct contagion in which the actual default event causes a direct default of another firm or a deterioration of credit quality as a consequence of the default event.

Figure 9.1 is an example of why we need to worry about correlation. We have already discussed empirical evidence that there are common factors in credit spreads, and a casual look at credit spreads for large issuers in different sectors indicates a strong correlation within the sector and some correlation across sectors. The difficulty is to sort out what kind of dependence underlies the covariation in spreads.

The art of correlation modeling is to specify a model structure which works for calculating or simulating distributions of large numbers of entities while having parameters which can be estimated and interpreted. The fundamental problem is that we need to calculate the distribution of the number of defaults among a large collection of issuers. This is very cumbersome unless some sort of homogeneity assumption is brought into play. This naturally leads to binomial distributions and

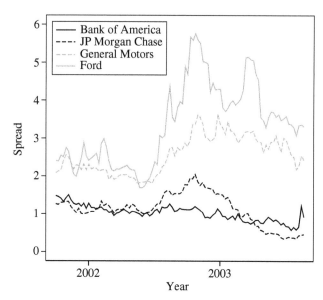

Figure 9.1. The evolution of yield spreads in percent for two pairs of corporate bonds. General Motors and Ford from the auto industry and JP Morgan Chase and Bank of America from banking.

in essence much of correlation modeling can be understood as variations over the binomial distribution using mixture distributions.

9.2 Homogeneous Loan Portfolios: Variations over the Binomial Distribution

9.2.1 The Basic Mixed Binomial Model

Mixed binomial models are an excellent framework for understanding a wide class of models. The immediate application of the binomial framework is for studying the distribution of the number of defaults over a given fixed time horizon. The role of the mixture distribution, which randomizes the default probability of the binomial, is to induce dependence, mimicking a situation where a common background variable affects a collection of firms. The default events of the firms are then conditionally independent given the mixture variable.

Recall the following facts about the binomial distribution. If X is binomially distributed (n, p), then

$$EX = np \quad \text{and} \quad VX = np(1 - p).$$

In particular, a Bernoulli random variable (taking the value 1 with probability p and 0 with probability $1 - p$) has mean p and variance $p(1 - p)$. When we start randomizing the default parameter p, the calculation of moments in the unconditional distribution involves first conditioning on the outcome of the mixture variable and then integrating out over its distribution. We therefore recall the following relationships for random variables X, Y defined on the same probability space:

$$EX = E(E(X \mid Y)), \tag{9.1}$$
$$VX = V(E(X \mid Y)) + E(V(X \mid Y)). \tag{9.2}$$

These will be useful when we consider binomial modeling in a random environment.

Assume that we have a collection of n firms. The default indicator of firm i is denoted X_i and it is equal to 1 if firm i defaults before some given time horizon and 0 otherwise. The default probability will of course depend on the chosen time horizon, but that will not concern us now. Assume that $\tilde{p}$ is a random variable which is independent of all the X_i. Assume that $\tilde{p}$ takes on values in the interval $[0, 1]$, and that, conditional on the value of $\tilde{p}$, the random variables $X_1, \ldots, X_n$ are independent and each have default probability $\tilde{p}$. We denote by f the density of $\tilde{p}$ and define $\bar{p} = E\tilde{p} = \int_0^1 pf(p)\,dp$. Then, using the rules in (9.1), we have

$$EX_i = \bar{p} \quad \text{and} \quad VX_i = \bar{p}(1 - \bar{p}),$$

and

$$\text{Cov}(X_i, X_j) = E(\tilde{p}^2) - \bar{p}^2, \quad i \neq j.$$

Note that the case where $\tilde{p}$ is a constant, we have 0 covariance and that by Jensen's inequality the covariance is always nonnegative in this setting. Finally, we have the default-event correlation, given as

$$\rho(X_i, X_j) = \frac{E\tilde{p}^2 - \bar{p}^2}{\bar{p}(1 - \bar{p})}.$$

Now consider the total number of defaults $D_n = \sum_{i=1}^n X_i$ among the n firms. Then $ED_N = n\bar{p}$ and

$$VD_n = n\bar{p}(1 - \bar{p}) + n(n - 1)(E\tilde{p}^2 - \bar{p}^2).$$

When $\tilde{p} = \bar{p}$, corresponding to no randomness, the variance is $n\bar{p}(1 - \bar{p})$, as in the binomial distribution. The other extreme is when $\tilde{p}$ is 1 with probability $\bar{p}$ and 0 otherwise. Then the variance is $n^2\bar{p}(1 - \bar{p})$, corresponding to perfect correlation between all default events. It then seems reasonable to believe that by choosing our density f (or point mass distribution), which is between the two extremes just considered, we can, for any fixed default frequency, obtain any default correlation in the interval $[0, 1]$. Note, however, that the correlation of default events only depends on the first and second moments of f, so any distribution f which gives the same default frequency and the same second moment will produce the same correlation structure. As we shall see later, however, the distributions of the number of defaults can be quite different.

From the expression for the variance,

$$V\left(\frac{D_n}{n}\right) = \frac{\bar{p}(1-\bar{p})}{n} + \frac{n(n-1)}{n^2}(E\tilde{p}^2 - \bar{p}^2) \to E\tilde{p}^2 - \bar{p} \quad \text{as } n \to \infty,$$

we observe that when considering the fractional loss for n large, the only remaining variance is that of the distribution of $\tilde{p}$. In fact, when n is large, the realized frequency of losses is close to the realized value of $\tilde{p}$, so the distribution of losses becomes that of $\tilde{p}$:

$$P\left(\frac{D_n}{n} < \theta\right) = \int_0^1 P\left(\frac{D_n}{n} < \theta \,\middle|\, \tilde{p} = p\right) f(p)\,\mathrm{d}p.$$

Since $(D_n/n) \to p$ for $n \to \infty$ when $\tilde{p} = p$, we have, as $n \longrightarrow \infty$,

$$P\left(\frac{D_n}{n} < \theta \,\middle|\, \tilde{p} = p\right) \longrightarrow \begin{cases} 0 & \text{if } \theta < p, \\ 1 & \text{if } \theta > p. \end{cases}$$

Therefore,

$$P\left(\frac{D_n}{n} < \theta\right) \xrightarrow[n \to \infty]{} \int_0^1 1_{\{\theta > p\}} f(p)\,\mathrm{d}p = \int_0^\theta f(p)\,\mathrm{d}p \equiv F(\theta).$$

Hence for large portfolios—that is portfolios containing many names—it is the distribution of $\tilde{p}$ which determines the loss distribution. The more variability that there is in the mixture distribution, the more correlation of default events there is, and hence the more weight there is in the tails of the loss distribution. Consider, for example, a beta distribution for $\tilde{p}$ that gives us a flexible class of distributions in the interval $[0, 1]$. The distribution is characterized by the two positive parameters α, β, and the mean and variance of the distribution are

$$E\tilde{p} = \frac{\alpha}{\alpha + \beta}, \qquad V\tilde{p} = \frac{\alpha\beta}{(\alpha + \beta)^2(\alpha + \beta + 1)},$$

and it is straightforward to check that if we look at combinations of the two parameters for which $\alpha/(\alpha + \beta) = \bar{p}$ for some default probability $\bar{p}$, the variance of the distribution will decrease as we increase α. This is illustrated in Figure 9.2.

As a concrete illustration, consider a stylized example of a CDO, in which 50 loans, assumed to have zero recovery in default, are posted as collateral in an asset-backed security construction where "equity," "junior note holders", and "senior note holders" each have claim to a portion of the loan, but in such a way that defaults in the pool hit the payouts to the equity holders first. If enough defaults occur to make equity worthless, the junior note holders will start absorbing the defaults and so forth. With an equity face value of 5, a junior note of 10, and senior notes with a face value of 35 we have the results in Table 9.1 for the expected payoff to each of the claim holders. As we can see, increasing the correlation decreases the value of

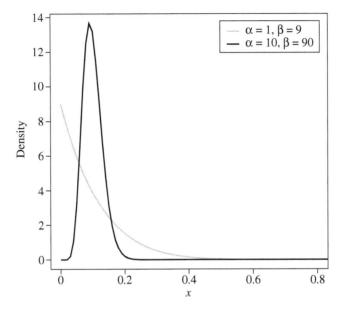

Figure 9.2. Two beta distributions both with mean 0.1 but with different variances.

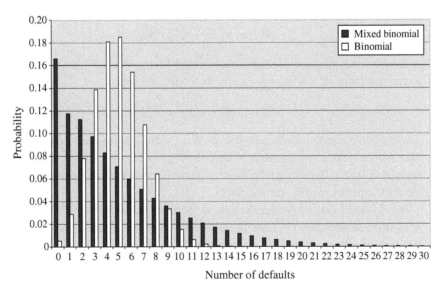

Figure 9.3. The distribution of the number of defaults among 50 issuers in the case of a pure binomial model with default probability 0.1 and in cases with beta distributions as mixture distributions over the default probability.

Table 9.1. The expected payoff to three tranches of a CDO with an underlying pool of 50 loans. Each loan has a face value of 1 and pays 0 in default. The face values are 35 for the senior tranche, 10 for the junior tranche and 5 for the equity tranche. The default probability is 0.1 for the binomial case and the two mixture distributions also have a mean of 0.1.

Expected payout	Binomial	Beta(10, 90) mixture	Beta(1, 9) mixture
Senior	34.999 98	34.999	34.803
Junior	9.168	8.985	8.293
Equity	0.832	1.016	1.904

the senior notes but increases the value of equity. As shown in Figure 9.3, keeping the default probability constant while having larger probabilities of many defaults requires the probability of very few defaults to increase as well. The increase in the probability of seeing very few defaults increases the value of equity.

The beta distribution is convenient to work with but has limited economic content. A choice of mixture distribution $F(\theta)$ that has an economic justification is given in the following section.

9.2.2 Choosing the Mixing Distribution Using Merton's Model

Consider n firms whose asset values follow a stochastic process of the form

$$dV_t^i = r V_t^i \, dt + \sigma V_t^i \, dB_t^i,$$

and assume that the geometric Brownian motion driving V^i can be decomposed into a common factor B^0 and a firm-specific factor B^i such that

$$B_t^i = \rho B_t^0 + \sqrt{1 - \rho^2} B_t^i,$$

where ρ is a nonnegative constant and $B^0, B^1, \ldots$ are independent standard Brownian motions. As a consequence of this, the log-asset values of the firms are all correlated with a (local) correlation of ρ. Note that we assume that the firms are identical in terms of drift and volatility.

Now assume that each firm defaults if the asset value at time T (the chosen horizon) is smaller than D^i. Contrary to the Merton model, assume that in this case that there is zero-recovery (this assumption can be relaxed). Hence, firm i defaults if

$$V_0^i \exp((r - \tfrac{1}{2}\sigma^2)T + \sigma B_T^i) < D^i,$$

i.e. if

$$\log V_0^i - \log D^i + (r - \tfrac{1}{2}\sigma^2)T + \sigma(\rho B_T^0 + \sqrt{1 - \rho^2} B_T^i) < 0.$$

We can write B_T^i as $\sqrt{T}\varepsilon_i$, where, for $i = 0, 1, \ldots,$ ε_i is a standard normal random variable, and therefore we can reexpress the inequality as

$$\log V_0^i - \log D^i + (r - \tfrac{1}{2}\sigma^2)T + \sigma(\rho\sqrt{T}\varepsilon_0 + \sqrt{1 - \rho^2}\sqrt{T}\varepsilon_i) < 0$$

or

$$\frac{\log V_0^i - \log D^i + (r - \tfrac{1}{2}\sigma^2)T}{\sigma\sqrt{T}} + \rho\varepsilon_0 + \sqrt{1 - \rho^2}\varepsilon_i < 0.$$

Now, conditional on a realization of the common factor, i.e. if $\varepsilon_0 = u$ for some $u \in \mathbb{R}$, firm i defaults if

$$\varepsilon_i < \frac{-(c_i + \rho u)}{\sqrt{1 - \rho^2}},$$

where

$$c_i = \frac{\log(V_0^i/D^i) + (r - \tfrac{1}{2}\sigma^2)T}{\sigma\sqrt{T}}.$$

Furthermore, assume that $c_i = c$ for all i; then, for given $\varepsilon_0 = u$, the probability of default is given through the distribution of ε_i as

$$P(u) = N\left(-\frac{c + \rho u}{\sqrt{1 - \rho^2}}\right).$$

Given $\varepsilon_0 = u$, defaults of the firms are independent, hence we are in a mixed binomial model in which the mixing distribution is that of the common factor ε_0. N transforms ε_0 into a distribution on $[0, 1]$.

The distribution function $F(\theta)$ for the distribution of the mixing variable $\tilde{p} := P(\varepsilon_0)$ is

$$F(\theta) = \text{Prob}(P(\varepsilon_0) \leqslant \theta) = \text{Prob}\left(N\left(-\frac{c + \rho u}{\sqrt{1 - \rho^2}}\right) \leqslant \theta\right)$$

$$= \text{Prob}\left(-\varepsilon_0 \leqslant \frac{1}{\rho}(\sqrt{1 - \rho^2}N^{-1}(\theta) + c)\right)$$

$$= N\left(\frac{1}{\rho}(\sqrt{1 - \rho^2}N^{-1}(\theta) + c)\right),$$

and if we use the fact that the unconditional default probability is $\bar{p} = N(-c)$ (just check when $V_T < D$), we can express $F(\theta)$ as

$$F(\theta) = N\left(\frac{1}{\rho}(\sqrt{1 - \rho^2}N^{-1}(\theta) - N^{-1}(\bar{p}))\right),$$

which is appealing since this only uses the correlation ρ and the default probability $\bar{p}$. But note that it is only within the given model structure that this dependence holds.

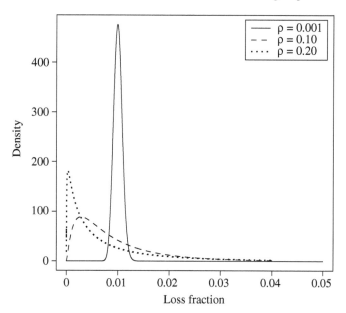

Figure 9.4. The figure shows the loss distribution in an infinitely diversified loan portfolio consisting of loans of equal size and with one common factor of default risk. The default probability is fixed at 1% but the correlation in asset values varies from nearly 0 to 0.2.

Now, with n firms, we can determine the probability that no more than a fraction θ default as

$$P\left(\frac{D_n}{n} \leqslant \theta\right) = \int_0^1 \sum_{k=0}^{n\theta} \binom{n}{k} P(u)^k (1 - P(u))^{n-k} f(u)\, du.$$

If n approaches infinity, we have already seen that

$$P\left(\frac{D_n}{n} \leqslant \theta\right) \xrightarrow[n \to \infty]{} \int_0^\theta f(u)\, du \equiv F(\theta).$$

$F(\theta)$ is thus the probability of having a fractional loss less then θ on a perfectly diversified portfolio with only factor risk. Having derived F as a function of $\bar{p}$ and ρ, we can show a typical consequence of correlation: probability mass is moved to the tails, meaning that for a given default probability $\bar{p}$, increasing correlation increases the probability of seeing large losses and of seeing small losses compared with a situation with no correlation. This is illustrated in Figure 9.4.

9.2.3 Randomizing the Loss

We can generalize the setup to a situation where the loss in default is a function of the underlying latent variable. For simplicity, assume that the underlying factor is the default probability $\tilde{p}$, whose distribution is given by a density function f. Assume that the expected loss given $\tilde{p}$ is $l(\tilde{p})$ and that this function is strictly monotone. It is natural to think of it as monotonically increasing so that the loss in default increases when systematic default risk is high, perhaps because of losses in the value of (insufficient) collateral.

It is easy to work with a model structure in which losses are random even after conditioning on the environment. One would then assume that losses were conditionally independent given the environment, and in the asymptotic argument this would reduce the parameter of interest to the expected loss, which is a function of the latent variable only.

Define the loss on the individual loan as

$$L_i(\tilde{p}) = l(\tilde{p})1_{\{D_i=1\}}.$$

Then

$$E(L_i \mid \tilde{p} = p) = l(p)p \equiv \Lambda(p),$$

and therefore we have convergence in L^2,

$$L := \frac{\sum_{i=1}^{n} L_i}{n} \xrightarrow[n\to\infty]{} l(\tilde{p})\tilde{p},$$

so

$$P(L \leqslant \theta) \xrightarrow[n\to\infty]{} \int_0^1 1_{\{l(p)p \leqslant \theta\}} f(p)\, \mathrm{d}p = F(\Lambda^{-1}(\theta)),$$

where F is the distribution function of $\tilde{p}$ and Λ, as defined above, can be thought of as a loss-weighted loss probability.

9.2.4 A Contagion Model

We describe the model proposed by Davis and Lo (2001), which incorporates contagion in a binomial-type model. In the model with a background variable it is the common dependence on the background variable $\tilde{p}$ that induces the correlation in the default events. While it is possible to obtain all correlations between 0 and 1, it requires assumptions of large fluctuations in $\tilde{p}$ to obtain significant correlation. A more direct way that does not push the marginal probabilities up as sharply while still inducing correlation is to have direct contagion. The model is constructed as follows. We need to distinguish between direct defaults and defaults triggered through a contagion event. Contagion means that once a firm defaults, it may bring down other firms with it. Accordingly, Y_{ij} is an "infection" variable, which, when equal to 1, implies that default of firm i immediately triggers default of firm j. Now assume that all X_i, Y_{ij} are independent Bernoulli variables. with $P(X_i = 1) = p$

and $P(Y_{ij} = 1) = q$. Let the default indicator of firm i be given as

$$Z_i = X_i + (1 - X_i)\left(1 - \prod_{j \neq i}(1 - X_j Y_{ji})\right).$$

Note that this expression is 1 either if there is a direct default of firm i or if there is no direct default *and* the entire second term of the sum is 0. This second term is 0 precisely when at least one of the factors X_j, Y_{ji} is 1, which happens when firm j defaults and infects firm i. Let the number of defaults be

$$D_n = Z_1 + \cdots + Z_n.$$

The first and second moments are computed explicitly in Davis and Lo (2001). Letting

$$\beta_n^{pq} = p^2 + 2p(1 - p)[1 - (1 - q)(1 - pq)^{n-2}]$$
$$+ (1 - p)^2[1 - 2(1 - pq)^{n-2} + (1 - 2pq + pq^2)^{n-2}],$$

they find that

$$ED_n = n(1 - (1 - p)(1 - pq)^{n-1}),$$
$$VD_n = n(n - 1)\beta_n^{pq} - (VD_n)^2.$$

The covariance between two default events is given as

$$\mathrm{Cov}(Z_i, Z_j) = \beta_n^{pq} - (VD_n/n)^2,$$

and hence the correlation between the individual firm defaults is

$$\rho := \mathrm{corr}(Z_i, Z_j) = \frac{\beta_n^{pq} - (VD_n/n)^2}{ED_n/n - (ED_n/n)^2}.$$

Before picking a particular set of parameters, consider first how the shape of the distribution varies with the level of contagion even when holding the marginal default probability constant. Note that to preserve the mean we must compensate for an increase in the infection parameter by decreasing the probability of direct default. This is done in Figure 9.5.

The contagion model can be generalized to a more realistic scenario in which contagion takes place within various isolated "compartments." This of course has the effect of lowering the default correlation for a given infection rate.

9.2.5 *Equal Correlations but Different Distributions*

To illustrate just how insufficient the correlation of default events is in describing the characteristics of a loss distribution, consider three cases in which we have the same expected number of defaults (i.e. the same probability of default for each issuer)

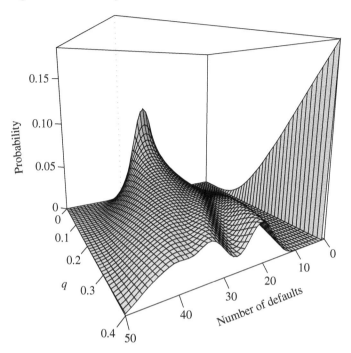

Probability

q

Number of defaults

Figure 9.5. The figure shows the distribution of defaults among 50 issuers in three different models when the total default probability, i.e. that resulting from the combined effect of direct default and contagion, is fixed at 0.5. Zero contagion gives a pure binomial model, whereas increasing the contagion brings more mass to high and low default numbers.

and the same correlation structure. The three cases shown in Figure 9.6 are from a beta mixture, a two-point mixture, and the contagion model of Davis and Lo. A difference like this will have a significant effect on tail probabilities, as shown in Figure 9.7.

9.2.6 *Estimating Default Correlation through Variation in Frequencies*

The variations over the binomial model that we have seen show how positive correlation among defaults tends to cluster defaults. Clustering of defaults should lead to larger fluctuations in default frequencies as years with many defaults are followed by years of few defaults compared with the overall default frequency. This insight can be used to estimate correlation from variations in frequency. To see this, consider a period of T years. Each year we observe a population of n firms and record for year t the number of defaults D_t. We assume that the default events contributing to D_i within a given year are correlated with parameter ρ. Assume that the default events from year to year are independent (or at least conditionally independent given

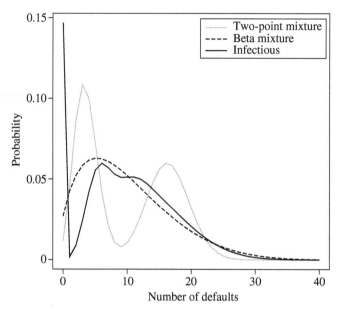

Figure 9.6.   The figure shows the distribution of defaults among 50 issuers when the total default probability, i.e. that resulting from the combined effect of direct default and contagion, is fixed at 0.2 and the correlation of the default-event indicators is equal to 0.1.

the default frequency). Note that

$$\operatorname{Var}\frac{D_t}{n} = \frac{\bar{p}(1-\bar{p})}{n} + \frac{n(n-1)}{n^2}(E\tilde{p}^2 - \bar{p}^2) \sim (E\tilde{p}^2 - \bar{p}^2),$$

where the last approximation works when the number of firms is large. Estimating the overall default frequency as the overall frequency

$$\hat{\bar{p}} = \frac{1}{Tn}\sum_{t=1}^{T} D_t,$$

we can use the empirical variance of the default frequencies

$$\widehat{\operatorname{Var}(D_t/n)} = \frac{1}{T}\sum_{t=1}^{T}\left(\frac{D_t}{n} - \hat{\bar{p}}\right)^2$$

as an estimator for $E\tilde{p}^2 - \bar{p}^2$. We now see that a moment-based estimator for the correlation is

$$\hat{\rho} = \frac{\widehat{\operatorname{Var}(D_t/n)}}{\hat{\bar{p}}(1-\hat{\bar{p}})}.$$

This is useful as a first estimate but its conditional nature makes it more attractive to try and estimate a full model of correlation.

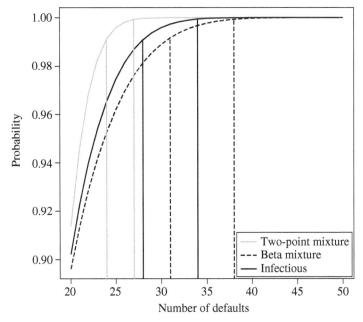

Figure 9.7. The figure shows 95 and 99 percentiles for the distribution of the number of defaults. As before, the default probability is 20% and the correlation is the same for all three cases considered: namely the contagion model, a two-point mixture, and a beta mixture.

9.2.7 Binomial Approximation Using Diversity Scores

The tractability of the binomial distribution makes it tempting to seek reductions of problems of multiple defaults to binomial distributions. This idea is pursued using so-called diversity scores, as explained for example in Cifuentes et al. (1998). The idea behind the approach can partly be captured as follows. If n loans each with face value 1 are independent, have the same default probability, and (for simplicity) have zero recovery, then the distribution of the loss is a binomial distribution with n as the number of trials. If all loans are perfectly correlated, then we may think of the portfolio as a single loan but with face value n. The idea is then to try to approximate the loss on a portfolio of n positively correlated loans with the loss on a smaller number of independent loans with larger face value. This is the idea we now pursue.

Imagine a pool of bonds or loans with the following characteristics. The face value of each bond is F_i, the probability of default within the relevant time horizon of each individual bond is p_i and we assume that we know the correlations between default events ρ_{ij} between pairs of bonds in the portfolio. With a total of n bonds, the total principal is then $\sum_{i=1}^n F_i$ and the mean and variance of the loss of principal at the end of the period are

$$EP = \sum_{i=1}^{n} p_i F_i, \tag{9.3}$$

$$VP = \sum_{i=1}^{n} \sum_{j=1}^{n} F_i F_j \rho_{ij} \sqrt{p_i(1-p_i)p_j(1-p_j)}, \tag{9.4}$$

where of course $\rho_{ii} = 1$ for all i. Due to the possible inhomogeneities in the default probabilities and face values it is hard to do calculations on, for example, the probability that more than k firms will default over the period or, even harder, on what the quantiles in the distribution of the remaining face value look like. Therefore, one may try instead to approximate the distribution of the remaining notional amount by a binomial distribution. In other words, construct a model portfolio consisting of D independent loans, each with the same face value F and the same default probability p, such that the total promised principal on the model portfolio and the mean and variance of the loss of principal on the model portfolio are the same as on the original portfolio. Equating the promised notional amounts forces $\sum_{i=1}^{n} F_i = DF$, and equating means and variances gives us

$$\sum_{i=1}^{n} p_i F_i = DFp \tag{9.5}$$

and

$$VP = F^2 Dp(1-p), \tag{9.6}$$

where VP is given above. Now solve the equations (noting that we also have $\sum_{i=1}^{n}(1-p_i)F_i = DF(1-p)$) to get

$$p = \frac{\sum_{i=1}^{n} p_i F_i}{\sum_{i=1}^{n} F_i}, \tag{9.7}$$

$$D = \frac{\sum_{i=1}^{n} p_i F_i \sum_{i=1}^{n}(1-p_i)F_i}{\sum_{i=1}^{n} \sum_{j=1}^{n} F_i F_j \rho_{ij} \sqrt{p_i(1-p_i)p_j(1-p_j)}}, \tag{9.8}$$

$$F = \frac{\sum_{i=1}^{n} F_i}{D}. \tag{9.9}$$

D is called the *diversity score*. We saw in the case with identical principals and identical correlations that the distribution of populations with the same characteristics may exhibit large variations in tail probabilities and hence, since all cases will have the same approximating model portfolio, varying degrees of accuracy of approximation.

9.2.8 Buckets and Multiple Binomials

The reduction to a single binomial distribution using a diversity-score approach is unsatisfactory when the underlying portfolio is very heterogeneous in terms of credit quality. If, for example, a loan portfolio consists of loans from two different rating classes, so that, for example, the high-rated and low-rated loans have default probabilities of 1% and 5%, respectively, over a 1-year horizon, then the true distribution of losses will be bimodal, and the binomial approximation will never be able to capture that. One can take this into account without giving up the tractability of binomial models by working instead with "buckets"—a principle which extends into all model structures that use some homogeneity assumption. We illustrate the principle through the "double-binomial method", and extensions to more categories is easy in principle as long as the scale of the problem can be handled numerically.

In the double-binomial approach, a pool of n loans is separated into two independent buckets with n_A in the first and n_B in the second bucket. Let the corresponding default probabilities be denoted p_A and p_B. Of course, these numbers could also come about as the result of a diversity-score analysis conducted on each pool. The probability of k defaults is then given as

$$P(D = k) = \sum_{i=0}^{k} \binom{n_A}{i} p_A^i (1 - p_A)^{n_A - i} \binom{n_B}{k - i} p_B^{k-i} (1 - p_B)^{n_B - (k-i)},$$

and this calculation for all $k = 0, \ldots, n$ gives the entire loss distribution. While this approach assumes that the two pools are uncorrelated, we may of course use the mixing of binomials to extend the model to take into account correlation within pools and between the pools.

Extending to more buckets is straightforward, in principle, but the numerical effort once we have more than a handful of buckets becomes significant. With M buckets, the number of ways in which a total number k of defaults can be split into a sum of M integers, and where the ordering matters, quickly becomes quite large.

9.2.9 Inhomogeneous Collections and Moment-Generating Functions

The diversity-score approximation used above is a crude way of approximating inhomogeneous loan portfolios through a binomial distribution (or a multiple binomial distribution), whose probabilities can, of course, be computed exactly. If one is content with having only the moment-generating function of the exact distribution, even for inhomogeneous and correlated portfolios, then there is an easy way around this.

Define the moment-generating function M_X for a random variable X as

$$M_X(s) = E \exp(sX),$$

where the domain of the function is all s, real and complex, for which the integral is finite. If one looks at numbers of the form $s = iu$, for which the integral is always finite, we have the characteristic function. If X is a positive random variable and we look at negative real numbers, we have the Laplace transform.

The moment-generating function of a sum of independent random variables is just the product of the individual moment-generating functions. Since $M_{aX}(s) = M_X(as)$, we can easily obtain the moment-generating function of a linear combination of independent random variables $Y = \sum_{i=1}^n a_i X_i$ as

$$M_Y(s) = \prod_{i=1}^n M_{X_i}(a_i s).$$

There are then many techniques for inverting the characteristic function or obtaining properties of the distribution directly. We refer to Martin et al. (2003) for more on this. The promise of the technique is that we avoid the impossible task of summing up probabilities over all different configurations of events leading to a given number of defaults—an impossible task in practice for even medium-sized portfolios.

The method extends to conditional-independence models in the usual fashion. Assume that there is some latent variable Z such that the individual distributions are independent given Z. To save numerical effort, consider the case where the random variable Z is discrete. If we denote by p_k the probability that $Z = k$, and we let $M_{X|k}(s)$ denote the moment-generating function of X given k, then we have the following unconditional moment-generating function of $Y = \sum_{i=1}^n a_i X_i$:

$$M_Y(s) = \sum_{k=1}^K p_k \prod_{i=1}^n M_{X_i|k}(a_i s).$$

Of course, the summation can be replaced by a numerical integration, but the loss of accuracy from the discretization need not be very important.

9.2.10 The Continuous-Time Analogue of the Binomial Model: the Pure Death Process

It is straightforward to generate a dynamic version of the static one-period binomial model in which one assumes that the firms have identical default intensities. We simply model the default process as a pure death process. Assume that we wish to model defaults of N firms over time. Consider therefore the state space $0, 1, \dots, N$, where a state represents the number of nondefaulted firms. To begin with, assuming that only one firm can default at a time and that every firm has a default intensity of λ, the intensity of the first default among n firms is $n\lambda$. Therefore, we define the intensity of the pure death process going from state n to state $n - 1$ as

$$\lambda_{n,n-1} = n\lambda, \quad n = 1, \dots, N,$$

and we let state 0 be absorbing. It is then easy to compute the distribution of the number of firms alive at some date t. If the starting population is N, then because we can view each firm as having an exponential lifetime with intensity parameter λ it is clear that the probability of there being k firms left at time t is

$$\binom{N}{k} \exp(-k\lambda t)(1 - \exp(-\lambda t))^{N-k},$$

corresponding to all the ways in which k firms survive and $N - k$ default within the given time period. Note the difference between the probability of this process having k defaults and the probability that N Poisson processes with intensity λ experience k defaults. The latter probability is larger since no firms leave the population in this case after a default. It is also straightforward to include a common background variable just as in the Cox setup: given an intensity process λ and assuming that, conditional on the sample path of this process, we have

$$P_{k,\lambda}(t) = \binom{N}{k} \exp\left(-k \int_0^t \lambda_s \, ds\right) \left(1 - \exp\left(-\int_0^t \lambda_s \, ds\right)\right)^{N-k},$$

and therefore we have, unconditionally,

$$E P_{k,x} = \binom{N}{k} E\left(\exp\left(-k \int_0^t \lambda(s) \, ds\right) \left(1 - \exp\left(-\int_0^t \lambda(s) \, ds\right)\right)^{N-k}\right),$$

which reduces to calculating functionals of the form $E(\exp(-k \int_0^t \lambda(s) \, ds))$ for $k = 1, \ldots, n$, which is straightforward in affine specifications for the state variable process. Again, the critical assumption is that of identical intensities.

When the number of firms becomes large, though, computing the distribution of defaults becomes a numerical problem due to the large binomial coefficients and the small numbers in the exponential-affine terms.

It may then be advantageous to use instead an approximation of the setup using a large pure death process in a random environment and then to compute the matrix exponential of the generator numerically. In fact, it is easy to see that if we are willing to settle for numerical computation of large generator matrices, we can incorporate models ranging from conditional independence to contagious defaults within a single framework as long as we remain in the homogeneous firm setting.

9.2.11 *Generalizing the Pure Death Process*

As noted in Appendix C that it is straightforward and fast to compute matrix exponentials of generators with, say, 1000 states. In this section we show that working with specifying generators of this kind, we may easily construct various models of dependence within the same framework. To see how this is done, consider the following three examples.

Example 1: Markov modulated intensity. Instead of having an affine process modifying the default intensities in the previous example we can incorporate a process for the environment into the generator matrix of defaults directly. The random environment is specified using a generator matrix A with M states. We let α_{ij} for $i \neq j$ equal an off-diagonal element of this matrix. Think of the state of this chain as determining the default intensity of a firm in our homogeneous pool. Hence, the default intensity of a firm is λ_K when the environment is in state K.

Now, letting (N, Z) denote the state of the Markov chain, where N records the number of surviving firms and Z the state of the environment, we have the following specification of the transition intensities:

$$(n, z) \rightarrow (n - 1, z) \quad \text{has intensity } n\lambda_z, \qquad (9.10)$$

$$(n, i) \rightarrow (n, j) \quad \text{has intensity } \alpha_{ij}. \qquad (9.11)$$

All other transition intensities are zero (even though you can easily specify joint transitions of defaults and the environment—a point we return to below). If one specifies the ordering of the states as being $(N, 1), \ldots, (N, M), (N - 1, 1), \ldots$, the generator becomes upper triangular, and computing the matrix exponential can be performed very quickly. Given an environment originally formulated as a jump-diffusion, the Markov chain can be chosen as an approximating chain.

Example 2: contagion through intensities. A simple way, again using indistinguishable firms, of having a mild degree of contagion is provided by Davis and Lo (2001) using the following approach. Instead of having a constant intensity of default equal to λ as in the example above, there is now higher intensity of default equal to $\lambda + \mu$ right after a firm has defaulted. This higher default intensity persists for an exponentially distributed amount of time after which (if there is no new default) it drops to the "normal level" λ. The parameter of the exponential distribution is ν. The precise description is as follows. Let the state space be $0, 1, \ldots, 2N$ and let state $2n$ for each n denote a state in which n firms are alive and the default level is normal, and let $2n + 1$ denote the state where there are n nondefaulted firms but the default intensity is high. Hence

$$\lambda_{2n+1,2n} = \nu,$$
$$\lambda_{2n+1,2n-1} = n(\lambda + \mu),$$
$$\lambda_{2n,2n-1} = n\lambda.$$

All other transition intensities are 0. Note that in this model, the actual defaults do not directly trigger other defaults, but they do increase default intensities. This is a weak-type contagion. The state space needed for this model is $\{1, \ldots, N\} \times \{0, 1\}$, taking into account that each state needs a modifier to describe whether we are still feeling the shock aftermath of a default. Of course, we can modify this to have more states and thus merge this example with the previous example, letting the environment be affected by defaults.

Example 3: direct contagion. Davis and Lo proposed the mild-contagion model above as a generalization of the binomial model, but it is also straightforward to look into a scheme with more direct contagion. Assume that each firm has an intensity of defaulting "directly" of λ^d and that given that a firm defaults it brings with it a binomially distributed number of other firms. Each default triggers a contagion with probability $q(n)$, which we allow to depend on the number of remaining firms so that we can keep the marginal default intensities of each firm fixed throughout the period. The intensity of a move away from the state n, which still counts the number of surviving firms, is $n\lambda^d$ since one of the firms must default directly for there to be a change of state. Given that a direct default occurs, the number of *additional* defaults is binomially distributed on $0, \ldots, n-1$. Let $b(n, q; x)$ denote the probability mass at the point x in a binomial distribution with n trials and a probability of success equal to q. Then the transition intensities are as follows:

$$n \to n-1 \quad \text{has intensity } n\lambda^d b(n-1, q(n), 0),$$
$$n \to n-2 \quad \text{has intensity } n\lambda^d b(n-1, q(n), 1),$$
$$\vdots$$
$$n \to 0 \quad \text{has intensity } n\lambda^d b(n-1, q(n), n-1).$$

If we want the marginal default intensity of a firm to stay the same, say $\bar{\lambda}$ throughout the entire period, then we must choose $q(n)$ so that

$$\bar{\lambda} = \lambda^d + (n-1)q(n-1)\lambda^d,$$

that is

$$q(n-1) = \frac{\bar{\lambda} - \lambda^d}{\lambda^d(n-1)}.$$

9.3 Asset-Value Correlation and Intensity Correlation

9.3.1 From Correlations in Asset Values to Correlated Rating Movements

The idea of this approach to correlation of rating movements is to associate rating changes with asset values crossing certain thresholds and then to translate the correlation in asset values into a correlation of rating movements. This is really a preview of the copula approach, which will be discussed later. For a rating system with classes $1, \ldots, K$, assume that the current ratings of firms A and B are i^A and i^B, respectively. Assume that we know the 1-year (or any other period one decides to look at) transition probabilities $p(i^A, j), p(i^B, j), j = 1, \ldots, K$, for each firm. Let

Φ denote the standard normal distribution function. Now, for firm A define constants $a(i^A, j)$ for $j = 1, \ldots, K - 1$ such that

$$p(i^A, K) = \Phi(a(i^A, K)),$$
$$p(i^A, K - 1) = \Phi(a(i^A, K - 2)) - \Phi(a(i^A, K - 1)),$$
$$\vdots$$
$$p(i^A, 1) = 1 - \Phi(a(i^A, 1)),$$

and proceed in the same way for firm B defining constants $b(i^B, j)$ for $j = 1, \ldots, K - 1$ using $p(i^B, j)$ instead of $p(i^A, j)$ on the left-hand side of the equations. With this done, let $\phi(x_1, x_2; \rho)$ denote the density at (x_1, x_2) of a bivariate normal random variable with mean vector $(0, 0)$ and covariance matrix $\left(\begin{smallmatrix} 1 & \rho \\ \rho & 1 \end{smallmatrix}\right)$. Now define the probability of joint transitions as the probability assigned to the corresponding rectangles by this bivariate density, i.e. let the joint transition probability $p[(i^A, i^B) \to (j^A, j^B)]$ be given as

$$p[(i^A, i^B) \to (j^A, j^B)] = \int_{b(i^B, j^B)}^{b(i^B, j^B - 1)} \int_{a(i^A, j^A)}^{b(i^A, j^A - 1)} \phi(x_1, x_2; \rho) \, dx_1 \, dx_2 \quad (9.12)$$

for $j = 1, \ldots, K$ with the convention $a(i^A, 0) = b(i^B, 0) = 0$.

Since it is natural to think of the thresholds being defined by the constants as levels which the logarithms of asset value have to cross for rating changes to take place, we may think of ρ as the correlation of the asset-value processes. Note, however, that this is only consistent with a model in which there is no default boundary before the end of the time period under study. For example, in a Black–Cox-type model, the distribution of asset value at maturity is not Gaussian, but rather is obtained from a conditional survival probability of Brownian motion.

It is possible to analytically compute correlation of default events for two issuers in a Merton-type model (see Zhou 2001a). However, from a practical perspective, the result does not seem that useful since the pairwise default correlations between individual default events are not sufficient for analyzing tail events and pricing tranches in a CDO structure.

9.3.2 *Intensity Correlation: the Large Variation Required*

The most obvious way of handling correlation between a large number of issuers is to impose a factor structure on the default intensities. While it is also possible with jump processes to let the default events have a factor structure, this quickly becomes cumbersome. We will address this briefly in the next section.

As with all factor modeling, the goal is to reduce the parameter specification so as to specify a marginal intensity for each issuer and to quantify the part of the marginal intensity which comes from a set of common factors. An example of this factor structure is used in Duffie and Gârleanu (2001), and we use their setup for illustrating the main points about correlation in intensity models.

A factor structure in intensities decomposes the structure of the intensity of an individual firm i into two independent components, one coming from a common factor and one being idiosyncratic:

$$\lambda^i(t) = \nu^c(t) + \nu^i(t).$$

Needless to say, the global factor can be split into sector components and general economy components without changing the approach conceptually but each additional split induces its own estimation problems of course.

To facilitate computation we consider only affine specifications. From our basic intensity modeling we know that in a Cox process setup this means that the survival probability of an individual issuer is

$$P(\tau^i > T) = E \exp\left(\int_0^T \lambda^i(s)\,ds \right)$$

$$= E \exp\left(\int_0^T \nu^i(s)\,ds \right) E \exp\left(\int_0^T \nu^c(s)\,ds \right).$$

Correlation between firms of course arises because of the common intensity component. Of course, this computation of marginal default probabilities allows us to specify the affine processes freely for each issuer, but when looking at many issuers in a pool underlying a CDO, for example, this reintroduces the problems we have encountered earlier with lack of homogeneity. So, again, it will be natural to consider homogeneous pools of issuers whose marginal intensities and whose split between global and idiosyncratic risk are the same. In this case, we are back to a mixed binomial model in which, after conditioning on the common factor, defaults are independent. Let us start by looking at the type of mixture one obtains by "mixing over an intensity process." Is it possible to induce correlation enough to see an effect? The answer is yes, but one generally requires large variations in the intensity and/or long time horizons to really see a large effect. Consider an intensity process of the affine family with exponentially distributed jumps:

$$d\lambda_t = \kappa(\theta - \lambda_t)\,dt + \sigma\sqrt{\lambda_t}\,dW_t + dJ_t, \tag{9.13}$$

where J is a compound Poisson process with jump intensity l and exponentially distributed jumps with mean μ. The parameters used for our calculations are shown in Table 9.2. Now imagine the following experiment. Assume that all firm defaults are driven by the same intensity process, but that the actual jumps are conditionally independent given the intensity process, i.e. our standard Cox process setting with identical intensities. The common intensity process implies that the default probability of firms over a fixed time horizon becomes randomized exactly as in a mixed binomial experiment. The mixing distribution is the distribution of the default probability given the intensity evolution $1 - \exp(-\int_0^T \lambda_s \, ds)$, where T is the fixed time horizon. Note that

$$P\left(1 - \exp\left(-\int_0^T \lambda_s \, ds\right) \leqslant x\right) = P\left(\exp\left(-\int_0^T \lambda_s \, ds\right) \geqslant 1 - x\right)$$
$$= P\left(\int_0^T \lambda_s \, ds \leqslant -\log(1 - x)\right),$$

and therefore we can find the mixing distribution if we can compute the distribution of $\int_0^T \lambda_s \, ds$. The characteristic function for this variable is given explicitly from results in Chapter E, so up to an inversion of a characteristic function we have the desired distribution. We show the mixing distribution for the two cases $l = 0$, corresponding to a pure CIR process, and $l = 0.2$, corresponding to a case where fairly drastic jumps increase the intensity at a random rate (but the intensity is drawn quickly towards its mean reversion rate also). The result is shown in Figure 9.8. We have also shown the expected default probability for the two cases, i.e. the default probability that one should use if all the intensity processes for the firms had the same distribution but were independent. The horizon is five years, and as we see the mixing distribution definitely has a strong effect. We will see next how it affects the distribution of the number of defaults.

In general, we do not have one common factor determining all the variation in the intensity. Correlation induces some degree of dependence, which puts us between the case of purely systematic risk and a case of purely idiosyncratic risk. To really analyze the effect of dependence, the best approach is to have a setting in which we can vary a correlation parameter without affecting the marginal default probabilities. This is possible using what Duffie and Gârleanu (2001) refer to as "basic affine processes."

Consider the following specifications for systematic risk:

$$dv_t^c = \kappa^c(\theta^c - v_t^c) \, dt + \sigma^c \sqrt{v_t^c} \, dW_t^c + dJ_t^c,$$

where

$$J_t^c = \sum_{i=1}^{N_t^c} \varepsilon_i^c$$

and N_t^c is a Poisson process with intensity $l^c \geqslant 0$ and $(\varepsilon_i)_{i=1}^{\infty}$ is a sequence of independent and identically distributed (i.i.d.) exponentially distributed random variables with mean μ^c. Assume that the idiosyncratic risk is specified in exactly the same way, replacing all superscripts "c" by "i." In particular, the driving Brownian

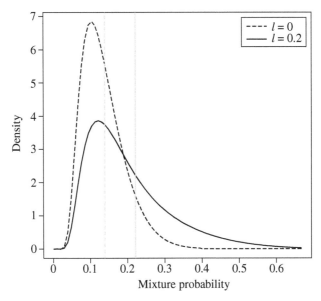

Figure 9.8. The mixture distribution for the probability of default over a 5-year time horizon for two different cases of a common background intensity process as described in (9.13) above. $\mu = 0$ corresponds to a pure CIR process for the background intensity, whereas the case in which $\mu = 0.2$ adds exponentially distributed jumps with a mean of 0.2 at an intensity also set to $l = 0.2$. The mixture distribution was found by inverting the affine characteristic function of the random variable $\int_0^T \lambda^i(s) \, ds$. The dotted lines are the mean values of the distribution. The parameters are from Duffie and Gârleanu (2001).

motions and the jump processes are independent. In this specification, jumps in the total intensity occur at a rate of

$$l = l^c + l^i,$$

and we let

$$\rho = l^c / l$$

denote the fraction of jumps in the individual firm's intensity that is due to common jumps. We now want to follow Duffie and Gârleanu (2001) and vary this dependence parameter while keeping the marginal intensities fixed. It turns out that if one assumes

$$\kappa := \kappa^c = \kappa^i, \quad \sigma := \sigma^c + \sigma^i \quad \text{and} \quad \mu := \mu^c + \mu^i,$$

then the sum of two affine processes ν^i and ν^c is again an affine processes with parameters κ, σ, μ as defined above and with jump rate and mean reversion level given as

$$l = l^i + l^c \quad \text{and} \quad \theta = \theta^i + \theta^c.$$

Table 9.2. Parameter inputs to the correlation experiment.

Parameter	$\lambda^i(0)$	κ	θ	σ	μ	l
Value	0.053	0.6	0.02	0.141	0.1	0.2

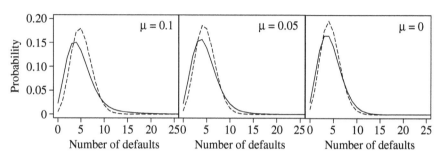

Figure 9.9. The distribution of the number of defaulters over a 1-year horizon. In all graphs, the case $\rho = 0$ corresponds to purely nonsystematic risk and the resulting distribution is a binomial distribution with default probability $1 - E\exp(-\int_0^1 \lambda^i(s)\,ds)$. $\rho = 1$ corresponds to purely systematic risk. (Dashed lines denote the case where there is no systematic risk and the solid lines denote the case where there is only systematic risk.)

This means that as long as we keep these two sums constant, we can vary the contribution from the systematic and idiosyncratic risk without changing the marginal rate. We now look at what variation can be obtained between the two extreme cases of purely nonsystematic risk and purely idiosyncratic risk where the parameters are chosen as in Case 1 of Duffie and Gârleanu (2001) and are shown in Table 9.2. Note that because of these extreme choices we do not have to worry about how to distribute out the mean reversion level to the individual processes.

In Figures 9.9 and 9.10 we look at the distribution of the number of defaulters among 100 firms when the total default intensity is fixed and where the only variation is in the correlation ρ. We consider only the extreme cases of $\rho = 0$ and $\rho = 1$, corresponding to the cases of purely nonsystematic and purely systematic risk, respectively.

It is clear that all cases with correlation must lie between these two cases. We vary the parameter μ, the mean jump size, over the values $0, 0.05$, and 0.1. The correlation effect is limited over the 1-year horizon, even for the case of purely systematic risk and $\mu = 0.2$. The effect is very significant over five years with $\mu = 0.1$ moving the point at which the probabilities become small by about 30.

9.3.3 Multivariate Exponential Distributions and Common Default-Event Factors

When using a factor model for the intensities as presented above, the intensities were correlated but the actual jump events were conditionally independent given the

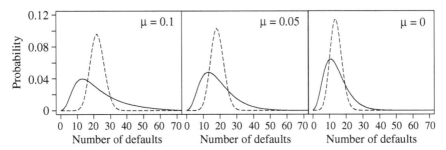

Figure 9.10. The distribution of the number of defaulters over a 5-year horizon. In all graphs, the case $\rho = 0$ corresponds to purely nonsystematic risk and the resulting distribution is a binomial distribution with default probability $1 - E \exp(-\int_0^5 \lambda^i(s)\,ds)$. $\rho = 1$ corresponds to purely systematic risk. (Dashed lines denote the case where there is no systematic risk and the solid lines denote the case where there is only systematic risk.)

sample paths of the intensities. In other words, the underlying Poisson processes used to define the default events were independent. It is also possible, at least in theory, to allow default events to have a factor structure. The easiest framework for considering this is that of multivariate exponential distributions, which we have already seen an example of in Section 5.9. We will not go into the details of the modeling here but give the basic idea for the case of a three-dimensional distribution. To generate a three-dimensional exponential distribution, consider a collection of independent exponentially distributed random variables E_1, E_2, E_3, E_{12}, E_{13}, E_{23}, E_{123} with corresponding intensities $\lambda_1, \lambda_2, \ldots, \lambda_{123}$. The interpretation of the exponentials is straightforward: the subscript denotes the collection of firms whose defaults are triggered by the exponential variable. Hence E_{12} triggers a simultaneous default of firms 1 and 2, whereas λ_1 triggers a default of firm 1 only. Now define the default time of firm i as the minimum of the exponential variables in which i is present in the subscript, i.e. for firm 1

$$\tau_1 = \min(E_1, E_{12}, E_{13}, E_{123}).$$

The definitions of τ_2, τ_3 are the obvious analogues, and it is also clear how the extension to more dimensions proceeds. Without stating the definition more formally than this we refer to distributions generated in this way for two or more variables as multidimensional exponential distributions. Some important properties are as follows.

(1) The univariate marginal distributions are exponential distributions. The distribution of (say) τ_1 has parameter $\lambda_1 + \lambda_{12} + \lambda_{13} + \lambda_{123}$.

(2) All lower-dimensional marginal distributions of a multivariate exponential distribution are multivariate exponential.

(3) The system as a whole has the memoryless property, meaning that if no firm has defaulted at time s, the distribution of the residual lifetimes is the same as the distribution of lifetimes at time 0.

This type of setting can be useful when the correlation of two particular issuers, and not that of a whole pool, is of interest, and one feels a need to induce a stronger correlation than can be obtained from the intensity factor models. As an example of this, think of modeling the effect on the premium of a single-name default swap of having correlation between the issuer of the reference security and the default protection seller. If the default protection seller has sold very large quantities of a particular CDS, the default event of the reference security could cause the protection seller to default. To see a significant reduction in the CDS premium arising from such dependence, one needs to make fairly strong dependence assumptions and one way of doing this is to use a structure similar to the multivariate exponential distribution.

The unsatisfactory part of this choice of distribution is the fact that if one firm defaults it either pulls another firm with it or leaves the surviving firms unharmed. One may modify this assumption by adding an extra probability parameter associated with each event, acting as a thinning parameter. For example, q_1 would then be the probability that when E_1 occurs first, this actually triggers a default of firm 1. This ends up also producing multivariate exponentials with a more flexible interpretation, but the effect of one firm's default is still either instantaneous or absent.

There are different ways around this problem. One is to specify other families of multivariate distributions. If the mean is large enough compared with the variance, so that negative values are unlikely, one might for example use the multivariate normal distribution as an approximation of joint failure times. Another approach, which is more satisfactory from an economic viewpoint, is treated in the following section.

9.3.4 Correlation through Updating of Latent Variables

If we believe that intensities depend on variables whose levels we cannot observe, then the actual defaults of one entity may lead us to update our knowledge of the latent variable. This is a typical contagion mechanism which is not due to the direct contagion but rather a revision of default intensities in light of what other defaults reveal about the true state of the economy. For an intensity illustration of this phenomenon, we follow Arjas (1989) and consider a simple setup in which a one-dimensional random variable at time 0 determines the random environment. The distribution of the random environment Z is given by the density $\Phi(dz)$ on the positive real line. Let the default time of firm i be denoted τ_i and given knowledge of the background variable we have an intensity of default given as

$$\lambda_t(i) = Za_i(t)1_{\{\tau_i \geqslant t\}}, \quad i = 1, 2,$$

where the $a_i(\cdot)$ are known functions for $i = 1, 2$. We are interested in a situation where we know the distribution of Z but not its realization, and we use information on waiting times and defaults to update our estimate of Z. We let T_1 denote the time of the first default and let X_1 denote the identity of the first issuer to default. Then before the arrival of the first default, the conditional density of Z is

$$\pi_t(dz) = \frac{\Phi(dz)\exp(-z\int_0^t a(s)\,ds)}{\int_0^\infty \Phi(dz)\exp(-z\int_0^t a(s)\,ds)},$$

where

$$a(t) = a_1(t) + a_2(t).$$

This density is obtained through a straightforward application of the Bayes rule:

$$P(Z \in dz \mid T_1 > t) = \frac{P(Z \in dz \mid T_1 > t)}{P(T_1 > t)}$$
$$= \frac{P(T_1 > t \mid Z \in dz)P(Z \in dz)}{P(T_1 > t)}.$$

Similar calculations yield the density of Z after the first jump, but before the second, i.e. on $\{T_1 < t < T_2\}$ we have

$$\pi_t(dz) = \frac{\Phi(dz)z\exp(-z\int_0^{T_1} a(s)\,ds - z\int_{T_1}^t a_{X_2}(s)\,ds)}{\int_0^\infty \Phi(dz)z\exp(-z\int_0^{T_1} a(s)\,ds - z\int_{T_1}^t a_{X_2}(s)\,ds)}.$$

Finally, after the second jump has occurred we obtain a time-independent value (since no more information is then arriving on the distribution of Z):

$$\pi(dz) = \frac{\Phi(dz)z^2\exp(-z\int_0^{T_1} a(s)\,ds - z\int_{T_1}^{T_2} a_{X_2}(s)\,ds)}{\int_0^\infty \Phi(dz)z^2\exp(-z\int_0^{T_1} a(s)\,ds - z\int_{T_1}^{T_2} a_{X_2}(s)\,ds)}.$$

From this conditional density we obtain the intensity of each firm at time t by computing

$$\lambda_t(i) = a_i(t)\int_0^\infty z\pi_{t-}^*(dz)1_{\{\tau_i \geqslant t\}}, \quad i = 1, 2, \ t \geqslant 0.$$

The jump event of course kills the intensity for the firm which defaulted but for the surviving firm there is a change in intensity caused by the revision of the density π.

In a model like this the intensity of default depends critically on what we observe. If we observe Z, it is a constant; if we observe only one jump process, then the intensity of the observed process is a deterministic function up to the default time; and if we observe both processes, the intensity of the surviving firm evolves deterministically until the default of the other firm, at which point there is a jump in the intensity. All of this is illustrated in Figure 9.11.

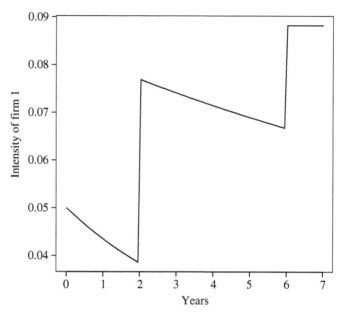

Figure 9.11. The development of the intensity of firm 1 in a model where firm 2 jumps first at time 2 and firm 1 jumps at time 6. The intensities are $0.05Z$ and $0.1Z$ and the multiplicative factor Z has an exponential distribution with mean 1.

9.4 The Copula Approach

In the context of credit risk modeling, copula functions are mainly used for creating families of multivariate distributions with given marginals. For example, both in basket default swaps and in CDOs, we can often calibrate the implied default probability for each individual reference security, but modeling the correlation is a real challenge. To get started, recall that if a one-dimensional continuous random variable X has distribution function F, i.e. $F(x) = P(X \leqslant x)$, then the distribution of the random variable $U = F(X)$ is a uniform distribution on $[0, 1]$. This also means that to simulate an outcome of X one may simulate an outcome u from a uniform distribution and then let the outcome of X be $x = F^{-1}(u)$.

A distribution function for a multivariate distribution is an increasing, right-continuous function which maps a subset of the real numbers into the unit interval $[0, 1]$. Apart from the obvious limiting requirements, a multivariate distribution function F mapping $\mathbb{R}^N$ into $[0, 1]$ must have the monotonicity property for vectors a and b:

$$a < b \Rightarrow F(b) - F(a) \geqslant 0,$$

where $a < b$ as usual means that $b - a$ is a vector with nonnegative entries and at least one strictly positive entry. This condition, however, is not enough to ensure that F is a distribution function. In two dimensions, for example, the probability assigned to a set of the form $[x_1, y_1] \times [x_2, y_2]$ by F is $F(x_2, y_2) - F(x_1, y_2) - F(x_2, y_1) + F(x_1, y_1)$ and we need more than the monotonicity requirement to make sure that this is positive. For a distribution function we simply require that it assigns positive mass to all rectangles. This is easy to state in two dimensions, but it is ugly in higher dimensions. An N-dimensional copula function is a multivariate distribution function C defined on $[0, 1]^N$ with the additional requirement that all one-dimensional marginal distributions are uniform, i.e.

$$C(1, \ldots, 1, v_i, 1, \ldots, 1) = v_i, \quad i = 1, \ldots, N, \; v_i \in [0, 1].$$

From N univariate distribution functions $(F_1, \ldots, F_N)$ and a copula function C, we can define an N-dimensional distribution function F by letting, for $x \in \mathbb{R}^N$,

$$F(x) = C(F_1(x_1), \ldots, F_N(x_N)).$$

As long as C is a distribution function on the unit "cube," it is easy to check that F is in fact a distribution function, and the requirement that C has uniform marginals ensures that the ith marginal distribution of F is F_i.

An important theorem in copula theory, known as Sklar's theorem, states that *any* joint distribution function which has $(F_1, \ldots, F_N)$ as marginal distributions can be obtained by a suitable choice of copula function C. In other words, going through all copula functions gives us all the possible types of dependence structures that are compatible with the given one-dimensional marginal distributions. If the joint distribution of $(F_1, \ldots, F_N)$ is continuous, the copula function is unique.

One may compare copula functions with correlation in the following way. The correlation between two random variables (with finite variance) is the covariance of the two variables after scaling each variable down (or up) so that their variances are 1. A copula function is a joint distribution function on the unit "cube" obtained by transforming the marginal distributions with their distribution functions. The way in which the density of the copula function deviates from a constant equal to 1 (which is the density which corresponds to independence) explains "areas of dependence" between quantiles. If the copula density is higher than 1 at a given point (say 0.7, 0.7) it means that the two variables are more likely to lie simultaneously at their 70% quantile than they would be if they were independent.

Copulas are very popular for simulating correlated default times. Assume that the default times of N issuers have marginal distribution functions $F_1, \ldots, F_N$, which for simplicity we assume to have an inverse function. Then the simulation of N correlated default times is done by first simulating an outcome $(u_1, \ldots, u_N)$ on the N-dimensional unit cube following the distribution specified by the preferred copula function, and let the default times be given as $\tau_1 = F_1^{-1}(u_1), \ldots, \tau_N = F_N^{-1}(u_N)$.

There is no single general method for simulating the outcome of a copula function which is practically feasible in several dimensions. It requires computation of conditional distributions in the copula distribution and this can be very cumbersome. Therefore, the univariate method of simulating a uniform random variable and transforming by the inverse distribution function is not as simple in several dimensions. Hence there are different simulation algorithms for different types of copulas. For example, it is fairly straightforward to simulate the outcome of a multivariate normal distribution and this leads directly to a copula function. If we assume that $(X_1, \ldots, X_N)$ is a multivariate normally distributed random variable with mean vector equal to $\mu_1, \ldots, \mu_N$ and covariance matrix Σ, then $(U_1, \ldots, U_N)$ are distributed according to the *Gaussian* copula if we let

$$U_i = \Phi^{-1}\left(\frac{X_i - \mu_i}{\sigma_i^2}\right).$$

Here the critical parameter for inducing correlation is the covariance matrix Σ. In all families of copula functions we have parameters that we can choose and the difficulty is finding something to calibrate these parameters against.

A quick and dirty method of simulating joint default times is to simulate a copula from a Gaussian copula, using the correlation of asset values as correlation parameter, and then to transform each coordinate into a default time using the inverse of the marginal distribution function. This is somewhat ad hoc, since there is no clear connection between the asset correlations and the correlation obtained in default times using this method. A slightly more reasonable approach matches the correlation parameter in the copula function to obtain the correct default event correlation between pairs of firms. The choice depends heavily on the time horizon, and again there is very little mathematical underpinning of this approach.

An approach that is, perhaps, more natural and which links up directly with the Cox process approach specified earlier is as follows. Recall that the default time in the case of conditional independence is simulated as follows:

$$\tau_i = \inf\left\{t : \int_0^t \lambda^i(X_s)\, \mathrm{d}s > E^i\right\},$$

where the variables E^i are independent exponential distributions with mean 1. A natural deviation from this approach is to replace the independent exponentials by multivariate exponential distributions, which allow for simultaneous jumps and marginal distributions which are exponentials.

An alternative which hooks up directly with copula functions is to rewrite the definition of τ_i as follows:

$$\tau_i = \inf\left\{t : \exp\left(\int_0^t \lambda^i(X_s)\, \mathrm{d}s\right) > U_i\right\},$$

where the U_i are now uniform random variables. Instead of choosing the uniform distributions to be independent, we can choose a copula function and induce correlation between default times in this way. An approach using Archimedean copula functions is presented in Rogge and Schönbucher (2003).

9.5 Network Dependence

The problem with the correlation modeling we have seen is that either we work with common background variables, in which case we may fear that important information about contagion is left out, or we try to incorporate contagion, in which case the models become simplified or have parameters which are hard to assign values to and which are rooted in empirical analysis. One attempt to move towards more fundamental modeling in which defaults of firms trigger the defaults of others is through the idea of a financial clearing network. Here we try to explicitly model networks in which firms hold claims on each other and in which a default causes a sequence of settlements which ultimately may result in more defaults. This section builds on the elegant paper by Eisenberg and Noe (2001).

Consider an economy consisting of n firms. Define a financial system as a pair (L, e), where L is an $n \times n$ matrix and e is a vector in $\mathbb{R}^n$. L_{ij} is the nominal liability of firm i to firm j, and e_i is the cash flow (operating income) that firm i receives from outside the system. We assume that all entries in L and e are nonnegative and that the diagonal of L is 0 so that no firm can hold nominal liabilities on itself.

We think of the system as having a clearing date at which all firms have to settle their nominal liabilities. In a world where all liabilities are met, firm i has a total liability at the clearing date equal to $\bar{p}_i$, where

$$\bar{p}_i = \sum_{j=1}^{n} L_{ij}.$$

$\bar{p}_i = (\bar{p}_1, \ldots, \bar{p}_n)$ denotes the vector of total obligations. In a world where all liabilities are met, i.e. where each firm is able to pay its total obligations, the nominal assets of the ith firm would be

$$e_i + \sum_{j=1}^{n} L_{ji}$$

and the net worth of the firm would be the difference between the total assets and the total obligation. The problem arises when at least one firm, say firm i, has larger nominal liabilities than nominal assets. This firm cannot pay all of its liabilities. This in turn affects the nominal assets of other firms, whose nominal assets include nominal liabilities from firm i. This effect will then spread through the network. In this situation, what is the appropriate payment made from each node which respects

limited liability and absolute priority? To define a "clearing payment vector," we
need a few definitions.

Define the matrix of relative liabilities

$$\Pi_{ij} = \begin{cases} L_{ij}/\bar{p}_i & \text{if } \bar{p}_i > 0, \\ 0 & \text{otherwise.} \end{cases}$$

We characterize the clearing payments in terms of the total payments made by each
node. This is sufficient since we will insist that if the total payment out of node i is
p_i, then the payment to (say) node j is proportional to the relative liability to that
node. Stated mathematically, $p_{ij} = \pi_{ij}\bar{p}_i$. A clearing payment vector $p^* \in [0, \bar{p}]$
is then defined as a vector satisfying

(1) $p_i^* \leqslant \sum_{j=1}^n \Pi_{ij}^t p_j^* + e_i$;

(2) for all $i \in N$ either $p_i^* = \bar{p}_i$ or

$$p_i^* = \sum_{j=1}^n \Pi_{ij}^t p_j^* + e_i.$$

In words, the first condition is a budget constraint or limited-liability clause, saying
that the total payment made by i must be covered by operating income and income
received through (possibly partial) payment on the nominal claims from other firms.
The second condition is an absolute priority condition saying that either liabilities
are paid in full, in which case there could be money left for equity, or they are not
paid in full, in which case all income is paid out to partially cover liabilities, leaving
zero for equity. Under a mild condition of regularity it is shown in Eisenberg and
Noe (2001) that such a clearing system exists and is unique.

There are two interesting ways of determining a clearing system: one is a "fictitious
default algorithm," which gives a clear impression of how the default contagion is
spread through the system; and the second method finds the clearing payment vector
through an extremely simple optimization problem.

The "fictitious default algorithm" works as follows. For each node i, check if
the node is "solvent" by looking at whether it is able to meet its liabilities given
that other firms honor their liabilities to i. If all nodes are solvent according to
this definition, the algorithm terminates and there are no defaults. If at least one
node is not able to meet its liabilities, then define its total payment to be the sum
of its endowment and the payments from the other firms. Divide the payments
proportionally between the different liabilities. The payment vector thus obtained
is p_0. Let $D(p_0)$ describe the set of defaulted firms in this first round. Now the fact
that at least one firm is not honoring its liabilities may cause other firms to default.
If at least one node is not able to meet its liabilities, define the total payment from

this firm to be the sum of its endowment and the payments it is due to receive from other firms. Do this for every firm which is not able to meet its liabilities. This defines a new payment vector p_1. This payment vector implies that all the firms that are owed money from the defaulted firms now have a reduced wealth. While the endowment is unchanged, they lose money on the reduced payments from defaulted firms. If, despite this reduction, all firms have enough wealth to pay all liabilities, the algorithm terminates. If, however, a firm has insufficient wealth after its income has become smaller, then it is added to the default pool, its payment is reduced as in step 1. The algorithm continues like this and terminates after at most n iterations, where n is the number of nodes. The result is a vector showing the total amount to be paid by each firm. Figure 9.3 below illustrates the procedure for data given on the same page.

An extremely simple way of obtaining the clearing payment vector directly is to consider a simple optimization problem. Let $f : [0, \bar{p}] \to \mathbb{R}$ be any function that is strictly monotone in all its coordinates. (One candidate is simply the sum of the coordinates.) Now look at

$$\max f(p), \quad \text{subject to } p \leqslant \Pi^t p + e.$$

The solution to this optimization problem is a clearing payment vector.

The model above provides interesting insights. A possible extension would be to randomize the endowments. For example, we could use a standard Merton setup in which a group of firms have issued debt but also hold liabilities on each other. This is an interesting alternative to a case where correlation is just a consequence of asset values moving jointly. The network dependence clearly incorporates the possibility of interbank lending and of counterparty default risk spreading through trading positions from one financial institution to another.

A second interesting feature would be to introduce nonsimultaneity in the system. As a final example on how hard it is to say something general about a financial clearing system, consider the following example, which is in Flamgaard (2002). Consider an income vector

$$e = (0.2, 0.3, 0.1, 0.54)$$

and a liability matrix of the form

$$L = \begin{pmatrix} 0 & 0.9375 & 0.0625 & 0 \\ 0 & 0 & 1.125 & 0.075 \\ 0.0125 & 0 & 0 & 0.1875 \\ 0 & 0.6 & 0.2 & 0 \end{pmatrix}.$$

The vector of total liabilities is then

$$\bar{p} = (1, 1.2, 0.2, 0.8).$$

Table 9.3. The table shows an example of the steps of the "fictitious default algorithm" needed to find a payment clearing vector. The endowments of the four firms and their mutual liabilities are defined in the text. For each step, the table shows the payment vector at the beginning of each iteration and the set of defaulting firms after each step.

n	Payment vector	$D(p^n)$
0	$p^0 = (1, 1.2, 0.2, 0.8)$	$\{1\}$
1	$p^1 = (0.2125, 1.2, 0.2, 0.8)$	$\{1, 2\}$
2	$p^2 = (0.2125, 1.099\,219, 0.2, 0.8)$	$\{1, 2, 4\}$
3	$p^2 = (0.2125, 1.099\,219, 0.2, 0.796\,201\,2)$	$\{1, 2, 4\}$

and the relative liability matrix is

$$\Pi = \begin{pmatrix} 0 & 0.9375 & 0.0625 & 0 \\ 0 & 0 & 0.9375 & 0.0625 \\ 0.0625 & 0 & 0 & 0.9375 \\ 0 & 0.75 & 0.25 & 0 \end{pmatrix}.$$

Finding the clearing vector using the direct solution method is easy. The result is

$$p^* = (0.2125, 1.099\,219, 0.2, 0.796\,201\,2)$$

and the resulting defaults are

$$D(p^*) = \{1, 2, 4\}.$$

If we run the clearing algorithm, the successive approximations are as in Table 9.3.

We now analyze whether first netting bilaterally has a stabilizing effect on the system. In the example above, if we apply bilateral netting before we run the clearing algorithm, this leads to the net liability matrix

$$NL = \begin{pmatrix} 0 & 0.9375 & 0.05 & 0 \\ 0 & 0 & 1.125 & 0 \\ 0 & 0 & 0 & 0 \\ 0 & 0.525 & 0.0125 & 0 \end{pmatrix}.$$

Using the same endowment as above, this leads to the net clearing vector

$$p^* = (0.2, 1.014\,873, 0, 0.5375)$$

and

$$D(p^*) = \{1, 2\},$$

i.e. there are fewer defaults with bilateral netting. Is this a general pattern? The following (counter-) example shows that it is not. If we consider instead the endowment vector

$$e = (0.2, 0.3, 0.1, 0.4)$$

and add 100 to the liabilities from 1 to 3 and from 3 to 1, then the clearing vector is

$$p^* = (100.2125, 1.2, 100.2, 0.6625),$$

and only 1 and 4 default in this case. If we first apply bilateral netting, then we get the clearing vector

$$p^* = (0.2, 0.880\,57, 0, 0.4),$$

but the resulting number of defaults is larger:

$$D(p^*) = \{1, 2, 4\},$$

with bilateral netting. The intuition is that firm 2 benefits from receiving a small fraction of a very large amount in the setting with no bilateral netting. It is interesting to note that this is in conflict with the intuition that "less connectedness" destabilizes, as hinted at in Allen and Gale (2000).

9.6 Bibliographical Notes

Modeling dependent defaults is a big area and at the time of writing there are many papers in circulation that are related to copula and intensity approaches. The best reference to the collection is simply the magnificent website www.defaultrisk.com, which is maintained by Greg Gupton. Here we will focus mainly on the sources I have relied on for preparing this chapter. The mixed binomial model is a standard tool in statistics and probability and I am not sure where it first entered into the credit risk literature, but Vasicek (1991) is certainly an early reference on loan portfolio losses modeled using that approach. Other papers dealing with portfolio credit risk, emphasizing mixed binomials and common dependence on factor variables, include Frey and McNeil (2003), Gordy (2000), and Wilson (1997a,b). We have emphasized the argument of Vasicek (1991) since it plays a large role in the Basel II process. The assumptions we have to make to work with analytical solutions are stiff. Working with more realistic model assumptions requires simulation. For more on simulation of defaults using intensity models, see Duffie and Singleton (1999b).

The example illustrating contagion through updating of latent variables is from Norros (1985). The subject of diversity scores is treated in Cifuentes et al. (1998). The papers by Frye (2003a,b) consider random loss in the asymptotic loan portfolio model. Empirical evidence on systematic components in recovery rates is studied, for example, in Acharya et al. (2003) and Altman et al. (2002). The model of correlated ratings based on correlated asset values is from Gupton et al. (1997). The binomial contagion model and one of the birth–death examples are from Davis and Lo (2001).

The notion of basic affine models is from Duffie and Gârleanu (2001), and their setup is used to illustrate the effects one can obtain by randomizing the intensity. There is a growing literature on copulas. We refer to Gregory and Laurent (2003b), Li (2000), Rogge and Schönbucher (2003) and Schubert and Schönbucher (2001), which contain further references.

One section was dedicated to the paper on financial network dependence by Eisenberg and Noe (2001). For an empirical study building on this approach, see Elsinger et al. (2003). For more on the topic of contagion, see Allen and Gale (2000).

Appendix A
Discrete-Time Implementation

Most of the explicit pricing formulas presented in this book are centered around computations related to Brownian motion and to affine processes. In many practical situations these solutions are not sufficient since securities and derivatives may have American features or complicated payoff structures which preclude explicit pricing formulas. Examples of this include the pricing of risky coupon debt with compound option features due to asset-sale restrictions and swap pricing with two-sided default risk, which we met in Chapter 7. A quick way to obtain numerical solutions is through discrete-time tree models for security prices. This section gives an overview of how this is solved conceptually for our two main cases. For the explicit implementation the reader will have to consult the cited references. The goal of this section is to convey the basic idea behind building discrete-time arbitrage-free models for bond prices.

A.1   The Discrete-Time, Finite-State-Space Model

We have given a probability space $(\Omega, \mathcal{F}, P)$ with Ω finite. Assume that there are $T + 1$ dates, starting at date 0. A security is defined in terms of two stochastic process—an ex-dividend price process S and a dividend process δ—with the following interpretation: $S_t(\omega)$ is the price of buying the security at time t if the state is ω. Buying the security at time t ensures the buyer (and obligates the seller to deliver) the remaining dividends $\delta_{t+1}(\omega), \delta_{t+2}(\omega), \ldots, \delta_T(\omega)$. We will follow the tradition of probability theory and almost always suppress the ω in the notation below. Of course, a buyer can sell the security at a later date, thereby transferring the right to future dividends to the new owner. Since there are no dividends after the final date T we should think of S_T as 0 and δ_T as a final liquidating dividend if the security is still traded at this point.

In all models considered in this appendix (and in almost every model encountered in practice), we will assume that the model contains a *money-market account* which provides locally riskless borrowing and lending. The interest rate on this account is defined through *the spot rate process*:

$$\rho = (\rho_0, \rho_1, \ldots, \rho_{T-1}),$$

which we require to be strictly greater than -1 at all times and in all states, and which we, for modelling purposes, think of as in fact being strictly positive. The money-market account is defined as a security which permits riskless borrowing and lending between period t and $t + 1$ at the rate ρ_t. Formally, the money-market account has the price process

$$S_t^0 = 1, \quad t = 0, 1, \ldots, T - 1,$$
$$S_T^0 = 0,$$

and the dividend process

$$\delta_t^0(\omega) = \rho_{t-1}(\omega) \quad \text{for all } \omega \text{ and } t = 1, \ldots, T - 1,$$
$$\delta_T^0(\omega) = 1 + \rho_{T-1}(\omega).$$

This means that if you buy one unit of the money-market account at time t, you will receive a dividend of ρ_t at time $t + 1$. Since ρ_t is known already at time t, the dividend received on the money-market account in the next period $t + 1$ is known at time t. Since the price is also known to be 1, you know that placing 1 in the money-market account at time t and selling the asset at time $t + 1$ will give you $1 + \rho_t$. This is why we refer to this asset as a locally riskless asset. You may of course also choose to keep the money in the money-market account and receive the stream of dividends. Starting with an initial investment of 1 and reinvesting the dividends in the money-market account will make this account grow according to the process R, defined as

$$R_t = (1 + \rho_0) \cdots (1 + \rho_{t-1}).$$

If this strategy of *rolling over* in the money-market account is carried out starting with 1 unit of account at date s, then the amount of money available at date t is given as

$$R_{s,t} \equiv (1 + \rho_s) \cdots (1 + \rho_{t-1}).$$

A.2 Equivalent Martingale Measures

In this section we give the least-technical statement of the notion of an equivalent martingale measure that we know of. We maintain the setup with a money-market account generated by the spot rate process ρ, and imagine now having N securities with price and dividend processes $S = (S^1, \ldots, S^N)$, $\delta = (\delta^1, \ldots, \delta^N)$. Define the corresponding discounted processes $\tilde{S}$, $\tilde{\delta}$ by defining, for each $i = 1, \ldots, N$,

$$\tilde{S}_t^i = \frac{S_t^i}{R_{0,t}}, \quad t = 0, \ldots, T,$$

$$\tilde{\delta}_t^i = \frac{\delta_t^i}{R_{0,t}}, \quad t = 1, \ldots, T.$$

We need to define conditional expectation at time t given the information contained in the security price processes up to and including time t. Because of the finite state space, which we call $\Omega = \{\omega_1, \ldots, \omega_S\}$, this can be done very easily. First we generate the partition of Ω at time t as follows.

(1) Pick $\omega_1 \in \Omega$.

(2) Define A_t^1 as the smallest subset of Ω on which all security price processes have the same evolution up to and including time t as they do on ω_1.

(3) Next, pick the lowest indexed ω, say ω', outside A_t^1, and define A_t^2 as the smallest subset of Ω on which all security price processes have the same evolution up to and including time t as they do on ω'.

(4) Now pick the lowest indexed ω outside $A_t^1 \cup A_t^2$ and define a member of the partition as above.

(5) Continue until after, say, $n(t)$ iterations all elements of Ω have been exhausted, thus obtaining a partition $A_t^1, \ldots, A_t^{n(t)}$ of Ω at time t. We refer to $A_t(\omega)$ as the set in this partition of which ω is a member.

Given a probability measure Q not necessarily equal to P on Ω, we can define conditional probabilities given information at time t as follows. Let

$$q(\omega \mid A_t(\omega)) = Q(\omega \mid A_t(\omega)) = \frac{Q(\{\omega\})}{Q(A_t(\omega))}.$$

This is the probability under Q that ω is the "true" state given that we know that ω is consistent with information in security prices up to time t. Then we can compute the associated conditional expectation of future prices (or dividends) as

$$E_t(S_u)(\omega) = \sum_{\omega \in A_t(\omega)} q(\omega \mid A_t(\omega)) S_u(\omega), \quad u > t.$$

This gives the necessary machinery for defining the notion of an equivalent martingale measure. A probability measure Q on $\mathcal{F}$ is an equivalent martingale measure (EMM) if, for all ω, $Q(\omega) > 0$ and, for all $i = 1, \ldots, N$,

$$\tilde{S}_t^i = E_t^Q \left(\sum_{j=t+1}^{T} \tilde{\delta}_j^i \right), \quad t = 1, \ldots, T. \tag{A.1}$$

The term martingale measure has the following explanation. Given a (one-dimensional) security price process S whose underlying dividend process only pays dividend δ_T at time T, the existence of an EMM will give us

$$\tilde{S}_t = E_t^Q(\tilde{\delta}_T), \quad i = 1, \ldots, T-1, \tag{A.2}$$

and therefore the process $(\tilde{S}_0, \tilde{S}_1, \ldots, \tilde{S}_{T-1}, \tilde{\delta}_T)$ is a martingale.

The fundamental reason for the interest in martingale measures is the fact that their existence means that the model for security markets is consistent in the sense that there are no arbitrage opportunities. To define an arbitrage opportunity we must first define the notion of a trading strategy. A trading strategy is a vector-valued stochastic process $\phi = (\phi^0, \phi^1, \ldots, \phi^N)$ whose value at time t gives the number of each security, which the strategy says should be held from time t and into the next time period $t + 1$. It must be adapted to the partitions generated by the security market prices, which means that the value of ϕ_t must be the same for all ω belonging to the same $A_t(\omega)$. This is merely a way of saying that the number of securities bought at time t can only use information about the true state of the world as revealed by security prices up to and including time t. The dividend process generated by a trading strategy is denoted δ^ϕ and it is defined as follows:

$$\delta^\phi(0) = -\phi(0) \cdot S(0),$$
$$\delta^\phi(t) = \phi(t) \cdot S(t) - \phi(t-1) \cdot S(t), \quad t = 1, \ldots, T.$$

The first equation is the amount used to "get started" at time 0. If this involves long positions in securities, the value is negative. The second equation is the cost of investing in the new portfolio at time t minus the value that is brought into time t. Note that we have no need to specify a trading strategy at time T. An arbitrage strategy is a trading strategy whose dividend process is nonnegative at all times and for all $\omega \in \Omega$ but for which there exists at least one $A_t(\omega)$ on which it is strictly positive.

In our security market model the following statements are equivalent.

(1) There are no arbitrage opportunities.

(2) There exists an equivalent martingale measure.

The way this is typically used to prices derivatives is as follows. Let the security model defined by (S, δ) (including the money-market account), on $(\Omega, P, \mathcal{F}, \mathbb{F})$, be arbitrage-free and complete. Then the augmented model obtained by adding a new pair (S^{N+1}, δ^{N+1}), consisting of a dividend process and the associated security price process, is arbitrage-free if and only if

$$\tilde{S}_t^{N+1} = E_t^Q \left(\sum_{j=t+1}^{T} \tilde{\delta}_j^{N+1} \right), \tag{A.3}$$

i.e.

$$\frac{S_t^{N+1}}{R_{0,t}} = E_t^Q \left(\sum_{j=t+1}^{T} \frac{\delta_j^{N+1}}{R_{0,j}} \right),$$

where Q is the unique equivalent martingale measure for (S, δ). In the special case where the discount rate is deterministic, the expression simplifies somewhat. For ease of notation assume that the spot interest rate is not only deterministic but also constant and let $R = 1 + \rho$. Then (A.3) becomes

$$S_t^{N+1} = R^t E_t^Q \left(\sum_{j=t+1}^{T} \frac{\delta_j^{N+1}}{R_{0,j}} \right)$$

$$= E_t^Q \left(\sum_{j=t+1}^{T} \frac{\delta_j^{N+1}}{R^{j-t}} \right).$$

A.3 The Binomial Implementation of Option-Based Models

The classical binomial model for pricing an option on a stock can be translated directly into the valuation problem for corporate securities. Instead of choosing a stock price as the underlying security, as in the classical binomial model, we instead let the firm's asset value be the underlying security. If the asset value is assumed to be a geometric Brownian motion as in the Merton model, we do as follows. Assume that we have chosen a discretization of time in which one year is divided into n periods of length $1/n$. We define the probabilities under the real world as follows:

$$u_n = \exp(\sigma\sqrt{1/n}),$$

$$d_n = \exp(-\sigma\sqrt{1/n}),$$

$$R_n = \exp(r/n),$$

$$p_n = \frac{1}{2} + \frac{1}{2}\frac{\mu}{\sigma}\sqrt{\frac{1}{n}}.$$

This gives the stock a dynamic which, as n goes to infinity, converges "weakly," which means that all expectations of a bounded continuous function of the path computed on the tree will converge to the value of the functional computed in the continuous-time model. The equivalent martingale measure is then given as

$$q_n = \frac{R_n - d_n}{u_n - d_n},$$

and this produces the European option price. Now we can introduce boundaries, as in the Black–Cox model, or have a more complicated boundary. We can also very easily implement the model with endogenous default boundaries working in the normal dynamic programming fashion backwards through the tree.

Most notably, we can deal with the case of asset-sale restrictions and "endogenous" bankruptcy, as explained in Chapter 2.

A.4   Term-Structure Modeling Using Trees

The classical approach in equity modeling is to take as given the P dynamics of the stock and to infer the no-arbitrage measure Q from the given parameters. This approach is more difficult for bonds. It is not easy *a priori* to specify bond-price processes for bonds of all maturities making sure at once that each bond ends up having value 1 at maturity. The trick is therefore to turn the procedure around and once we have the results from the previous section we see immediately why it produces an arbitrage-free model.

Define a zero-coupon bond maturing at time t as a security whose dividend process is zero except at time t, where it is 1, for all ω. Assume for a moment that we have a given specification of the short-rate process and a given Q. Simply define the time t price $p(t, T)$ of a zero-coupon bond maturing at date T as

$$p(t, T) = E_t^Q\left[\frac{1}{R(t, T)}\right].$$

Dividing both sides by $R(0, t)$, we have

$$\frac{p(t, T)}{R(0, t)} = E_t^Q\left[\frac{1}{R(0, T)}\right],$$

and from this we see that the discounted price process is a martingale since it is the conditional expectation of a random quantity independent of t. Hence it corresponds exactly to the formula (A.2). Therefore the market is born arbitrage-free with the prespecified measure Q as martingale measure. The problem then is to choose Q and to choose the dynamics of ρ in such a way that observed features of the bond market are reproduced. Typically, these features are the initial term structure, i.e. the prices $p(0, t)$ for all maturities t, or the volatilities of yields across the maturity spectrum.

Assume that we have a calibration procedure which allows us to fit a term-structure model for zero-coupon bonds. Choosing a simple binomial model for illustration, we can think of the state of the short-rate process at time $t = n\Delta t$ as an integer having counted the total number of up-jumps of the short rate up to that time. Hence the state space at the nth date is then the integers $\{0, 1, \ldots, n\}$. The calibration procedure then gives us values for the short rate ρ at all dates and in all states, i.e. a description of $\rho_t(i)$ for all $n = 0, \ldots, N$ and $i \leqslant n$. Depending on the calibration method it may also give us conditional probabilities of states $i + 1$ or i occurring at time n given the state at time $n - 1$. But these probabilities are also sometimes just chosen as fixed and all of the calibration is then done through the values of the short rate. Now assume that we work with a default intensity model where the default intensity λ is independent of the short rate. Assume also that we work with fractional recovery of market value equal to δ. We then calibrate another model for the loss-adjusted default intensity $(1 - \delta)\lambda$ using prices of defaultable zero-coupon

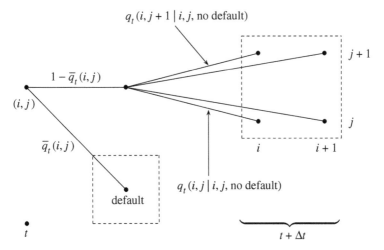

Figure A.1. The figure illustrates one time step as seen from one node of an event tree. There are two independent factors controlling the short rate and the default intensity. The current state is (i, j), which means that the short rate is $\rho_t(i)$ and the default intensity is $\lambda_t(j)$. The possible values at time $t + 1$ are $\rho_{t+1}(i)$, $\rho_{t+1}(i + 1)$ for the short rate and $\lambda_{t+1}(j)$, $\lambda_{t+1}(j + 1)$ for the default intensity. Default can also happen.

bonds. Just as for the short rate we obtain values $\lambda_n(j)$ for the loss-adjusted intensity at time n as a function of the state $j \in \{0, 1, \ldots, n\}$. Now combine the two models to price defaultable claims by combining the two state spaces and adding a default node. The principle is shown in Figure A.1. The value of the default probability at $t = n\Delta t$ when the state is (i, j) is

$$\bar{q}_t(i, j) = 1 - \exp(-\lambda_t(j)\Delta t).$$

The notes contain further references to how this works in trinomial trees and with dependence between the short rate and the default intensity.

A.5 Bibliographical Notes

The notation of this section and the formulation of the fundamental theorem in this version can be found in Duffie (2001). Here one will also find a description of the forward induction method and the calibration methods of Black–Derman–Toy and Ho–Lee. A careful exposition of how to calibrate trees for credit-risky bonds, building on the approach of Hull and White (1994a,b), can be found in Schönbucher (2002). For a calibration approach starting with observed forward rates, as in the model of Heath et al. (1992), see Das and Sundaram (2000).

Appendix B
Some Results Related to Brownian Motion

We record in this appendix for convenience a few results on Brownian motion which are used in the text. First we look at first-passage-time distributions, and the value of receiving a payment at the time of first passage if this occurs before a finite maturity date. Then we look at some expressions for expected values of time-independent functions of Brownian motions which are used in models with perpetual claims.

Throughout this appendix, the process W is a standard Brownian motion on a probability space $(\Omega, \mathcal{F}, P)$, i.e. $W_0 = 0$, W has independent increments and $W_t - W_s$ is normally distributed with mean 0 and variance $t - s$ for $0 \leqslant s < t$. If W is a standard Brownian motion, then the process X defined by $X_t = \sigma W_t + \mu t$ is a Brownian motion with drift μ and volatility σ. For short, we will refer to X as a (μ, σ)-Brownian motion.

B.1 Boundary Hitting Times

The results we need for the distribution of first-passage times and for conditional distributions given that a Brownian motion with drift has not hit an upper boundary can be found, for example, in the concise treatment of Harrison (1990). In this section we simply restate these results for a lower boundary, which is the case we typically need for default modeling.

Consider a (μ, σ)-Brownian motion X starting at some positive level $X_0 = x_0$, and think of the lower barrier as being at 0. Hence x_0 represents the distance to a lower barrier. Let m_t be the minimum of the process up to time t:

$$m_t = \inf\{X_s : 0 \leqslant s \leqslant t\}.$$

Then, using the same techniques as Harrison (1990), we have the joint distribution of the process and its running minimum, given as

$$
P^{x_0}(X_t > x, \, m_t > y)
$$
$$
= \Phi\left(\frac{x_0 - x + \mu t}{\sigma\sqrt{t}}\right) - \exp\left(\frac{-2\mu(x_0 - y)}{\sigma^2}\right)\phi\left(\frac{2y - x_0 - x + \mu t}{\sigma\sqrt{t}}\right). \quad \text{(B.1)}
$$

Denote by τ the first-passage time to 0:

$$\tau := \inf\{X_t = 0 \mid X_0 = x_0\}.$$

Then, since $\tau > t \Leftrightarrow m_t > 0$, we note by inserting $x = 0$, $y = 0$ in (B.1) above that

$$P(\tau > t) = \Phi\left(\frac{x_0 + \mu t}{\sigma\sqrt{t}}\right) - \exp\left(-\frac{2\mu x_0}{\sigma^2}\right)\Phi\left(\frac{-x_0 + \mu t}{\sigma\sqrt{t}}\right). \qquad \text{(B.2)}$$

The associated first-passage density is obtained by differentiating $P(\tau \leqslant t) = 1 - P(\tau > t)$ with respect to t. When the drift is positive, there is a positive probability of never hitting the boundary, so the density is defective. When the drift is 0 the boundary is hit with probability 1, but the hitting time has infinite expectation. For more on this, see, for example, Karatzas and Shreve (1988).

B.2   Valuing a Boundary Payment when the Contract Has Finite Maturity

For models such as the Black–Cox model, where bonds have finite maturity and default occurs when the asset value hits a (lower) boundary, we need to compute the present value of a payment of 1 made at the time the boundary is hit but only if this occurs before maturity T.

Let X be a $(\mu, 1)$-Brownian motion with $X_0 = 0$ and with

$$\tau_b = \inf\{t \geqslant 0 : X_t = b\}.$$

We are interested in computing

$$V(b, T) = E^\mu(\exp(-\alpha\tau_b)1_{\{\tau_b \leqslant T\}})$$

$$= \int_0^T \exp(-\alpha\tau_b)P^\mu(\tau_b \in ds),$$

where $P^\mu(\tau_b \in ds)$ is the density of τ_b. Note that with $\alpha = 0$ this is just $P^\mu(\tau_b \leqslant T)$, an expression which is known analytically. When $\alpha \neq 0$ the trick is to make α part of a drift change of the driving Brownian motion, and obtain an expression involving $P^{\tilde{\mu}}(\tau_b \leqslant T)$ for a different $\tilde{\mu}$. Therefore we refer explicitly to the drift assumption in our notation for the density of τ_b.

From Karatzas and Shreve (1988) we know that

$$P^\mu(\tau_b \leqslant T) = \int_0^T \exp(\mu b - \tfrac{1}{2}\mu^2 s)P^0(\tau_b \in ds),$$

i.e. the density of τ_b can also be expressed as

$$\exp(\mu b - \tfrac{1}{2}\mu^2 s)P^0(\tau_b \in ds).$$

Therefore

$$V(b, T) = \int_0^T \exp(-\alpha s) \exp(\mu b - \tfrac{1}{2}\mu^2 s) P^0(\tau_b \in ds)$$

$$= \frac{\exp(\mu b)}{\exp(b\sqrt{\mu^2 + 2\alpha})} \int_0^T \exp(\sqrt{\mu^2 + 2\alpha} b - \tfrac{1}{2}(\mu^2 + 2\alpha)s) P^0(\tau_b \in ds)$$

$$= \frac{\exp(\mu b)}{\exp(b\sqrt{\mu^2 + 2\alpha})} P^{\sqrt{\mu^2 + 2\alpha}}(\tau_b \leqslant T), \tag{B.3}$$

and we are back on home ground.

In the Black–Cox model we are looking at

$$\inf\{0 \leqslant t \leqslant T : \sigma W_t + (r - a - \tfrac{1}{2}\sigma^2 - \gamma)t = \log(C/V_0) - \gamma T\},$$

which is the same as

$$\inf\left\{0 \leqslant t \leqslant T : W_t + \frac{(r - a - \tfrac{1}{2}\sigma^2 - \gamma)t}{\sigma} = \frac{\log(C/V_0) - \gamma T}{\sigma}\right\},$$

and hence we can use the expression for $V(b, T)$ with

$$b = \frac{\log(C/V_0) - \gamma T}{\sigma} \quad \text{and} \quad \mu = \frac{r - a - \tfrac{1}{2}\sigma^2 - \gamma}{\sigma}.$$

Defining $\tilde{\mu} = \sqrt{\mu^2 + 2\alpha}$ we can rewrite

$$P^{\tilde{\mu}}(\tau_b \leqslant t) = N\left(\frac{b - \tilde{\mu}t}{\sqrt{t}}\right) + \exp(2\mu b) N\left(\frac{b + \tilde{\mu}t}{\sqrt{t}}\right),$$

and this gives us all the quantities we need to evaluate (B.3).

B.3 Present Values Associated with Brownian Motion

We finally consider the calculation of present values of "perpetual" claims whose cash flows are derived from a geometric Brownian motion. To signal that the process need not be the value of a firm's assets, we refer to a state variable process ξ starting in $\xi_0 > 0$ and satisfying the SDE under a pricing measure Q:

$$d\xi_t = \mu\xi_t \, dt + \sigma\xi_t \, dW_t.$$

A perpetual claim is a claim whose cash flow depends only on ξ and not on the passing of time itself. That is, the claim may terminate its payments in finite time, but then only because of changes in ξ and not because of a fixed maturity. We assume a constant riskless interest rate of r and let β_t denote the discount factor $\exp(-rt)$. We will study both payment flows and lump-sum payments. We consider a claim whose price is of the form $F(\xi_t)$, where F is a twice continuously differentiable function. We want to derive an ordinary differential equation for F. The interpretation is that paying the price $F(\xi_t)$ entitles the buyer to a future dividend stream from the security (or a liquidation value at a boundary). We define D_t as the cumulative dividends paid up to time t. The dividends will be of the form $a + b\xi_t$ and then

$$D_t = \int_0^t a + b\xi_s \, ds.$$

Claims which pay a lump sum when ξ hits a certain level will be considered to have no dividend flow, but the price process of the claim will then be forced to equal the lump-sum payment at this point. This we can do very easily when there is only one "liquidating" payment. The discounted gains process is then[1]

$$
\begin{aligned}
dG_t &= d(\beta_t F(\xi_t)) + \beta_t \, dD_t \\
&= \beta_t \, dF(\xi_t) + F(\xi_t) \, d\beta_t + \beta_t \, dD_t \\
&= \beta_t \{F'(\xi_t)\mu\xi_t + \tfrac{1}{2}\sigma^2\xi_t^2 F''(\xi_t) \, dt - rF(\xi_t) + (a + b\xi_t)\} \, dt \\
&\qquad + \beta_t F'(\xi_t)\sigma\xi_t \, dW_t.
\end{aligned}
$$

For this to be a martingale under Q, which it must be if Q is the measure under which we price all claims, the drift term must be 0 and this leads us to consider the second-order ODE

$$\tfrac{1}{2}\sigma^2 x^2 F''(x) + \mu x F'(x) + a + bx = rF(x),$$

which merely states that if you hold the claim F over an infinitesimal period of time, you receive a capital gain from the evolution in F and a dividend flow, and under the risk-neutral measure this payoff is equal to that obtained by letting the amount F earn the riskless rate.

Now let us turn to the solution of the ODE. The homogeneous part of the differential equation is

$$\tfrac{1}{2}\sigma^2 x^2 F''(x) + \mu x F'(x) - rF(x) = 0,$$

and this is easy to solve, at least if you get the idea of trying solutions of the form Cx^β. Insert x^β into the equation:

$$\tfrac{1}{2}\sigma^2 x^2 \beta(\beta - 1)x^{\beta-2} + \mu x \beta x^{\beta-1} - rx^\beta = 0,$$

i.e. we want

$$x^\beta[\tfrac{1}{2}\sigma^2\beta(\beta - 1) + \mu\beta - r] = 0.$$

---

[1] For the formalism of gains processes and prices processes see Duffie (2001).

This gives two possible value for β, namely

$$\delta = \frac{-\mu + \frac{1}{2}\sigma^2}{\sigma^2} + \sqrt{\frac{(\mu - \frac{1}{2}\sigma^2)^2 + 2\sigma^2 r}{\sigma^2}}, \tag{B.4}$$

$$-\gamma = \frac{-\mu + \frac{1}{2}\sigma^2}{\sigma^2} - \sqrt{\frac{(\mu - \frac{1}{2}\sigma^2)^2 + 2\sigma^2 r}{\sigma^2}}, \tag{B.5}$$

where we have used a notation that makes it easy to distinguish the positive exponent from the negative. Hence the general solution to the homogeneous equation is

$$A_1 x^{-\gamma} + A_2 x^\delta, \tag{B.6}$$

where the constants have to determined from boundary conditions.

For the nonhomogeneous part we will assume $\mu < r$. Guessing a particular solution of the form $A + Bx$ gives us the particular solution

$$A = a/r,$$
$$B = b/(r - \mu),$$

and hence a complete solution of the differential equation is given as

$$A_1 x^{-\gamma} + A_2 x^\delta + \frac{a}{r} + \frac{bx}{r - \mu}. \tag{B.7}$$

We first consider the case where we can fix boundary conditions at an upper boundary ξ_U and a lower boundary ξ_L, where the current value ξ_0 satisfies $\xi_L < \xi_0 < \xi_U$. Consider a claim which pays off 1 when ξ hits the upper boundary without first hitting the lower boundary, and pays off 0 when the lower boundary is hit before the upper boundary. This corresponds to setting $f(\xi_U) = 1$, $f(\xi_L) = 0$ and $g = 0$, and we are left with only the homogeneous part of the solution. Therefore, at the lower boundary this gives us the coefficients A_1, A_2 by solving two equations in two unknowns. Defining

$$\Sigma = \xi_U^{-\gamma}\xi_L^\delta - \xi_L^{-\gamma}\xi_U^\delta,$$

we obtain

$$E_0(\exp(-r\tau_U)1_{\{\tau_U < \tau_L\}}) = \frac{1}{\Sigma}(\xi_L^\delta \xi_0^{-\gamma} - \xi_L^{-\gamma}\xi_0^\delta) \tag{B.8}$$

for the value of the claim paying 1 if the upper boundary is hit first. A similar expression applies, of course, for the value of a claim paying 1 when the lower boundary is hit before the upper boundary:

$$E_0(\exp(-r\tau_L)1_{\{\tau_L < \tau_U\}}) = \frac{1}{\Sigma}(-\xi_U^\delta \xi_0^{-\gamma} + \xi_U^{-\gamma}\xi_0^\delta). \tag{B.9}$$

Finally, for the two-boundary case, we record the value of a payout received until the first time the boundary is hit and given a starting value of ξ_0. Again, this must have the form

$$E \int_0^{\tau_D} \exp(-rt)(a + b\xi_t)\, dt = A_1 \xi_0^{-\gamma} + A_2 \xi_0^{\delta} + \frac{a}{r} + \frac{b\xi_0}{r - \mu}. \qquad (B.10)$$

The boundary conditions are that the claim has value 0 at the upper and the lower boundary, and solving the resulting two equations in two unknowns we obtain

$$A_1 = \frac{1}{\Sigma}\left(\frac{a}{r} + \frac{b\xi_0}{r - \mu}\right)(\xi_U^{\delta} - \xi_L^{\delta}),$$

$$A_2 = \frac{1}{\Sigma}\left(\frac{a}{r} + \frac{b\xi_0}{r - \mu}\right)(\xi_L^{-\gamma} - \xi_U^{-\gamma}).$$

When there are no boundaries we can compute the present value of a perpetual dividend flow without using the ODE. But we do need to assume $\mu < r$. To compute the expected discounted value in this case, just use the fact that $E\xi_t = \xi_0 \exp(\mu t)$ and the assumption that $\mu < r$ to conclude that

$$E \int_0^{\infty} \exp(-rt)(a + b\xi_t)\, dt = \frac{a}{r} + \frac{\xi_0}{r - \mu}. \qquad (B.11)$$

When there is only one boundary, and we assume $\mu < r$ if $b \neq 0$, one can show that the following reasoning using boundary conditions as ξ goes to infinity is justified. Let $\xi_0 > \xi_L$, and think of a contract promising a payoff of 1 upon hitting this boundary. Assume no upper boundary. The general solution to the homogeneous problem must then have $A_2 = 0$, since that is required for the price of the claim to go to 0 as the boundary becomes more and more remote, i.e. $\xi_0 \to \infty$. Solving $A_1 \xi_L^{-\gamma} = 1$ we obtain $A_1 = \xi_L^{\gamma}$ and therefore the price of the claim starting as a function of the current position ξ_L is

$$E \exp(-r\tau_L) = \left(\frac{\xi_L}{\xi_L}\right)^{\gamma}, \qquad (B.12)$$

where τ_L is the first hitting time of the lower boundary. Another way to compute the value P_B of a unit paid upon hitting the boundary would be to consider

$$P_B(\xi_0) = \int_0^{\infty} \exp(-rt) f(t, \xi_0; \xi_L)\, dt,$$

where $f(t, \xi_0, \xi_L)$ is the density of the first-passage time of ξ_0 to ξ_L, but the differential equation is simpler to handle.

The price of a claim paying an affine cash flow up until ξ hits the lower boundary is found by noting that again we must have $A_2 = 0$ since, as the distance to the boundary becomes remote, the solution must converge to the perpetual claim defined above. The result is

$$E \int_0^{\tau_L} \exp(-rt)(a+b\xi_t) \, dt = \frac{a}{r}\left(1-\left(\frac{\xi_L}{\xi_0}\right)^\gamma\right) + \frac{b\xi_0}{r-\mu}\left(1-\left(\frac{\xi_L}{\xi_0}\right)^{1+\gamma}\right). \quad \text{(B.13)}$$

B.4 Bibliographical Notes

An extremely concise introduction to Brownian motion and important functionals related to Brownian motion is given in Harrison (1990). Dixit (1993) also contains much useful material in this direction, as does Karatzas and Shreve (1988). The mathematics of gain processes in continuous time and its role in continuous-time models is given in Duffie (2001).

Appendix C
Markov Chains

C.1 Discrete-Time Markov Chains

For ease of reference, this appendix reviews the concepts and results on Markov chains that we need in this book.

Let $\eta = (\eta_0, \eta_1, \dots)$ be a stochastic process defined on some probability space $(\Omega, \mathcal{F}, \text{Pr})$. Assume that the state space is finite and equal to $\{1, \dots, K\}$. The process η is said to be a Markov chain if, for every time n and every combination of states $\{i_0, i_1, \dots, i_n\}$, we have

$$\text{Pr}(\eta_n = i_n \mid \eta_0 = i_0, \eta_1 = i_1, \dots, \eta_{n-1} = i_{n-1}) = \text{Pr}(\eta_n = i_n \mid \eta_{n-1} = i_{n-1}).$$
$$(\text{C.1})$$

The Markov chain is said to be time-homogeneous if $\text{Pr}(\eta_{n+1} = j \mid \eta_n = i)$ does not depend on n, and then we define the one-period transition probability from i to j as

$$p_{ij} = \text{Pr}(\eta_{n+1} = j \mid \eta_n = i)$$

for any n. We collect these transition probabilities in a matrix

$$P = \begin{pmatrix} p_{11} & \cdots & p_{1K} \\ \vdots & \ddots & \vdots \\ p_{K1} & \cdots & p_{KK} \end{pmatrix},$$

where $\sum_{j=1}^{K} p_{ij} = 1$ for all i (i.e. rows sum to 1). A consequence of the Markov property is that n-step transition probabilities can be obtained by taking the nth power of the (one-period) transition matrix, i.e.

$$p_{ij}^{(n)} := \text{Pr}\{\eta_n = j \mid \eta_0 = i\} = (P^n)_{ij},$$

where $(P^n)_{ij}$ is the ijth element of the matrix obtained by raising P to the power n. This matrix multiplication adds up the probabilities of each possible path and thus obtains the n-step transition probability.

A Markov chain which is time inhomogeneous still satisfies the equation (C.1) but we may no longer define P_{ij} as independent of calendar time. Therefore, we will write

$$P(t, t+1) = \begin{pmatrix} p_{11}(t, t+1) & \cdots & p_{1K}(t, t+1) \\ \vdots & \ddots & \vdots \\ p_{K1}(t) & \cdots & p_{KK}(t, t+1) \end{pmatrix}$$

for the transition-probability matrix between time t and time $t + 1$ and we now have the following connection between multi-period and one-period transition probabilities:

$$P(t, u) = P(t, t+1)P(t+1, t+2) \cdots P(u-1, u).$$

C.2   Continuous-Time Markov Chains

In several applications it turns out to be more flexible to work with a continuous-time formulation in which we can consider transitions over any time horizon, i.e. not just consider horizons which are multiples of the basic period length. The continuous-time setting requires estimation of transition intensities, but this is straightforward. We can then compute estimates of transition probabilities from the intensity estimates.

C.2.1   The Time-Homogeneous Case

The definition of a continuous-time Markov chain is obtained from the discrete-time definition simply by making the time parameter continuous. Hence for a stochastic process η indexed by a continuous parameter t with values in a finite state space, the Markov property holds if

$$\text{Prob}(\eta_t = j \mid \eta_{s_0} = i_0, \ \eta_{s_1} = i_1, \dots, \eta_{s_{n-1}} = i_{n-1}, \ \eta_s = i)$$
$$= \text{Prob}(\eta_t = j \mid \eta_s = i)$$

whenever $s_0, s_1, \dots, s_{n-1} < s$.

For a homogeneous Markov chain, the family of transition matrices satisfies

$$P(u - s) = P(t - s)P(u - t), \quad \text{for } s < t < u.$$

A time-homogeneous Markov chain on a finite state space can be described by an associated *generator matrix*, i.e. a $K \times K$ matrix Λ for which

$$P(t) = \exp(\Lambda t),$$

where the exponential of the matrix Λt (obtained by multiplying all entries of Λ by t) is defined as

$$\exp(\Lambda t) = I + \sum_{k=1}^{\infty} \frac{\Lambda^k t^k}{k!}.$$

Hence all the transition probabilities can be obtained from the generator. Note that we are ignoring the role of initial distributions since we will always consider the chains as starting in a known state.

The elements of a generator matrix satisfy

$$\lambda_{ij} \geqslant 0 \quad \text{for } i \neq j,$$
$$\lambda_i = \sum_{j \neq i} \lambda_{ij},$$

i.e. all elements off the diagonal are nonnegative and the diagonal elements make the sum of the rows equal to 0. A row of zeros corresponds to an absorbing state.

It is useful for our interpretation of the parameters of the generator to recall the way in which a Markov chain can be simulated from its generator. Consider an example with three states and a generator given by

$$\Lambda = \begin{pmatrix} -\lambda_1 & \lambda_{12} & \lambda_{13} \\ \lambda_{21} & -\lambda_2 & \lambda_{23} \\ \lambda_{31} & \lambda_{32} & -\lambda_3 \end{pmatrix}.$$

Let $\text{Ex}(\lambda)$ denote the exponential distribution with mean $1/\lambda$. To simulate the chain proceed as follows.

(1) Fix an initial state of the Markov chain, say state 1.

(2) Simulate the outcome of an $\text{Ex}(\lambda_1)$-distributed random variable. Let the chain stay in state 1 for this amount of time.

(3) Jump to either state 2 with probability

$$\frac{\lambda_{12}}{\lambda_{12} + \lambda_{13}} = \frac{\lambda_{12}}{\lambda_1},$$

or state 3 with probability λ_{13}/λ_1.

(4) If the new state is 2, simulate an $\text{Ex}(\lambda_2)$-distributed random variable and stay in the state for that amount of time.

(5) Now jump to state 3 with probability λ_{23}/λ_2, and to state 1 with probability λ_{21}/λ_2.

(6) Continue the simulation until the elapsed time exceeds the desired time horizon.

A row consisting of all zeros marks an *absorbing state*. If the chain hits such a state, it remains there and never makes another transition. Hence the simulation stops. It is convenient to work with the default states as absorbing states even if firms may, in practice, recover and leave the default state. If we ask what the probability is that a firm will default before time T, then this can be read from the transition matrix $P(T)$ when we have defined default to be an absorbing state. If the state is not absorbing, but P allows the chain to jump back into the nondefault rating categories, then the transition-probability matrix for time T will only give the probability of being in default *at* time T and this (smaller) probability is typically not the one we are interested in for risk-management purposes.

C.2.2 Computing the Matrix Exponential

Computing the exponential of a matrix is not straightforward, but it is a function available in many mathematical software packages. We present two ways that usually work for rating transition matrices.

A simple case is when there exists a matrix B such that

$$B^{-1}\Lambda B = D,$$

where D is a diagonal matrix of "eigenvalues" $d_1, \dots, d_K$. Then $\exp(Dt)$ is just the diagonal matrix with entries $\exp(d_1 t), \dots, \exp(d_K t)$, and

$$P(t) = B\exp(Dt)B^{-1}.$$

This is easy to compute if B has been found, which of course requires diagonalization algorithms. These exist in many software packages.

A second possibility is to work directly on the series definition of the exponential. Recall the definition of the matrix exponential

$$\exp(\Lambda) = \sum_{k=0}^{\infty} \frac{\Lambda^k}{k!},$$

which suggests that we evaluate the exponential by choosing a large number of terms from the power series. But the diagonal elements are negative, and in some applications involving birth–death processes they may be large in numerical value as well. This creates numerical problems because we end up adding large quantities with opposite signs. We can get around this issue by using the following procedure. Choose $\lambda = \max\{|\lambda_i| : i = 1, \dots, K\}$, where λ_i is the ith diagonal element of Λ. Let I_K denote the $K \times K$ identity matrix and note that

$$\exp(\lambda I_K + \Lambda) = \exp(\lambda I_K)\exp(\Lambda)$$

since λI_K and Λ commute.[1] Since $\exp(\lambda I_K) = \text{diag}(\exp(\lambda), \dots, \exp(\lambda))$ we see that

$$\exp(\Lambda) = \exp(-\lambda)\exp(\lambda I_K + \Lambda).$$

[1] For matrices, we only have $\exp(A+B) = \exp(A)\exp(B)$ when A and B commute. Scalar multiples of the identity matrix are the only matrices which commute with all other matrices of the same dimension.

Since $\lambda I_K + \Lambda$ has all elements positive, the truncated sum will be a good approximation for a manageable number of terms. This can be done even for large matrices (say 1000×1000).

A final possibility, which is not spelled out in detail here, is to work with the expression for the transition probabilities as a solution to the forward and backward equations,

$$\frac{\partial P(t)}{\partial t} = P(t)\Lambda = \Lambda P(t),$$

and some numerical scheme for solving ODE systems could then be applied.

C.2.3 Time-Nonhomogeneous Chains

For applications to pricing we need the concept of a nonhomogeneous chain. In complete analogy with the discrete-time case, the definition of the Markov property does not change when we drop the assumption of time-homogeneity, but the description of the family of transition matrices requires that we keep track of calendar dates instead of just time lengths.

Hence the family of transition matrices for a nonhomogeneous chain satisfies

$$P(s, u) = P(s, t)P(t, u) \quad \text{for } s < t < u.$$

For the purpose of specifying the dynamics it is again more natural to work with intensities, but unfortunately the translation from intensities to probabilities requires numerical techniques except for very special cases.

The natural extension of the Chapman–Kolmogorov equations to the inhomogeneous setting is the pair of forward–backward equations given by

$$\frac{\partial P(t, u)}{\partial u} = P(t, u)\Lambda(u) \quad \text{(forward)},$$

$$-\frac{\partial P(t, u)}{\partial t} = \Lambda(t)P(t, u) \quad \text{(backward)},$$

where $u > t$. There is no explicit solution, so proceeding numerically using, for example, the forward equation we would get that

$$\frac{P(t, u + h) - P(t, u)}{h} \simeq P(t, u)\Lambda(u),$$

i.e.

$$P(t, u + h) \cong h P(t, u)\Lambda(u) + P(t, u)$$
$$= P(t, u)[\Lambda(u)h + I],$$

which shows how we work out $P(t, u + h)$ from $P(t, u)$. The initial condition is of course $P(t, t) = I$.

C.2.4 *The Embedding Problem for Markov Chains*

In Chapter 4 we compared the estimation of rating transitions based on discrete-time observations with estimation based on continuous-time observation. One advantage of the continuous-time method is best understood if we first briefly consider the embedding problem for Markov chains. Typically, the shortest period for which the major rating agencies report transition intensities is one year. In practical risk management it is important to be able to analyze the risk of credit events and credit migration over shorter periods of time. For example, when pricing bonds with step-up provisions it is convenient to work easily with periods down to one day. If one only has observations of 1-year transition probabilities, a way of solving this problem is to find a generator matrix Λ for a given 1-year transition matrix P such that $P = \exp(\Lambda)$. By then setting $P(t) = \exp(\Lambda t)$ we would be able to compute transition probabilities over arbitrary time horizons that are consistent with the 1-year transition probability. This problem of finding a generator which is consistent with a given P is known as the embedding problem for Markov chains. The problem does not have a solution in general (we will see why shortly). And even when a solution exists, it need not be unique. An exposition of much of the existing literature on this topic can be found in Israel et al. (2001). Three sufficient conditions, each of which is sufficient for the problem *not* to have a solution, are as follows.

(1) There are states i and j such that j is accessible from i but $p_{ij} = 0$.

(2) $\det(P) \leqslant 0$.

(3) $\det(P) > \prod_i p_{ii}$.

The first condition is the critical one from our perspective, since that is the one which is almost always true in practice. In the context of a rating system, it is always the case that the nondefault states communicate, that is, it is possible over the course of time to go from any nondefault state $i \in \{1, \ldots, K-1\}$ to any other nondefault state $j \in \{1, \ldots, K-1\}$; that is, for some n we will have $p_{ij}^{(n)} > 0$. But we often see the 1-year migration rates reported with $p_{ij} = 0$ for pairs of states (i, j). Such states rule out a solution to the embedding problem since a continuous-time chain must have either $p_{ij}(t) > 0$ for all t or $p_{ij}(t) = 0$ for all t. Intuitively speaking, what can happen over a period of time may also happen over arbitrarily small periods of time. Note that the generator matrix, which in essence describes what can happen instantaneously, may have $\lambda_{ij} = 0$, corresponding to a situation in which the direct transition from i to j is not possible, but it will still be the case that $p_{ij}(t) > 0$ if there is a sequence of states that leads from i to j. The second condition is a simple consequence of the fact that the determinant of the matrix exponential satisfies

$$\det(\exp(\Lambda)) = \exp(\mathrm{tr}\,\Lambda),$$

which we see from the right-hand side is strictly positive. The third condition is more technical in nature and we will not comment on it here. As we will see below, a good way to avoid having the problem of embedding in the first place is to estimate rating transitions based on continuous-time data. As a final word on how difficult it is to deal with "logarithms" of matrices, note that even in the case where the discrete-time transition probability can be diagonalized, i.e.

$$P = BDB^{-1}$$

and the eigenvalues $d_1, \ldots, d_n$ which form the diagonal in the diagonal matrix D are strictly positive, we do not necessarily have a solution. It is tempting to take logarithms of the eigenvalues and compute

$$Q = B \operatorname{diag}(\log(d_1), \ldots, \log(d_n)) B^{-1}.$$

While this gives a solution to the equation $\exp(Q) = P$ it does not necessarily produce a generator matrix, since the off-diagonal elements may be strictly negative. For more on this issue and on how to find approximate solutions of this nature, see Israel et al. (2001).

C.3 Bibliographical Notes

A nice textbook with an introduction to both discrete-time and continuous-time Markov chains is Resnick (1992). The method for computing matrix exponentials by adding a diagonal matrix is the "uniformization method" and it can be found in Neuts (1995). For the connection between intensities and transition probabilities for time-inhomogeneous Markov chains see Gill and Johansen (1990) and Andersen et al. (1993). An overview of the embedding problem and ways to obtain approximate solutions is given in Israel et al. (2001).

Appendix D
Stochastic Calculus for Jump-Diffusions

This appendix gives an overview of some basic tools involving processes with jumps. The reader is assumed to be familiar with diffusion processes and the Itô formula for such processes. This appendix gives the extension of Itô's formula to processes with a finite number of jumps on finite intervals. It also describes how the distribution of jump-diffusions can change under an equivalent change of measure. We define the concepts in a framework which is more general, namely within a class of processes known as special semimartingales. Working within this class gives us a way of defining what we mean by a jump-diffusion and it also carries additional dividends. For example, special semimartingales represent the most general class of processes within which we can formulate "beta" relationships, i.e. equations which describe the excess returns on processes in terms of their local covariation with a state price density process (which then in turn can be related to the return on a market portfolio). We look at how this can be formulated.

D.1   The Poisson Process

The Poisson process is the fundamental building block of jump processes. It is just as essential to modeling jump processes as Brownian motion is to diffusion modeling.

Given a filtered probability space $(\Omega, \mathcal{F}, P, F)$, a Poisson process N with intensity $\lambda \geqslant 0$ is the unique process satisfying the following properties:

(i) $N_0 = 0$;

(ii) N has independent increments; and

(iii) $P(N_t - N_s = k) = ((\lambda(t-s))^k / k!) \exp(-\lambda(t-s))$ for $k \in N_0$ and $t > s \geqslant 0$.

Just as one needs to prove the existence of a Brownian motion (after all, the defining properties could be self-contradictory), one also has to "construct" a Poisson process. This is a lot easier than for Brownian motion. The construction is simply done by letting $\varepsilon_1, \varepsilon_2, \ldots$ be a sequence of independent, identically, and exponentially distributed random variables with

$$P(\varepsilon_1 \leqslant t) = 1 - \exp(-\lambda t),$$

and then define the arrival times of jumps as

$$\tau_1 = \varepsilon_1,$$
$$\tau_2 = \tau_1 + \varepsilon_2,$$
$$\vdots$$
$$\tau_n = \tau_{n-1} + \varepsilon_n.$$

Now let N_t be the number of jumps which fall in the interval $[0, t]$, i.e. let

$$N_t = \max\{n : \tau_n \leqslant t\}.$$

We will not prove here that this gives us a Poisson process, but see Resnick (1992), for example, for a proof. The Poisson process is a counting process, i.e. the sample paths of N are constant between jumps, and increases by one at jump times.

D.2   A Fundamental Martingale

Since the Poisson process is increasing, it cannot be a martingale. But subtracting a "compensator" of the form λt will turn it into a martingale:

$$M_t = N_t - \lambda t$$

is a martingale, since, for $t > s$,

$$
\begin{aligned}
E[M_t - M_s \mid \mathcal{F}_s] &= E[N_t - N_s - \lambda(t - s) \mid \mathcal{F}_s] \\
&= E[N_t - N_s \mid \mathcal{F}_s] - \lambda(t - s) \\
&= \lambda(t - s) - \lambda(t - s) = 0,
\end{aligned}
$$

where the second equality is due to the fact that N has independent increments, and the third emerges by using the mean of the Poisson distribution. The intuition is that over a small time interval Δt the process will either decrease by λt (with probability $1 - \lambda \Delta t$) or increase by $1 - \lambda \Delta t$ (with probability $\lambda \Delta t$) and this has mean 0.

   Note that from the martingale property, or as a direct consequence of the definition,

$$E N_t = \lambda t.$$

D.3   The Stochastic Integral and a First Look at Itô's Formula for a Jump Process

Given a Poisson process N with intensity λ, consider the stochastic differential equation

$$dX_t = \mu_t \, dt + h_t \, dN_t, \quad X_0 = x_0,$$

where μ_t is an adapted process satisfying $\int_0^t |\mu_s| \, ds < \infty$ for all t and h is an adapted and left-continuous process satisfying $\int_0^t |h_s| \, ds < \infty$. It is comforting to know that the stochastic integral defined above does not require the same technical effort as one involving Brownian motion. In fact, the equation is to be interpreted as a path-by-path integral so that

$$X_t(\omega) - x_0 = \int_0^t \mu_s(\omega)\,ds + \int_0^t h_s(\omega)\,dN_s(\omega).$$

Note that the stochastic integral with respect to the Poisson process is really just a finite sum. As in the construction of N, let τ_i denote the ith jump of N. Then

$$\int_0^t h_s(\omega)\,dN_s(\omega) = \sum_{0 \leqslant s \leqslant t} h_s \Delta N_s$$

$$= \sum_{i=0}^{N_t} h(\tau_i).$$

Hence, between jumps we have

$$\frac{dX_t(\omega)}{dt} = \mu_t(\omega),$$

and at the jump times we have

$$\Delta X_t \equiv X_t - X_{t-} = h_t \Delta N_t = h_t.$$

Now let $Z_t = F(X_t, t)$ for a differentiable function F. Between jumps, we can then apply the chain rule ω by ω to obtain

$$\frac{dZ_t(\omega)}{dt} = \frac{\partial F}{\partial t}(X_t(\omega), t) + \frac{\partial F}{\partial x}(X_t(\omega), t)\mu_t(\omega).$$

At the jump times we have (this time suppressing the dependence on ω)

$$\Delta Z_t = F(X_t, t) - F(X_{t-}, t-)$$
$$= F(X_t, t) - F(X_{t-}, t) \quad \text{using continuity of } F$$
$$= F(X_{t-} + h_t, t) - F(X_{t-}, t),$$

so we end up with

$$dZ_t = \left(\frac{\partial F}{\partial t}(X_t, t) + \frac{\partial F}{\partial x}(X_t, t)\mu_t\right)dt + (F(X_{t-} + h_t, t) - F(X_{t-}, t))\,dN_t.$$

This way of thinking about Itô's formula when jumps are involved is very helpful when looking at more complicated jump processes.

D.4   The General Itô Formula for Semimartingales

In this section we first present a version of Itô's formula which is general enough to handle the processes encountered in this book. Assume throughout that the semi-martingale X satisfies the following property:

$$\sum_{0 \leqslant s \leqslant t} |\Delta X_s| < \infty.$$

Certainly, a process which only jumps a finite number of times on any finite time interval satisfies this property. With this property satisfied, we can define the continuous part of the process X as

$$X_t^c = X_t - \sum_{0 \leqslant s \leqslant t} \Delta X_s.$$

This continuous part of X also has a continuous martingale part, and we refer to the quadratic variation of this as $\langle X^c \rangle$. We have not formally defined the predictable quadratic variation but we will do that below and will write it out for the case of a jump-diffusion.

Let f be a function depending on x and t which is C^2 in the x variable and C^1 in the t variable. Then $f(X_t, t)$ is also a semimartingale and

$$f(X_t) - f(X_0)$$
$$= \int_0^t f'(X_s)\, dX_s^c + \int_0^t \tfrac{1}{2} f''(X_s)\, d\langle X^c \rangle_s + \sum_{0 \leqslant s \leqslant t} \{f(X_s, s) - f(X_{s-}, s)\}.$$

D.5   The Semimartingale Exponential

The semimartingale exponential is crucial in defining the connection between cumulative returns and prices. When seeking continuous-time formulations of asset-pricing restrictions on returns—a goal which also requires the mathematics of portfolio returns to be tractable—it turns out that the most convenient mathematical representation of the connection between prices and returns is obtained using the semimartingale exponential. Semimartingale exponentials are also crucial in the formulation of measure changes.

The fundamental result we use is the following: the solution to the equation

$$Z_t = Z_0 + \int_0^t Z_{s-}\, dX_s$$

is given by

$$Z_t = Z_0 \mathcal{E}(X)_t \equiv Z_0 \exp(X_t^c - \tfrac{1}{2}\langle X^c \rangle_t) \prod_{0 \leqslant s \leqslant t} (1 + \Delta X_s). \tag{D.1}$$

We emphasize that again we use the assumption that the semimartingale X satisfies the finite jump property. When applied to modeling security prices, X is a cumulative return process and Z is the price process of a security. For the main examples where the return process is a diffusion or a jump-diffusion, see Section D.9.

To stress the convenience of working with semimartingale exponentials note the following.

(1) We can analyze whether a price process S is a martingale by looking at the the return process R directly. For many of the processes we work with it will be the case that

$$S_t = \mathcal{E}(R_t)$$

is a martingale if and only if

$$R_t = \frac{1}{S_t}\, dS_t$$

is a martingale. The precise theorem would have to involve local martingales, but we will not run into complications along these lines in this book.

(2) If $R = (R_t^1, \ldots, R_t^N)$ is a vector of return processes, then the return of a portfolio strategy ω_t is

$$R_t^\omega = \omega_t'\, dR_t,$$

i.e. the wealth W of using this strategy (for a self-financing strategy) satisfies $W_t = W_0 \mathcal{E}(R_t^\omega)$.

D.6 Special Semimartingales

The general theory of processes involves many classes of process that are defined through measurability conditions and sample path properties. We will not need much of this theory in this book, but there are a few places in the book where we need the concepts of a local martingale, of predictable quadratic variation, and of a special semimartingale, so here is a very short introduction to these concepts. Furthermore, we introduce enough notation to hint at the more general measure-change theorems, since these more general theorems are helpful in understanding the structure of risk premiums in the vast majority of models used in the literature.

Given a probability field $(\Omega, \mathcal{F}, P)$, let $\mathbb{F} = (\mathcal{F}_t)_{t \in \mathcal{T}}$ be a filtration on this space, i.e. an increasing sequence of σ-algebras. For almost all applications in this book, think of a finite time horizon T such that $\mathcal{T} = [0, T]$ and assume that $\mathcal{F}_T = \mathcal{F}$. Occasionally, we use $T = \infty$ and the definitions in this chapter carry over to this case as well.

Usually we think of a stochastic process X as a family of stochastic variables $(X_t)_{t \in \mathcal{T}}$ indexed by time and we say that the process is *adapted* to the filtration $\mathbb{F}$ (and write also $\mathcal{F}_t$-adapted) if X_t is measurable with respect to $\mathcal{F}_t$ for all $t \in \mathcal{T}$. When formulating technical requirements of measurability and also when we consider random measures, it is useful to think of a stochastic process as a mapping

$$X : \Omega \times \mathcal{T} \longrightarrow \mathbb{R},$$

where the product space $\Omega \times \mathcal{T}$ is then equipped with the product σ-algebra of $\mathcal{F}$ and the Borel field $B(\mathcal{T})$ on $\mathcal{T}$. Holding ω fixed, we then have a function of t which is a *sample path* of the process. If all sample paths are right continuous and have limits from the left, we say the process is RCLL or cadlag, depending on whether we want an abbreviation from English or French. We also use the notation LCRL or caglad, with the obvious meaning. The Poisson process and all martingales that we consider are (and can be) chosen to be RCLL. The adapted LCRL and RCLL processes define two important sigma fields.

The smallest sigma field on $\Omega \times \mathcal{T}$ for which all adapted RCLL processes are measurable is called the optional sigma field, denoted $\mathcal{O}$. All processes measurable with respect to this field are optional.

The smallest sigma field on $\Omega \times \mathcal{T}$ for which all adapted LCRL processes are measurable is called the predictable sigma field, denoted $\mathcal{P}$. All processes measurable with respect to this field are predictable. Unless we introduce artificial delays into processes (defining a process to jump at a later date when something happens now), we will not have any reason here to distinguish between a left-continuous and adapted process and a predictable process. A typical way of making a process predictable is to replace right limits by left limits. Hence, if X is an adapted RCLL process and we let X_- be the process obtained by replacing all right limits by left limits, we obtain a predictable process.

X is said to have *finite variation* if its sample paths are of finite variation. This means that for every $t \in \mathcal{T}$ and every ω, the variation

$$\text{Var}(X)_t(\omega) = \lim_{n \to \infty} \sum_{1 \leqslant k \leqslant n} |X_{tk/n}(\omega) - X_{t(k-1)/n}(\omega)| \qquad (D.2)$$

is finite. It is equivalent to saying that each sample path can be written as the difference between two increasing functions. All processes which arise by integrating paths with respect to Lebesgue measure have finite variation and so do all jump processes with finitely many jumps on any finite interval. The only processes we will encounter in this book with infinite variation are diffusion processes. They have the interesting property of having finite quadratic variation, meaning that, for each (t, ω),

$$[X]_t := \lim_{n \to \infty} \sum_{1 \leqslant k \leqslant n} |X_{tk/n}(\omega) - X_{t(k-1)/n}(\omega)|^2 < \infty.$$

A process which is continuous cannot have both finite variation and finite quadratic variation, but a jump process with finitely many jumps has both measures of variation finite. In fact, if X is a process with finite variation and jumps, we have (assuming $X_0 = 0$)

$$[X]_t := \sum_{s \leqslant t} \Delta X_s(\omega)^2,$$

where $\Delta X_s = X_s - X_{s-}$ is the amount by which the process jumps at time s. Jump processes with infinitely many jumps on finite intervals also have infinite variation, but we will not encounter these here.

An adapted process M is a *local* martingale if there exists an increasing sequence of stopping times (τ_n) such that $\tau_n \to T$ with probability 1 as $n \to \infty$ and the stopped process $M(\tau_n \wedge t)$ is a uniformly integrable martingale. Note that the stopped process is still defined on all of $\mathcal{T}$ but it retains the value it has at the random time τ_n on the interval $[\tau_n, T]$. The idea of localization extends to other properties as well. For example, a Brownian motion W is locally bounded, since we can define $\tau_n = \inf\{t \geqslant 0 : |W_t| \geqslant n\} \wedge T$. In fact, any process with bounded jumps is locally bounded, since we can use the same sequence of stopping times as above. Clearly, the stopped process will never exceed in absolute value the level n plus the maximal jump size. It is also clear that the sequence of stopping times will converge to the terminal date when n increases.

There are two other classes of processes which are important for stating results below and which have "localized" versions. An adapted finite-variation process A is said to have integrable variation on $\mathcal{T}$ if $E(\mathrm{Var}(A)_T) < \infty$. Here, the variation is defined as in (D.2), and as usual T is allowed to be ∞.

A process M is said to be a square-integrable martingale if $EM_t^2 < \infty$ for all $t \in \mathcal{T}$. A locally square-integrable martingale permits the definition of a predictable quadratic variation process $\langle M \rangle$. This process is defined as the unique predictable and increasing process with $\langle M \rangle_0 = 0$ for which

$$M_t^2 - \langle M \rangle_t \text{ is a local martingale.}$$

X is a *semimartingale* if it permits a decomposition $X = X_0 + M + A$ into a local martingale M and a finite-variation process A. If in this decomposition the finite-variation process A can be chosen to be predictable, then X is a *special semimartingale*. When we insist that both the martingale part and the finite-variation part start at zero, this decomposition is unique. We need to go into fairly exotic processes to see the distinction between special semimartingales and the general class of semimartingales. The Cauchy process is a Lévy process with independent, Cauchy distributed increments. These increments do not have a finite mean, and since they are unpredictable jumps, any decomposition of the process into a local martingale and a finite-variation part must assign the large jumps to the finite-variation part. But this makes the finite-variation part nonpredictable. Since the jumps are not predictable, the finite-variation part is not predictable either. Once we give up predictability in the decomposition, there are infinitely many decompositions since we can vary the definition of "large jumps." All processes encountered in this book are special semimartingales.

D.7   Random Measures, Local Characteristics, and Equivalent Martingale Measures

In this section we discuss how to find equivalent martingale measures by looking at the local characteristics of the return process. Unless stated otherwise, all processes discussed in this section are assumed to have the value 0 at time 0. We now proceed through three decompositions to define the local characteristics of a special semi-martingale. Assume that the return process is a special semimartingale, i.e. there exists a unique decomposition of R,

$$R = R_0 + M + A, \tag{D.3}$$

in which M is a local martingale and A is predictable and of finite variation. M in turn can be decomposed into a continuous martingale part and a purely discontinuous martingale part, $M = M^c + M^d$, and since the continuous part is locally square integrable, it has a predictable quadratic variation process $\langle M^c \rangle$.

To describe how the jumps of a process behave, we need the concept of an integer-valued random measure. Let E be a subset of $\mathbb{R}$ (denoted the mark space) equipped with the Borel field. A random measure μ on $\mathcal{T} \times E$ is a family $\mu = (\mu(\omega; dt, dx) : \omega \in \Omega)$ of nonnegative measures on $(\mathcal{T} \times E, B(\mathcal{T}) \otimes B(E))$ which satisfy $\mu(\omega; \{0\} \times E) = 0$. Now define

$$\tilde{\Omega} = \Omega \times \mathcal{T} \times E$$

and define the predictable and optional sigma fields on $\tilde{\Omega}$ as

$$\tilde{\mathcal{O}} = \mathcal{O} \otimes B(E),$$
$$\tilde{\mathcal{P}} = \mathcal{P} \otimes B(E),$$

and call a function $W : (\omega, t, x) \rightarrow R$ an optional (predictable) function if it is measurable with respect to $\tilde{\mathcal{O}}$ ($\tilde{\mathcal{P}}$). For an optional function W we define the integral process

$$W * \mu_t(\omega)$$
$$= \begin{cases} \int_{\mathcal{T} \times E} W(\omega, s, x)\mu(\omega, ds, dx) & \text{if } \int_{\mathcal{T} \times E} |W(\omega, s, x)|\mu(\omega, ds, dx) < \infty, \\ \infty & \text{otherwise.} \end{cases}$$

A random measure is optional (predictable) if for any optional (predictable) function the stochastic process $W * \mu_t$ is optional (predictable). With all these tools in place, we can define a random measure by extracting the jumps from R:

$$\mu^R(dt, dx) = \sum_s 1_{\{\Delta R_s \neq 0\}} \delta_{(s, \Delta R_s)}(dt, dx).$$

This measure can be shown to be integer valued and, for each ω, has the value 1 at (t, x) if R for that ω has a jump at time t of size x. Just as we have a compensating intensity for a counting process, we have a compensating measure for a random measure which can turn expectations into simple integrals: the measure ν^R is a compensating measure for μ^R if for every predictable function W for which $|W| *$ $\mu \in \mathcal{A}_{\mathrm{loc}}^+$ we have that $W * \mu^R - W * \nu^R$ is a local martingale.

We are now finally ready to define the local characteristics of the special semi-martingale R as the triple (A, β, ν), where

(1) $A(t, \omega)$ is the predictable process of finite variation in the canonical decomposition (D.3);

(2) $\beta(t, \omega) = \langle M^c \rangle(t, \omega)$ is a predictable, increasing process; and

(3) $\nu(\omega; dt, dx)$ is the compensating measure of the jump measure μ^R.

With these general definitions in place, we can define the most important class of processes, namely "diffusions with jumps." These are processes for which the characteristics are of the form

$$A_t(\omega) = \int_0^t a(s, X_{s-}(\omega))\, ds,$$

$$\beta_t(\omega) = \int_0^t b(s, X_{s-}(\omega))\, ds,$$

$$\nu(\omega; ds \times dx) = \lambda(s, X_{s-}(\omega))\, ds \times \Phi_s(X_{s-}(\omega), dx),$$

where

(1) $a : [0, T] \times R \to R$ is Borel;

(2) $b : [0, T] \times R \to R$ is nonnegative, Borel;

(3) $\lambda : [0, T] \times R \to R$ is nonnegative, Borel;

(4) $\Phi_s(x, dy)$ is a transition kernel, i.e. for fixed (s, x), $\Phi_s(x, dy)$ is a probability measure on some subset E of $R \backslash \{0\}$, and for a fixed Borel set B of E, $\Phi_s(x, B)$ is a measurable from $\mathcal{T} \times R$ into $[0, 1]$.

In what follows we will generally suppress ω and often t also. Keeping in mind that an equality sign between two processes means that almost all sample paths of the processes are the same (i.e. the processes are *indistinguishable*), this should not cause any confusion. This notion of local characteristics is used in Métivier (1982). As shown there, the triple satisfies the following "generalized Dynkin formula."

For any C^2-function ϕ the process

$$M_t^\phi = \phi(R_t) - \phi(R_0) - \int_0^t \phi'(R_{s-}) \, dA_s - \frac{1}{2} \int_0^t \phi''(R_{s-}) \, d\beta_s$$

$$- \int_0^t \int_E (\phi(R_{s-} + x) - \phi(R_{s-}) - \phi'(R_{s-})x) \nu(ds, dx)$$

is a local martingale.[1]

For financial modelling it is important to know whether a given semimartingale is special (so that instantaneous covariance can be defined) and in some cases if it is even locally square integrable. Both regularity conditions are determined by the tails of the jump distribution (see Jacod and Shiryaev 1987, Proposition 2.29).

We are now able to state the main result, which we will use to find equivalent martingale measures below. Let E be the mark space of μ^R, which in our applications will be a subset of $[-1, \infty)$, and let $\tilde{\mathcal{P}}$ denote the predictable field on $\tilde{\Omega} = \Omega \times \mathcal{T} \times E$.

Let R be a special semimartingale under P and under an equivalent measure $\tilde{P}$. Assume for simplicity that $R_0 = 0$ and let the canonical decompositions be given as

$$R = M + A \quad \text{and} \quad R = \tilde{M} + \tilde{A},$$

respectively. Then there exists a $\tilde{\mathcal{P}}$-measurable mapping $Y : \tilde{\Omega} \to (0, \infty)$ and a predictable process $z : \Omega \times [0, T] \to (-\infty, \infty)$ such that the characteristics of R under $\tilde{P}$ are given by

$$\tilde{A}_t = A_t + z \cdot \beta_t + x(Y(x) - 1) * \nu_t, \tag{D.4}$$

$$\tilde{\beta}_t = \beta_t, \tag{D.5}$$

$$\tilde{\nu}(dt, dx) \equiv Y(t, x)\nu(dt, dx). \tag{D.6}$$

From this we observe that R is a local martingale under $\tilde{P}$ if and only if

$$A_t + z \cdot \beta_t + x(Y - 1) * \nu_t = 0. \tag{D.7}$$

If (D.7) is satisfied, and if R is in fact a martingale under $\tilde{P}$, we say that $\tilde{P}$ is an equivalent martingale measure, and if in addition the density process Z is square integrable, we say that the measure is an L^2-equivalent martingale measure.

This result is important in that it describes through the set of pairs (Y, z) the types of local characteristics that R can have under an equivalent measure. In other words, it gives us a necessary condition that the local characteristics must satisfy under the new measure if there is to be equivalence between the old and the new measure. The

---

[1] A more general version of local characteristics which cover semimartingales in general is given in Jacod and Memin (1976). This involves defining a "truncation function" $h(x) = x 1_{|x| \leqslant 1}$, which strips a semimartingale of its large jumps such that the remaining part has bounded jumps, and is therefore special and allows a unique decomposition. For more detail, see, for example, Jacod and Memin (1976) and Jacod and Shiryaev (1987).

invariance of β under equivalent changes of measure corresponds to the well-known fact that we cannot change the variance parameter of a diffusion under an equivalent change of measure.

It turns out that the pair (Y, z) also describes the density process of an equivalent measure. Expressions for the density process are available in great generality in, for example, Section III.5 of Jacod and Shiryaev (1987). By imposing the assumption of quasi-left continuity on the return process, we know (see Jacod and Shiryaev 1987, II.1.19) that there is a version of v such that $v(\{t\} \times E) = 0$ for all t. This simplifies the exposition considerably, and it still covers the large class of jump-diffusions, which is used in this book. With quasi-left continuity we get the following directly from Theorem 3.8 of Jacod and Memin (1976).

Let R be a special semimartingale with canonical decomposition $R = M + A$. Assume that $|Y - 1| * v \in \mathcal{A}_{\text{loc}}$ and let z_t be a predictable process for which $z^2 \cdot \beta \in \mathcal{A}_{\text{loc}}$. Define

$$
\left.
\begin{aligned}
\eta_t &= z \cdot M_t^c + (Y - 1) * (\mu^R - v)_t, \\
Z_t &= \mathcal{E}(\eta)_t \equiv \exp(\eta_t - \tfrac{1}{2}z^2 \cdot \beta_t) \prod_{s \leqslant t}((1 + \Delta \eta_s) \exp(-\Delta \eta_s)).
\end{aligned}
\right\}
\tag{D.8}
$$

If $EZ_T = 1$ and $P(Z_T > 0) = 1$, then the relation $dP' = Z\,dP$ defines an equivalent measure on $(\Omega, \mathcal{F}_T)$ and R is a semimartingale under $\tilde{P}$. If R is special under the equivalent measure P, its characteristics are given by expressions (D.4)–(D.6).

These results define the following strategy when looking for an equivalent martingale measure. Look at the characteristics of R and try to find pairs (Y, z) for which the equation (D.7) is satisfied. Look at the process Z_T defined in terms of (Y, z) in (D.8). If $EZ_T = 1$, then we have an equivalent measure under which the process R is a local martingale, and we have an explicit expression for the density process.

We can define the conditional mean jump size at time s, given that the process is at X_{s-} before the jump, as follows under the two measures:

$$
k(s, X_{s-}) := \int_E x \Phi_s(X_{s-}(\omega), dx) < \infty \quad \text{for all } s,
$$

$$
\tilde{k}(s, X_{s-}) := \int_E x \tilde{\Phi}_s(X_{s-}(\omega), dx) < \infty \quad \text{for all } s,
$$

where $\tilde{\Phi}$ is the transition kernel under the equivalent measure P. Then we may write (D.7) as

$$
\int_0^t a(s, X_{s-})\,ds + \int_0^t z(s)b(s, X_{s-})\,ds + \int_0^t \tilde{k}(s, X_{s-})\tilde{\lambda}(s, X_{s-})\,ds
$$

$$
- \int_0^t k(s, X_{s-})\lambda(s, X_{s-})\,ds = 0 \quad \text{a.s. all } t.
$$

A sufficient condition for this to hold is that the functions satisfy

$$a(s, x) + z(s)b(s, x) + \tilde{k}(s, x)\tilde{\lambda}(s, x) - k(s, x)\lambda(s, x) = 0 \quad \text{for all } (s, x).$$

Consider the case with time-independent and nonrandom coefficients: Equation (D.7) then becomes

$$a + zb + \tilde{\lambda}\tilde{k} - \lambda k = 0. \tag{D.9}$$

In the canonical decomposition of the return process we have $a = c + \lambda k$, and we then have the simplest possible solution where the coefficients in the return process as well as the density process are nonrandom and independent of time:

$$a + zb + \tilde{\lambda}\tilde{k} = 0.$$

We see how the change of measure is accomplished: the drift a is eliminated through a change of measure that introduces drift in the continuous martingale part of R and in the jump part by changing the mean jump size and the intensity. It is important to note that when markets are incomplete, this equality can be satisfied in several ways: many different choices of Y may produce the same combination of intensity $\tilde{\lambda}$ and mean jump size $\tilde{k}$ under the new measure $\tilde{P}$.

D.8 Asset Pricing and Risk Premiums for Special Semimartingales

We are now ready to see the connection between excess returns and density processes for an equivalent measure. The price of asset i is given as a semimartingale S^i. Associated with asset i is a cumulative dividend process D_i which is also a semimartingale. D_i is assumed to have finite variation.

The interpretation is that $S_i(t)$ represents the price at which the ith security can be bought at time t. $D_i(t)$ is the cumulative dividend paid by the asset up to time t. Purchasing asset i at time t gives the right to all dividends paid after time t.

Let

$$G_i(t) = S_i(t) + D_i(t)$$

denote the gains process associated with holding asset i. We also assume that a money-market account B_t is given, described as

$$B_t = \exp\left(\int_0^t r_s \, ds \right),$$

where r is an adapted semimartingale. The discounted gains process is then defined as

$$G_i^*(t) = \frac{S_i(t)}{B(t)} + \int_0^t \frac{1}{B(u)} \, dD_i(u).$$

We will also work under the assumption that there exists an equivalent martingale measure Q on $(\Omega, \mathcal{F}_T)$ defined through a strictly positive random variable L_T (which to preserve mass 1 satisfies $E^P[L_T] = 1$):

$$Q(A) = E^P[1_A L_T].$$

Under Q the discounted gains process is a local martingale.

We sidestep the issue of how exactly this is connected with a no-arbitrage condition. The reader will have to consult Duffie (2001) for a textbook presentation or the work by Delbaen and Schachermayer (1994) building, of course, on the fundamental insights in Harrison and Kreps (1979) and Harrison and Pliska (1981, 1983).

Our goal in this section is to describe the connection between the density process L and the excess return of securities under the measure P. This description relies on a notion of covariance for stochastic processes called quadratic covariation, which we now describe. The definition requires that we work with special semimartingales, which we do in all continuous-time specifications in this book. First, let M, N be local martingales. The predictable quadratic covariation of M, N is the unique predictable process $\langle M, N \rangle$ for which

$$MN - \langle M, N \rangle \text{ is a local martingale.}$$

Now let $X = M + A$ and $Y = N + B$ be special semimartingales. Then

$$\langle X, Y \rangle_t = \langle M, N \rangle_t + \sum_{0 \leqslant s \leqslant t} \Delta X_s \Delta Y_s.$$

In the cases we will consider, the jumps of X and Y will be in the martingale components and then $\langle X, Y \rangle_t = \langle M, N \rangle_t$.

But then we may write M and N as the sum of their continuous and purely discontinuous parts, respectively, and find

$$\langle M, N \rangle = \langle M^c, N^c \rangle + \sum_{0 \leqslant s \leqslant t} \Delta M_s^d \Delta N_s^d.$$

Associated with L_T is a density process

$$L_t = E^P[L_T \mid \mathcal{F}_t],$$

which is a martingale.

Now the following theorem from Back (1991) describes the connection between excess return on assets and the density process. Let $S_i(t) = M_i(t) + A_i(t)$ be the decomposition of the ith asset into a local martingale and a predictable process of finite variation. Let $L(t)$ be the density process of an equivalent martingale measure. Assume that $L(t)M_i(t)$ is a special semimartingale. Then

$$\int_0^t \frac{1}{S_i(u-)} \, dA_i(u) - \int_0^t r_u \, du = -\int_0^t \frac{1}{S_i(u-)} \frac{1}{L(u-)} \, d\langle G, L \rangle(u).$$

Remark: we could have used $\rho_t = \exp(-\int_0^t r_u\, du)L_t$, which is a state price density process, in the statement of the theorem, but we have chosen to exploit the special structure on the locally risk-free asset.

Now we will move to a simpler statement of this result which exploits the structure we have in almost all our models in continuous-time modeling.

We can also express the density process as

$$L(t) = \mathcal{E}(\ell)_t$$

for a special semimartingale ℓ which satisfies $\Delta \ell_t > -1$.

In all continuous-time models used in this book, the return process of an underlying asset has the form

$$s_i(t) = m_i(t) + a_i(t),$$

where m_i is a martingale and

$$a_i(t) = \int_0^t \alpha_i(s)\, ds$$

for some adapted, piecewise-continuous process α_i. Furthermore, $L_t = \mathcal{E}(\ell_t)$ and

$$\langle \ell, m_i \rangle_t = \int_0^t c_i(u)\, du$$

for some piecewise-continuous adapted process c_i.

In this case, in an interval $[0, t]$ with no dividend payments we have for almost every t

$$\alpha_i(t) - r_t = -c_i(t),$$

i.e. the excess return on asset i is the quadratic covariation between the martingale part of the cumulative return and the "stochastic logarithm" of the density process.

Therefore, to understand risk premiums we must understand the structure of the density processes and their covariation with asset returns.

D.9 Two Examples

We will now show how all of these concepts apply in three models: the standard Black–Scholes model; Merton's jump-diffusion model; and a pure jump model.

D.9.1 The Black–Scholes Model

This model contains only one asset besides the money-market account and we therefore omit the subscript:

$$dB(t) = rB(t)\, dt,$$
$$dS(t) = \mu S(t)\, dt + \sigma S(t)\, dW_t,$$

i.e.

$$B(t) = \exp(rt),$$
$$S(t) = S_0 \exp((\mu - \tfrac{1}{2}\sigma^2)t + \sigma W_t).$$

The associated return processes for the stock is

$$ds(t) = \mu\, dt + \sigma\, dW_t,$$

i.e.

$$s_t = \mu t + \sigma W_t.$$

Hence the continuous martingale part of the return is σW_t. Also, $a(t) = \mu t$ and so $\alpha(t) = \mu$.

The density process for the equivalent martingale measure is

$$L_t = \mathcal{E}(-\lambda W_t)$$

with $\lambda = (\mu - r)/\sigma$ and we have $d\langle m, \ell\rangle = -\lambda\sigma\, dt$, so $c(t) = -\lambda\sigma$, and we see that the excess return is given as

$$\mu - r = -c.$$

λ is the "market price of risk."

D.9.2 *A Jump-Diffusion Model*

In an extension of the Black–Scholes setting, Merton considers return processes of the form

$$s_t = \mu t + \sigma W_t + \sum_{i=1}^{N_t} \varepsilon_i,$$

in which N is a Poisson process with intensity λ, the ε_i form a sequence of i.i.d. random variables distributed on a subset of $[-1, \infty)$ with distribution Φ. Φ may be discrete or have a density $\phi(x)$.

The price process associated with s_t is

$$S_t = \mathcal{E}(s)_t = \exp((\mu - \tfrac{1}{2}\sigma^2)t + \sigma W_t) \prod_{i=1}^{N_t}(1 + \varepsilon_i).$$

So, between the jumps of the price process, it behaves like a geometric Brownian motion. Note that $\sum_{i=1}^{N_t} \varepsilon_i$ is not a martingale but we can correct for the jump-induced drift by letting

$$\kappa = \int x\Phi(dx)$$

and writing

$$S_t = (\mu + \lambda\kappa)t + \sigma W_t + \sum_{i=1} N_t\varepsilon_i - \lambda\kappa t.$$

This is not a complete model and an infinite collection of equivalent martingale measures exists.

We characterize a subset of these by considering the change in drift, the change in jump distribution, and the change in intensity to be time independent and nonrandom.

Let h be a change in jump distribution by assuming that $h(x) > 0$ on the support of Φ, and

$$\int xh(x)\Phi(dx) = 1.$$

Assume also that $\int xh(x)\Phi(dx) < \infty$.

Define $\tilde{\Phi}(dx) = h(x)\Phi(dx)$ and $\tilde{\kappa} = \int \tilde{\Phi}(dx)$. It is possible to change the drift through the Brownian motion and the intensity of N to $\tilde{\lambda}$. For the new measure Q to be a martingale measure we must have

$$\tilde{\mu} + \tilde{\lambda}\tilde{\kappa} = r.$$

This is obtained by using

$$L_t = \mathcal{E}(\ell_t)$$

with

$$\ell_t = -\kappa W_t + \lambda(1 - v)t + \sum_{i=1}^{N_t}(h(\varepsilon_i) - 1).$$

In this case

$$\langle \ell, m \rangle = \kappa\sigma + v\lambda\tilde{\kappa} = \kappa\sigma + \tilde{\lambda}\tilde{\kappa}$$

and so we have

$$\mu + \lambda\kappa - r = -\langle \ell, m \rangle = \kappa\sigma + \tilde{\lambda}\tilde{\kappa},$$

i.e.

$$\kappa = -\frac{\mu + \lambda\kappa - r - \tilde{\lambda}\tilde{\kappa}}{\sigma}.$$

D.10   Bibliographical Notes

Some standard references on the material presented here are Jacod and Shiryaev (1987) and Protter (1990) but I also benefited greatly from Paulsen (1999) and Brémaud (1981). The results on equivalence of measures are from Jacod and Memin (1976, Theorem 3.3), and can also be found in Jacod and Shiryaev (1987, p. 160). Lando (1994) also considers jump-diffusion option pricing from the viewpoint of semimartingale characteristics.

Appendix E

A Term-Structure Workhorse

This appendix gives completely explicit closed-form solutions to certain functionals of a univariate affine jump-diffusion with exponentially distributed jumps. It includes as special cases the classical models of Vasicek (1977) and Cox et al. (1985), along with the solutions found in the appendix of Duffie and Gârleanu (2001). The tools for the analysis are provided in Duffie et al. (2000), where multivariate affine models are also covered, but the explicit closed-form solutions presented here are, as far as we know, due to Christensen (2002). While it is reasonably fast to implement the ODEs which appear in affine modeling, it is still much less of a hurdle and faster computationally to simply copy down a closed-form expression given here. We also provide a completely closed-form solution for a characteristic function that is important for determining option prices and threshold-dependent payoffs.

We take as given a probability space $(\Omega, \mathcal{F}, P)$. P can be both a physical measure governing the true transition dynamics of our state variable, or it can be a martingale measure used for computing prices. Whenever we work with affine models (or quadratic models) and are concerned both with pricing and estimation, we typically pick the density process in such a way that the dynamics are affine (or quadratic) under both the physical measure and the martingale measure. Hence the formulas derived here will be useful for calculating actual survival probabilities, implied survival probabilities, bond prices, and prices of derivative securities.

The workhorse is the following affine jump-diffusion:

$$dX_t = \kappa(\mu - X_t)\,dt + \sqrt{\sigma_0^2 + \sigma_1^2 X_t}\,dW_t + dJ_t,$$

where

$$J_t = \sum_{i=1}^{N_t} \varepsilon_i$$

and N_t is a Poisson process with intensity $\lambda \geqslant 0$ and $(\varepsilon_i)_{i=1}^{\infty}$ is a sequence of i.i.d. exponentially distributed random variables with

$$P(\varepsilon_i \leqslant x) = 1 - \exp\left(-\frac{1}{\eta}x\right)$$

for some $\eta > 0$. Hence, the mean jump size of the exponential distribution is η. Note the two "classical" special cases: the Vasicek model corresponds to letting $\lambda = 0$ and $\sigma_1^2 = 0$ to get

$$dX_t = \kappa(\mu - X_t)\,dt + \sigma_0\,dW_t;$$

and the CIR model comes about by letting $\lambda = 0$ and $\sigma_0^2 = 0$ to get

$$dX_t = \kappa(\mu - X_t)\,dt + \sigma_1\sqrt{X_t}\,dW_t.$$

This specification does not cover all affine univariate processes—even when we insist on exponentially distributed jumps. The intensity could be an affine function of the state variable, but this case is not covered here. The affine dependence forces us to worry about the prospect of negative intensities of the jump process (controlling the intensity of another jump process). It saves a lot of explanation to just have a constant intensity. In our applications we will typically have one but not both of σ_0^2 and σ_1^2 different from 0. We include the possibility of having both different from 0, but note that we must then have $\kappa(\mu + (\sigma_0^2/\sigma_1^2)) > \frac{1}{2}\sigma_1^2$ to make sure that $\sigma_0^2 + \sigma_1^2 X_t$ remains positive. Only then is the drift away from the critical boundary $-\sigma_0^2/\sigma_1^2$ large enough to keep $\sigma_0^2 + \sigma_1^2 X_t$ from becoming negative.

We are interested in computing the following functional:

$$\Pi^X(T, X_0, \rho, \bar{u}) = E\left[\exp\left(-\int_0^T \rho X_s\,ds\right)\exp(\bar{u}X_T)\right].$$

When there is a square root diffusion term (as in the CIR model), we cannot choose ρ and $\bar{u}$ completely freely. In this case think of ρ as nonnegative (although we will see that the domain can be extended) when we are in the CIR case for the volatility. Although not completely accurate, think of ρ as positive when $\sigma_1^2 > 0$ and unrestricted when $\sigma_1^2 = 0$. Think of $\bar{u}$ as nonpositive. Note that the case $\rho = 1$, $\bar{u} = 0$ gives the expression for a zero-coupon bond price when X is thought of as a short rate, and survival probabilities in a Cox setting when X is a default intensity. We will need $\rho \neq 1$, for example, in our stochastic rating transition example.

This functional has a completely closed-form expression:

$$\Pi^X(T, X_0, \rho, \bar{u}) = \exp(\alpha(T) + \beta(T)X_0),$$

where

$$\beta(T) = \frac{-2\rho[e^{\gamma T} - 1] + \bar{u}e^{\gamma T}(\gamma - \kappa) + \bar{u}(\gamma + \kappa)}{2\gamma + (\gamma + \kappa - \bar{u}\sigma_1^2)[e^{\gamma T} - 1]},$$

$$\alpha(T) = \frac{2\kappa\mu}{\sigma_1^2}\ln\left[\frac{2\gamma e^{(\gamma+\kappa)T/2}}{2\gamma + (\gamma + \kappa - \bar{u}\sigma_1^2)(e^{\gamma T} - 1)}\right] + \frac{1}{2}\sigma_0^2\frac{[2\rho + \bar{u}(\gamma + \kappa)]^2}{[\gamma - \kappa + \bar{u}\sigma_1^2]^2}T$$
$$\qquad - \frac{2\sigma_0^2\kappa}{\sigma_1^4}\ln\left[\frac{2\gamma + (\gamma + \kappa - \bar{u}\sigma_1^2)[e^{\gamma T} - 1]}{2\gamma}\right]$$

$$- \frac{2\sigma_0^2}{\sigma_1^2} \frac{[e^{\gamma T} - 1](\rho + \kappa\bar{u} - \frac{1}{2}\sigma_1^2\bar{u}^2)}{2\gamma + (\gamma + \kappa - \bar{u}\sigma_1^2)[e^{\gamma T} - 1]}$$

$$+ \frac{\lambda\eta[2\rho + \bar{u}(\gamma + \kappa)]}{\gamma - \kappa + \bar{u}\sigma_1^2 - \eta[2\rho + \bar{u}(\gamma + \kappa)]} T$$

$$- \frac{2\lambda\eta}{\sigma_1^2 - 2\eta\kappa - 2\rho\eta^2}$$

$$\times \ln\left[1 + \frac{[\gamma + \kappa - \bar{u}\sigma_1^2 + \eta(2\rho - \bar{u}(\gamma - \kappa))](e^{\gamma T} - 1)}{2\gamma(1 - \bar{u}\eta)}\right]$$

and

$$\gamma = \sqrt{\kappa^2 + 2\rho\sigma_1^2} \quad \text{for } \rho > -\frac{\kappa^2}{2\sigma_1^2}.$$

For convenience, we record the special cases of Vasicek ($\sigma_1^2 = 0$, $\lambda = 0$),

$$\beta^V(T) = \bar{u}e^{-\kappa T} - \frac{\rho}{\kappa}[1 - e^{-\kappa T}],$$

$$\alpha^V(T) = \kappa\mu\left[\frac{\rho}{\kappa}T - \frac{\bar{u}\kappa + \rho}{\kappa^2}[1 - e^{-\kappa T}]\right]$$

$$- \frac{1}{2}\sigma^2\left[\left(\frac{\rho}{\kappa}\right)^2 T + \frac{(\bar{u}\kappa + \rho)^2}{2\kappa^3}[1 - e^{-2\kappa T}] - \frac{2\rho(\bar{u}\kappa + \rho)}{\kappa^3}[1 - e^{-\kappa T}]\right],$$

and of CIR ($\sigma_0^2 = 0$, $\lambda = 0$),

$$\beta^{\text{CIR}}(T) = \frac{-2\rho[e^{\gamma T} - 1] + \bar{u}e^{\gamma T}(\gamma - \kappa) + \bar{u}(\gamma + \kappa)}{2\gamma + (\gamma + \kappa - \bar{u}\sigma^2)[e^{\gamma T} - 1]},$$

$$\alpha^{\text{CIR}}(T) = \frac{2\kappa\mu}{\sigma^2}\ln\left[\frac{2\gamma e^{(\gamma+\kappa)T/2}}{2\gamma + (\gamma + \kappa - \bar{u}\sigma^2)(e^{\gamma T} - 1)}\right],$$

$$\gamma = \sqrt{\kappa^2 + 2\sigma^2\rho}.$$

This functional allows computation of characteristic functions of X_T by letting $\rho = 0$ and letting $\bar{u} = iu$ for some real number u. The formula holds even when inserting the complex number $\bar{u}$. It also allows us to compute an important ingredient in an option-pricing formula in which $\exp(uX_T)$ could be the price of a claim at time T as a function of the state variable at that time.

However, the affine setting has a very powerful extension to a more general type of functional:

$$G_{\bar{u},b}(T, X_0, \rho, y) = E\left[\exp\left(-\int_0^T \rho X_s \, ds\right) \exp(\bar{u}X_T)1_{\{bX_T \leqslant y\}}\right]. \quad \text{(E.1)}$$

Note that letting $\bar{u} = 0$ makes it possible to compute expectations of payments contingent upon a threshold being passed at time T. This is just what we would need for option pricing and for payments contingent upon the passing of a threshold, as for example in the case of credit triggers.

While there is not a closed-form expression for (E.1) there is an alternative route which will give us the prices we need up to a one-dimensional integral. By thinking of (E.1) as a function of y, we have an increasing function on $\mathbb{R}$, which then defines a measure on $\mathbb{R}$ as in the theory of Stieltjes integrals. The astonishing fact is that the Fourier transform of this measure has an affine form and this transform can be inverted to obtain an expression for prices.

In general, the method relies on solving ODEs, but as shown in Christensen (2002) there is an explicit solution for the Fourier transform when we are in the special setting studied here with the additional assumption $\sigma_0 = 0$. Inverting the Fourier transform gives us the following expression for (E.1), which is analytic up to an integral:

$$G_{\bar{u},b}(T, X_0, \rho, y)$$
$$= \tfrac{1}{2}\psi(\bar{u}, T, X_0, \rho) - \frac{1}{\pi}\int_0^\infty \frac{\mathrm{Im}[e^{-ivy}\psi(\bar{u}+ivb, T, X_0, \rho)]}{v}\, dv, \quad \text{(E.2)}$$

where

$$\psi(z, T, X_0, \rho) = E\left[\exp\left[-\int_0^T \rho X_s\, ds\right]\exp[zX_T]\,\Big|\,\mathcal{F}_0\right]$$
$$= \exp(\alpha_\psi(T) + \beta_\psi(T)X_0)$$

and

$$\alpha_\psi(T) = \frac{2\kappa\mu}{\sigma_1^2}\ln\left[\frac{2\gamma e^{(\gamma+\kappa)T/2}}{2\gamma + (\gamma+\kappa - z\sigma_1^2)(e^{\gamma T}-1)}\right]$$
$$+ \frac{\lambda\eta[2\rho + \bar{u}(\gamma+\kappa)]}{\gamma - \kappa + z\sigma_1^2 - \eta[2\rho + z(\gamma+\kappa)]}T$$
$$- \frac{2\lambda\eta}{\sigma_1^2 - 2\eta\kappa - 2\rho\eta^2}$$
$$\times \ln\left[1 + \frac{[\gamma+\kappa - z\sigma_1^2 + \eta(2\rho - z(\gamma-\kappa))](e^{\gamma T}-1)}{2\gamma(1-z\eta)}\right],$$

$$\beta_\psi(T) = \frac{-2\rho[e^{\gamma T}-1] + ze^{\gamma T}(\gamma-\kappa) + z(\gamma+\kappa)}{2\gamma + (\gamma+\kappa - z\sigma_1^2)[e^{\gamma T}-1]},$$

$$\gamma = \sqrt{\kappa^2 + 2\rho\sigma_1^2} \quad \text{and} \quad z \in \mathcal{C}.$$

To make the formula completely user friendly, we follow Christensen (2002) and give an explicit expression for the imaginary part which appears in (E.2):

$$\text{Im}[e^{-ivy}\psi(\bar{u}+ivb, T, X_0, \rho)]$$
$$= e^{UX(0)}[S\cos(WX(0)-vy)+R\sin(WX(0)-vy)],$$

where the intermediate variables are defined as

$$R = (J^2+K^2)^{D/2}e^G$$
$$\times [E\cos(H+D\arctan(K/J))-F\sin(H+D\arctan(K/J))],$$

$$S = (J^2+K^2)^{D/2}e^G$$
$$\times [F\cos(H+D\arctan(K/J))+E\sin(H+D\arctan(K/J))],$$

$$U = \frac{\delta+\varepsilon e^{\gamma T}+\phi e^{2\gamma T}}{N},$$

$$W = \frac{4vb\gamma^2 e^{\gamma T}}{N}.$$

These variables are finally defined through the parameters of the model as

$$E = (\tilde{x}^2+\tilde{y}^2)^{\kappa\mu/\sigma_1^2}\cos\left(\frac{2\kappa\mu}{\sigma_1^2}\arctan\left(\frac{\tilde{y}}{\tilde{x}}\right)\right),$$

$$F = (\tilde{x}^2+\tilde{y}^2)^{\kappa\mu/\sigma_1^2}\sin\left(\frac{2\kappa\mu}{\sigma_1^2}\arctan\left(\frac{\tilde{y}}{\tilde{x}}\right)\right),$$

where

$$\tilde{x} = \frac{2\gamma e^{(\gamma+\kappa)T/2}[\gamma-\kappa+\bar{u}\sigma_1^2+(\gamma+\kappa-\bar{u}\sigma_1^2)e^{\gamma T}]}{(2\gamma+(\gamma+\kappa)[e^{\gamma T}-1]-\bar{u}\sigma_1^2[e^{\gamma T}-1])^2+v^2b^2\sigma_1^4[e^{\gamma T}-1]^2},$$

$$\tilde{y} = \frac{2\gamma e^{(\gamma+\kappa)T/2}vb\sigma_1^2[e^{\gamma T}-1]}{(2\gamma+(\gamma+\kappa)[e^{\gamma T}-1]-\bar{u}\sigma_1^2[e^{\gamma T}-1])^2+v^2b^2\sigma_1^4[e^{\gamma T}-1]^2},$$

$$D = \frac{-2\eta v}{\sigma_1^2-2\eta\kappa-2\eta^2\rho},$$

$$G = \frac{v\eta T[(2\rho+\bar{u}(\gamma+\kappa))(\gamma-\kappa-2\eta\rho+\bar{u}[\sigma_1^2-\eta(\gamma+\kappa)]) + v^2b^2(\gamma+\kappa)[\sigma_1^2-\eta(\gamma+\kappa)]]}{(\gamma-\kappa-2\eta\rho+\bar{u}[\sigma_1^2-\eta(\gamma+\kappa)])^2+v^2b^2[\sigma_1^2-\eta(\gamma+\kappa)]^2},$$

$$H = \frac{v\eta Tvb[(\gamma+\kappa)(\gamma-\kappa-2\eta\rho+\bar{u}[\sigma_1^2-\eta(\gamma+\kappa)]) - (2\rho+\bar{u}(\gamma+\kappa))[\sigma_1^2-\eta(\gamma+\kappa)]]}{(\gamma-\kappa-2\eta\rho+\bar{u}[\sigma_1^2-\eta(\gamma+\kappa)])^2+v^2b^2[\sigma_1^2-\eta(\gamma+\kappa)]^2},$$

$$J = 1 + \frac{(e^{\gamma T} - 1)[(\gamma + \kappa + 2\eta\rho)(1 - \bar{u}\eta) + (\sigma_I^2 + \eta(\gamma - \kappa))[\bar{u}(\bar{u}\eta - 1) + v^2 b^2 \eta]]}{2\gamma(1 - \bar{u}\eta)^2 + 2\gamma v^2 b^2 \eta^2},$$

$$K = \frac{(e^{\gamma T} - 1)vb[2\eta\kappa + 2\eta^2\rho - \sigma_I^2]}{2\gamma(1 - \bar{u}\eta)^2 + 2\gamma v^2 b^2 \eta^2},$$

$$N = (2\gamma + (\gamma + \kappa)[e^{\gamma T} - 1] - \bar{u}\sigma_I^2[e^{\gamma T} - 1])^2 + v^2 b^2 \sigma_I^4 [e^{\gamma T} - 1]^2,$$

$$\delta = 2\rho(\gamma - \kappa) + 4\sigma_I^2\rho\bar{u} + \bar{u}^2\sigma_I^2(\gamma + \kappa) + v^2 b^2 \sigma_I^2(\gamma + \kappa),$$

$$\varepsilon = 4\kappa\rho + 4\kappa^2\bar{u} - 2\kappa\bar{u}^2\sigma_I^2 - 2v^2 b^2 \sigma_I^2\kappa,$$

$$\phi = -2\rho(\gamma + \kappa) + 4\sigma_I^2\rho\bar{u} - \bar{u}^2\sigma_I^2(\gamma - \kappa) - v^2 b^2 \sigma_I^2(\gamma - \kappa),$$

and, finally, in line with the earlier results, γ is defined throughout by

$$\gamma = \sqrt{\kappa^2 + 2\sigma_I^2\rho}.$$

The expressions are of course cumbersome, but they are explicit. Hence no ODE solver needs to be invoked.

References

Acharya, V. V. and J. Carpenter. 2002. Corporate bond valuation and hedging with stochastic interest rates and endogenous bankruptcy. *Review of Financial Studies* 15:1355–1383.

Acharya, V., S. Das, and R. Sundaram. 2002. Pricing credit derivatives with rating transitions. *Financial Analysts Journal* 58:28–44.

Acharya, V., S. Bharath, and A. Srinivasan. 2003. Understanding the recovery rates on defaulted securities. Working paper, London Business School, University of Michigan, and University of Georgia.

Allen, F. and D. Gale. 2000. Financial contagion. *Journal of Political Economy* 108:1–33.

Altman, E. 1968. Financial ratios: discriminant analysis, and the prediction of corporate bankruptcy. *Journal of Finance* 23:589–609.

Altman, E. and D. L. Kao. 1992a. The implications of corporate bond rating drift. *Financial Analysts Journal* 48(3):64–75.

Altman, E. and D. L. Kao. 1992b (March). Rating drift in high yield bonds. *Journal of Fixed Income* 1(4):15–20.

Altman, E., B. Brady, A. Resti, and A. Sironi. 2002. The link between default and recovery rates: implications for credit risk models and procyclicality. *Journal of Business*, in press.

Ammann, E. 2002. *Credit risk valuation: methods, models, and applications*. Springer.

Andersen, P. K., Ø. Borgan, R. Gill, and N. Keiding. 1993. *Statistical models based on counting processes*. Springer.

Anderson, R. and S. Sundaresan. 1996. Design and valuation of debt contracts. *Review of Financial Studies* 9:37–68.

Anderson, T. W. 1984. *An introduction to multivariate statistical analysis*, 2nd edn. New York: Wiley.

Arjas, E. 1989. Survival models and martingale dynamics. *Scandinavian Journal of Statistics* 16:177–225.

Artzner, P. and F. Delbaen. 1990. "Finem lauda" or the risk in swaps. *Insurance: Mathematics and Economics* 9:295–303.

Artzner, P. and F. Delbaen. 1995. Default risk insurance and incomplete markets. *Mathematical Finance* 5:187–195.

Arvanitis, A. and J. Gregory. 2001. *Credit—the complete guide to pricing, hedging and risk management*. London: Risk Books.

Arvanitis, A., J. Gregory, and J.-P. Laurent. 1999. Building models for credit spreads. *Journal of Derivatives* 6:27–43.

Back, K. 1991. Asset pricing for general processes. *Journal of Mathematical Economics* 20:371–395.

Bakshi, G., D. Madan, and F. Zhang. 2001. Understanding the role of recovery in default risk models: empirical comparisons and implied recovery rates. Working paper. University of Maryland.

Bangia, A., F. Diebold, A. Kronimus, C. Schagen, and T. Schuermann. 2002. Ratings migration and the business cycle, with applications to credit portfolio stress testing. *Journal of Banking and Finance* 26:445–474.

Bank of International Settlements. 2001. The emergence of new benchmark yield curves. *Fourth Quarterly Review: International Banking and Financial Market Developments*, pp. 48–57.

Bank of International Settlements. 2003. The international debt securities market. *Second Quarterly Review: International Banking and Financial Developments*, pp. 31–40.

Beaver, W. 1966. Financial ratios and the prediction of failure. *Journal of Accounting Research. Supplement. Empirical Research in Accounting: Selected Studies 1966* 4:77–111.

Becherer, D. 2001. Rational hedging and valuation with utility-based preferences. PhD Thesis. Technical University, Berlin.

Belanger, A., S. Shreve, and D. Wong. 2001. A unified model for credit derivatives. *Mathematical Finance*, in press.

Bernhardsen, Ø. 2001. A model of bankruptcy prediction. Working paper, Norges Bank.

Bhattacharya, R. and E. Waymire. 1990. *Stochastic processes with applications*. New York: Wiley.

Bicksler, J. and A. Chen. 1986. An economic analysis of interest rate swaps. *Journal of Finance* 41(3):645–655.

Bielecki, T. and M. Rutkowski. 2002. *Credit risk: modeling, valuation and hedging*. Berlin, Heidelberg: Springer Finance.

BIS. 2003. Credit risk transfer. Working Group Report, Committee on the Global Financial System.

Björk, T. 1998. *Arbitrage theory in continuous time*. London: Oxford University Press.

Black, F. and J. Cox. 1976. Valuing corporate securities: some effects of bond indenture provisions. *Journal of Finance* 31:351–367.

Black, F. and M. Scholes. 1973. The pricing of options and corporate liabilities. *Journal of Political Economy* 81:637–654.

Bluhm, C., L. Overbeck, and C. Wagner. 2002. *An introduction to credit risk modeling*. London: Chapman & Hall/CRC.

Blume, M., F. Lim, and A. MacKinlay. 1998. The declining credit quality of us corporate debt: myth or reality. *Journal of Finance* 53:1389–1413.

Bohn, J. R. 2000. A survey of contingent-claims approaches to risky debt valuation. *Journal of Risk Finance* 1:1–18.

Brémaud, P. 1981. *Point processes and queues—martingale dynamics*. Springer.

Brennan, M. J. and E. S. Schwartz. 1984. Valuation of corporate claims: optimal financial policy and firm valuation. *Journal of Finance* 39:593–609.

Briys, E. and F. de Varenne. 1997. Valuing risky fixed dept: an extension. *Journal of Financial and Quantitative Analysis* 32:239–248.

Brown, K., W. Harlow, and D. Smith. 1994. An empirical analysis of interest rate swap spreads. *Journal of Fixed Income* 3:61–78.

Buonocore, A., A. G. Nobile, and L. Ricciardi. 1987. A new integral equation for the evaluation of first-passage-time probability densities. *Advances in Applied Probability* 19:784–800.

Cantor, R. and D. Hamilton. 2004. Rating transitions and defaults conditional on watchlist, outlook and rating history. Special comment, Moody's Investors Service, New York.

Carey, M. and M. Hrycay. 2001. Parameterizing credit risk models with rating data. *Journal of Banking and Finance* 25:195–270.

Carey, M. and W. F. Treacy. 2000. Credit risk rating systems at large US banks. *Journal of Banking and Finance* 24:167–201.

Carty, L. 1997. Moody's rating migration and credit quality correlation, 1920–1996. Special comment, Moody's Investors Service, New York.

Chen, R. and L. Scott. 2003. Multi-factor Cox–Ingersoll–Ross models of the term structure: estimates and tests from a Kalman filter model. *The Journal of Real Estate Finance* 27(2):143–172.

Christensen, J. H. 2002. Kreditderivater og deres prisfastsættelse. Thesis, Institute of Economics, University of Copenhagen.

Christensen, J. H., E. Hansen, and D. Lando. 2004. Confidence sets for continuous-time rating transition probabilities. Working paper, Copenhagen Business School and University of Copenhagen.

Christensen, P., C. Flor, D. Lando, and K. Miltersen. 2002. Dynamic capital structure with callable debt and debt renegotiation. Working paper, Odense University and Copenhagen Business School.

Cifuentes, A., I. Efrat, J. Gluck, and E. Murphy. 1998. Buying and selling credit risk. In *Credit derivatives. Applications for risk management, investment and portfolio optimization*, pp. 105–116. Risk Magazine.

Collin-Dufresne, P. and R. S. Goldstein. 2001. Do credit spreads reflect stationary leverage ratios? *Journal of Finance* 56:1929–1957.

Collin-Dufresne, P. and B. Solnik. 2001. On the term structure of default premia in the swap and LIBOR markets. *Journal of Finance* 56(3):1095–1115.

Collin-Dufresne, P., R. S. Goldstein, and J. Martin. 2001. The determinants of credit spread changes. *Journal of Finance* 56:2177–2207.

Collin-Dufresne, P., R. Goldstein, and J. Hugonnier. 2003a. A general formula for valuing defaultable securities. Working paper, Carnegie Mellon University.

Collin-Dufresne, P., R. Goldstein, and J. Helwege. 2003b. Is credit event risk priced? Modeling contagion via the updating of beliefs. Working paper, Carnegie Mellon University.

Cooper, I. and A. Mello. 1991. The default risk of swaps. *Journal of Finance* 46:597–620.

Cossin, D. and H. Pirotte. 2001. *Advanced credit risk analysis—financial approaches and mathematical models to assess, price, and manage credit risk.* New York: Wiley.

Cossin, D., T. Hricko, D. Aunon-Nerin, and Z. Huang. 2002. Exploring the determinants of credit risk in credit default swap transaction data: is fixed-income markets' information sufficient to evaluate credit risk? Working paper, HEC, University of Lausanne.

Cox, D. and D. Oakes. 1984. *Analysis of survival data.* London: Chapman and Hall.

Cox, J., J. Ingersoll, and S. Ross. 1985. A theory of the term structure of interest rates. *Econometrica* 53:385–407.

Crosbie, P. 2002. Modeling default risk. Web page posted by the KMV Corporation.

Dai, Q. and K. J. Singleton. 2000. Specification analysis of affine term structure models. *Journal of Finance* 55(5):1943–1978.

Das, S. 1995. Credit risk derivatives. *Journal of Derivatives* 2(3):7–23.

Das, S. and R. Sundaram. 2000. A discrete-time approach to arbitrage-free pricing of credit derivatives. *Management Science* 46(1):46–63.

Das, S. and P. Tufano. 1996. Pricing credit-sensitive debt when interest rates, credit ratings and credit spreads are stochastic. *Journal of Financial Engineering* 5:161–198.

Davis, M. and V. Lo. 2001. Infectious defaults. *Quantitative Finance* 1:382–387.

Davydenko, S. A. and I. A. Strebulaev. 2003. Strategic behavior, capital structure, and credit spreads: an empirical investigation. Working paper, London Business School.

de Jong, F. 2000. Time series and cross-section information in affine term-structure models. *Journal of Business and Economic Statistics* 18(3):300–318.

Delbaen, F. and W. Schachermayer. 1994. A general version of the fundamental theorem of asset pricing. *Mathematische Annalen* 300:463–520.

Delianedis, G. and R. Geske. 1999. Credit risk and risk neutral default probabilities: information about rating migrations and defaults. Working paper, The Anderson School, UCLA.

Dixit, A. 1993. The art of smooth pasting. In *Fundamentals of Pure and Applied Economics*, pp. 1–71. Harwood Academic Publishers.

Driessen, J. 2002. Is default event risk priced in corporate bonds? Working paper, University of Amsterdam.

Duan, J. 1994. Maximum likelihood estimation using price data of the derivatives contract. *Mathematical Finance* 4:155–167. (Correction: 2000 *Mathematical Finance* 10(4):461–462.)

Duan, J.-C. and J.-G. Simonato. 1999. Estimating exponential-affine term structure models by Kalman filter. *Review of Quantitative Finance and Accounting* 13(2):111–135.

Duffee, G. 1999. Estimating the price of default risk. *Review of Financial Studies* 12:197–226.

Duffie, D. 1999a. Correlated event times with jump-diffusion intensities. Working paper, Stanford University.

Duffie, D. 1999b (January/February). Credit swap valuation. *Financial Analysts Journal* 55(1):73–87.

Duffie, D. 2001. *Dynamic asset pricing theory*, 3nd edn. Princeton, NJ: Princeton University Press.

Duffie, D. and N. Gârleanu. 2001 (January/February). Risk and valuation of collateralized debt obligations. *Financial Analysts Journal* 57(1):41–59.

Duffie, D. and M. Huang. 1996. Swap rates and credit quality. *Journal of Finance* 51(3):921–949.

Duffie, D. and D. Lando. 2001. Term structures of credit spreads with incomplete accounting information. *Econometrica* 69(3):633–664.

Duffie, D. and J. Liu. 2001 (May/June). Floating–fixed credit spreads. *Financial Analysts Journal* 57(3):76–86.

Duffie, D. and K. Singleton. 1997. An econometric model of the term structure of interest-rate swap yields. *Journal of Finance* 52(4):1287–1321.

Duffie, D. and K. Singleton. 1999a. Modeling term structures of defaultable bonds. *Review of Financial Studies* 12(4):687–720.

Duffie, D. and K. Singleton. 1999b. Simulating correlated defaults. Working paper, Stanford University.

Duffie, D. and K. Singleton. 2003. *Credit risk: pricing, measurement, and management.* Princeton, NJ: Princeton University Press.

Duffie, D., M. Schroder, and C. Skiadas. 1996. Recursive valuation of defaultable securities and the timing of resolution of uncertainty. *Annals of Applied Probability* 6:1075–1090.

Duffie, D., J. Pan, and K. Singleton. 2000. Transform analysis and asset pricing for affine jump diffusions. *Econometrica* 68:1343–1376.

Duffie, D., L. H. Pedersen, and K. J. Singleton. 2003. Modeling sovereign yield spreads: a case study of Russian debt. *Journal of Finance* 58:119–160.

Efron, B. 1975. The efficiency of logistic regression compared to normal discriminant analysis. *Journal of the American Statistical Association* 70:892–898.

Eisenberg, L. and T. H. Noe. 2001. Systemic risk in financial systems. *Management Science* 47(2):236–249.

El Karoui, N. and L. Martellini. 2002. A theoretical inspection of the market price for default risk. Working paper, École Polytechnique, France, and University of Southern California.

Elliott, R. J. and M. Jeanblanc. 1998. Some facts on default risk. Working paper, University of Alberta, Canada, and University d'Evry, France.

Elliott, R. J., M. Jeanblanc, and M. Yor. 2000. On models of default risk. *Mathematical Finance* 10:179–195.

Elsinger, H., A. Lehar, and M. Summer. 2003. Risk assessment for banking systems. Working paper.

Elton, E. J., M. J. Gruber, D. Agrawal, and C. Mann. 2001. Explaining the rate spread on corporate bonds. *Journal of Finance* 56(1):247–277.

Eom, Y., J. Helwege, and J. Huang. 2003. Structural models of corporate bond pricing: an empirical analysis. *Review of Financial Studies*, in press.

Ericsson, J. and J. Reneby. 2001. The valuation of corporate liabilities: theory and tests. Working paper, McGill University, Montreal.

Ericsson, J. and J. Reneby. 2002. Estimating structural bond pricing models. Working paper, McGill University, Montreal.

Finger, C. 2002. CreditGrades. Technical document, RiskMetrics Group, Inc.

Fischer, E., R. Heinkel, and J. Zechner. 1989. Dynamic capital structure choice: theory and tests. *Journal of Finance* 44:19–40.

Fisher, L. 1959. Determinants of risk premiums on corporate bonds. *Journal of Political Economy* 67:217–237.

Flamgaard, S. 2002. Financial contagion? Systemic risk in network models. (In Danish.) Master's thesis, University of Copenhagen.

Fledelius, P., D. Lando and J. P. Nielsen. 2004. Non-parametric analysis of rating-transition and default data. Working paper, Copenhagen Business School and Royal & Sun Alliance.

Fons, J. 1994 (September/October). Using default rates to model the term structure of credit risk. *Financial Analysts Journal* 50:25–32.

Fons, J. and A. Kimball. 1991. Corporate bond defaults and default rates 1970–1990. *Journal of Fixed Income* 1(1):36–47.

Fons, J., A. Kimball, and D. Girault. 1991. Corporate bond defaults and default rates 1970–1991. Moody's Special Report, January 1991.

Frey, R. and A. McNeil. 2003. Dependence modelling, model risk and model calibration in models of portfolio credit risk. *Journal of Risk*, in press.

Frydman, H. 1984. Maximum-likelihood estimation in the mover–stayer model. *Journal of the American Statistical Association* 79:632–638

Frydman, H., J. Kallberg, and D. Kao. 1985. Testing the adequacy of Markov chain and mover–stayer models as representations of credit behavior. *Operations Research* 33(6):1203–1214.

Frye, J. 2003a. Collateral damage. In *Credit risk modelling*, ed. M. B. Gordy, pp. 115–120. London: Risk Books.

Frye, J. 2003b. Depressing recoveries. In *Credit risk modelling*, ed. M. B. Gordy, pp. 121–130. London: Risk Books.

Geske, R. 1977. The valuation of corporate liabilities as compound options. *Journal of Financial and Quantitative Analysis* 12(4):541–552.

Geyer, A. L. and S. Pichler. 1999. A state-space approach to estimate and test multifactor CIR models of the term structure. *Journal of Financial Research* 22:107–130.

Giesecke, K. 2003. Default and information. Working paper, Cornell University.

Gill, R. and S. Johansen. 1990. A survey of product-integration with a view towards applications in survival analysis. *Annals of Statistics* 18(4):1501–1555.

Goldstein, R., N. Ju, and H. Leland. 2001. An EBIT-based model of dynamic capital structure. *Journal of Business* 74(4):483–512.

Gordy, M. B. 2000. A comparative anatomy of credit risk models. *Journal of Banking and Finance* 24:119–149.

Gordy, M. B. 2003. A risk-factor model foundation for rating-based bank capital rules. *Journal of Financial Intermediation* 12:199–232.

Grandell, J. 1976. *Doubly stochastic Poisson processes*. Lecture Notes in Mathematics, vol. 529. Springer.

Grandell, J. 1991. *Aspects of risk theory*. Springer.

Gregory, J. and J.-P. Laurent. 2003a. I will survive. *Risk* June:103–107.

Gregory, J. and J.-P. Laurent. 2003b. Basket default swaps, CDOs and factor copulas. Working paper, BNP Paribas and University of Lyon.

Grinblatt, M. 2001. An analytic solution for interest rate swap spreads. *International Review of Finance* 2:113–149.

Guha, R. 2002. Recovery of face value at default: theory and empirical evidence. Working paper, London Business School.

Gupton, G. and R. Stein. 2002. LossCalc™: Moody's model for predicting loss given default (LGD). Special Comment. Moody's Investors Service.

Gupton, G., C. Finger, and M. Bhatia. 1997. CreditMetrics—technical document. Morgan Guaranty Trust Company.

Harrison, J. 1990. *Brownian motion and stochastic flow systems*. Malabar, FL: Robert E. Krieger.

Harrison, J. and D. Kreps. 1979. Martingales and arbitrage in multiperiod securities markets. *Journal of Economic Theory* 20:381–408.

Harrison, J. and S. Pliska. 1981. Martingales and stochastic integrals in the theory of continuous trading. *Stochastic Processes and their Applications* 11:215–260.

Harrison, J. and S. Pliska. 1983. A stochastic calculus model of continuous trading: complete markets. *Stochastic Processes and their Applications* 15:313–316.

Harvey, A. 1990. *Forecasting, structural time series models and the Kalman filter*. Cambridge: Cambridge University Press.

He, H. 2001. Modeling term structures of swap spreads. Working paper, Yale University.

Heath, D., R. Jarrow, and A. Morton. 1992. Bond pricing and the term structure of interest rates: a new methodology for contingent claims valuation. *Econometrica* 60:77–105.

Helwege, J. and C. M. Turner. 1999. The slope of the credit yield curve for speculative-grade issuers. *Journal of Finance* 54:1869–1884.

Hilberink, B. and C. Rogers. 2002. Optimal capital structure and endogenous default. *Finance and Stochastics* 6(2):237–263.

Hillegeist, S., E. Keating, D. Cram, and K. Lundstedt. 2002. Assessing the probability of bankruptcy. Working paper, Northwestern University.

Ho, T. and R. Singer. 1982. Bond indenture provisions and the risk of corporate debt. *Journal of Financial Economics* 10:375–406.

Ho, T. and R. Singer. 1984. The value of corporate debt with a sinking-fund provision. *Journal of Business* 57:315–336.

Houweling, P. and T. Vorst. 2002. An empirical comparison of default swap pricing models. Working paper, Erasmus University Rotterdam.

Huang, J. and M. Huang. 2003. How much of the corporate-treasury yield spread is due to credit risk? Working paper, Stanford University.

Hübner, G. 2001. The analytic pricing of asymmetric defaultable swaps. *Journal of Banking and Finance* 25:295–316.

Huge, B. 2000. Three essays on defaultable claim valuation. PhD Thesis, Department of Statistics and Operations Research, University of Copenhagen.

Huge, B. and D. Lando. 1999. Swap pricing with two-sided default in a rating-based model. *European Finance Review* 3:239–268.

Hull, J. and A. White. 1994a. Numerical procedures for implementing term structure models. I. Single-factor models. *Journal of Derivatives* 2:7–16.

Hull, J. and A. White. 1994b. Numerical procedures for implementing term structure models. II. Two-factor models. *Journal of Derivatives* 2:37–48.

Hull, J. and A. White. 2001a. Valuing credit default swaps. I. No counterparty default risk. *Journal of Derivatives* 8:29–40.

Hull, J. and A. White. 2001b. Valuing credit default swaps. II. Modeling default correlation. *Journal of Derivatives* 8:12–22.

Israel, R., J. Rosenthal, and J. Wei. 2001. Finding generators for Markov chains via empirical transition matrices, with applications to credit ratings. *Mathematical Finance* 11:245–265.

Jacod, J. and J. Memin. 1976. Caractéristiques locales et conditions de continuité absolue pour les semi-martingales. *Zeitschrift für Wahrscheinlichkeitstheorie und Verwandte Gebiete* 35:1–37.

Jacod, J. and A. Shiryaev. 1987. *Limit theorems for stochastic processes.* Springer.

Jarrow, R. 2001 (September/October). Default parameter estimation using market prices. *Financial Analysts Journal* 57(5):75–92.

Jarrow, R. and S. Turnbull. 1995. Pricing options on financial securities subject to credit risk. *Journal of Finance* 50:53–85.

Jarrow, R. and S. Turnbull. 1997. When swaps are dropped. *Risk* 10(5):70–75.

Jarrow, R. and F. Yu. 2001. Counterparty risk and the pricing of defaultable securities. *Journal of Finance* 56(5):1765–1799.

Jarrow, R., D. Lando, and S. Turnbull. 1997. A Markov model for the term structure of credit risk spreads. *Review of Financial Studies* 10(2):481–523.

Jarrow, R., D. Lando, and F. Yu. 2003. Default risk and diversification: theory and applications. *Mathematical Finance*, in press.

Jones, E., S. Mason, and E. Rosenfeld. 1984. Contingent claims analysis of corporate capital structures: an empirical investigation. *Journal of Finance* 39:611–625.

Kane, A., A. J. Marcus, and R. L. McDonald. 1984. How big is the tax advantage to debt? *Journal of Finance* 39(3):841–855.

Kane, A., A. J. Marcus, and R. L. McDonald. 1985. Debt policy and the rate of return premium to leverage. *Journal of Financial and Quantitative Analysis* 20(4):479–499.

Karatzas, I. and S. Shreve. 1988. *Brownian motion and stochastic calculus.* Springer.

Kijima, M. 2000. Valuation of a credit swap of the basket type. *Review of Derivatives Research* 4:81–97.

Kijima, M. and K. Komoribayashi. 1998. A Markov chain model for valuing credit risk derivatives. *Journal of Derivatives* 6:97–108.

Kijima, M. and Y. Muromachi. 2000. Credit events and the valuation of credit derivatives of basket type. *Review of Derivatives Research* 4:55–79.

Kim, J., K. Ramaswamy, and S. Sundaresan. 1993. Does default risk in coupons affect the valuation of corporate bonds? *Financial Management* 22:117–131.

Kronborg, D., T. Tjur, and B. Vincents. 1998. Credit scoring: discussion of methods and a case study. Preprint no. 7/1998, Copenhagen Business School.

Küchler, U. and M. Sørensen. 1997. *Exponential families of stochastic processes*. Springer.

Kusuoka, S. 1999. A remark on default risk models. In *Advances in mathematical economics*, vol. 1, pp. 69–82. Springer.

Lambrecht, B. and W. Perraudin. 1996. Creditor races and contingent claims. *European Economic Review* 40:897–907.

Lando, D. 1994. Three essays on contingent claims pricing. PhD Thesis, Cornell University.

Lando, D. 1998. On Cox processes and credit risky securities. *Review of Derivatives Research* 2:99–120.

Lando, D. and A. Mortensen. 2003. Mispricing of step-up bonds in the European telecom sector. Working paper, Copenhagen Business School.

Lando, D. and T. Skødeberg. 2002. Analyzing rating transitions and rating drift with continuous observations. *Journal of Banking and Finance* 26:423–444.

Leblanc, B., O. Renault, and O. Scaillet. 2000. A correction note on the first passage time of an Ornstein–Uhlenbeck process to a boundary. *Finance and Stochastics* 4(1):109–111.

Leland, H. E. 1994. Corporate debt value, bond covenants, and optimal capital structure. *Journal of Finance* 49:157–196.

Leland, H. E. and K. Toft. 1996. Optimal capital structure, endogenous bankruptcy, and the term structure of credit spreads. *Journal of Finance* 51:987–1019.

Li, D. X. 2000. On default correlation: a copula function approach. *The Journal of Fixed Income* 9(4):43–54.

Litzenberger, R. 1992. Swaps: plain and fanciful. *Journal of Finance* 42:831–850.

Liu, J., F. Longstaff, and R. E. Mandell. 2002. The market price of credit risk: an empirical analysis of interest rate swap spreads. Working paper, Anderson School of Business, UCLA.

Löffler, G. 2002. An anatomy of rating through the cycle. Working paper, Goethe-Universität Frankfurt. *Journal of Banking and Finance*, in press.

Löffler, G. 2003. Avoiding the rating bounce: why rating agencies are slow to react to new information. Working paper, Goethe-Universität Frankfurt.

Longstaff, F. and E. Schwartz. 1995a. A simple approach to valuing risky fixed and floating rate debt. *Journal of Finance* 50:789–819.

Longstaff, F. and E. Schwartz. 1995b, June. Valuing credit derivatives. *Journal of Fixed Income* 5:6–12.

Lucas, D. and J. Lonski. 1992. Changes in corporate credit quality 1970–1990. *Journal of Fixed Income* 1(4):7–14.

Lund, J. 1997. Non-linear Kalman filtering techniques for term-structure models. Working paper, Aarhus School of Business.

Madan, D. and H. Unal. 1998. Pricing the risks of default. *Review of Derivatives Research* 2:121–160.

Martin, R., K. Thompson, and C. Browne. 2003. Taking to the saddle. In *Credit risk modelling*, ed. M. B. Gordy, pp. 137–144. London: Risk Books.

Mason, S. and S. Bhattacharya. 1981. Risky debt, jump processes, and safety covenants. *Journal of Financial Economics* 9:281–307.

Mella-Barral, P. and W. Perraudin. 1997. Strategic debt service. *Journal of Finance* 52:531–556.

Merton, R. C. 1974. On the pricing of corporate debt: the risk structure of interest rates. *Journal of Finance* 29:449–470.

Merton, R. C. 1990. *Continuous-time finance*. Cambridge, MA: Blackwell.

Métivier, M. 1982. *Semimartingales, a course on stochastic processes*. Berlin: Walter de Gruyter.

Minton, B. 1997. An empirical examination of basic valuation models for plain vanilla US interest rate swaps. *Journal of Financial Economics* 44:251–277.

Neuts, M. 1995. *Algorithmic probability: a collection of problems*. Chapman and Hall.

Nickell, P., W. Perraudin, and S. Varotto. 2000. Stability of ratings transitions. *Journal of Banking and Finance* 24:203–227.

Nielsen, J. P. and C. Tanggaard. 2001. Boundary and bias correction in kernel hazard estimation. *Scandinavian Journal of Statistics* 28:675–698.

Norros, I. 1985. Systems weakened by failures. *Stochastic Processes and Their Applications* 20:181–196.

Paulsen, J. 1999. Stochastic calculus with applications to risk theory. Lecture notes, University of Bergen and University of Copenhagen.

Press, J. and S. Wilson. 1978. Choosing between logistic regression and discriminant analysis. *Journal of the American Statistical Association* 73:699–706.

Protter, P. 1990. *Stochastic integration and differential equations—a new approach*. Springer.

Ramlau-Hansen, H. 1983. Smoothing counting processes by means of kernel functions. *Annals of Statistics* 11:453–466.

Rendleman, R. 1992. How risks are shared in interest rate swaps. *Journal of Financial Services Research* 7:5–34.

Resnick, S. I. 1992. *Adventures in stochastic processes*. Boston, MA: Birkhäuser.

Rogge, E. and P. Schönbucher. 2003. Modeling dynamic portfolio credit risk. Working paper, Imperial College and ETH Zürich.

Rule, D. 2001. The credit derivatives market: its development and possible implications for financial stability. *Financial Stability Review* 10:117–140.

Sarig, O. and A. Warga. 1989. Some empirical estimates of the risk structure of interest rates. *Journal of Finance* 46:1351–1360.

Schönbucher, P. 1998. The term structure of defaultable bond prices. *Review of Derivatives Research* 2:161–192.

Schönbucher, P. 2000. Credit risk modelling and credit derivatives. Dissertation, University of Bonn.

Schönbucher, P. 2002. A tree implementation of a credit spread model for credit derivatives. *Journal of Computational Finance* 6(2):1–38.

Schönbucher, P. 2003. *Credit derivatives pricing models: models, pricing and implementation*. Chichester, UK: Wiley.

Schubert, D. and P. Schönbucher. 2001. Copula dependent default risk in intensity models. Working paper, Bonn University.

Schuermann, T. 2003. What do we know about loss-given-default. Working paper, Federal Reserve Bank of New York.

Shimko, D., N. Tejima, and D. Deventer. 1993. The pricing of risky debt when interest rates are stochastic. *Journal of Fixed Income* 3:58–65.

Shumway, T. 2001. Forecasting bankruptcy more efficiently: a simple hazard model. *Journal of Business* 74:101–124.

Skødeberg, T. 1998. Statistical analysis of rating transitions—a survival analytic approach. Master's Thesis, University of Copenhagen.

Sobehart, J., S. Keenan, and R. Stein. 2000. Benchmarking quantitative default risk models. Moody's Investor Service. Rating methodology, March 2000.

Solnik, B. 1990. Swap pricing and default risk: a note. *Journal of International Financial Management and Accounting* 2(1):79–91.

Song, S. 1998. A remark on a result of Duffie and Lando. Working paper, Prepublication 82, Equipe d'Analyse et Probalités, Department of Mathematics, Université d'Evry, Val d'Essonne, France.

Sorensen, E. and T. Bollier. 1984 (May–June). Pricing swap default risk. *Financial Analysts Journal* 40:23–33.

Stumpp, P. and M. Coppola. 2002. Moody's analysis of US corporate rating triggers heightens need for increased disclosure. Moody's special comment.

Sun, T., S. Sundaresan, and C. Wang. 1993. Interest rate swaps: an empirical investigation. *Journal of Financial Economics* 34:77–99.

Sundaresan, S. 1991. Valuation of swaps. In *Recent developments in international banking*, ed. S. Khoury, Chapter XII, pp. 407–440. Elsevier Science Publishers (North Holland).

Tolk, J. 2001. Understanding the risks in credit default swaps. Special Report, Moody's Investors Service, New York.

Turnbull, S. 1987. Swaps: a zero sum game. *Financial Management* 16:15–21.

Uhrig-Homburg, M. 1998. Endogenous bankruptcy when issuance is costly. Working paper, Department of Finance, University of Mannheim.

Vasicek, O. 1977. An equilibrium characterization of the term structure. *Journal of Financial Economics* 5:177–188.

Vasicek, O. 1991. Limiting loan loss probability distribution. Working paper, KMV Corporation.

Vassalou, M. and Y. Xing. 2002. Default risk in equity returns. Working paper, Columbia University. *Journal of Finance*, in press.

Wall, L. and J. J. Pringle. 1988 (November/December). Interest rate swaps: a review of the issues. *Economic Review*, 22–37.

Wilson, T. 1997a (September). Portfolio credit risk. I. *Risk* 10(9):111–117.

Wilson, T. 1997b (October). Portfolio credit risk. II. *Risk* 10(10):56–61.

Yu, F. 2003. Accounting transparency and the term structure of credit spreads. *Journal of Financial Economics*, in press.

Zhou, C. 2001a (Summer). An analysis of default correlation and multiple defaults. *Journal of Banking and Finance* 14(2):555–576.

Zhou, C. 2001b (November). The term structure of credit spreads with jump risk. *Journal of Banking and Finance* 25(11):2015–2040.

Index

www.ingramcontent.com/pod-product-compliance
Ingram Content Group UK Ltd.
Pitfield, Milton Keynes, MK11 3LW, UK
UKHW022007020225
454516UK00004B/18/J